The Delinquent HOUSEWIFE!

3

NEMU YOKO

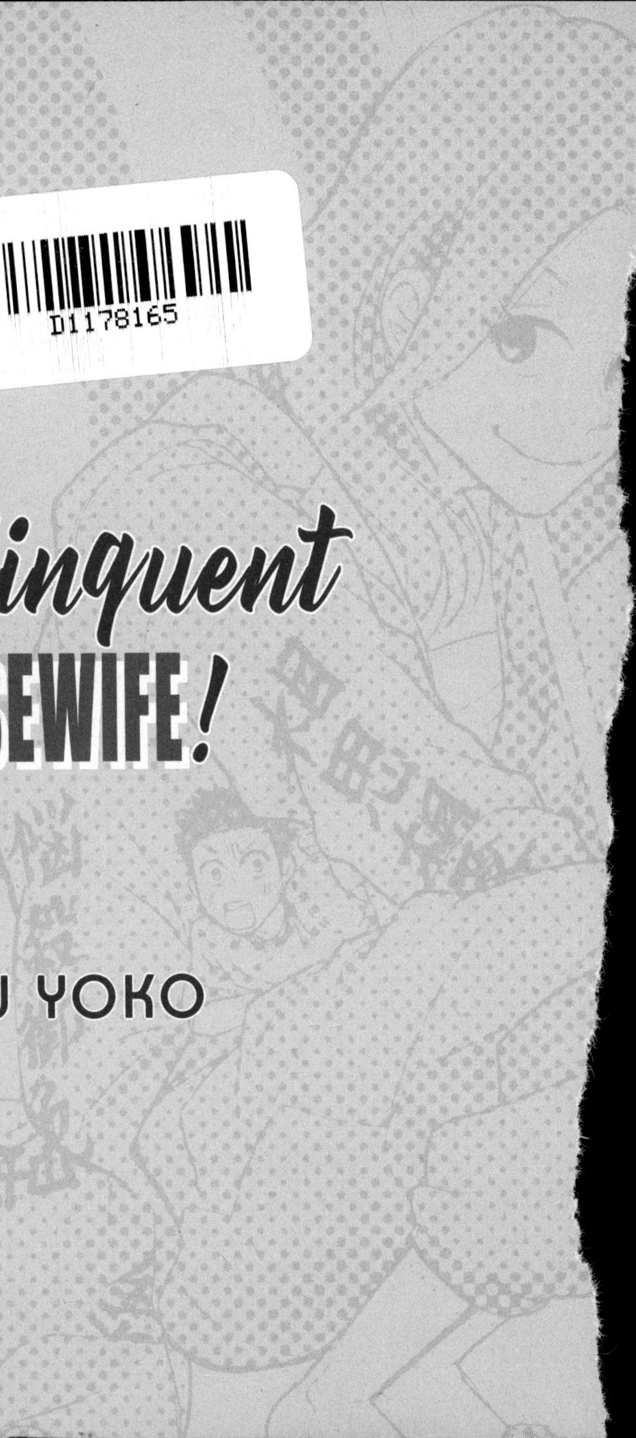

CONTENTS

20

LOVE'S FIRST FEVER

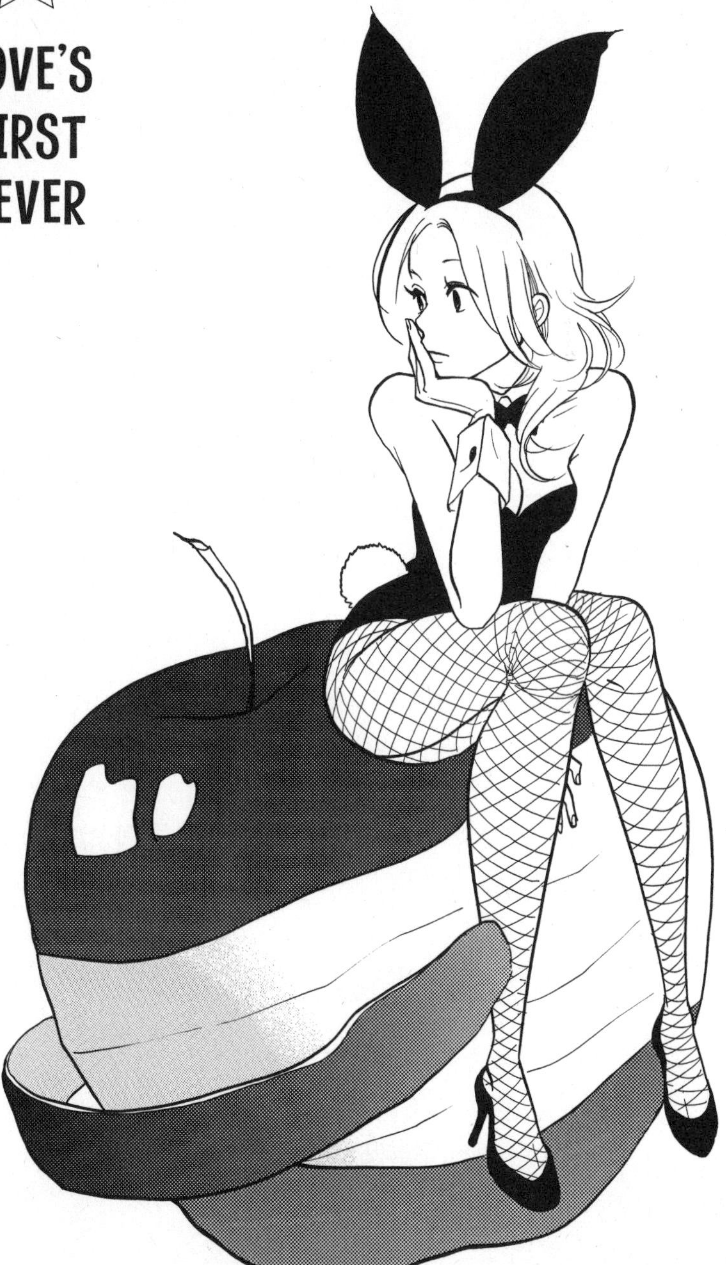

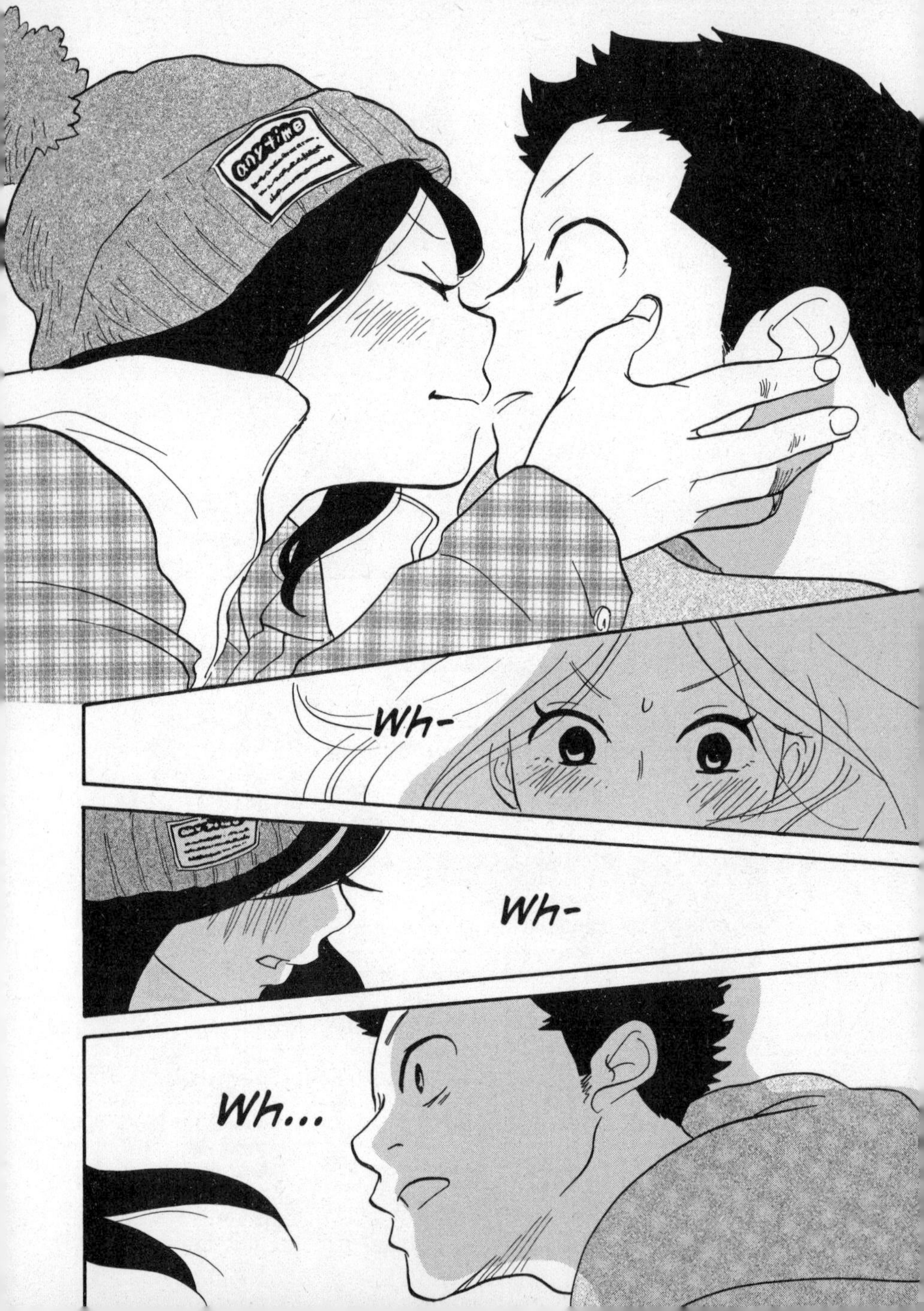
any time
Wh-
Wh-
Wh...

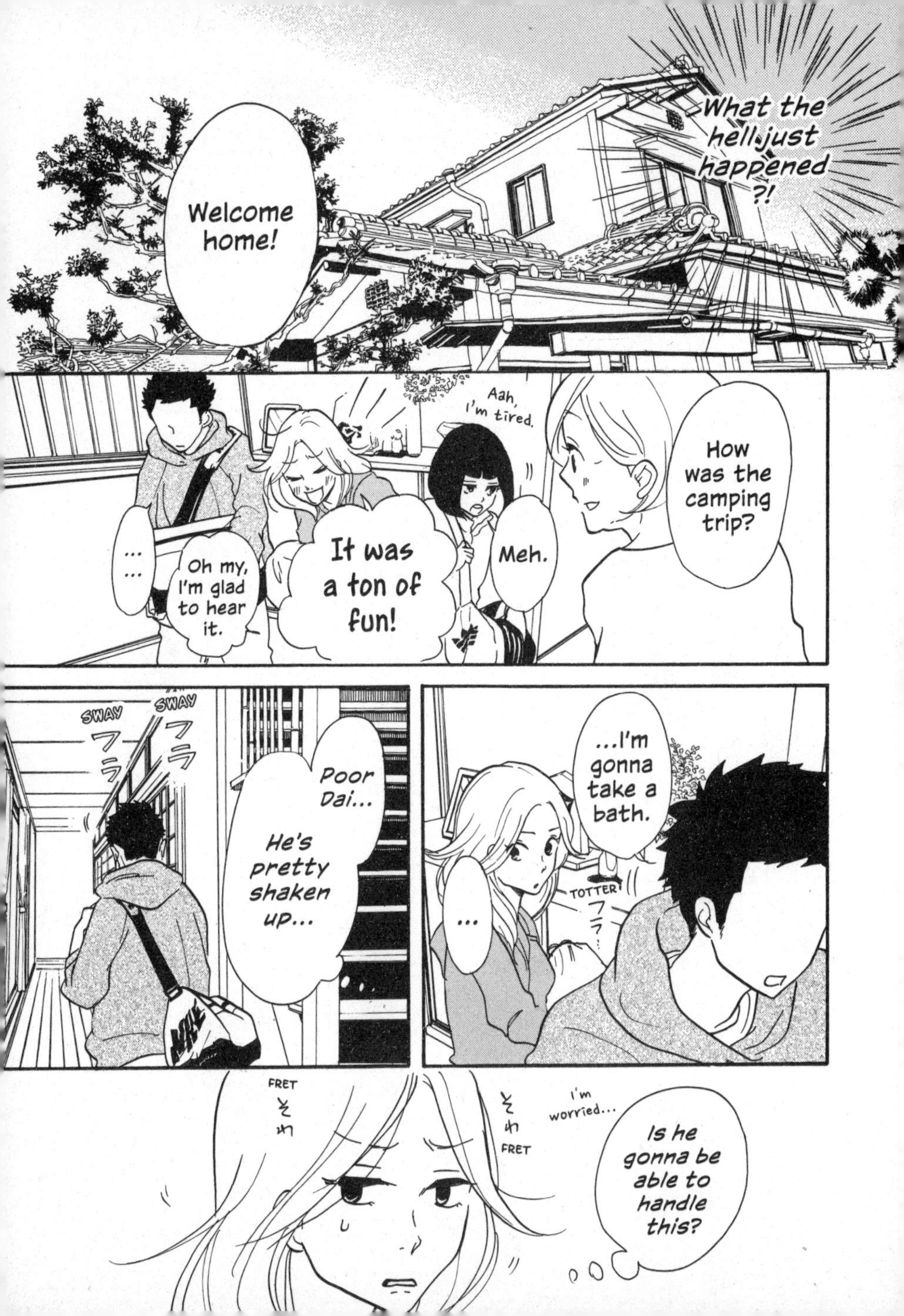
What the hell just happened?!
Welcome home!
How was the camping trip?
Aah, I'm tired.
Meh.
It was a ton of fun!
Oh my, I'm glad to hear it.
......
...I'm gonna take a bath.
TOTTER
フラ
...
Poor Dai...
He's pretty shaken up...
SWAY
フラ
SWAY
フラ
Is he gonna be able to handle this?
I'm worried...
FRET
それ
FRET
それ

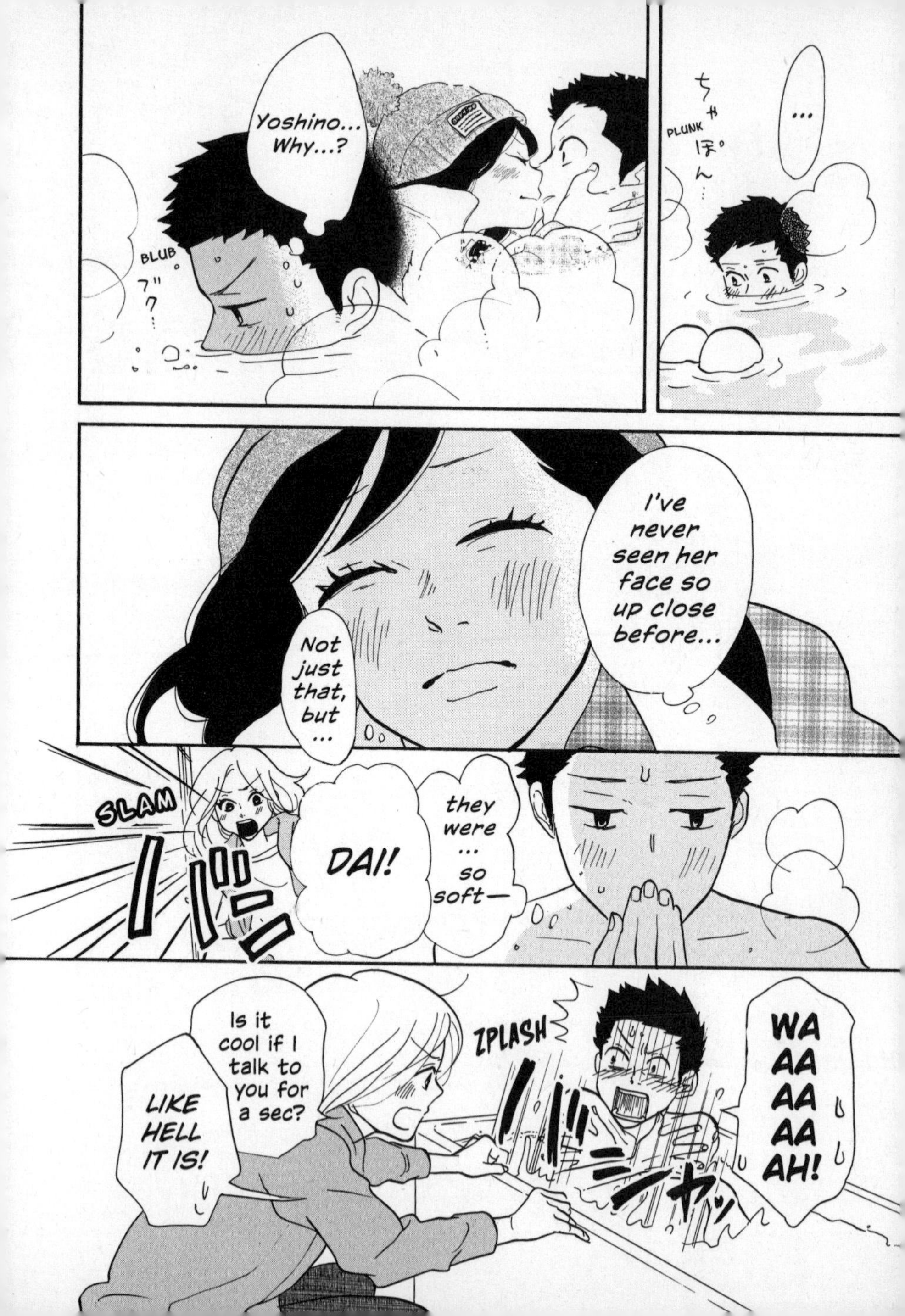
...
PLUNK
ちゃぽん…
Yoshino... Why...?
BLUB
ブク…
I've never seen her face so up close before...
Not just that, but ...
they were ... so soft—
DAI!
SLAM
WAAAAAAAAAH!
ZPLASH
Is it cool if I talk to you for a sec?
LIKE HELL IT IS!

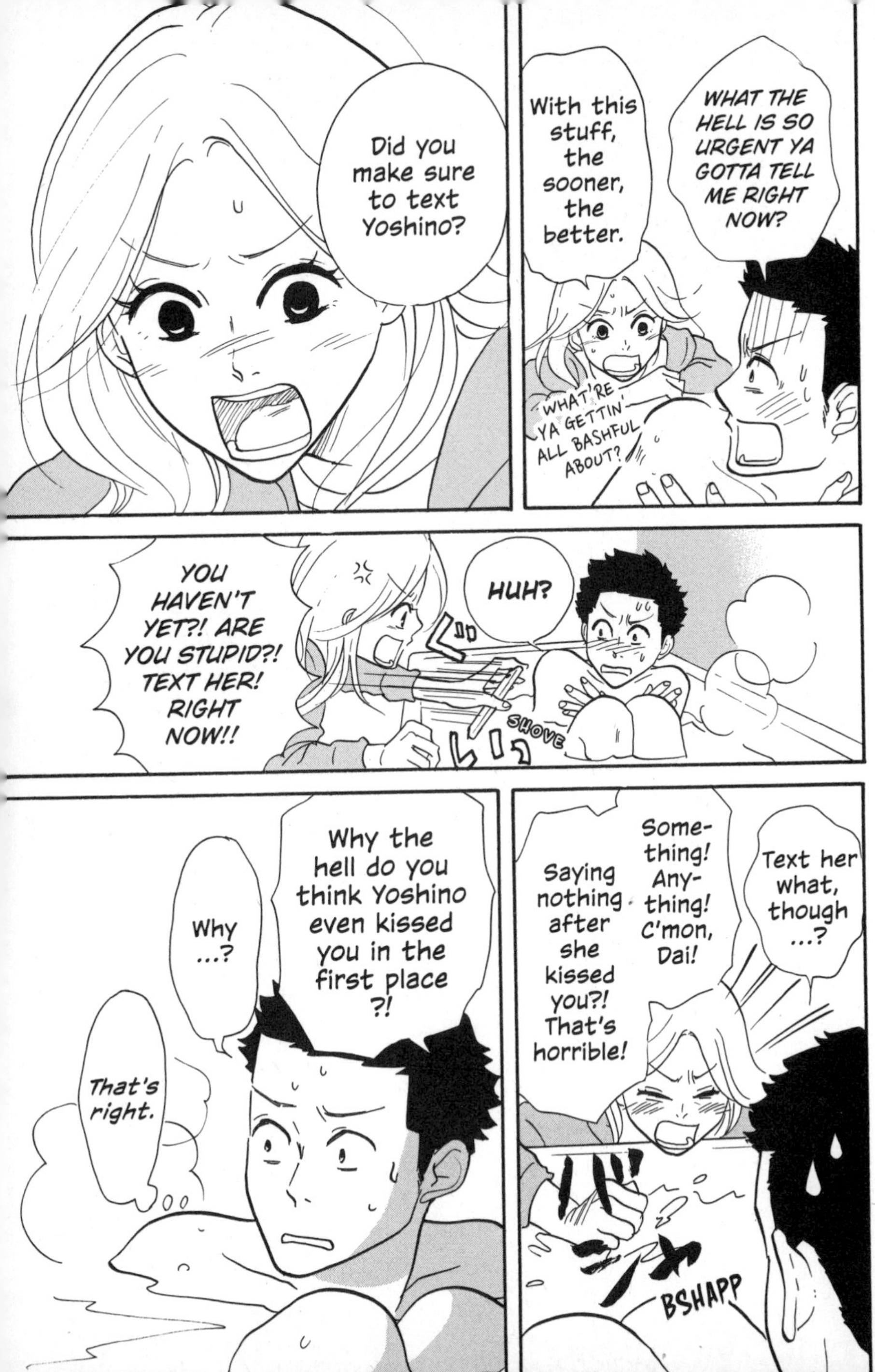
WHAT THE HELL IS SO URGENT YA GOTTA TELL ME RIGHT NOW?
With this stuff, the sooner, the better.
WHAT'RE YA GETTIN' ALL BASHFUL ABOUT?
Did you make sure to text Yoshino?
HUH?
YOU HAVEN'T YET?! ARE YOU STUPID?! TEXT HER! RIGHT NOW!!
SHOVE
Text her what, though ...?
Some-thing! Any-thing! C'mon, Dai!
Saying nothing after she kissed you?! That's horrible!
BSHAPP
Why the hell do you think Yoshino even kissed you in the first place ?!
Why ...?
That's right.

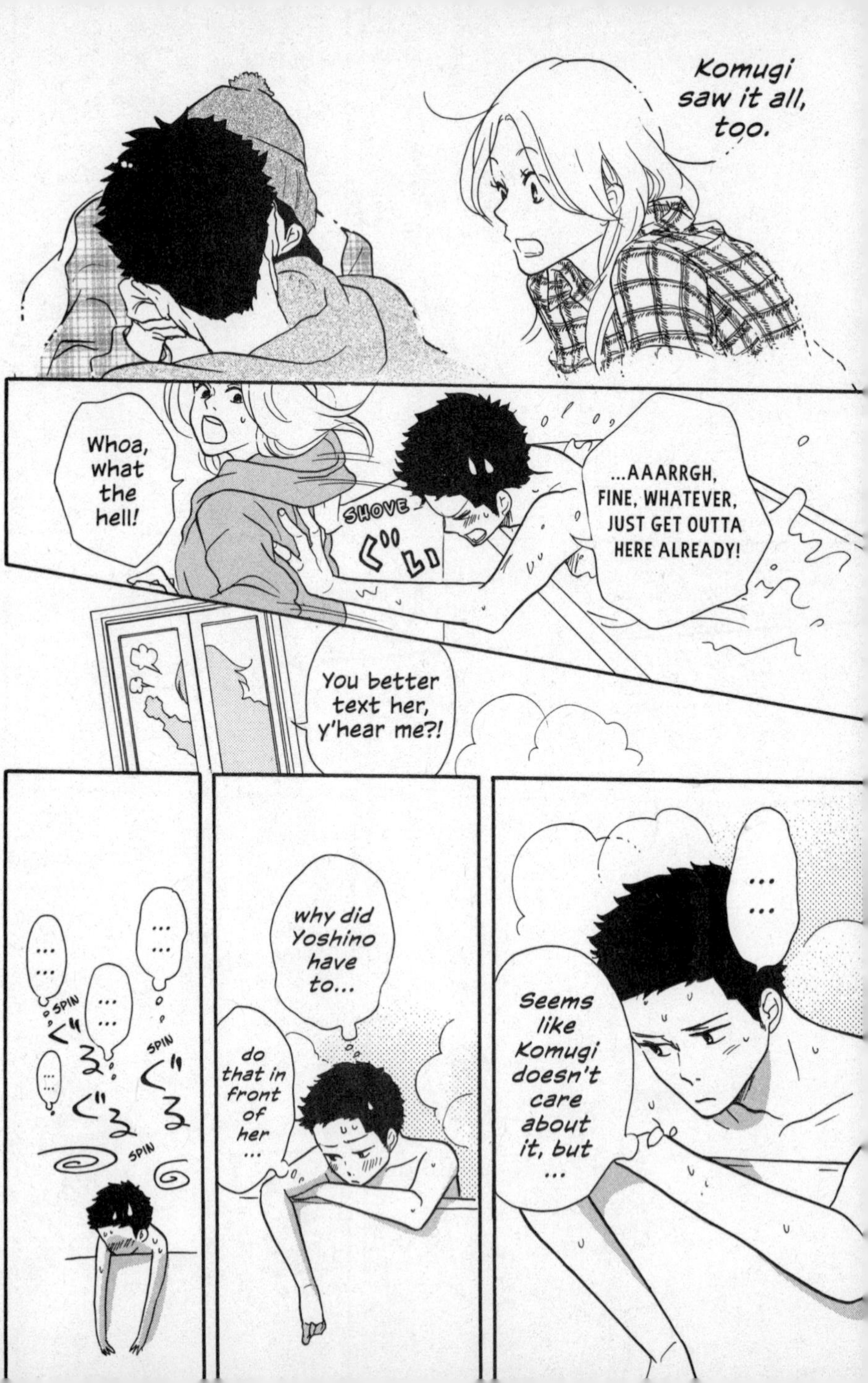
Komugi saw it all, too.
...AAARRGH, FINE, WHATEVER, JUST GET OUTTA HERE ALREADY!
Whoa, what the hell!
SHOVE
You better text her, y'hear me?!
... ...
Seems like Komugi doesn't care about it, but ...
why did Yoshino have to...
do that in front of her ...
... ...
... ...
... ...
SPIN
SPIN
SPIN

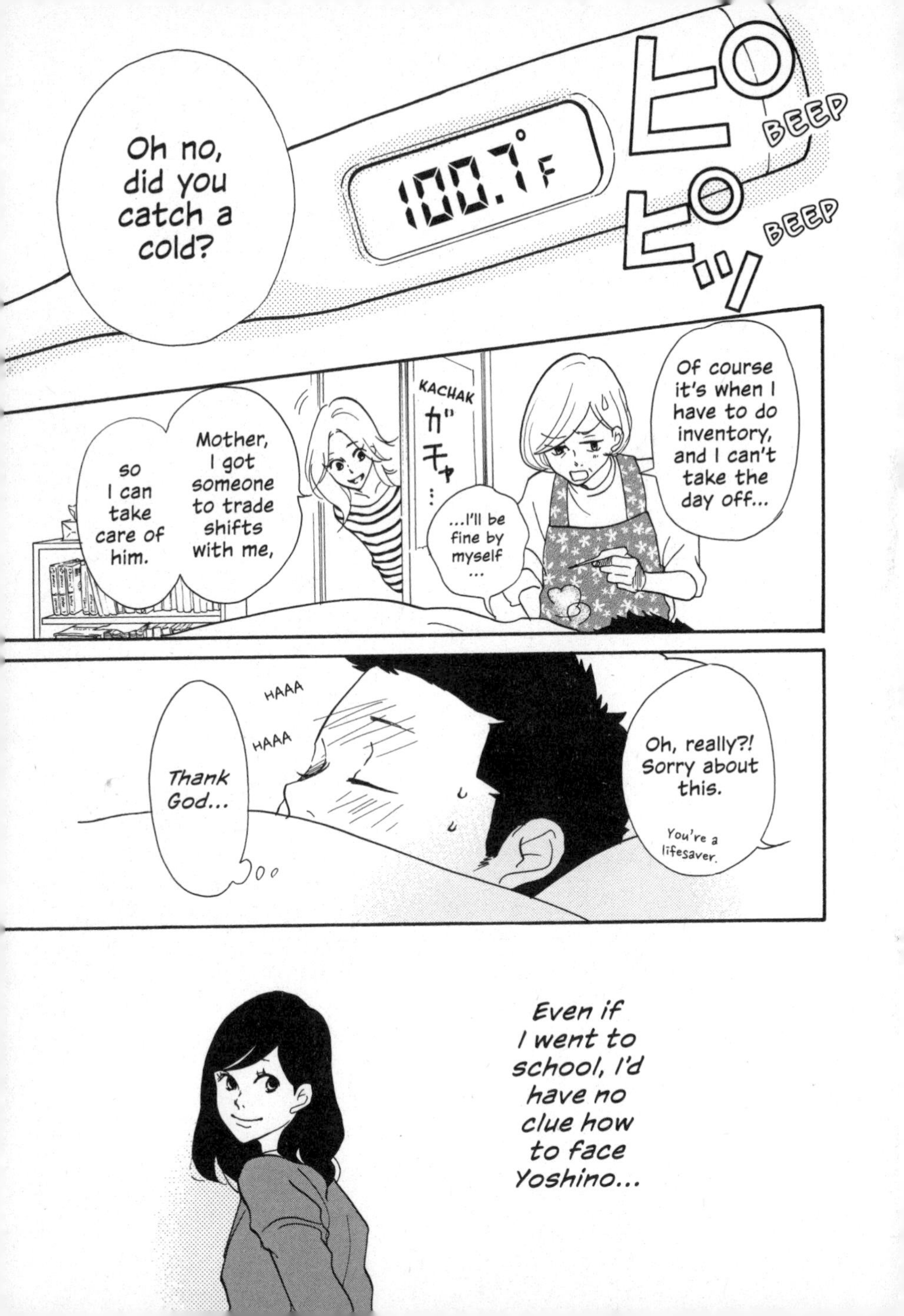
100.7°F
ピ
BEEP
ピッ
BEEP
Oh no, did you catch a cold?
Of course it's when I have to do inventory, and I can't take the day off...
...I'll be fine by myself...
KACHAK
ガチャ
Mother, I got someone to trade shifts with me,
so I can take care of him.
Oh, really?! Sorry about this.
You're a lifesaver.
HAAA
HAAA
Thank God...
Even if I went to school, I'd have no clue how to face Yoshino...

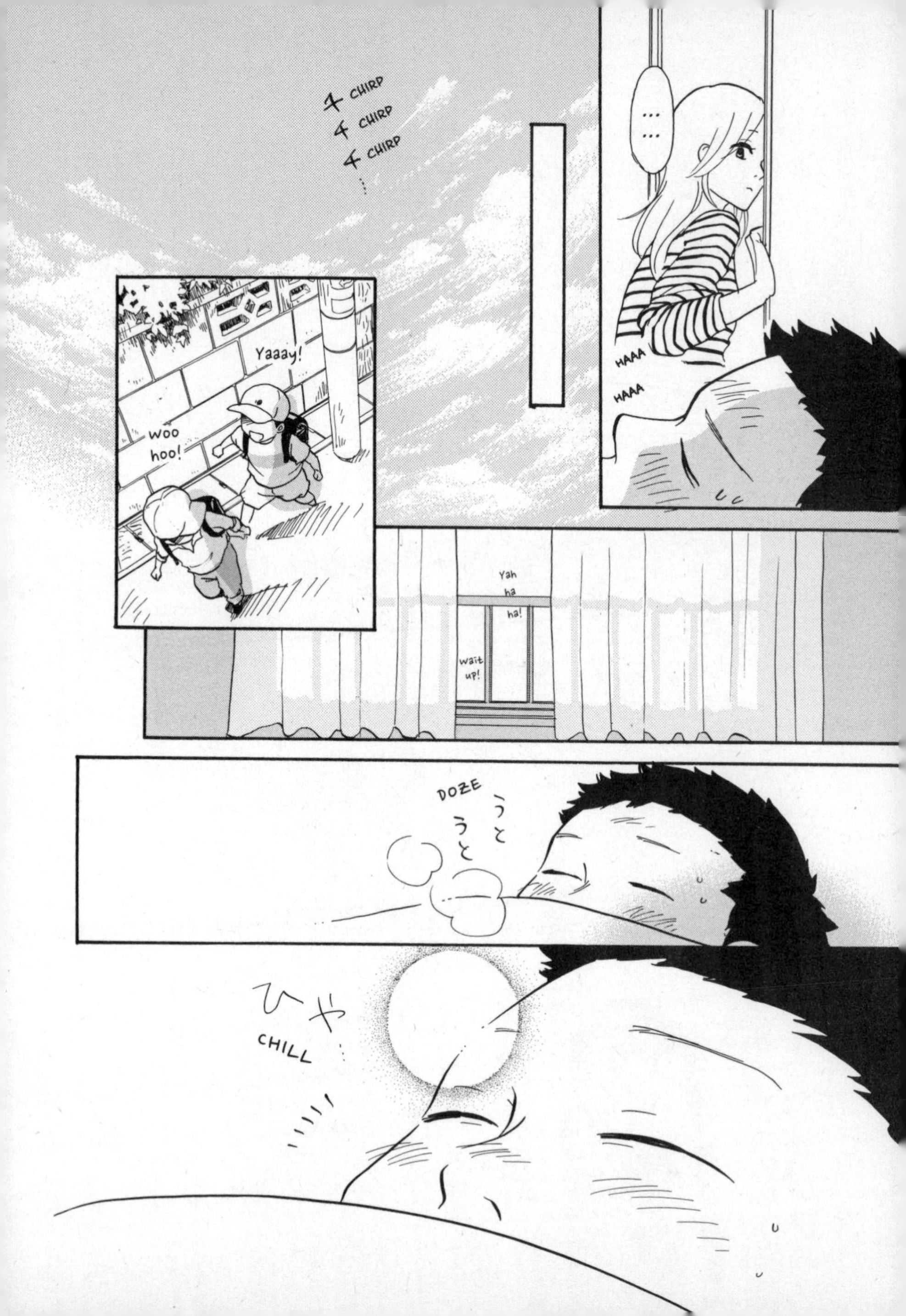

CHIRP
CHIRP
CHIRP
....
....
HAAA
HAAA
Yaaay!
woo hoo!
Yah ha ha!
Wait up!
DOZE
うと うと
ひや
CHILL

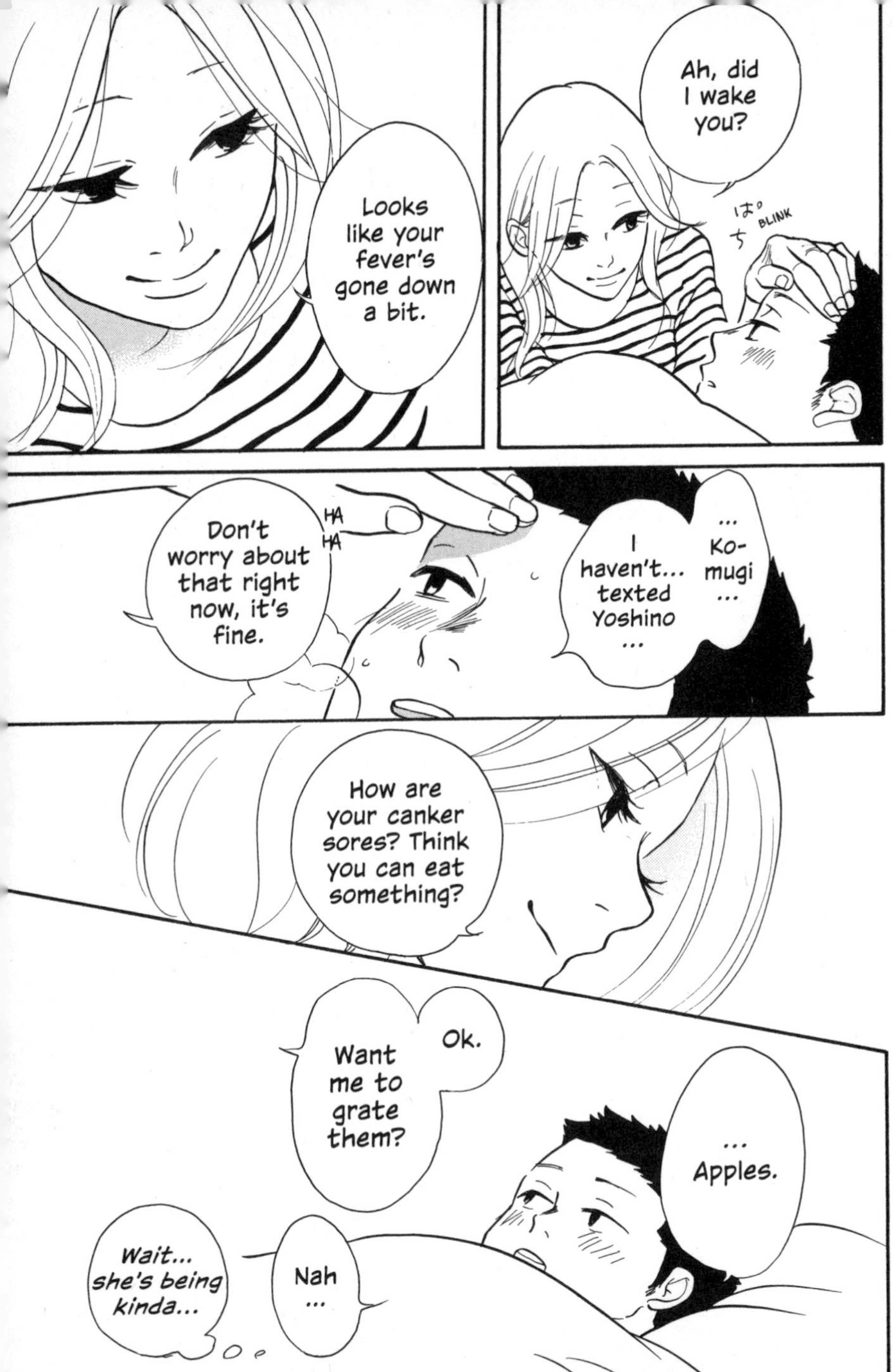
Ah, did I wake you?
ぱち BLINK
Looks like your fever's gone down a bit.
... Ko-mugi ...
I haven't... texted Yoshino ...
HA HA
Don't worry about that right now, it's fine.
How are your canker sores? Think you can eat something?
... Apples.
Ok.
Want me to grate them?
Nah ...
Wait... she's being kinda...

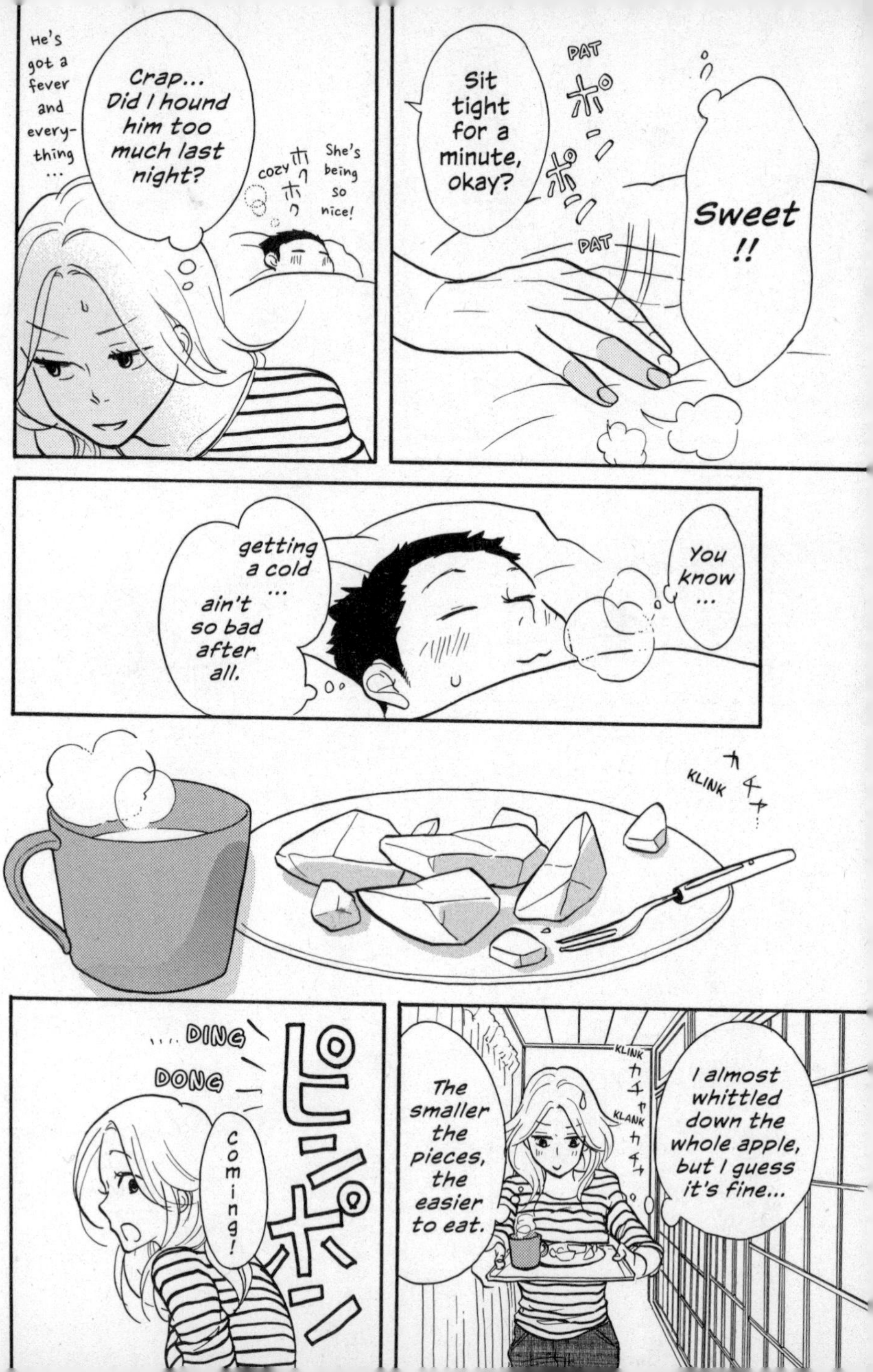
Sit tight for a minute, okay?
PAT
ポン
PAT
ポン
Sweet !!
She's being so nice!
cozy
ホクホク
Crap... Did I hound him too much last night?
He's got a fever and everything...
You know...
getting a cold... ain't so bad after all.
KLINK
カチャ...
I almost whittled down the whole apple, but I guess it's fine...
KLINK
カチャ
KLANK
カチャ
The smaller the pieces, the easier to eat.
ピンポーン
....DING
DONG
Coming!

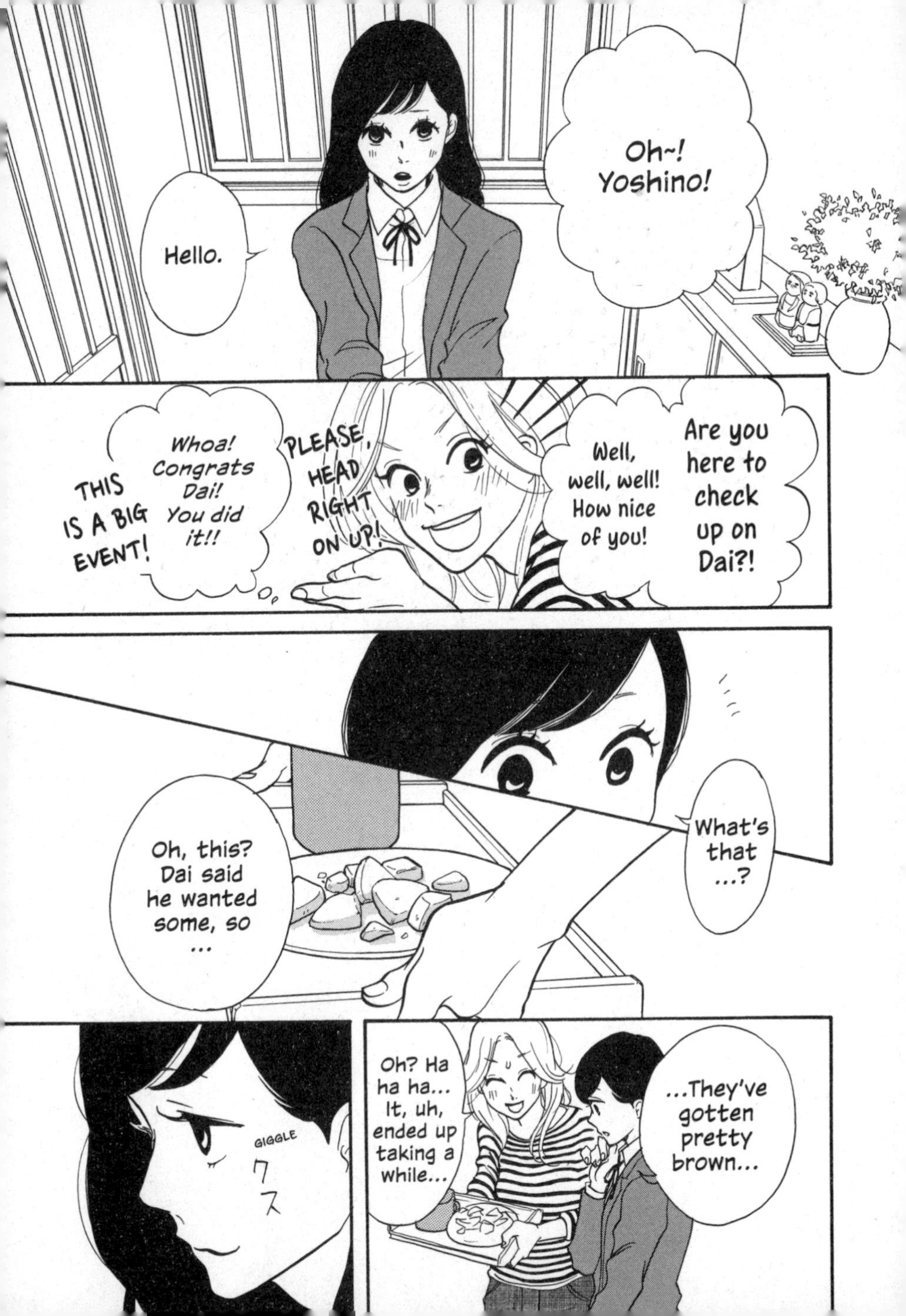
Oh~! Yoshino!
Hello.
Are you here to check up on Dai?!
Well, well, well! How nice of you!
PLEASE, HEAD RIGHT ON UP!
Whoa! Congrats Dai! You did it!!
THIS IS A BIG EVENT!
What's that ...?
Oh, this? Dai said he wanted some, so ...
...They've gotten pretty brown...
Oh? Ha ha ha... It, uh, ended up taking a while...
GIGGLE
クス

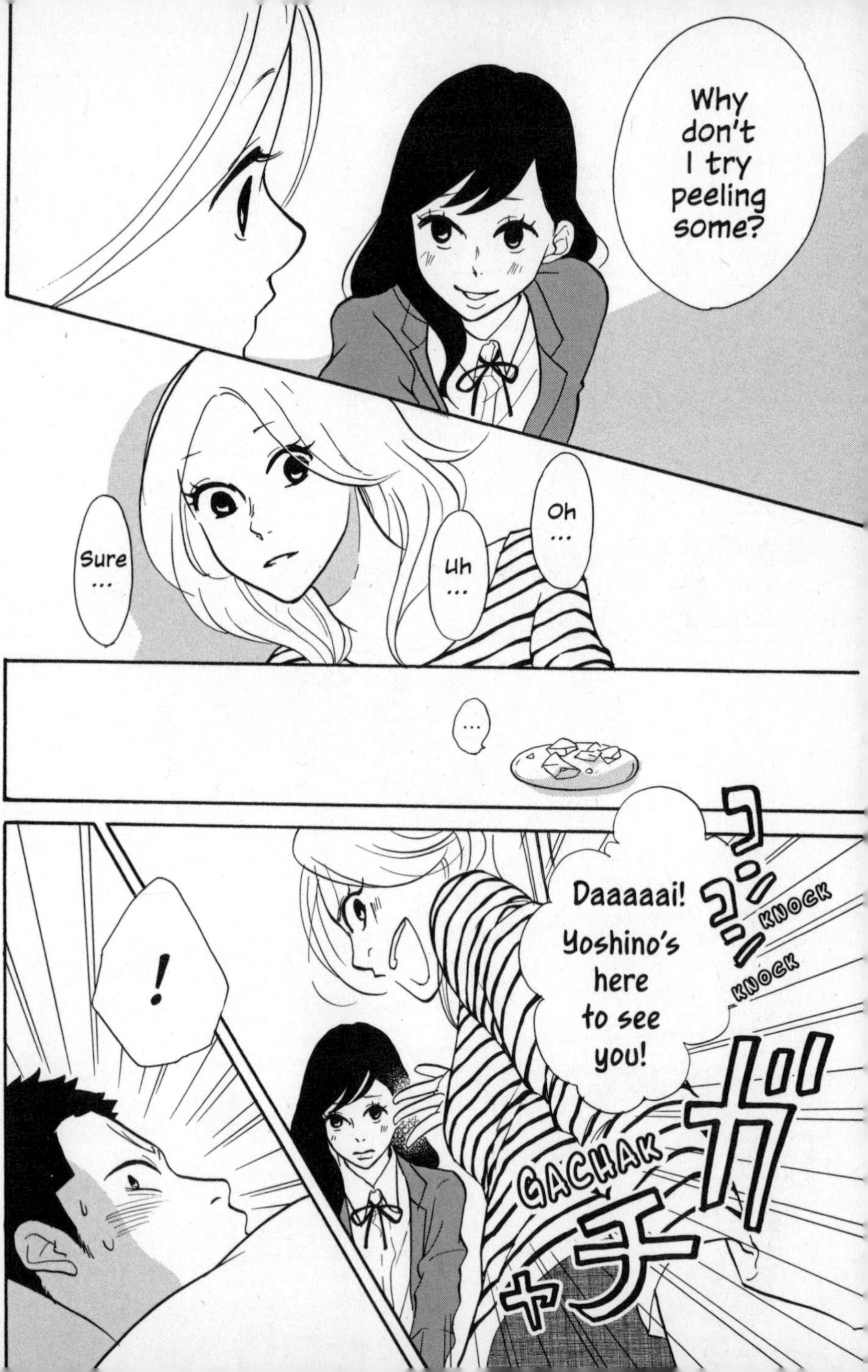

Why don't I try peeling some?
Oh ...
Uh ...
Sure ...
...
コンコン
KNOCK KNOCK
Daaaaai! Yoshino's here to see you!
ガチャ
GACHAK
!

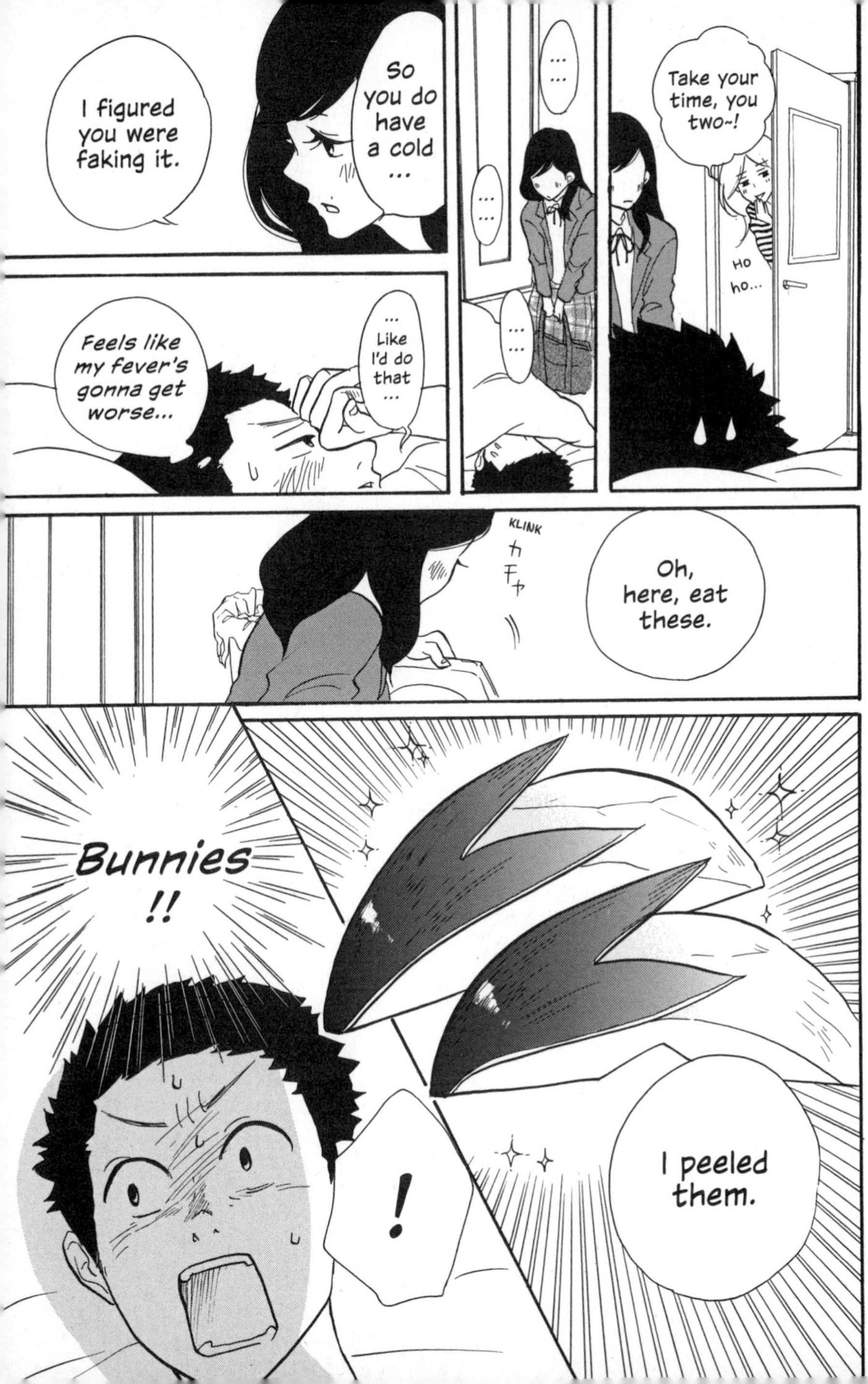
Take your time, you two~!
Ho ho...
......
......
......
So you do have a cold ...
I figured you were faking it.
... Like I'd do that ...
Feels like my fever's gonna get worse...
KLINK
カチャ
Oh, here, eat these.
I peeled them.
!
Bunnies !!

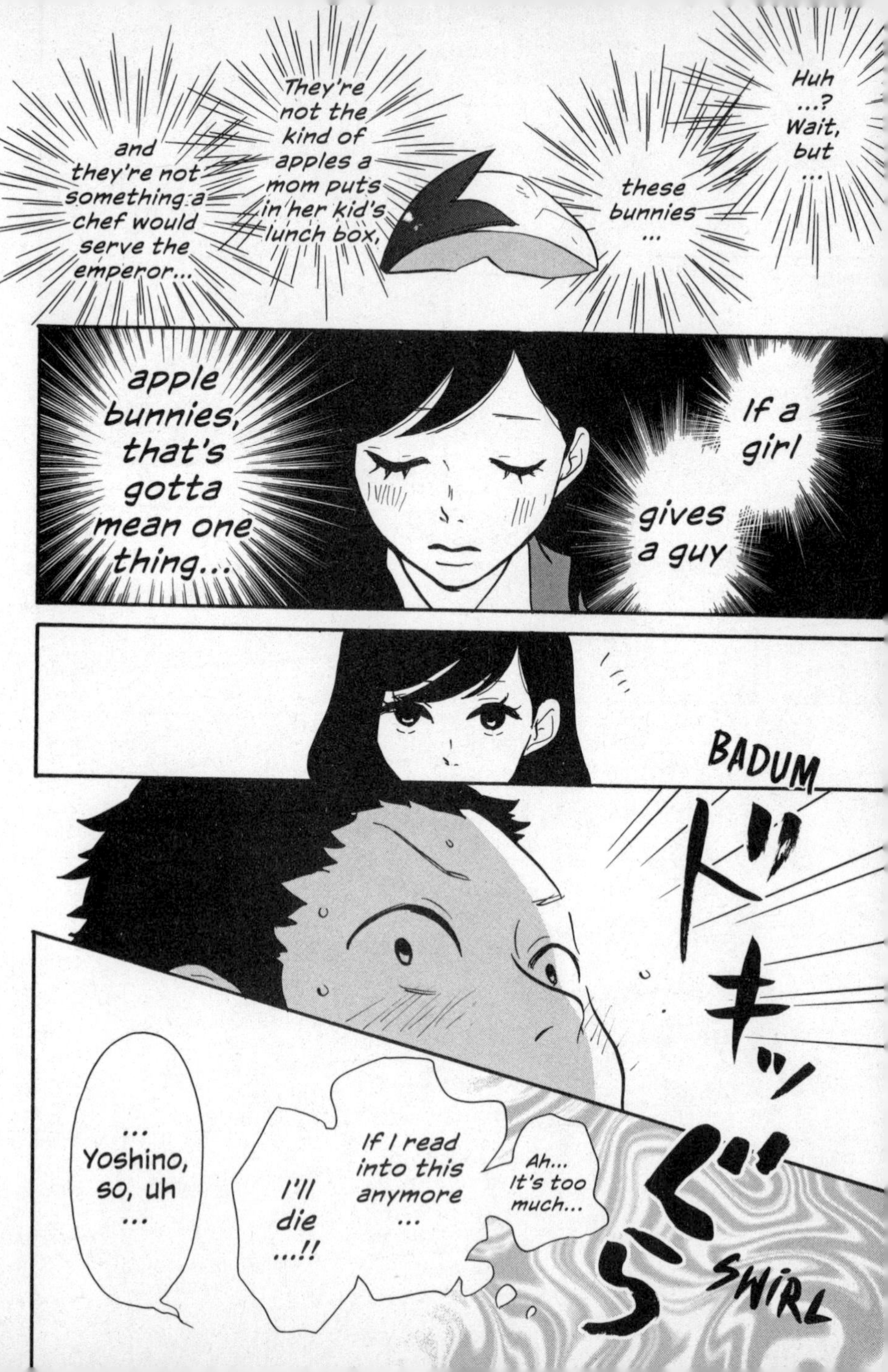
Huh ...? Wait, but ...
these bunnies ...
They're not the kind of apples a mom puts in her kid's lunch box,
and they're not something a chef would serve the emperor...
If a girl
gives a guy
apple bunnies, that's gotta mean one thing...
BADUM
ドキッ
Ah... It's too much...
If I read into this anymore ...
I'll die ...!!
... Yoshino, so, uh ...
ぐら
SWIRL

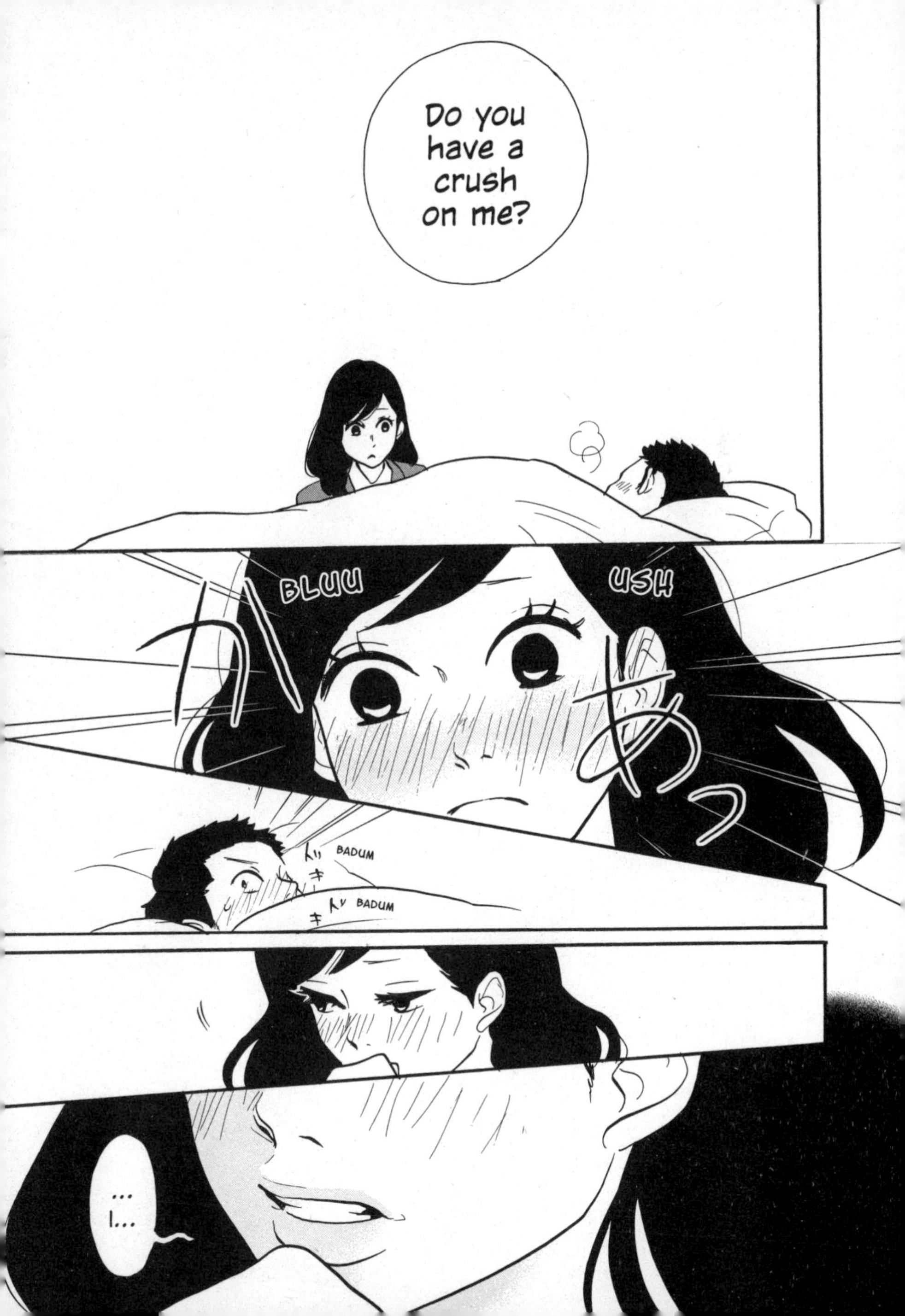

Do you have a crush on me?
BLUU
USH
BADUM
BADUM
... I...

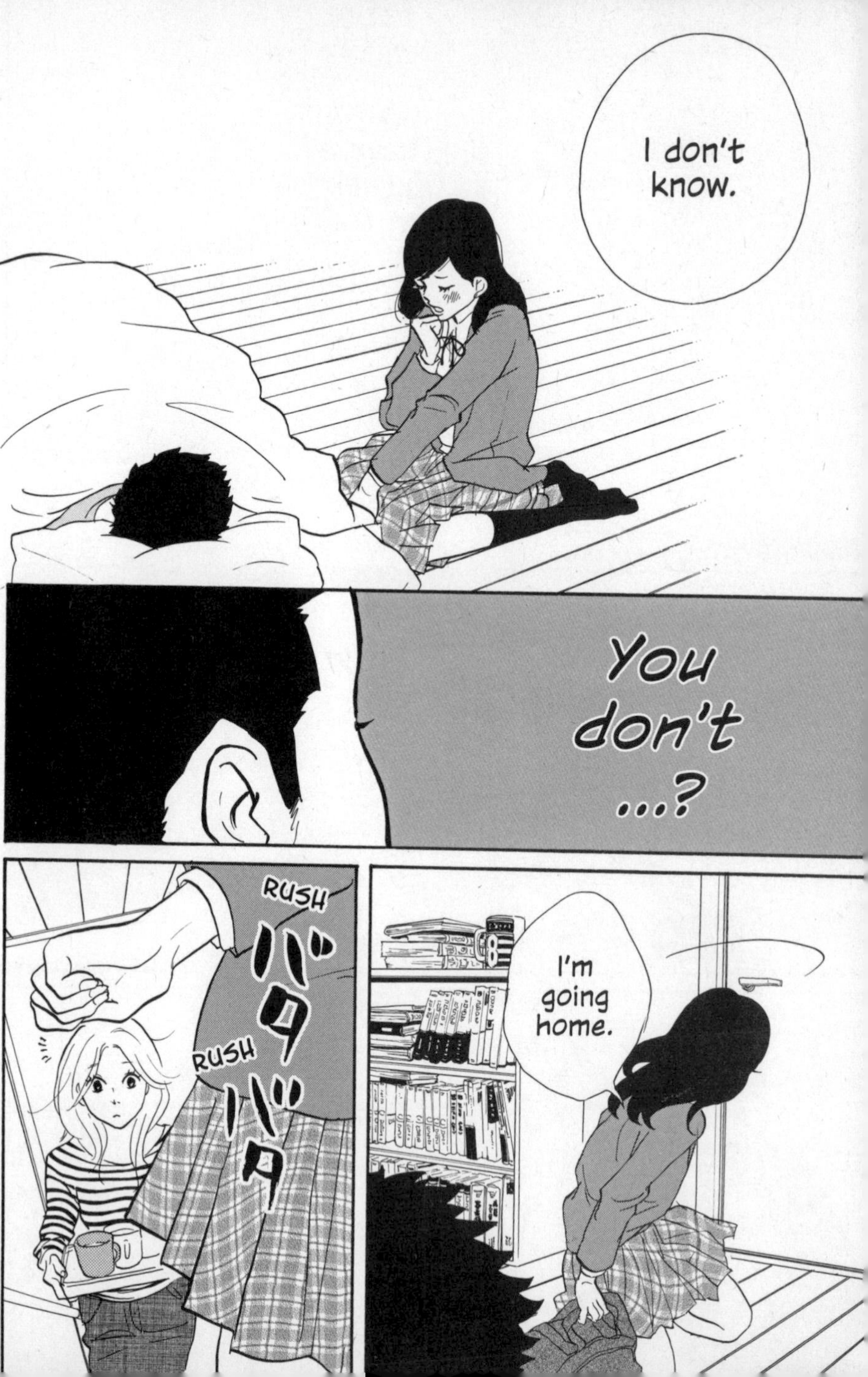
I don't know.
You don't ...?
I'm going home.
RUSH
RUSH
バタバタ

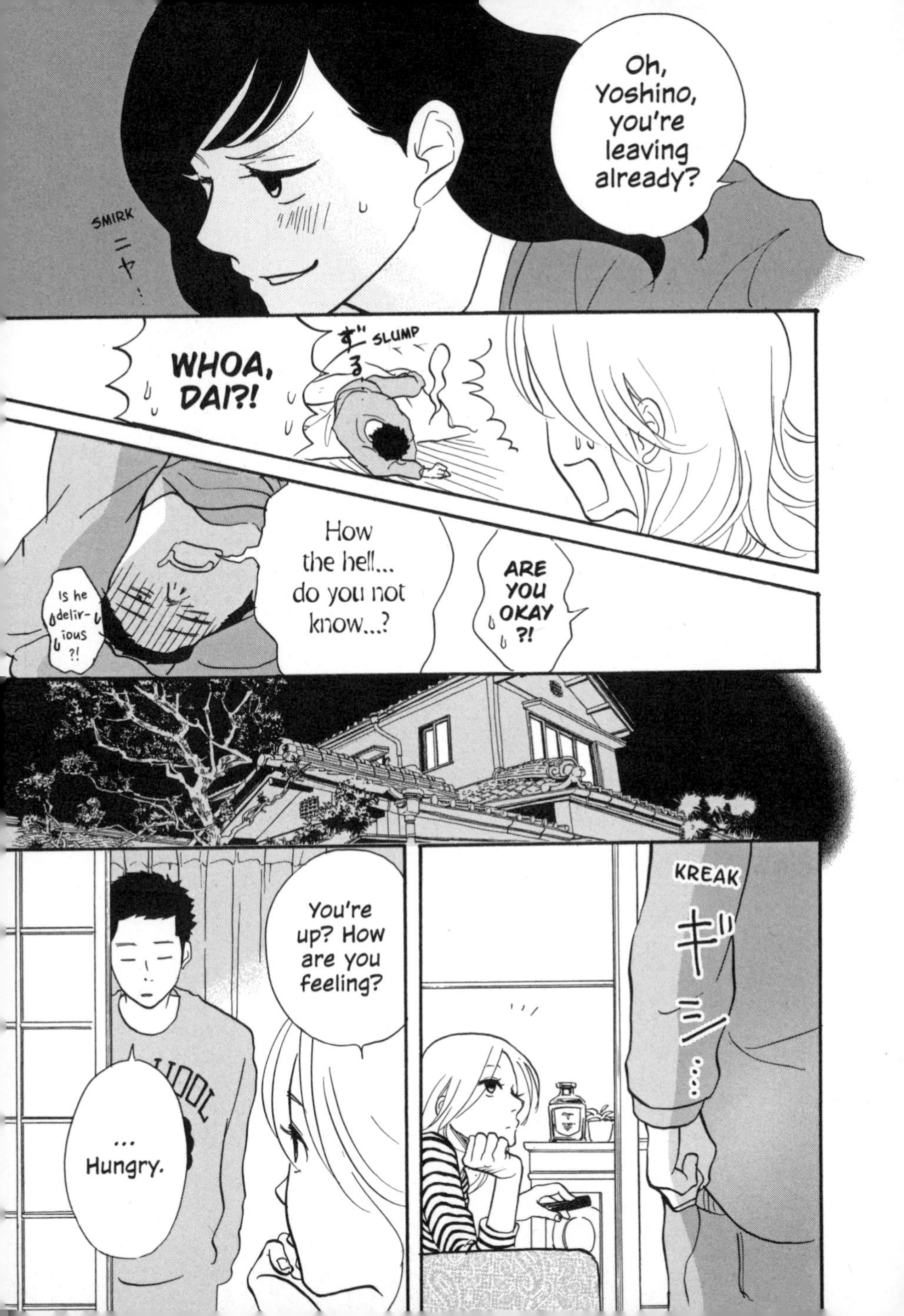
Oh, Yoshino, you're leaving already?
SMIRK
ニヤ
SLUMP
ずる
WHOA, DAI?!
ARE YOU OKAY?!
How the hell... do you not know...?
Is he delirious?!
KREAK
ギシ…
You're up? How are you feeling?
... Hungry.

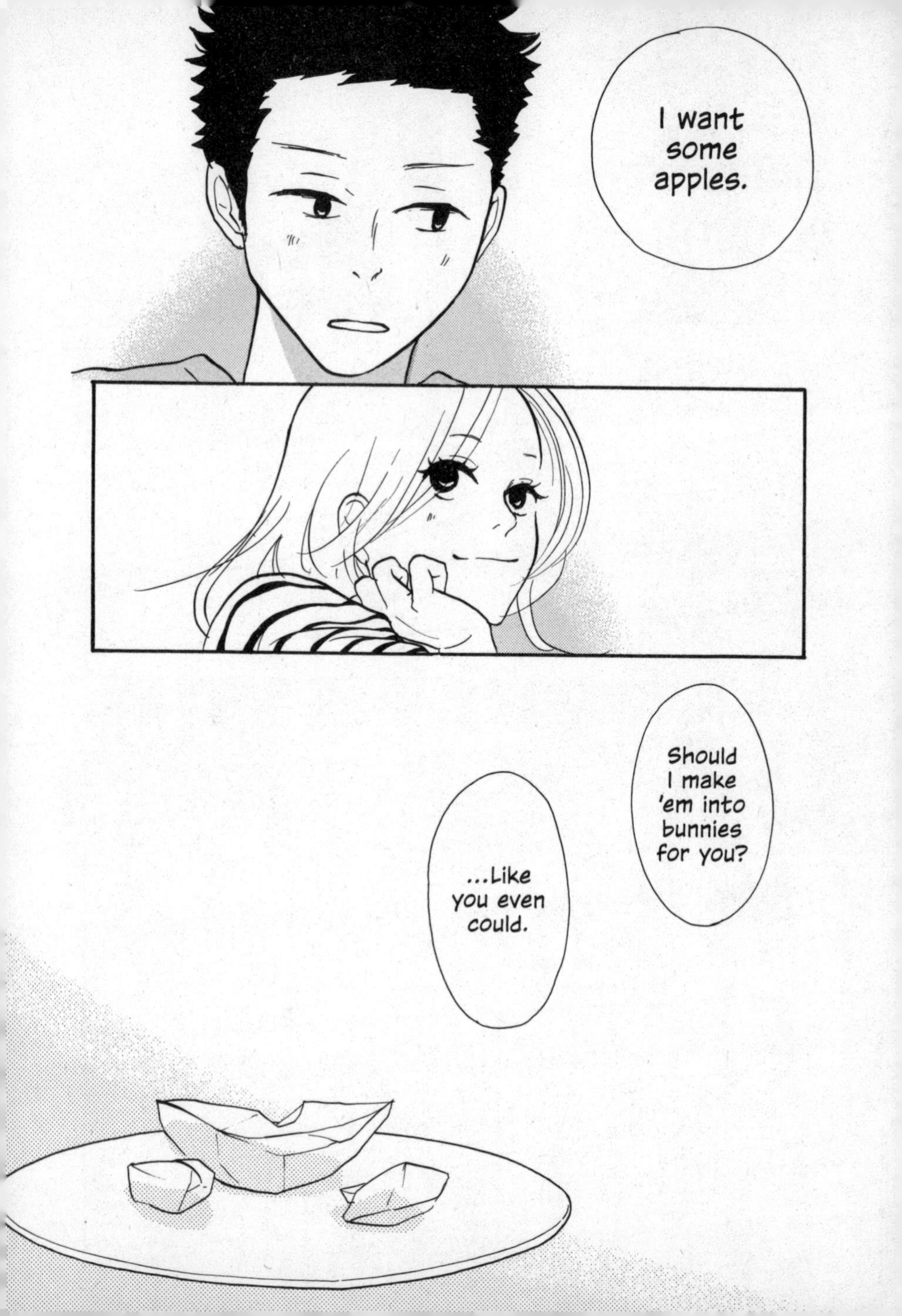
I want some apples.
Should I make 'em into bunnies for you?
...Like you even could.

21

THE DOOR OF YOUTH

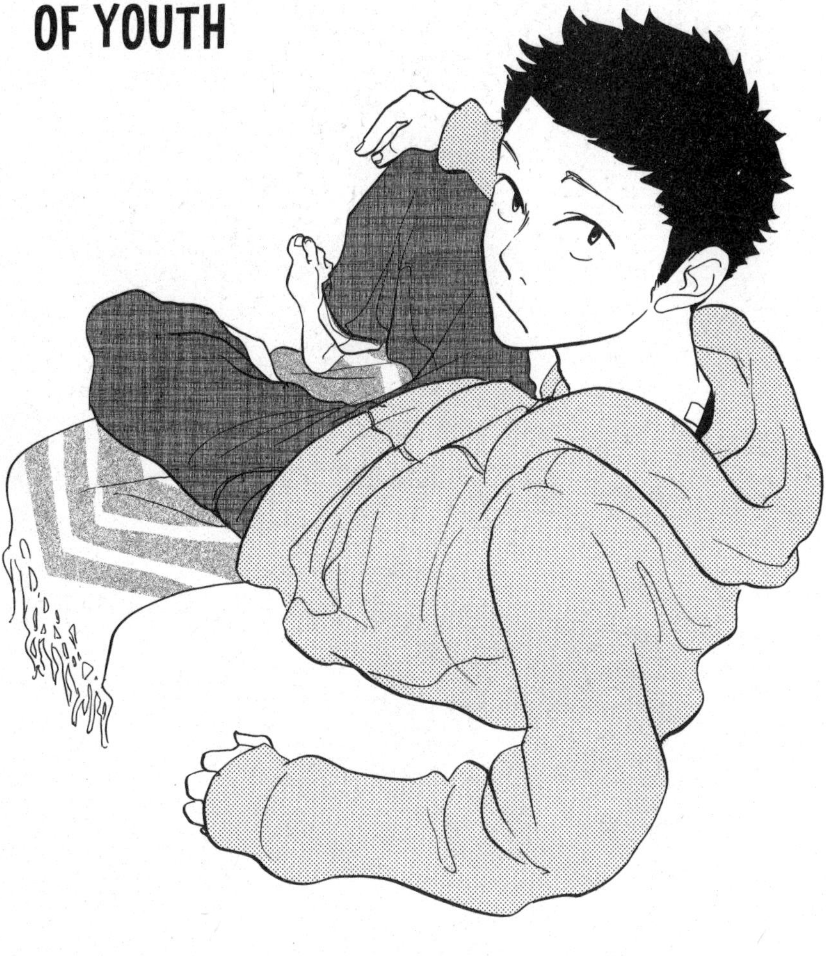

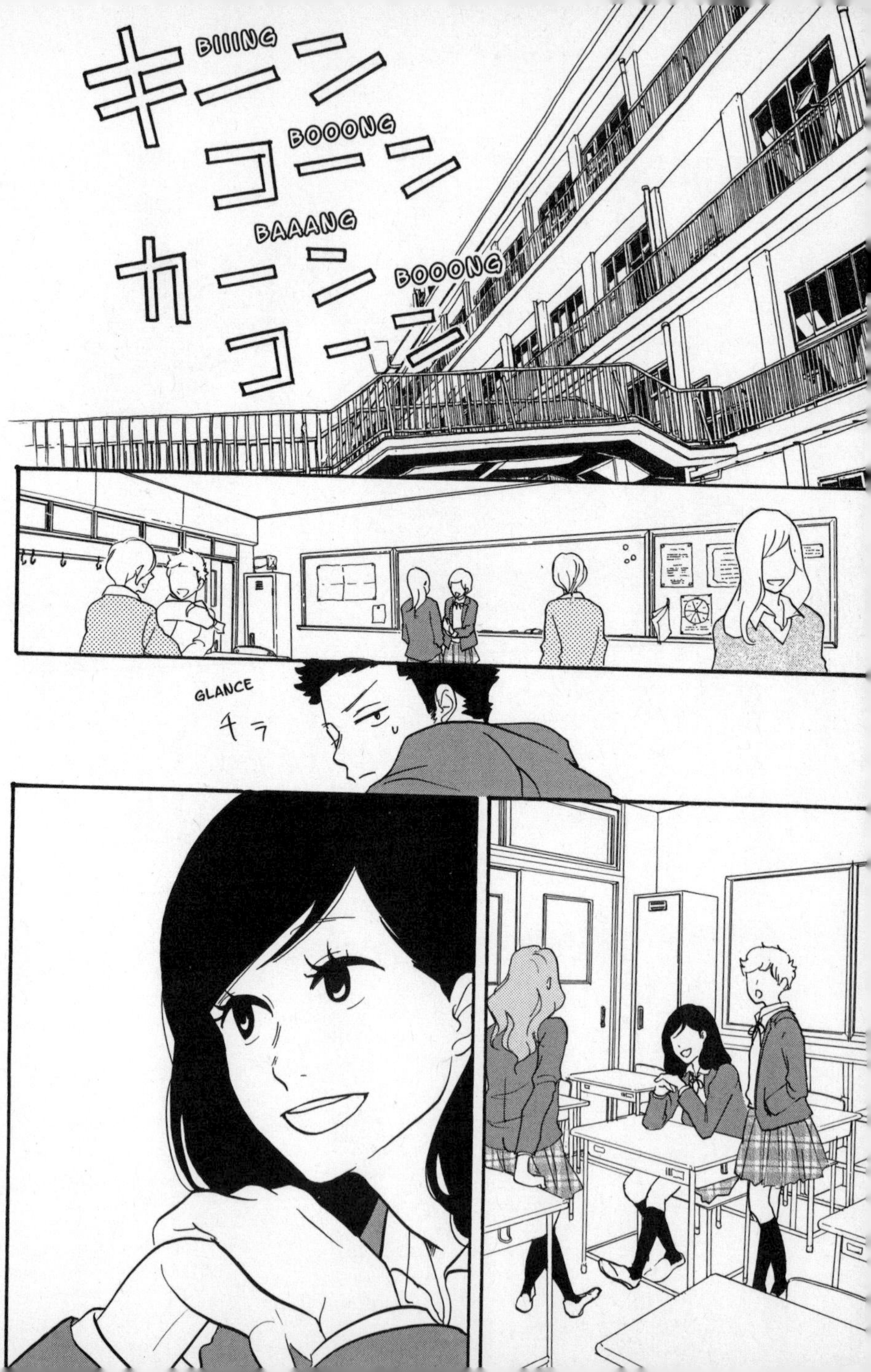
BIIING
キーン
BOOONG
コーン
BAAANG
カーン
BOOONG
コーン
GLANCE
チラ

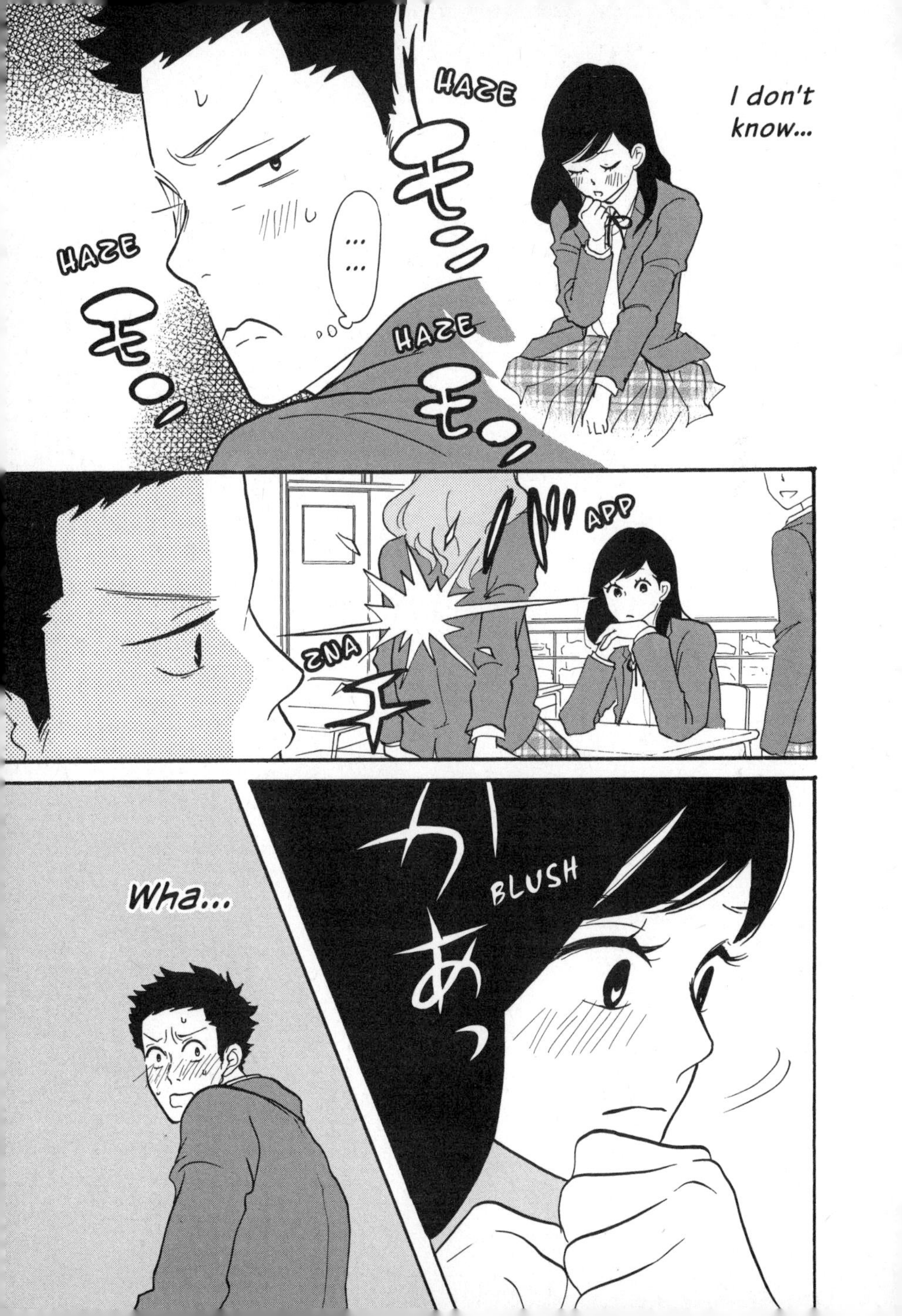

I don't know...
HAZE
......
HAZE
HAZE
APP
BLUSH
Wha...

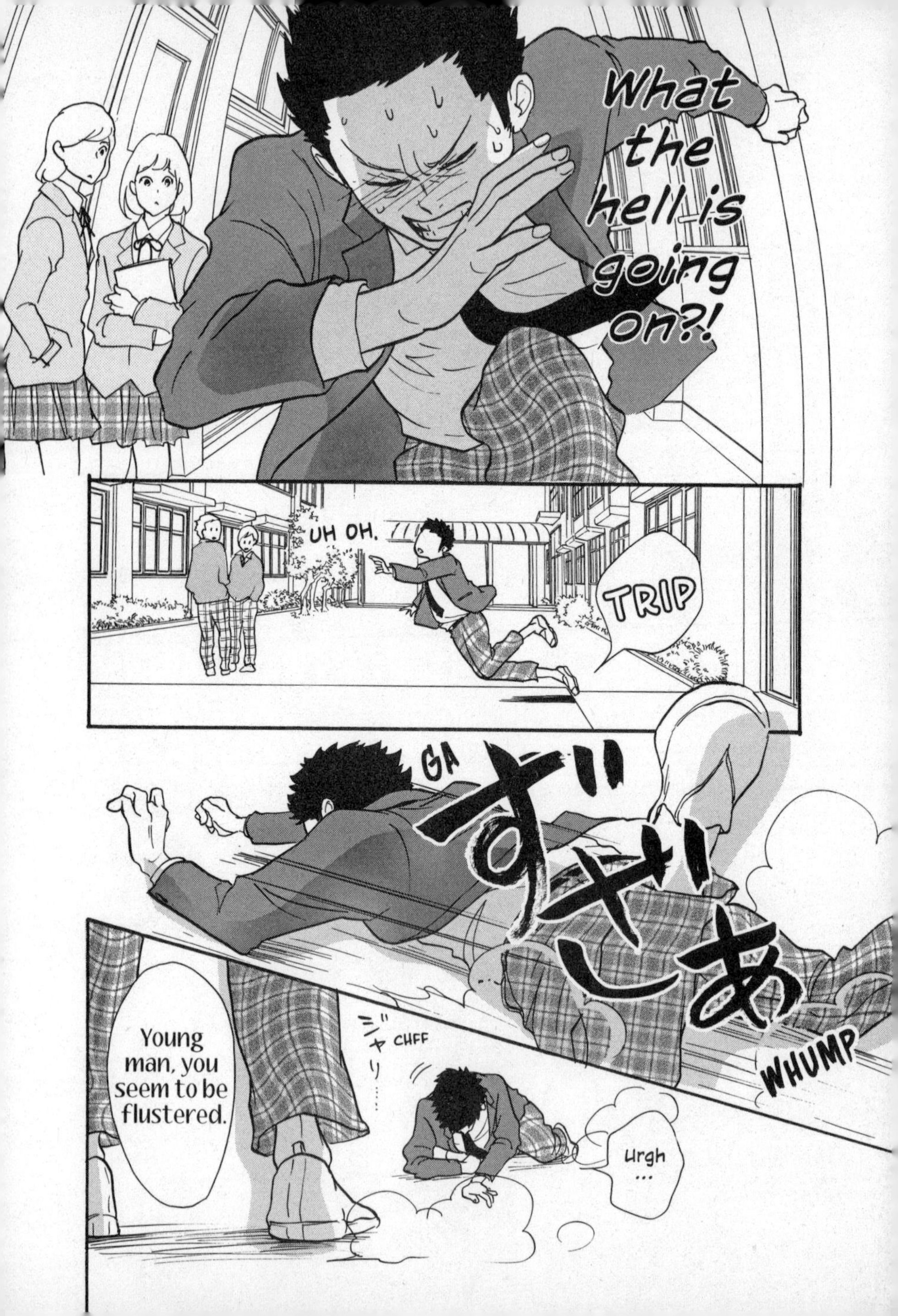
What the hell is going on?!
UH OH.
TRIP
GA
ずざあ
WHUMP
...
Urgh ...
ジャリ……
CHFF
Young man, you seem to be flustered.

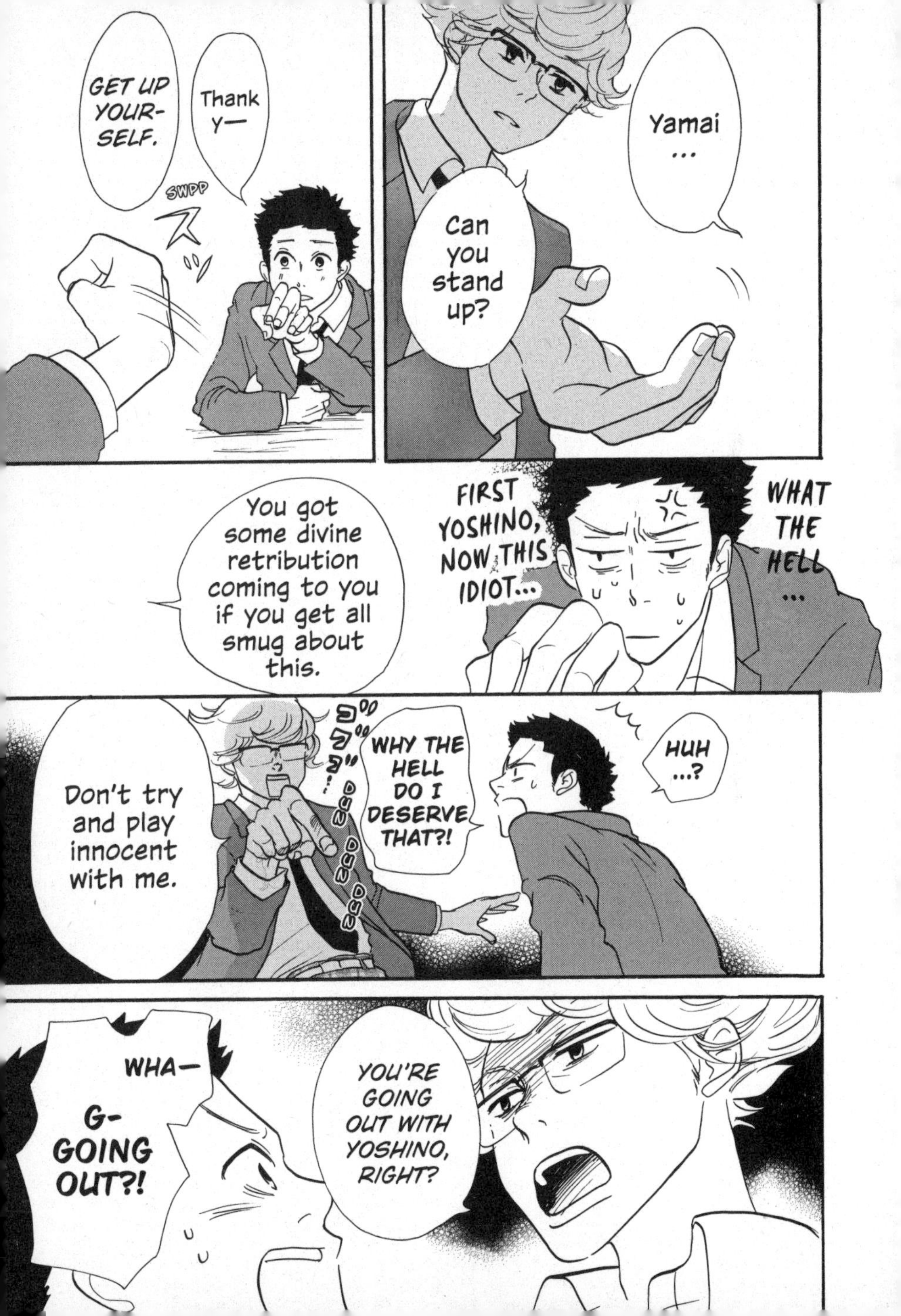
Yamai ...
Can you stand up?
Thank Y—
GET UP YOURSELF.
SWPP
WHAT THE HELL ...
FIRST YOSHINO, NOW THIS IDIOT...
You got some divine retribution coming to you if you get all smug about this.
HUH ...?
WHY THE HELL DO I DESERVE THAT?!
DUN DUN DUN DUN
Don't try and play innocent with me.
YOU'RE GOING OUT WITH YOSHINO, RIGHT?
WHA—
G-GOING OUT?!

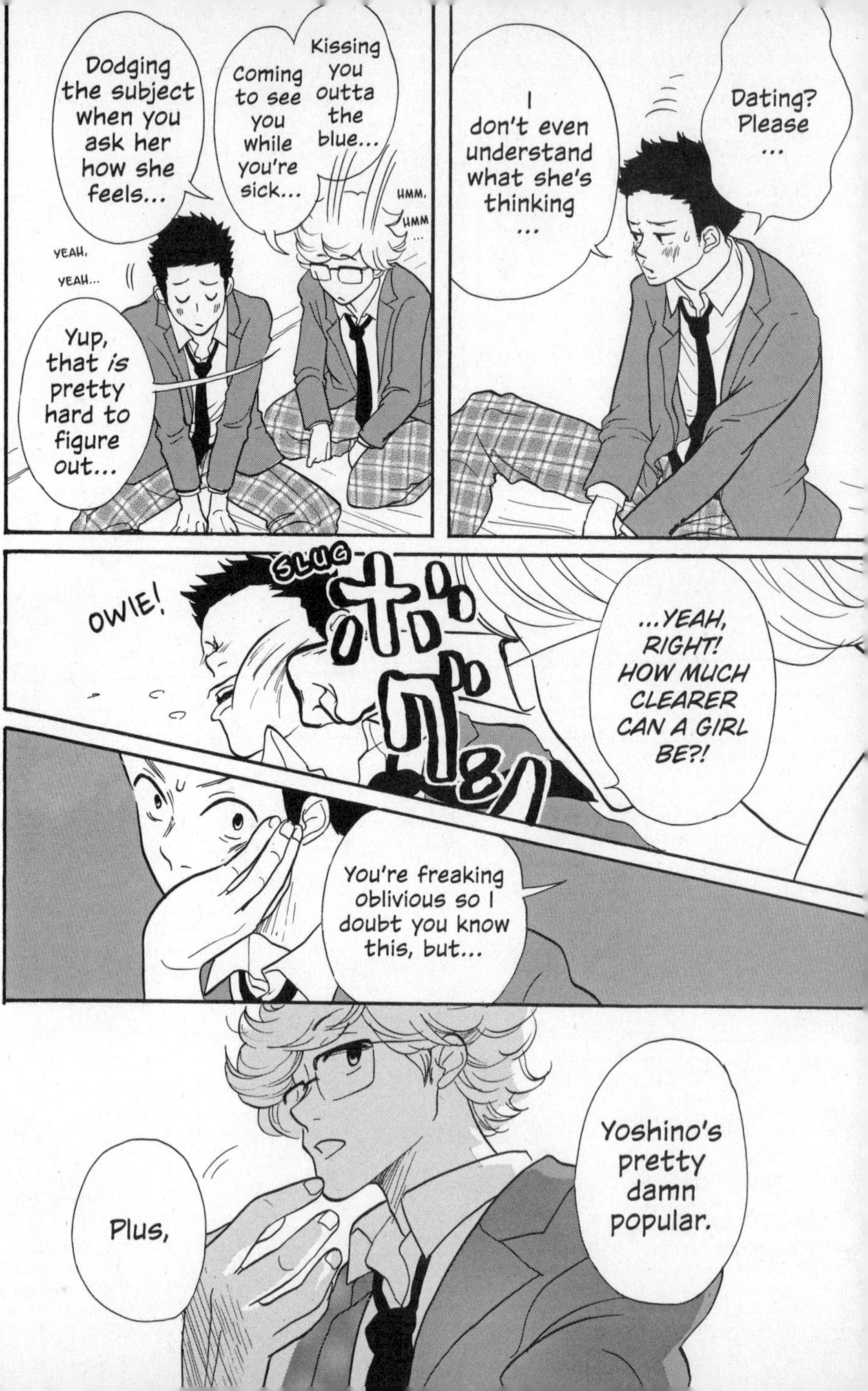
Dating? Please ...
I don't even understand what she's thinking ...
Kissing you outta the blue...
Coming to see you while you're sick...
HMM, HMM ...
Dodging the subject when you ask her how she feels...
YEAH, YEAH...
Yup, that *is* pretty hard to figure out...
SLUG
...YEAH, RIGHT! HOW MUCH CLEARER CAN A GIRL BE?!
OWIE!
You're freaking oblivious so I doubt you know this, but...
Yoshino's pretty damn popular.
Plus,

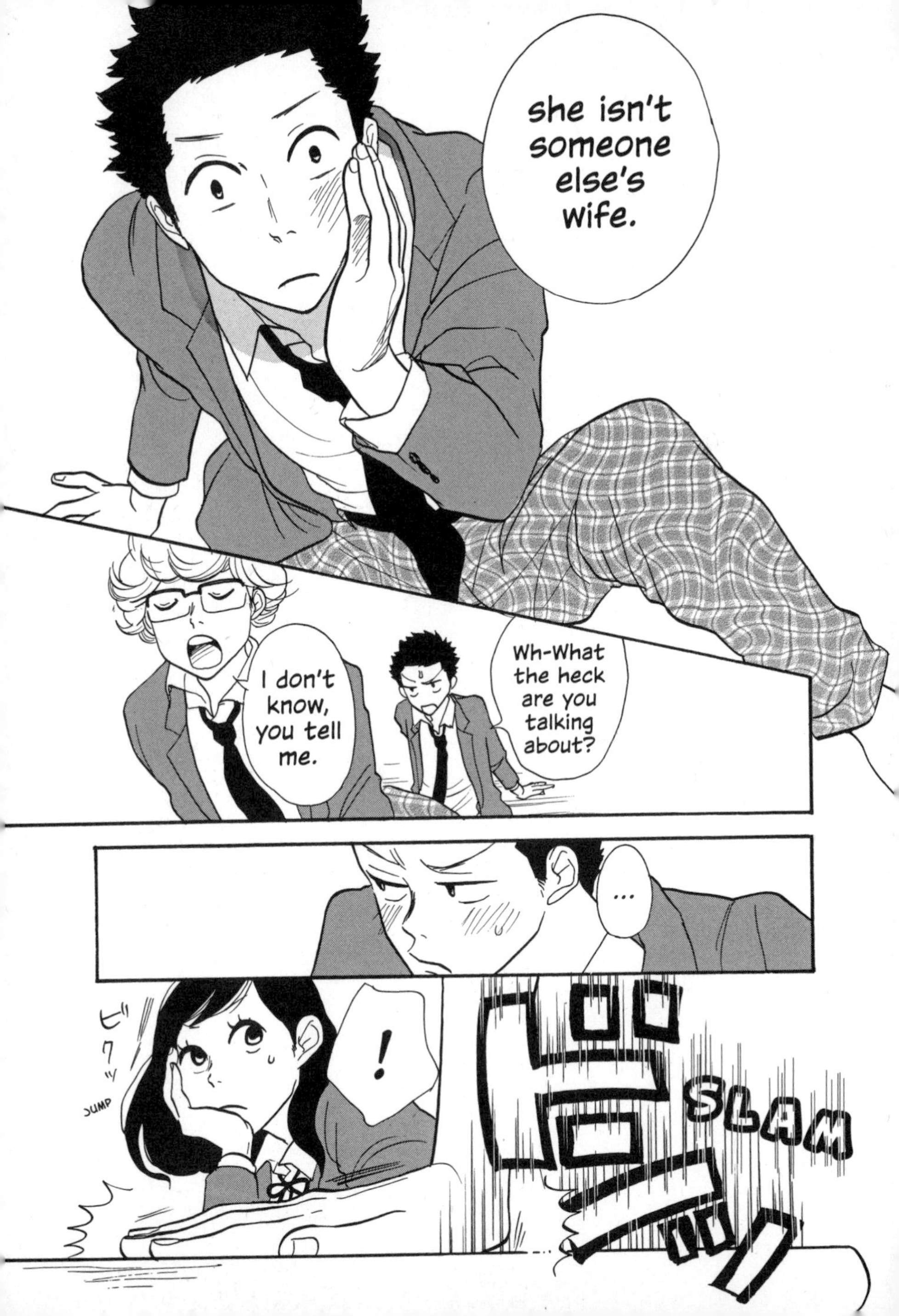
she isn't someone else's wife.
Wh-What the heck are you talking about?
I don't know, you tell me.
...
SLAM
!
ビクッ
JUMP

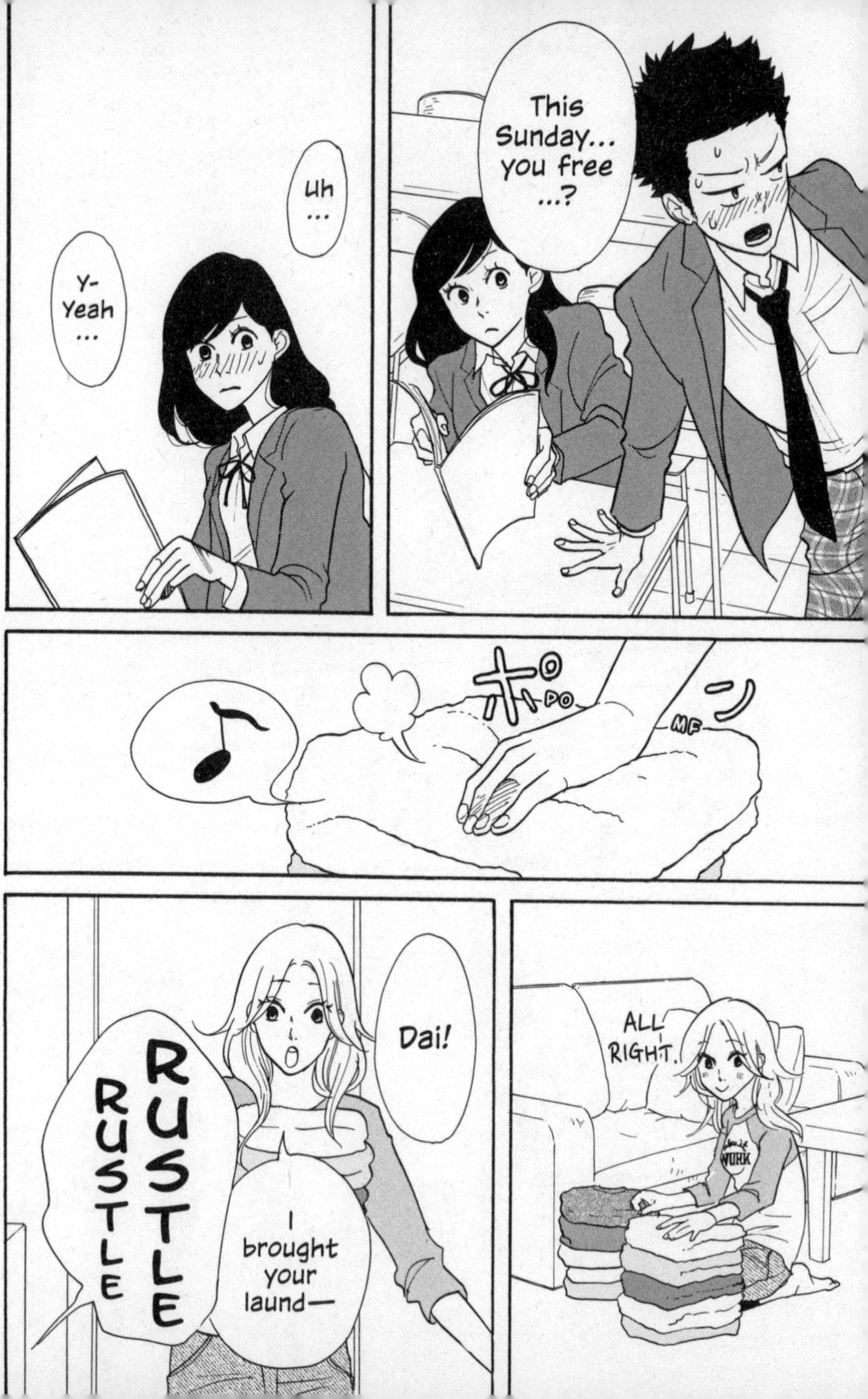
This Sunday... you free ...?
Uh ...
Y-Yeah ...
ポ
PO
ン
MF
ALL RIGHT.
Dai!
I brought your laund—
RUSTLE RUSTLE

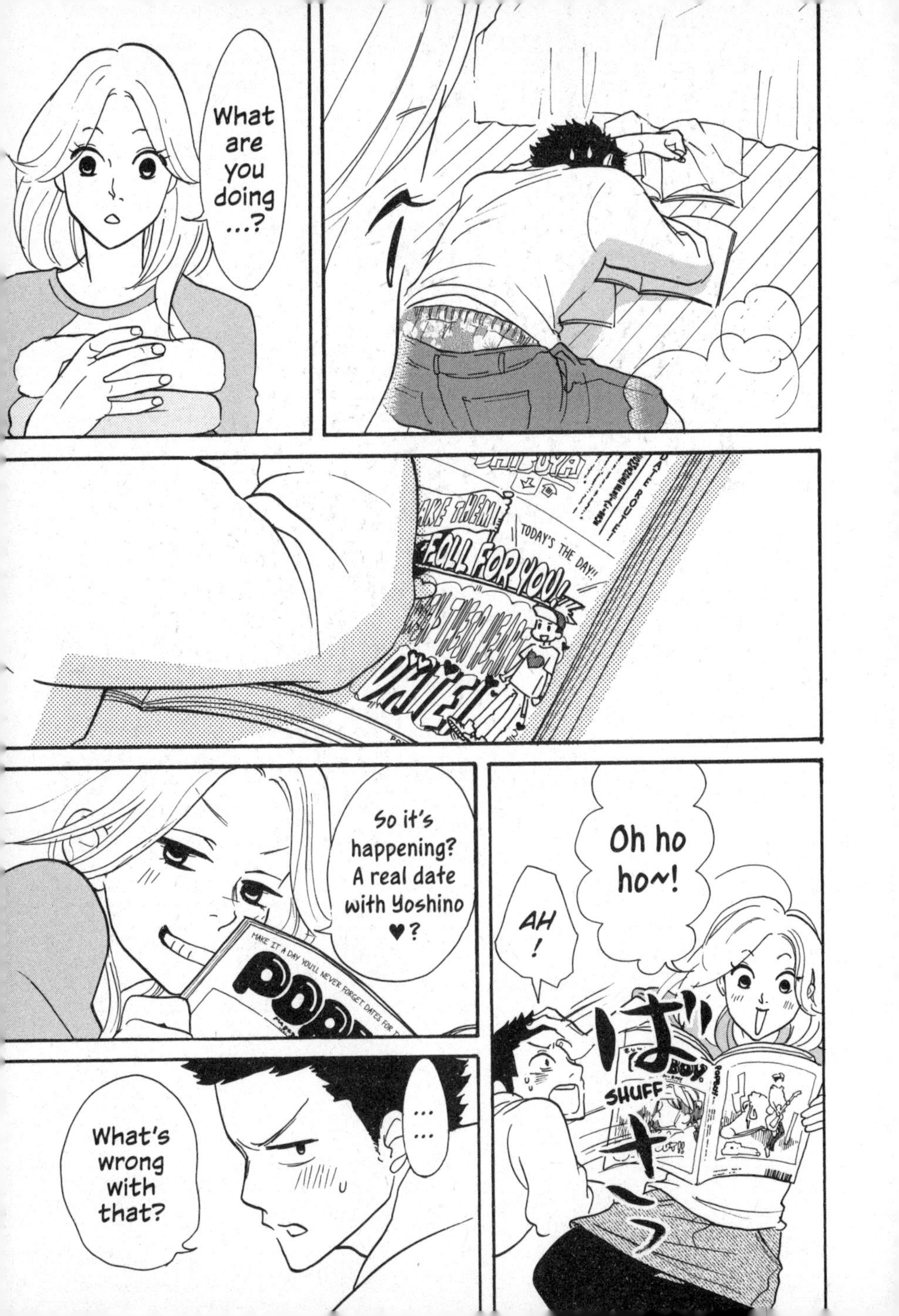
What are you doing ...?
TODAY'S THE DAY!!
FALL FOR YOU!!
Oh ho ho~!
AH!
SHUFF
So it's happening? A real date with Yoshino ♥?
MAKE IT A DAY YOU'LL NEVER FORGET DATES FOR
......
What's wrong with that?

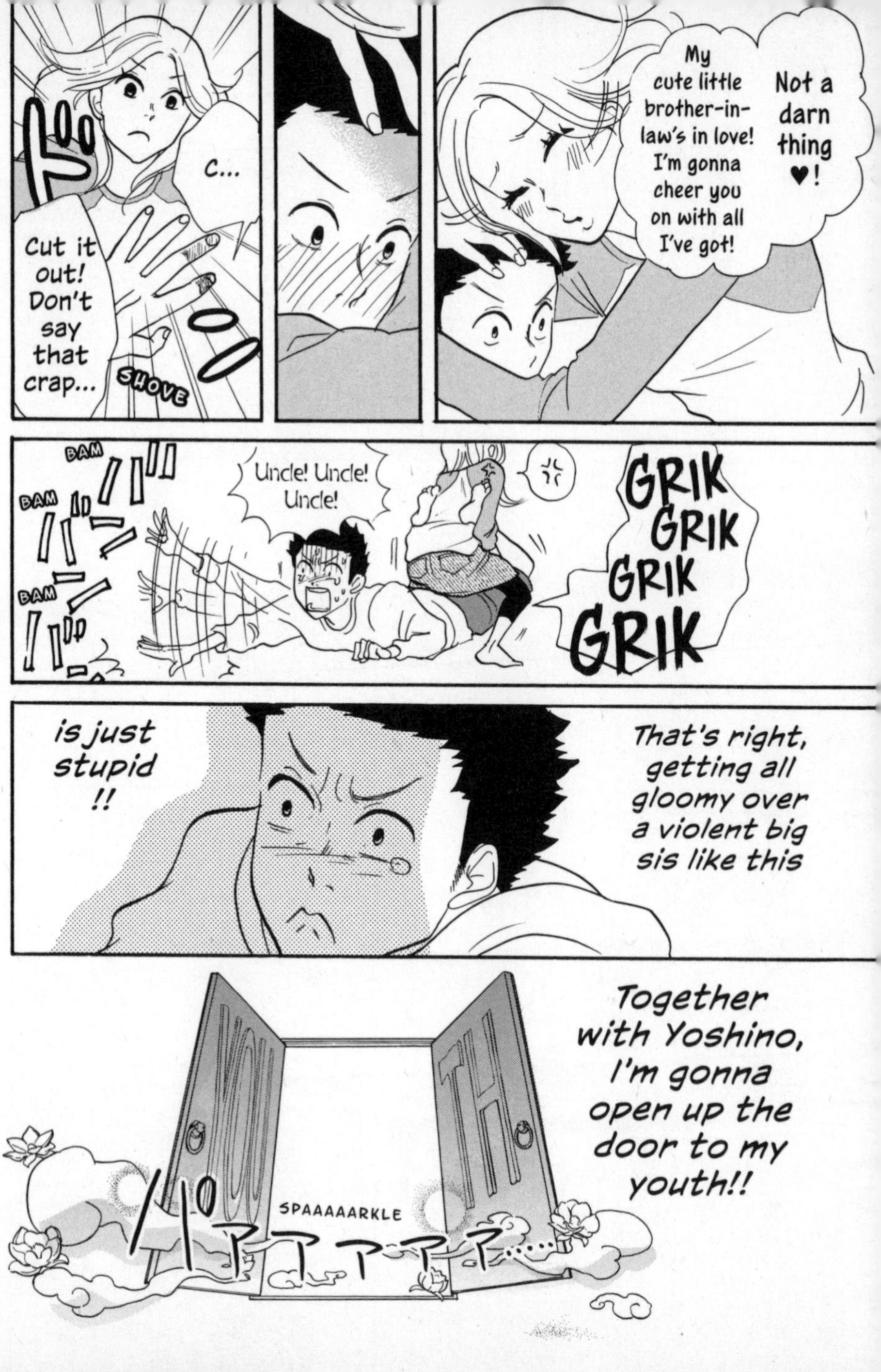
Not a darn thing ♥!
My cute little brother-in-law's in love! I'm gonna cheer you on with all I've got!
C...
Cut it out! Don't say that crap...
SHOVE
GRIK GRIK GRIK GRIK
Uncle! Uncle! Uncle!
BAM
BAM
BAM
That's right, getting all gloomy over a violent big sis like this
is just stupid !!
Together with Yoshino, I'm gonna open up the door to my youth!!
SPAAAAARKLE

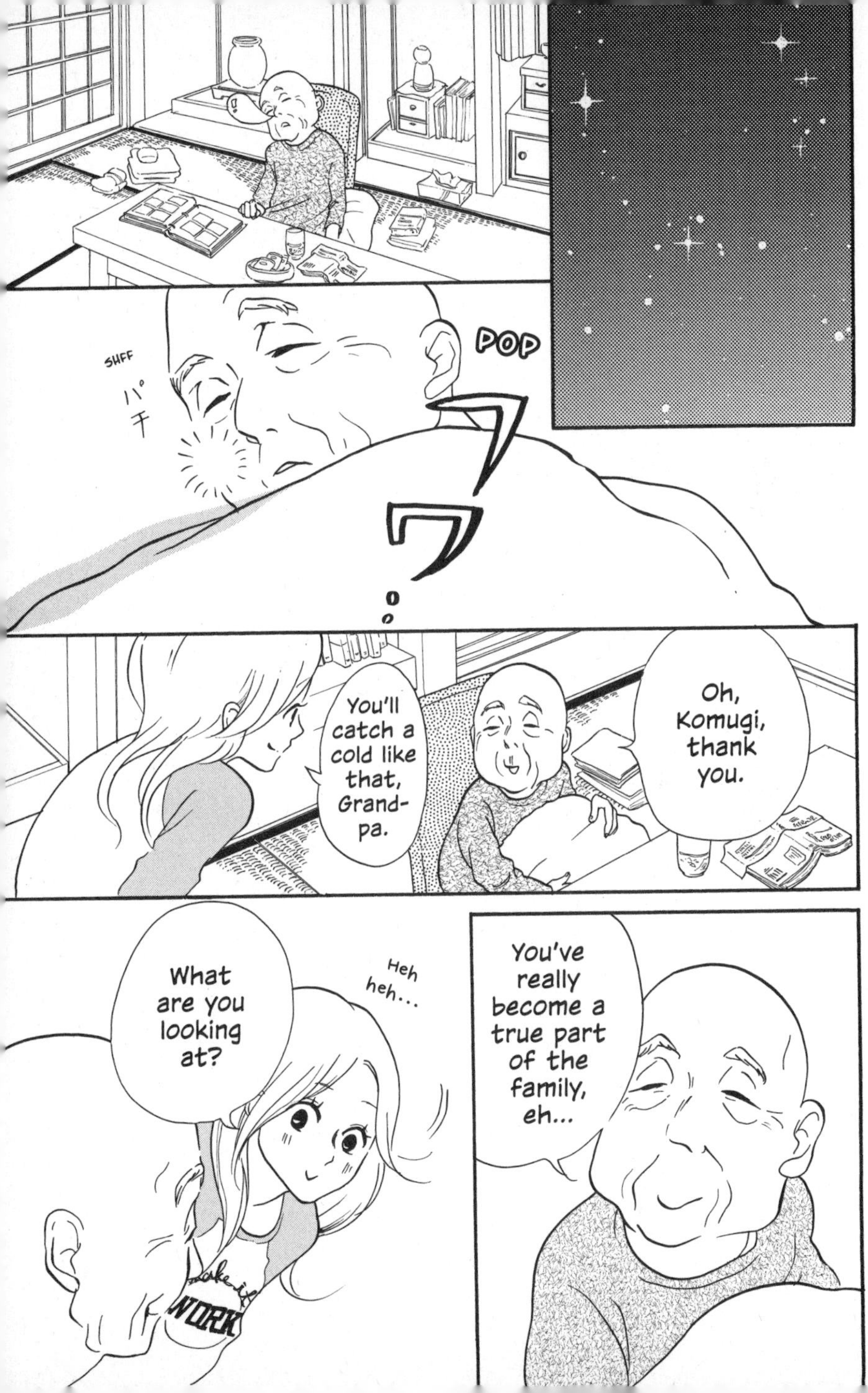
SHUFF
パチ
POP
フワ
Oh, Komugi, thank you.
You'll catch a cold like that, Grand-pa.
You've really become a true part of the family, eh...
Heh heh...
What are you looking at?
WORK

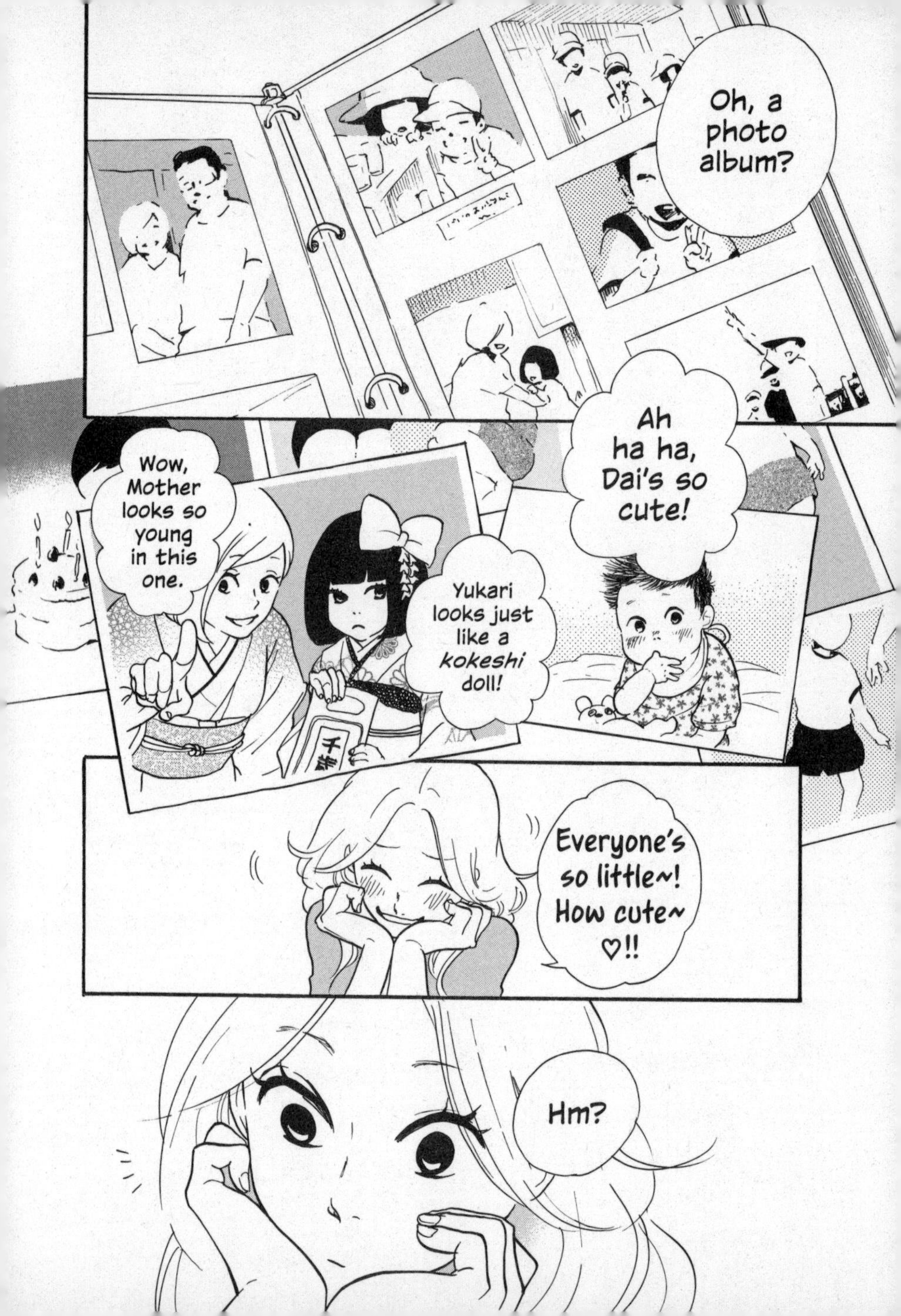
Oh, a photo album?
Ah ha ha, Dai's so cute!
Yukari looks just like a *kokeshi* doll!
Wow, Mother looks so young in this one.
Everyone's so little~! How cute~ ♡!!
Hm?

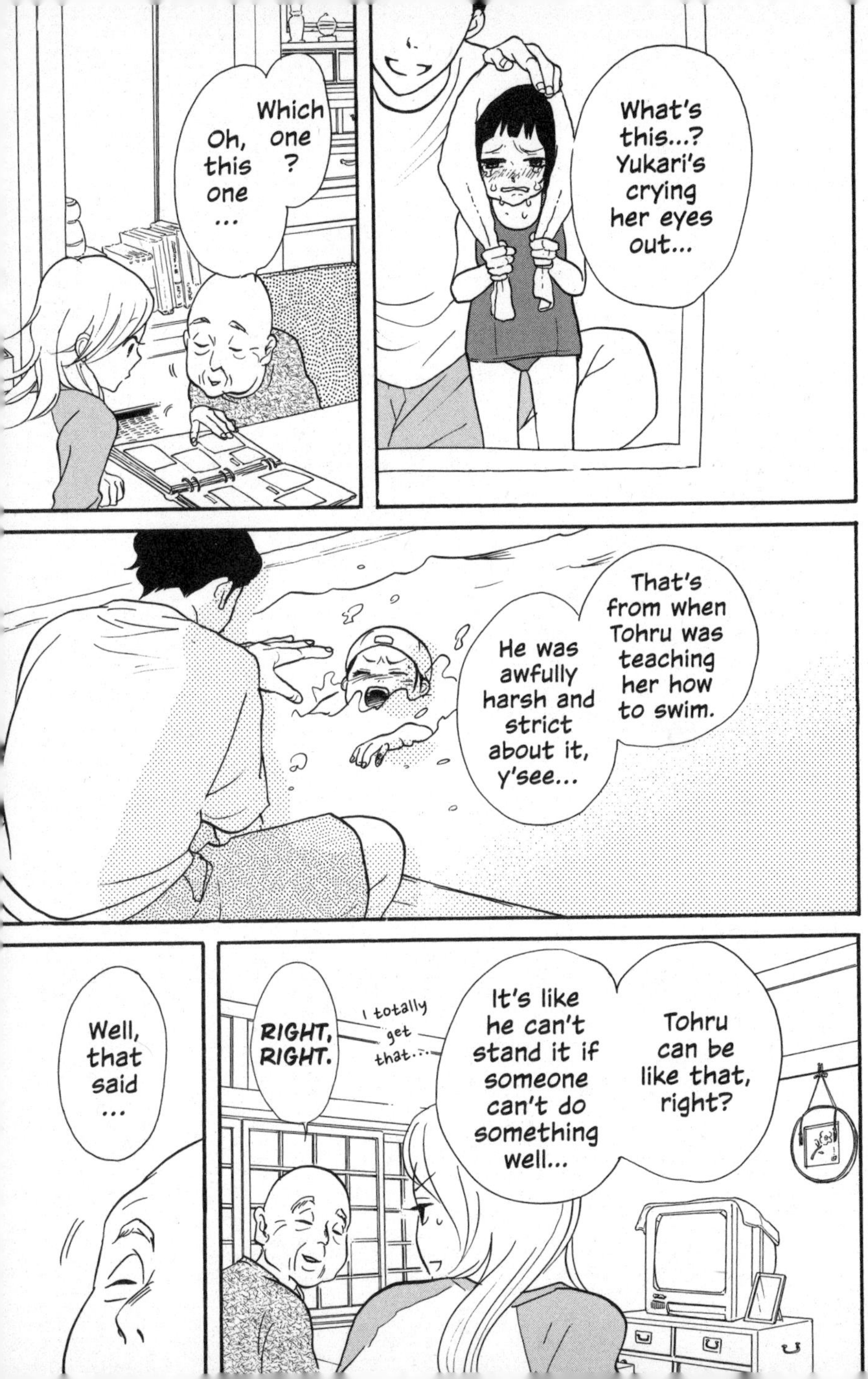
What's this...? Yukari's crying her eyes out...
Which one?
Oh, this one...
That's from when Tohru was teaching her how to swim.
He was awfully harsh and strict about it, y'see...
Tohru can be like that, right?
It's like he can't stand it if someone can't do something well...
I totally get that...
RIGHT, RIGHT.
Well, that said...

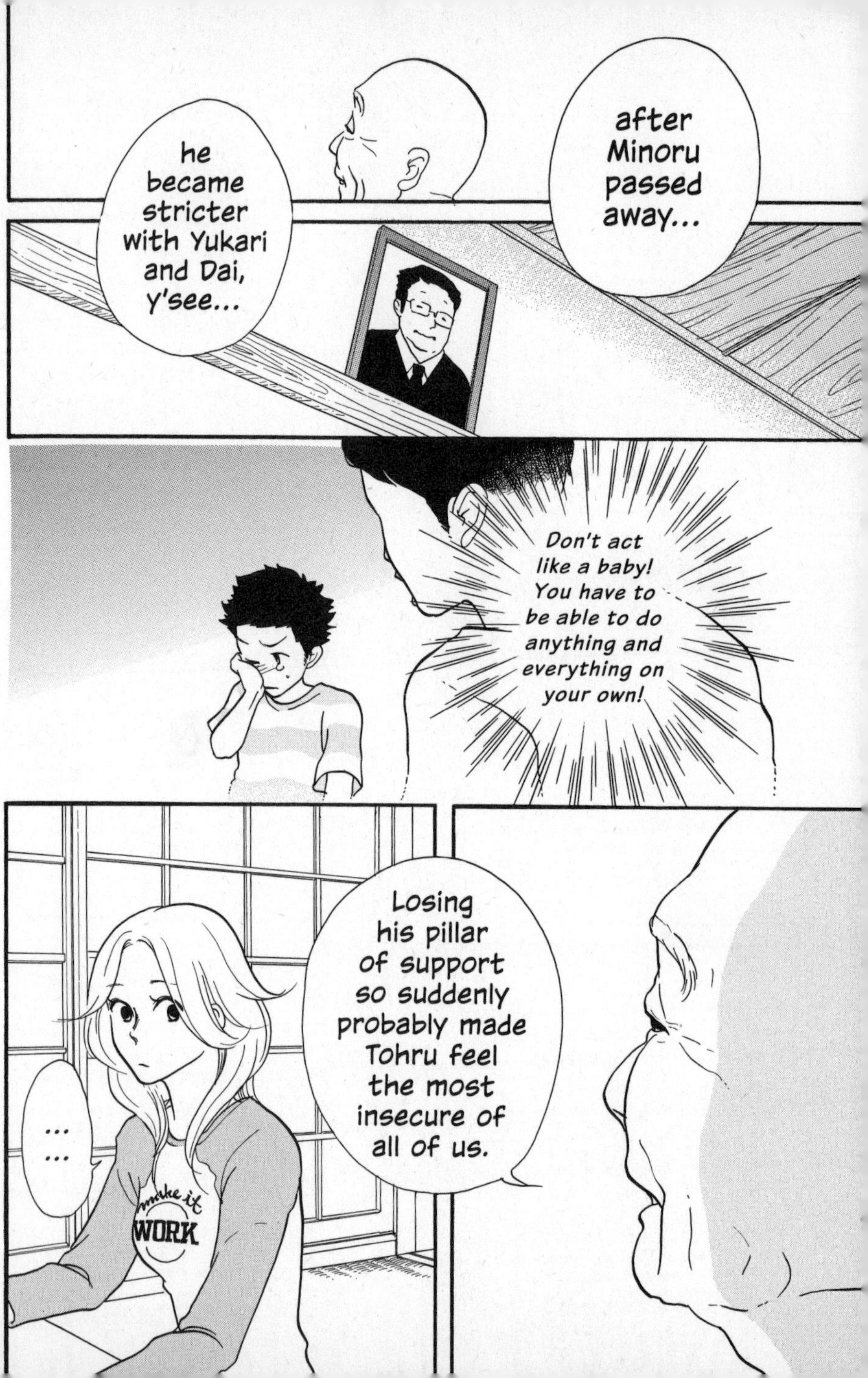
after Minoru passed away...
he became stricter with Yukari and Dai, y'see...
Don't act like a baby! You have to be able to do anything and everything on your own!
Losing his pillar of support so suddenly probably made Tohru feel the most insecure of all of us.
......
make it WORK

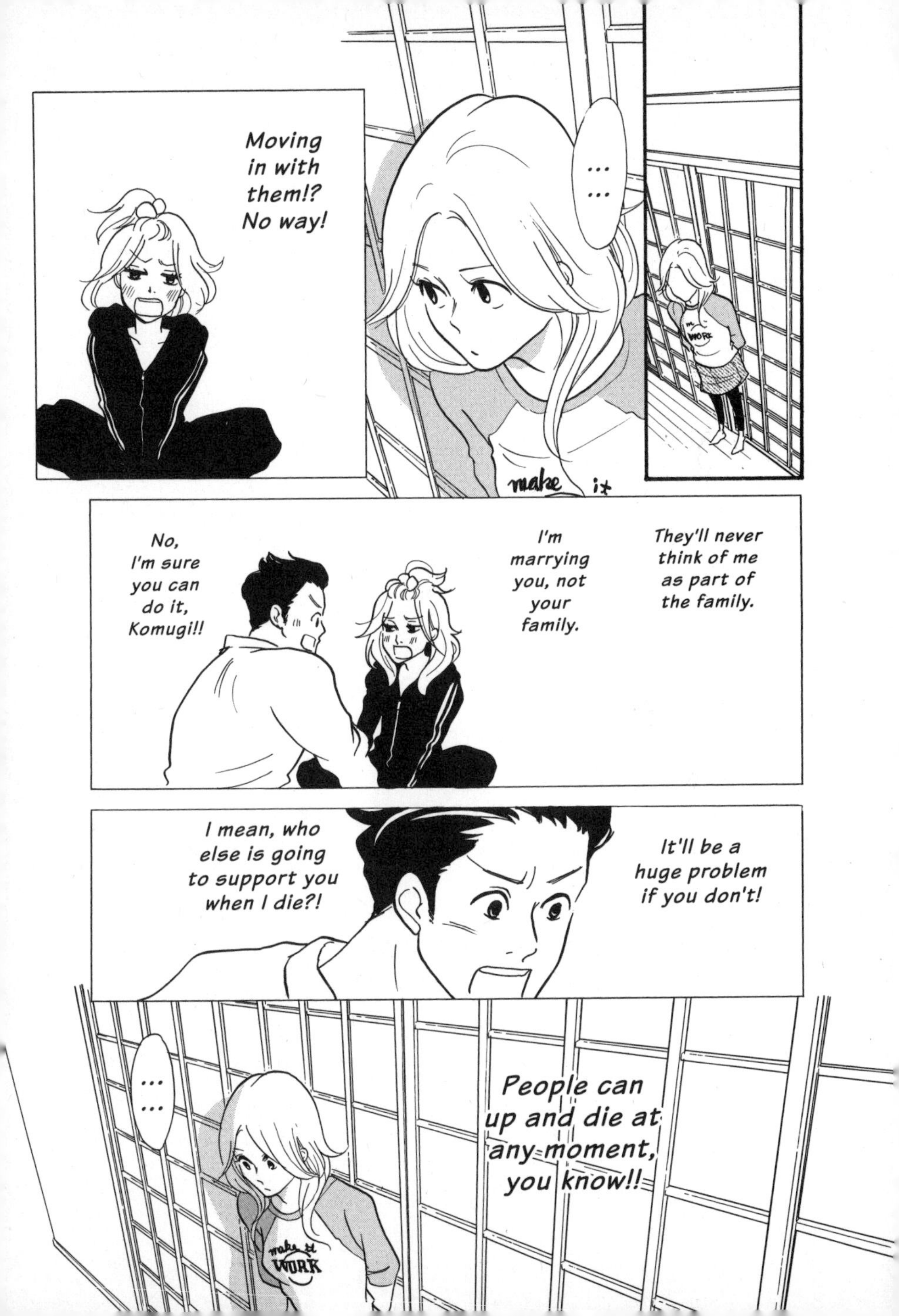
... ...
Moving in with them!? No way!
They'll never think of me as part of the family.
I'm marrying you, not your family.
No, I'm sure you can do it, Komugi!!
It'll be a huge problem if you don't!
I mean, who else is going to support you when I die?!
People can up and die at any moment, you know!!
... ...

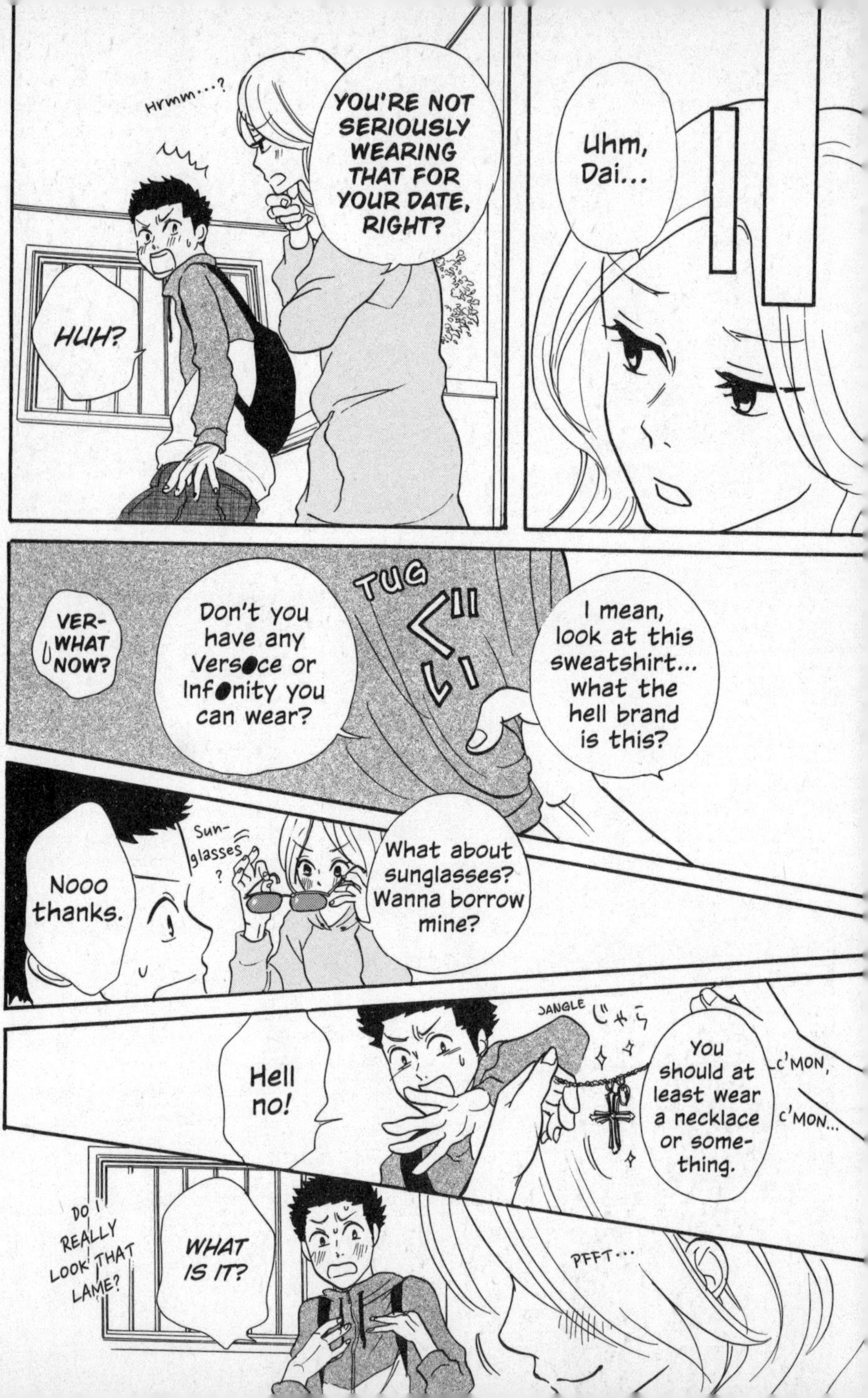
Uhm, Dai...
YOU'RE NOT SERIOUSLY WEARING THAT FOR YOUR DATE, RIGHT?
Hrmm...?
HUH?
I mean, look at this sweatshirt... what the hell brand is this?
TUG
Don't you have any Vers●ce or Inf●nity you can wear?
VER-WHAT NOW?
What about sunglasses? Wanna borrow mine?
Sun-glasses?
Nooo thanks.
You should at least wear a necklace or some-thing.
C'MON, C'MON...
JANGLE
Hell no!
PFFT...
WHAT IS IT?
DO I REALLY LOOK THAT LAME?

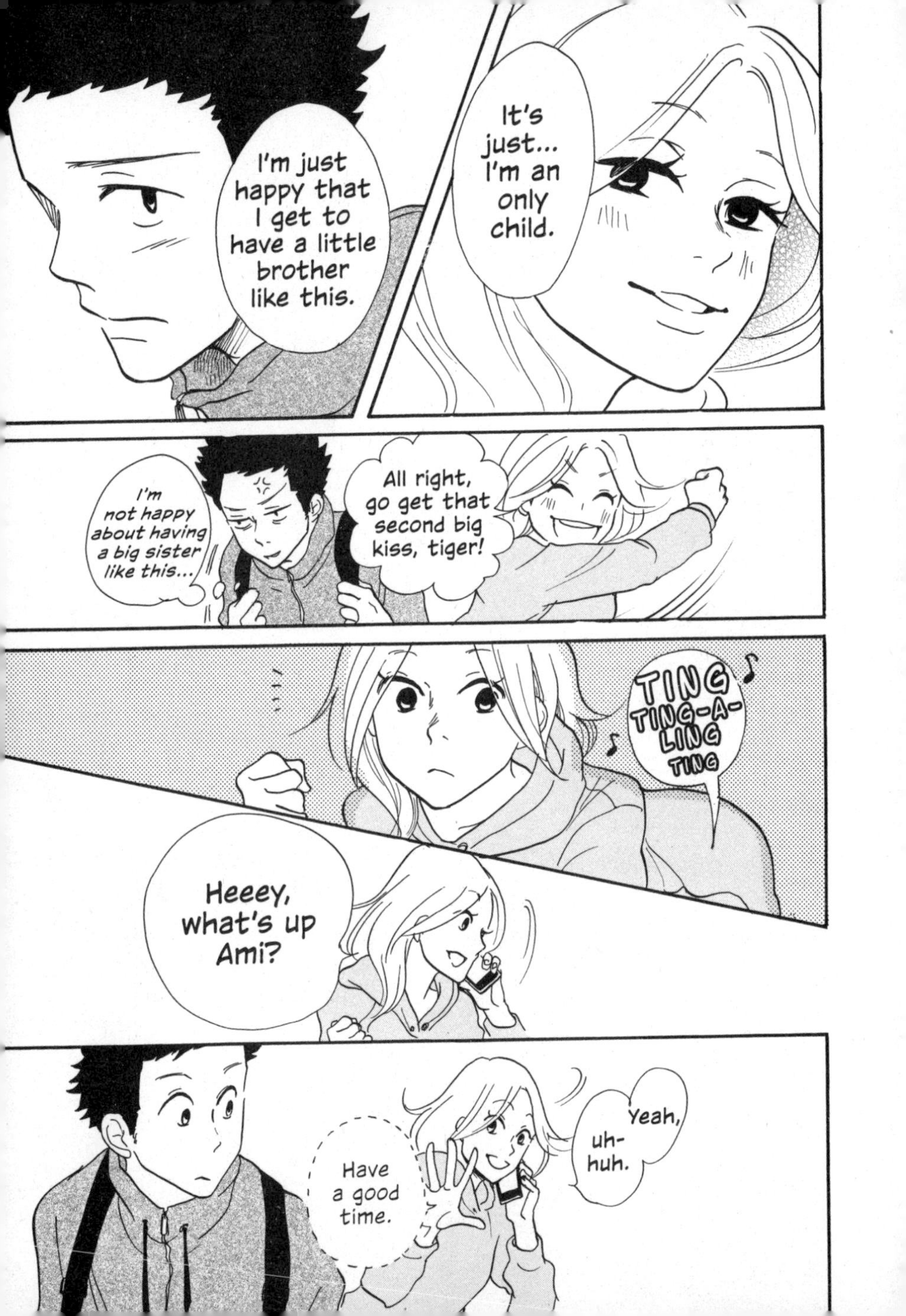

It's just... I'm an only child.
I'm just happy that I get to have a little brother like this.
All right, go get that second big kiss, tiger!
I'm not happy about having a big sister like this...
TING TING-A-LING TING
...
Heeey, what's up Ami?
Yeah, uh-huh.
Have a good time.

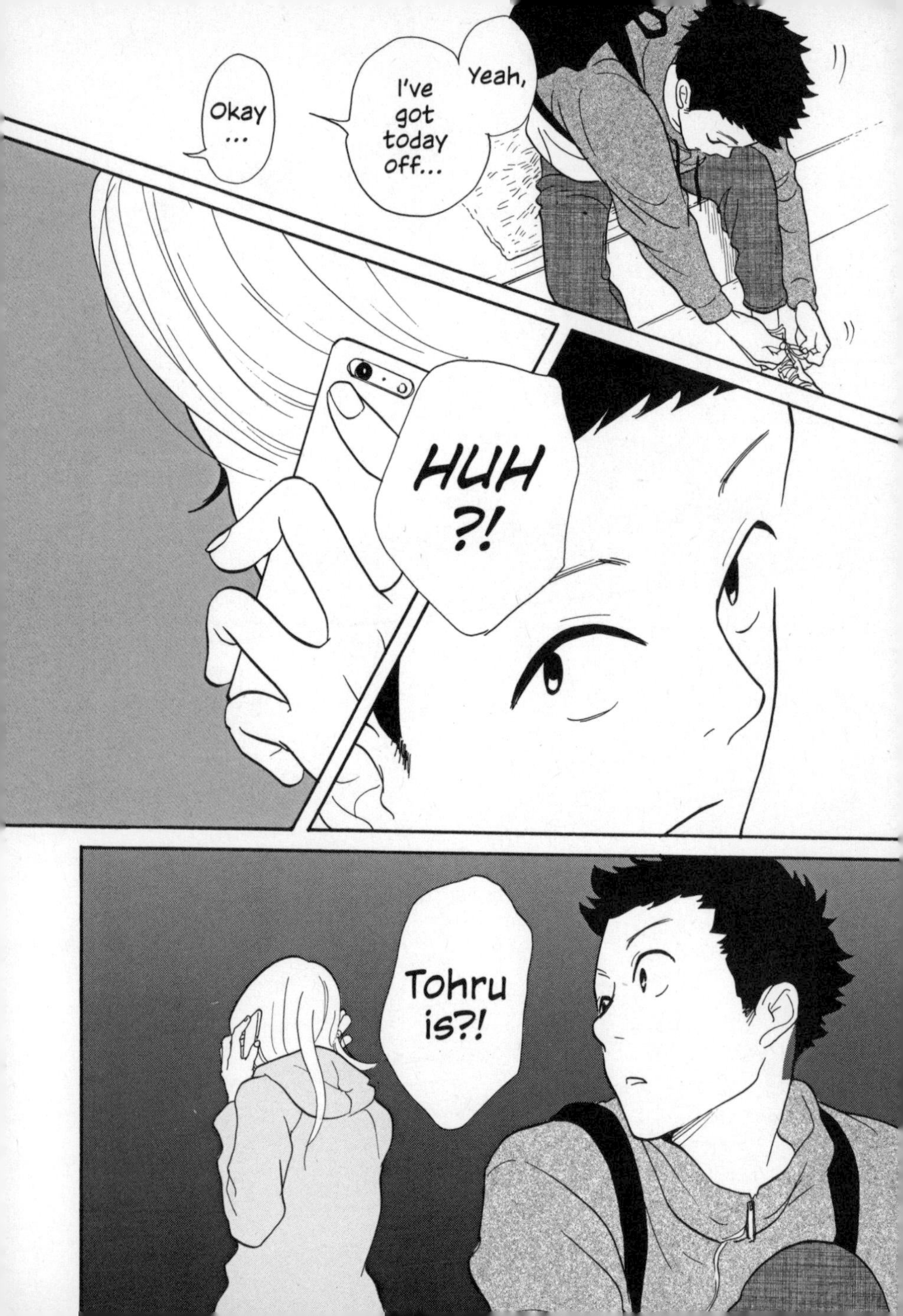
Yeah, I've got today off...
Okay...
HUH?!
Tohru is?!

22 NYAM

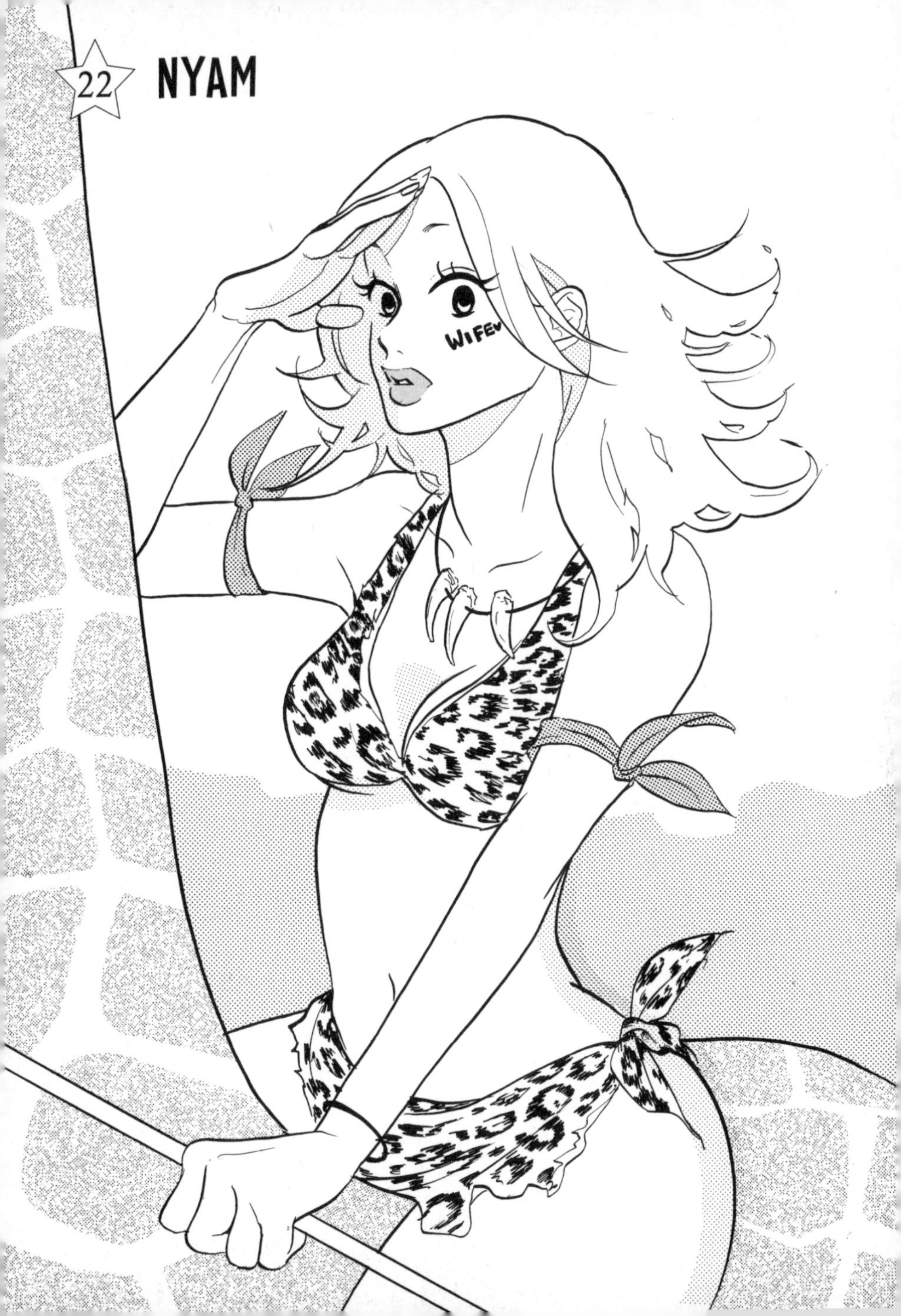
WIFE♥

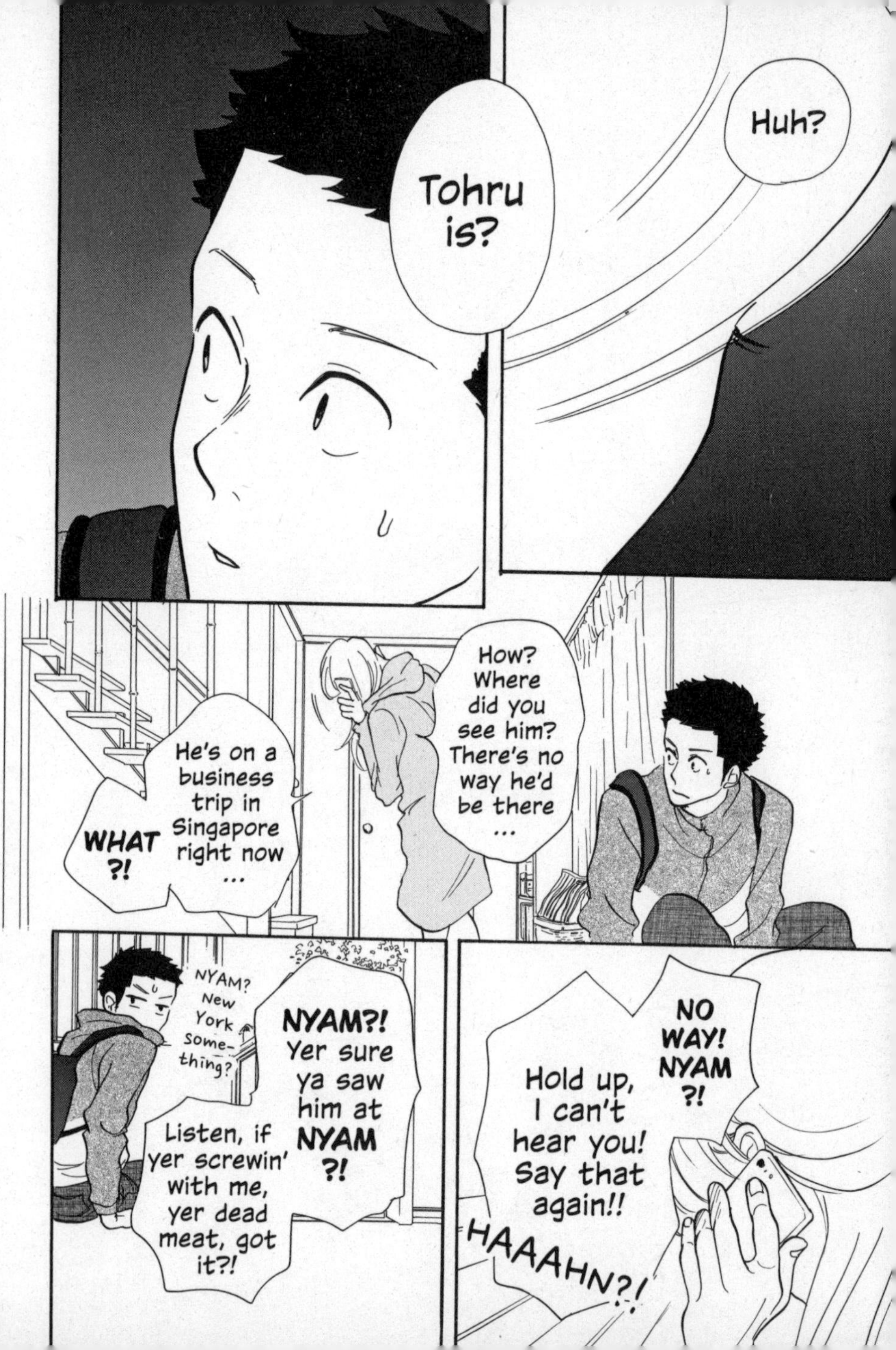
Huh?
Tohru is?
How? Where did you see him? There's no way he'd be there ...
He's on a business trip in Singapore right now ...
WHAT ?!
NO WAY! NYAM ?!
Hold up, I can't hear you! Say that again!!
HAAAAHN?!
NYAM?! Yer sure ya saw him at NYAM ?!
NYAM? New York Some- thing?
Listen, if yer screwin' with me, yer dead meat, got it?!

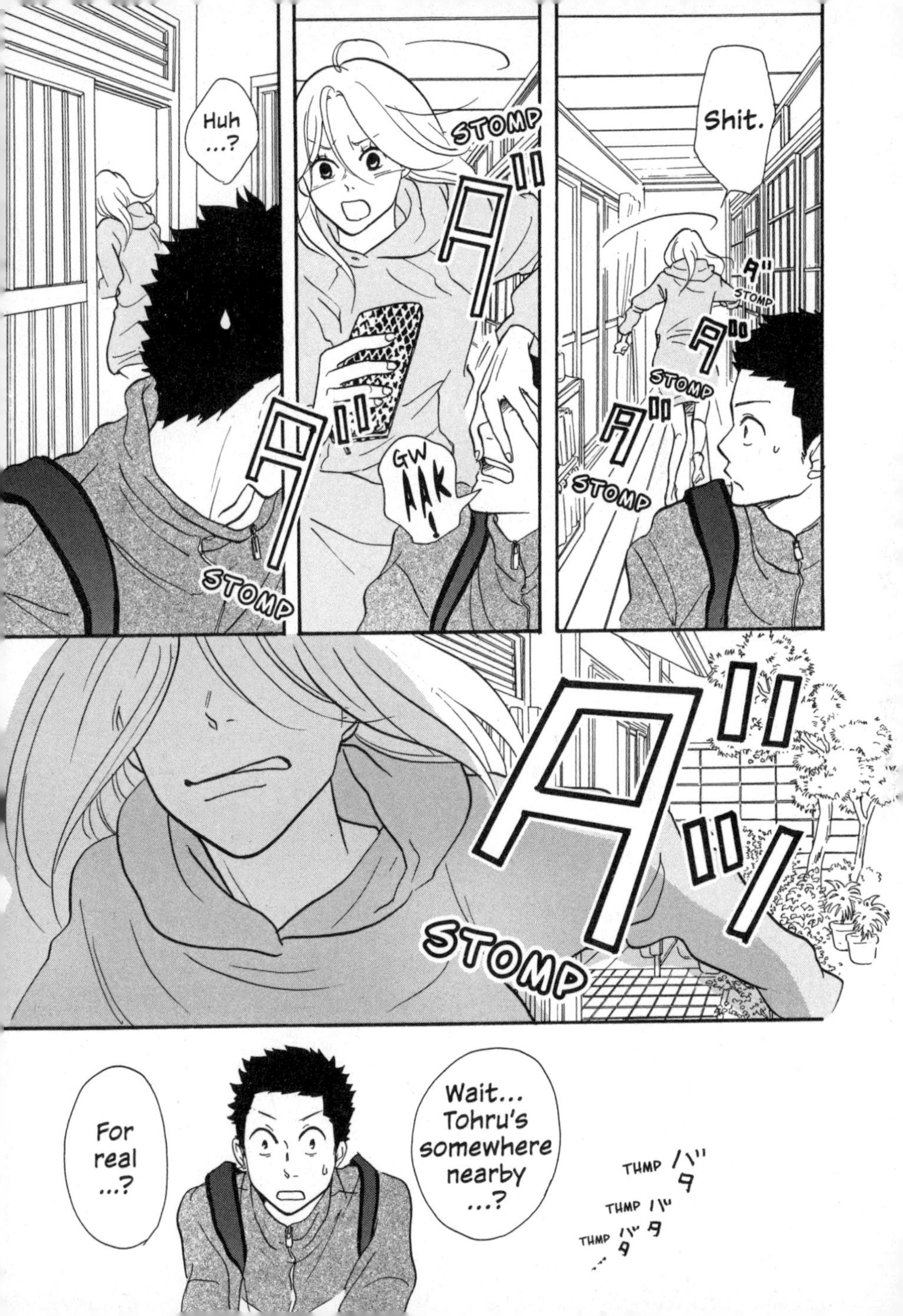
Shit.
ダ
STOMP
ダ
STOMP
ダ
STOMP
STOMP
ダ
GW AAK!
Huh ...?
ダ
STOMP
ダッ
STOMP
バタ THMP
バタ THMP
バタ THMP
Wait... Tohru's somewhere nearby ...?
For real ...?

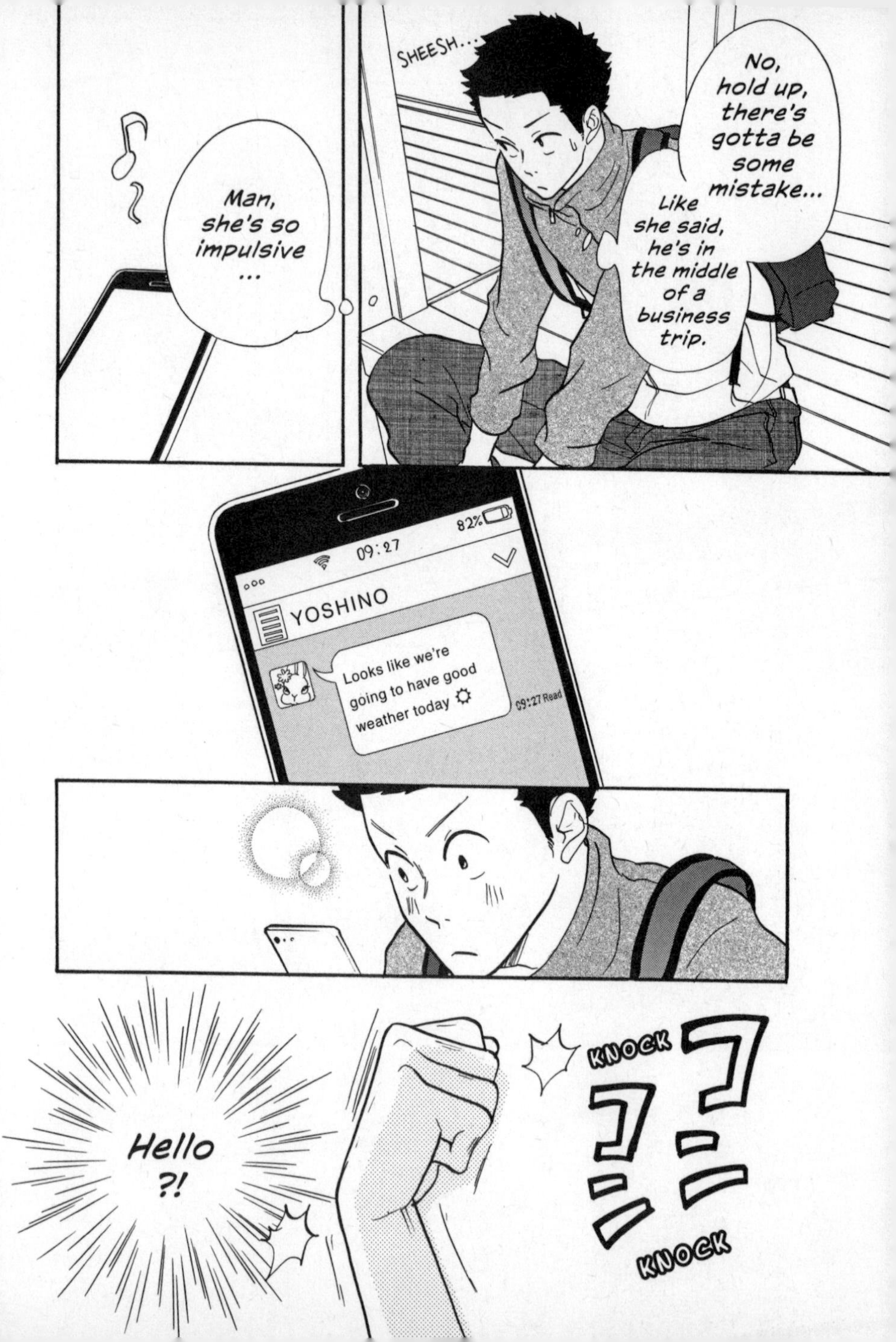
SHEESH...
No, hold up, there's gotta be some mistake...
Like she said, he's in the middle of a business trip.
Man, she's so impulsive ...
82%
09:27
YOSHINO
Looks like we're going to have good weather today
09:27 Read
KNOCK
KNOCK
Hello ?!

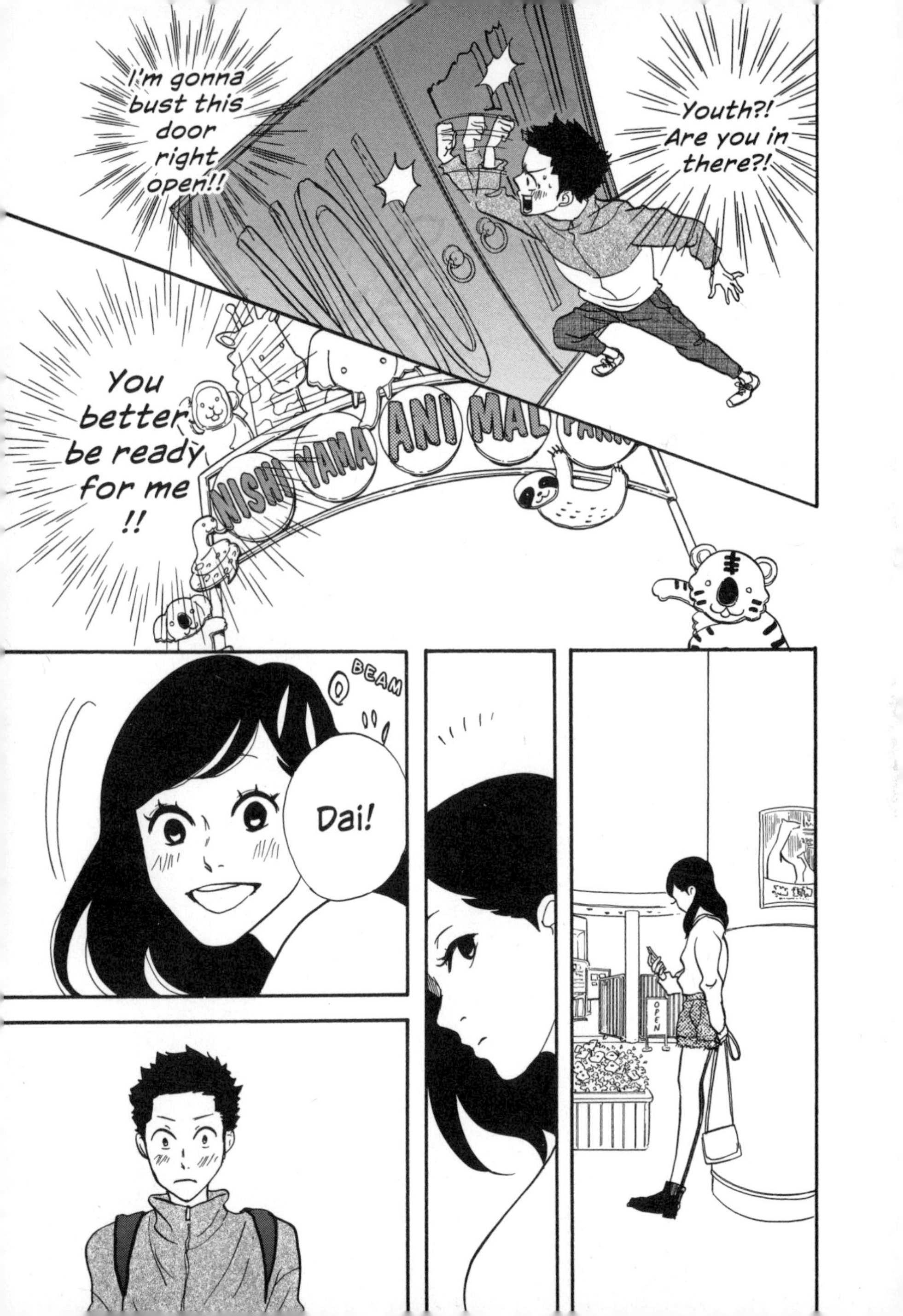
Youth?! Are you in there?!
I'm gonna bust this door right open!!
You better be ready for me !!
NISHI YAMA ANI MAL
OPEN
BEAM
Dai!

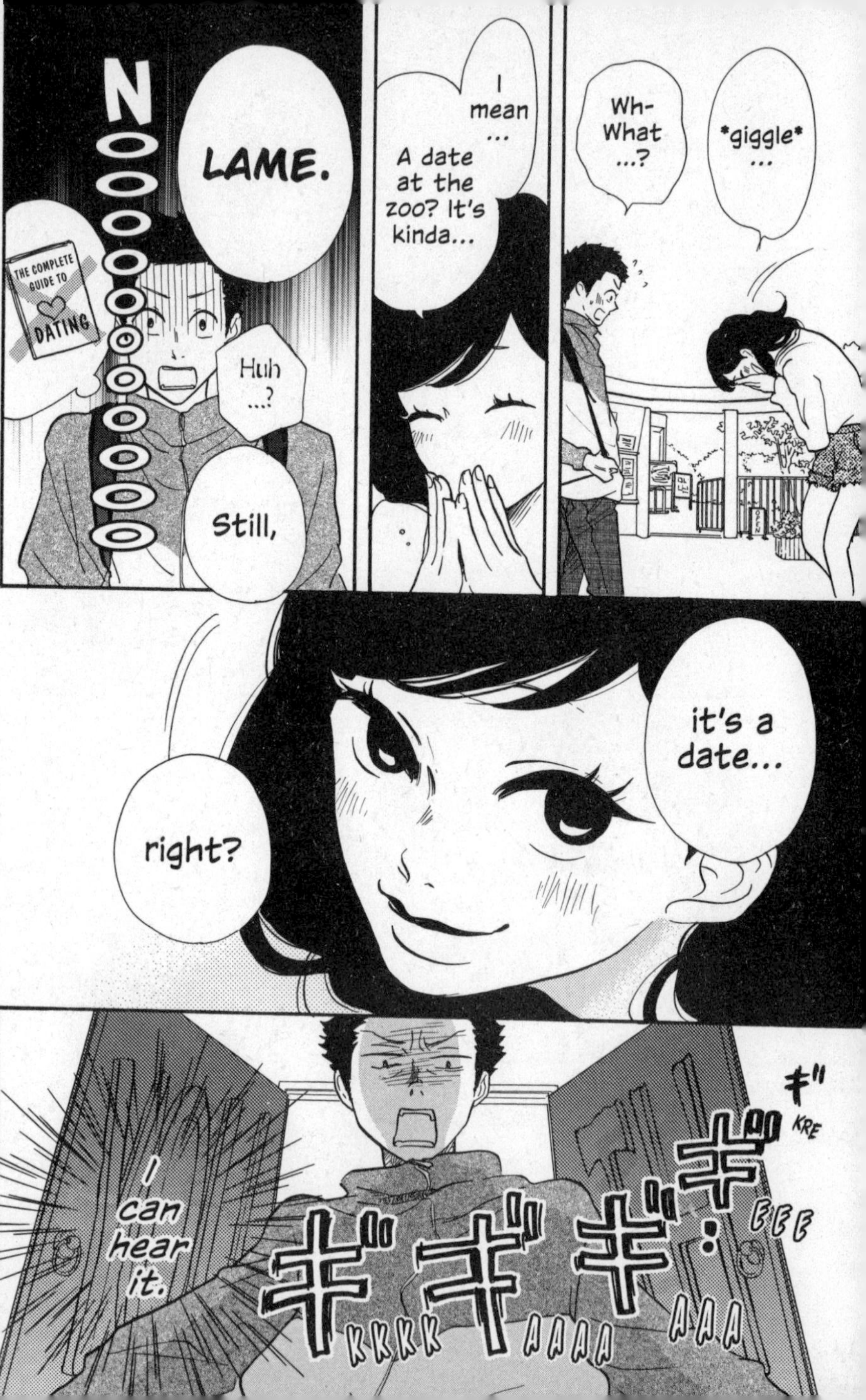
giggle ...
Wh- What ...?
I mean ...
A date at the zoo? It's kinda...
LAME.
NOOOOOOOOOOOOO
THE COMPLETE GUIDE TO DATING
Huh ...?
Still,
it's a date...
right?
ギ゛ギ゛ギ゛ギ゛ギ゛
KRE
EEE
AAA
AAAA
KKKK
I can hear it.

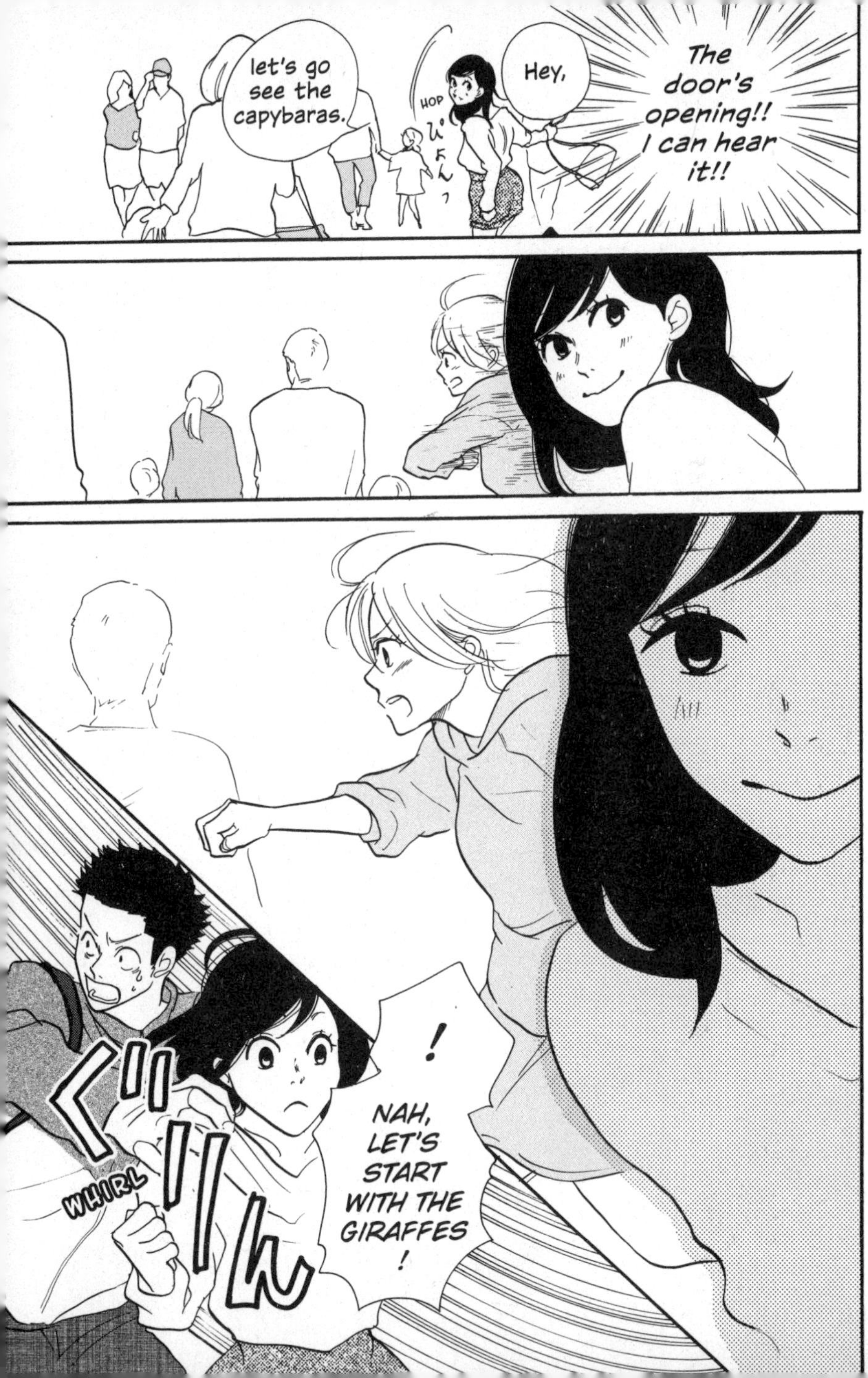
The door's opening!! I can hear it!!
Hey,
HOP
ぴょんっ
let's go see the capybaras.
!
NAH, LET'S START WITH THE GIRAFFES!
WHIRL

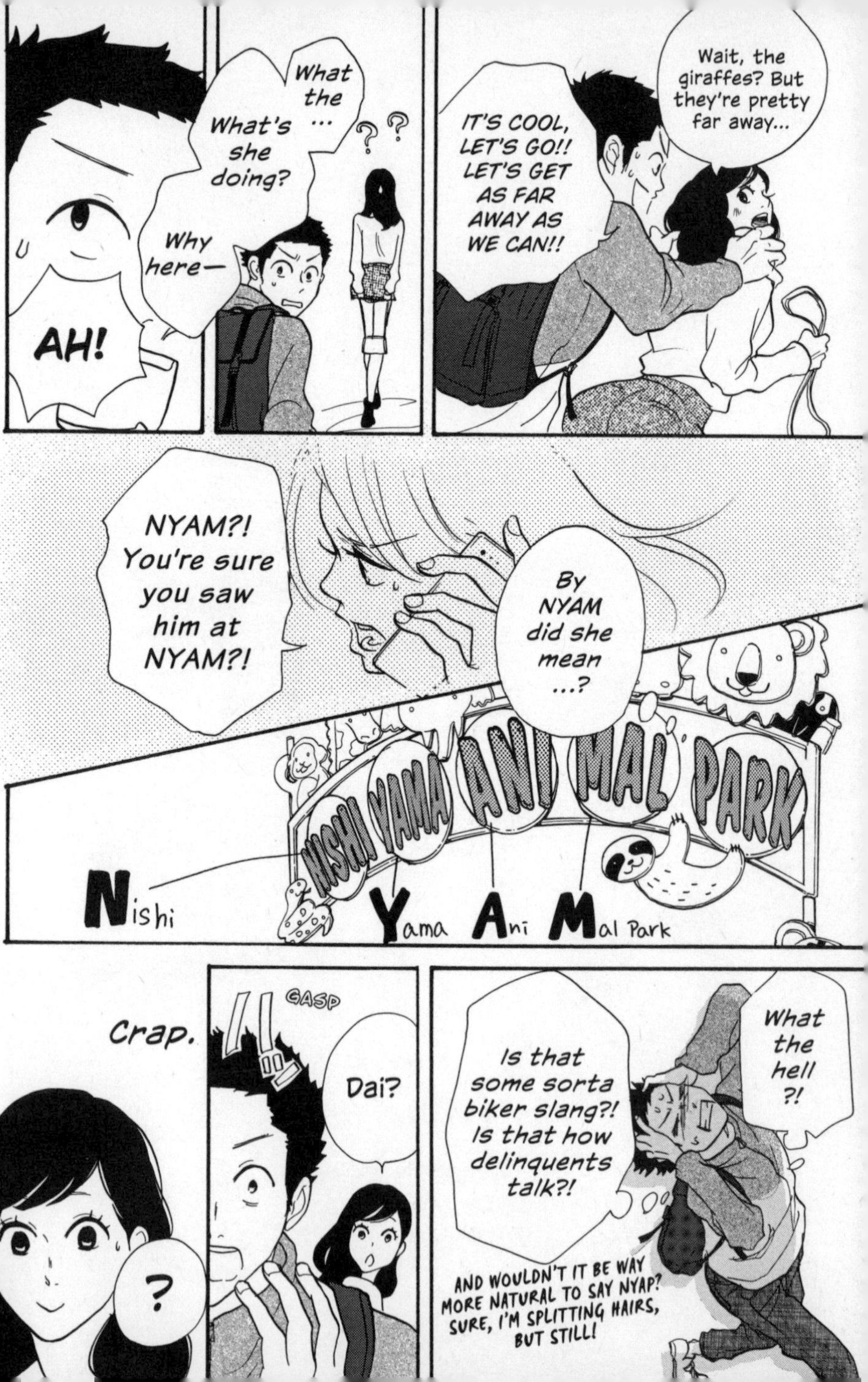
Wait, the giraffes? But they're pretty far away...
IT'S COOL, LET'S GO!! LET'S GET AS FAR AWAY AS WE CAN!!
What the ...
What's she doing?
Why here—
AH!
NYAM?! You're sure you saw him at NYAM?!
By NYAM did she mean ...?
NISHI YAMA ANI MAL PARK
Nishi Yama Ani Mal Park
What the hell ?!
Is that some sorta biker slang?! Is that how delinquents talk?!
AND WOULDN'T IT BE WAY MORE NATURAL TO SAY NYAP? SURE, I'M SPLITTING HAIRS, BUT STILL!
GASP
Dai?
Crap.
?

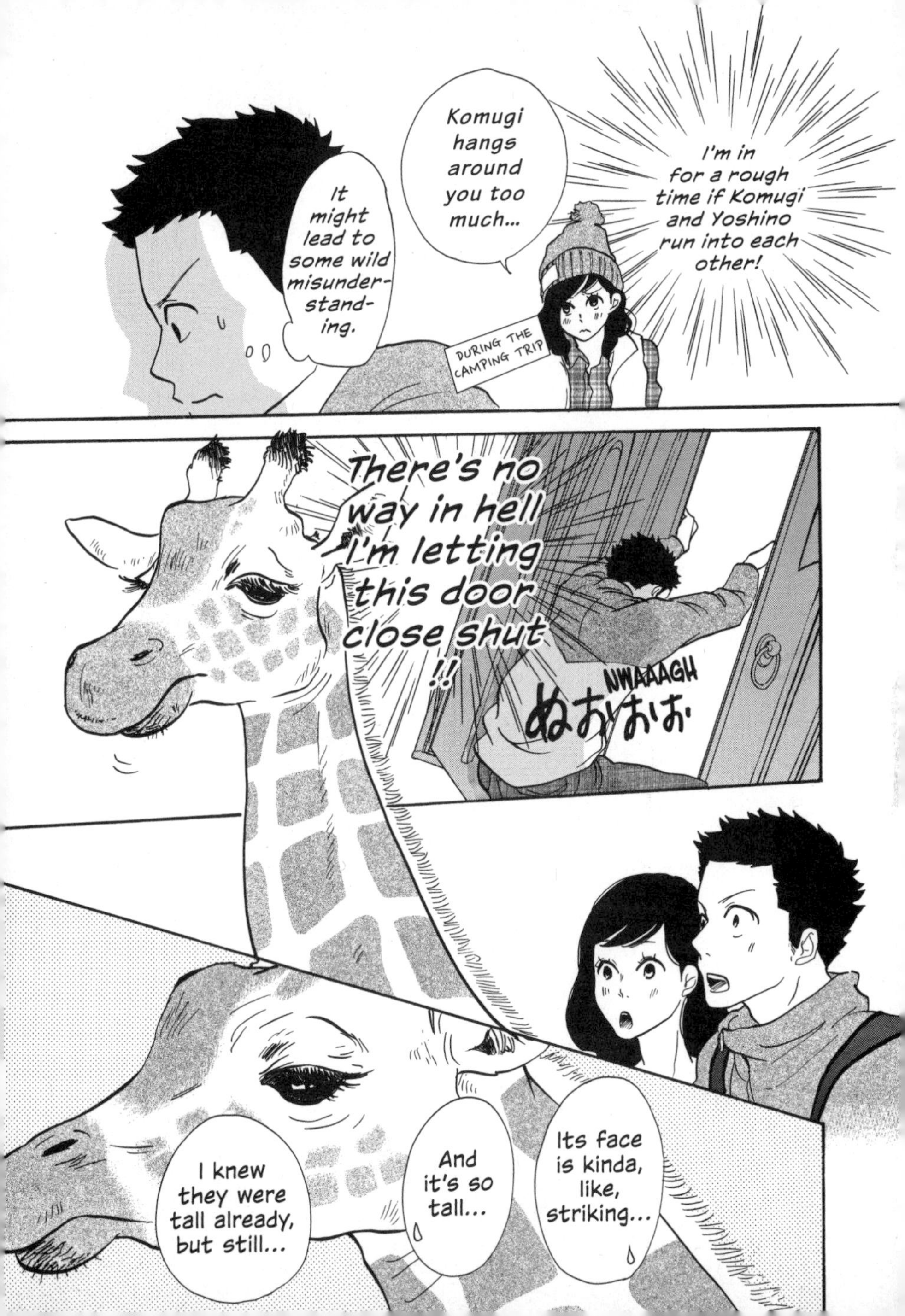
I'm in for a rough time if Komugi and Yoshino run into each other!
Komugi hangs around you too much...
It might lead to some wild misunder-stand-ing.
DURING THE CAMPING TRIP
There's no way in hell I'm letting this door close shut!!
NWAAAGH
ぬおおお
Its face is kinda, like, striking...
And it's so tall...
I knew they were tall already, but still...

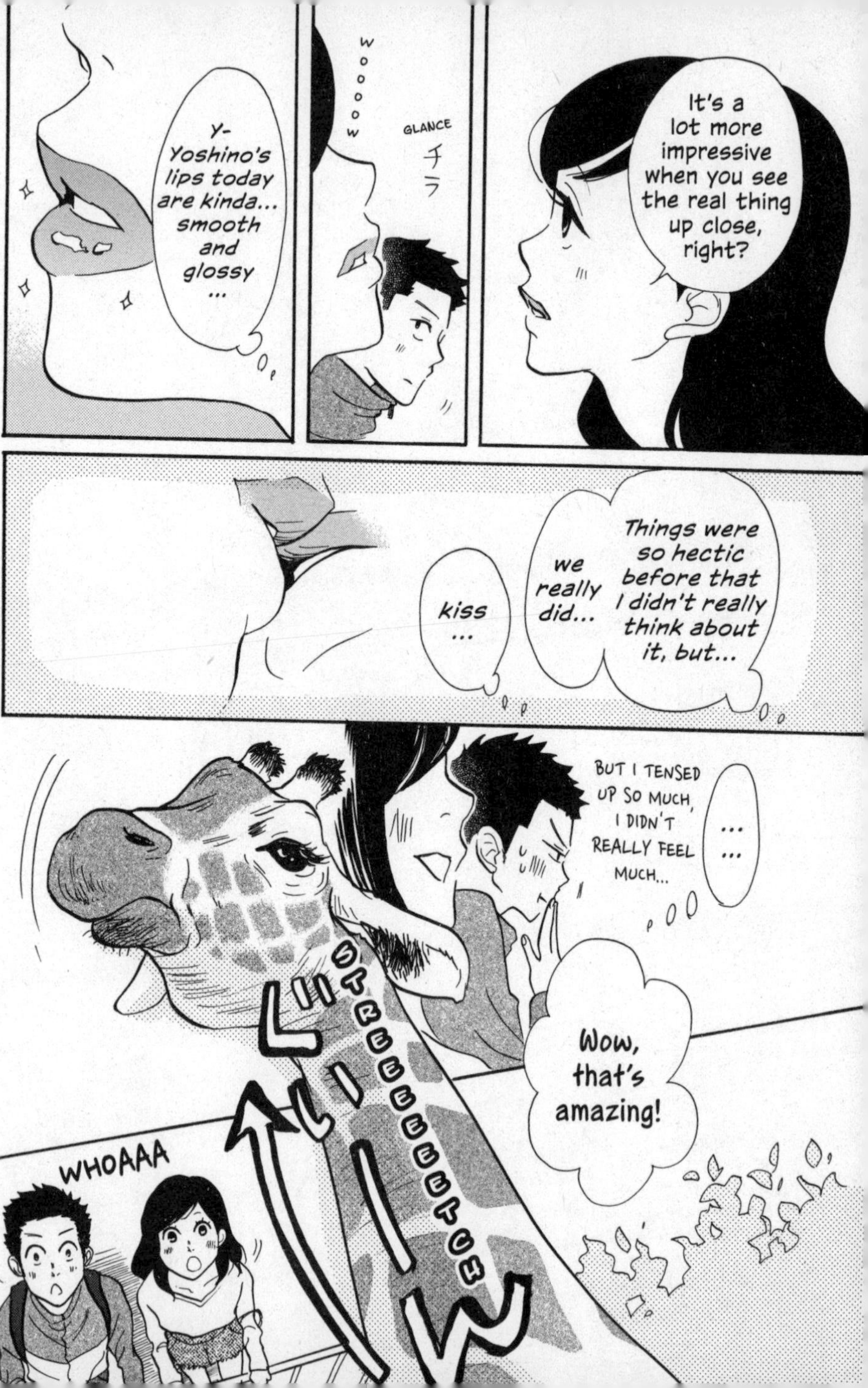
It's a lot more impressive when you see the real thing up close, right?
WOOOOOW
GLANCE
チラ
Y-Yoshino's lips today are kinda... smooth and glossy ...
Things were so hectic before that I didn't really think about it, but...
we really did...
kiss ...
BUT I TENSED UP SO MUCH, I DIDN'T REALLY FEEL MUCH...
... ...
Wow, that's amazing!
STREEEEEEETCH
WHOAAA

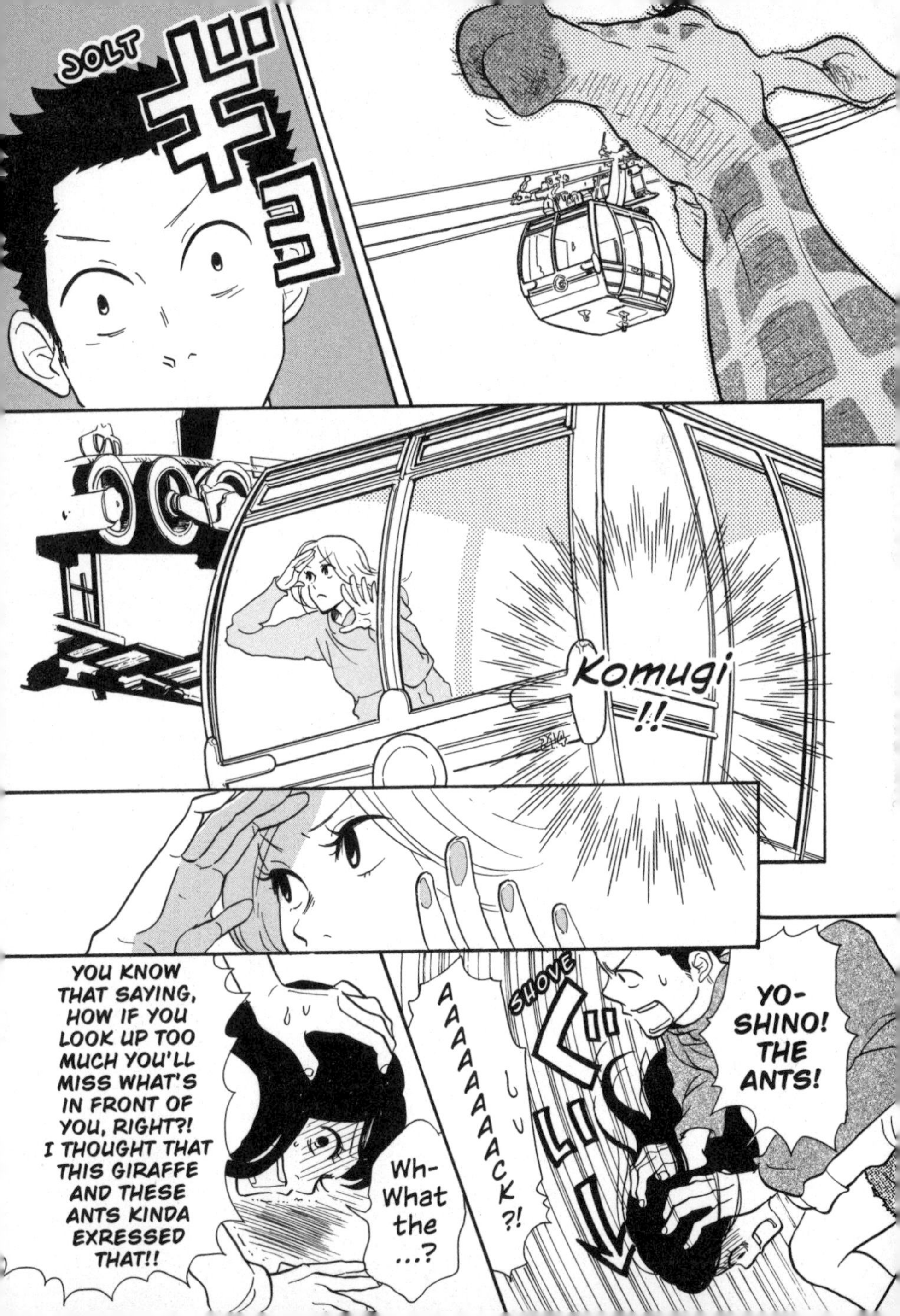
JOLT
Komugi !!
YO-SHINO! THE ANTS!
SHOVE
AAAAAAAACK?!
Wh- What the ...?
YOU KNOW THAT SAYING, HOW IF YOU LOOK UP TOO MUCH YOU'LL MISS WHAT'S IN FRONT OF YOU, RIGHT?! I THOUGHT THAT THIS GIRAFFE AND THESE ANTS KINDA EXRESSED THAT!!

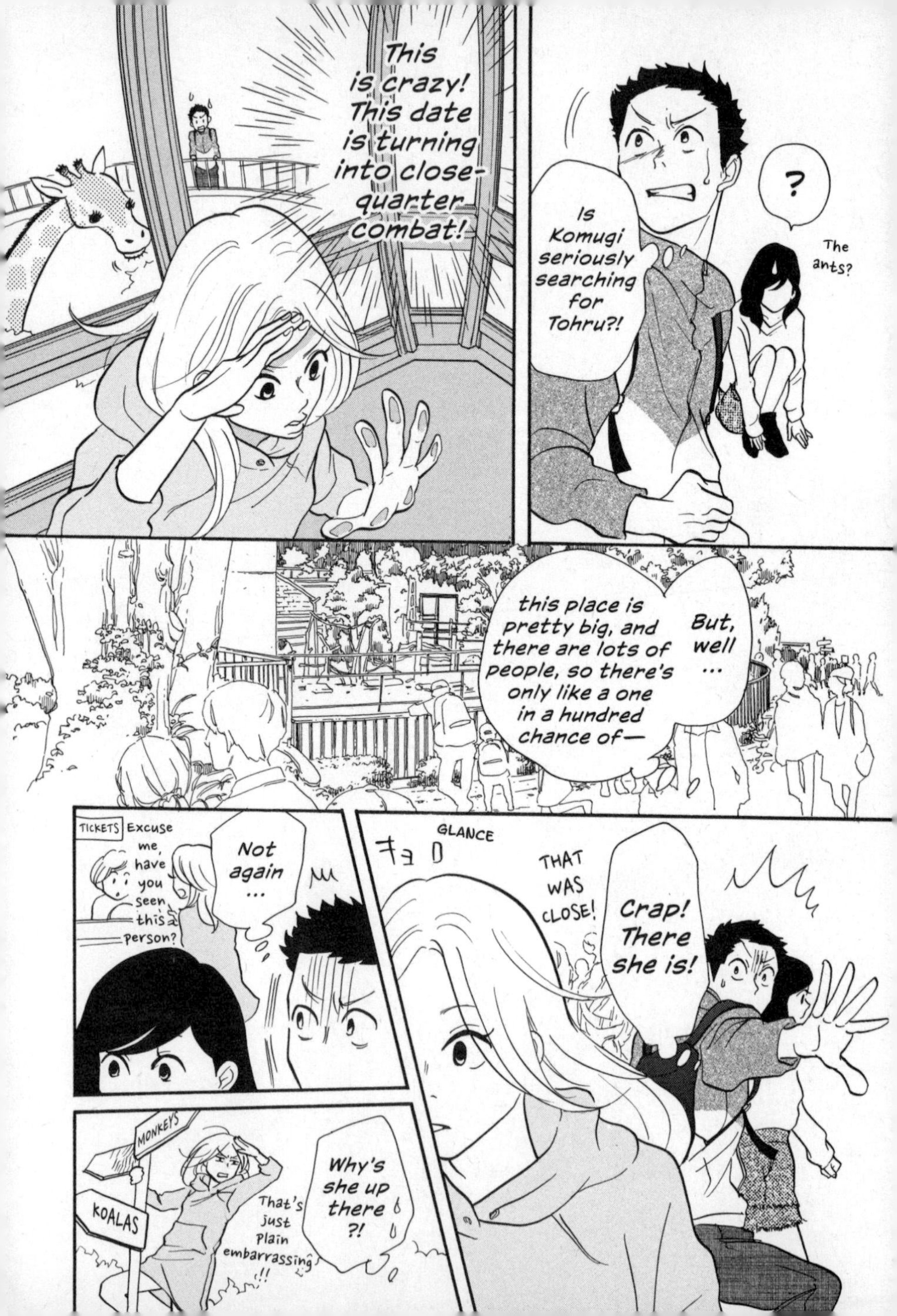
?
The ants?
Is Komugi seriously searching for Tohru?!
This is crazy! This date is turning into close-quarter combat!
But, well ...
this place is pretty big, and there are lots of people, so there's only like a one in a hundred chance of—
Crap! There she is!
THAT WAS CLOSE!
キョロ
GLANCE
Not again ...
Excuse me, have you seen this person?
TICKETS
Why's she up there?!
That's just plain embarrassing!!
MONKEYS
KOALAS

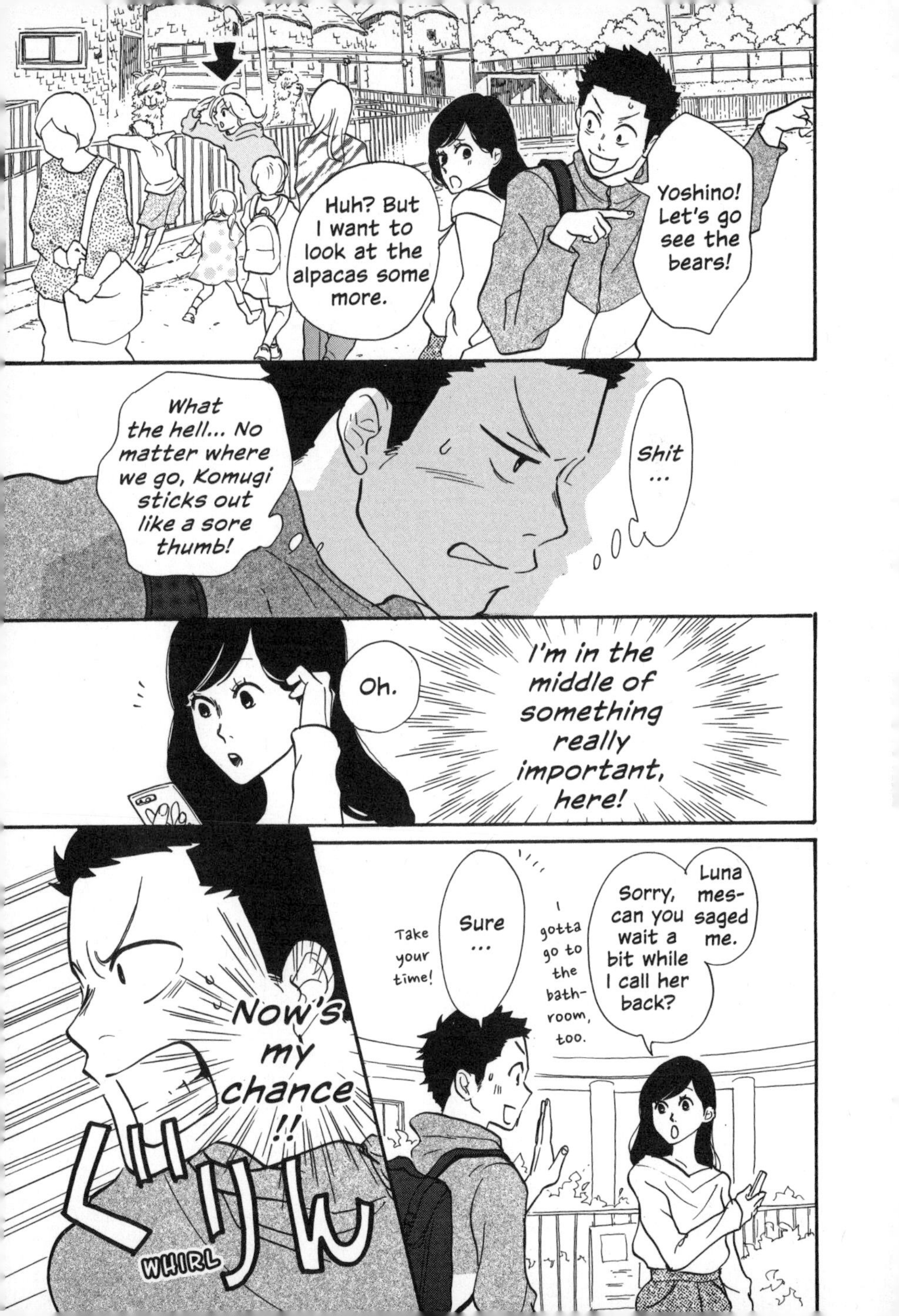

Yoshino! Let's go see the bears!
Huh? But I want to look at the alpacas some more.
Shit ...
What the hell... No matter where we go, Komugi sticks out like a sore thumb!
I'm in the middle of something really important, here!
Oh.
Luna messaged me.
Sorry, can you wait a bit while I call her back?
I gotta go to the bathroom, too.
Sure ...
Take your time!
Now's my chance !!
くりん
WHIRL

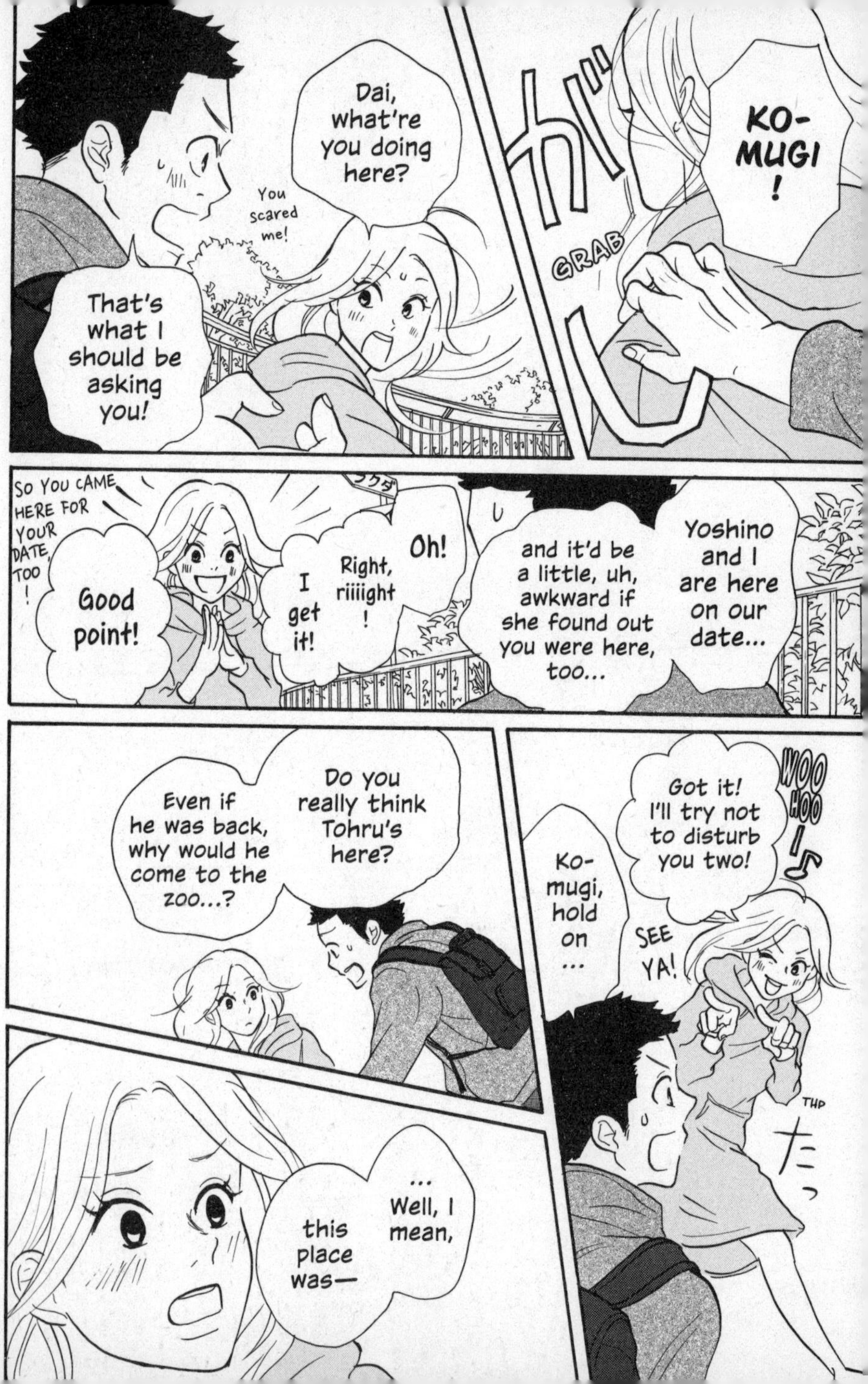
KO-MUGI!
GRAB
Dai, what're you doing here?
You scared me!
That's what I should be asking you!
Yoshino and I are here on our date...
and it'd be a little, uh, awkward if she found out you were here, too...
Oh!
Right, riiiight!
I get it!
SO YOU CAME HERE FOR YOUR DATE, TOO!
Good point!
WOO HOO ♪
Got it! I'll try not to disturb you two!
Ko-mugi, hold on...
SEE YA!
THP
Do you really think Tohru's here?
Even if he was back, why would he come to the zoo...?
... Well, I mean, this place was—

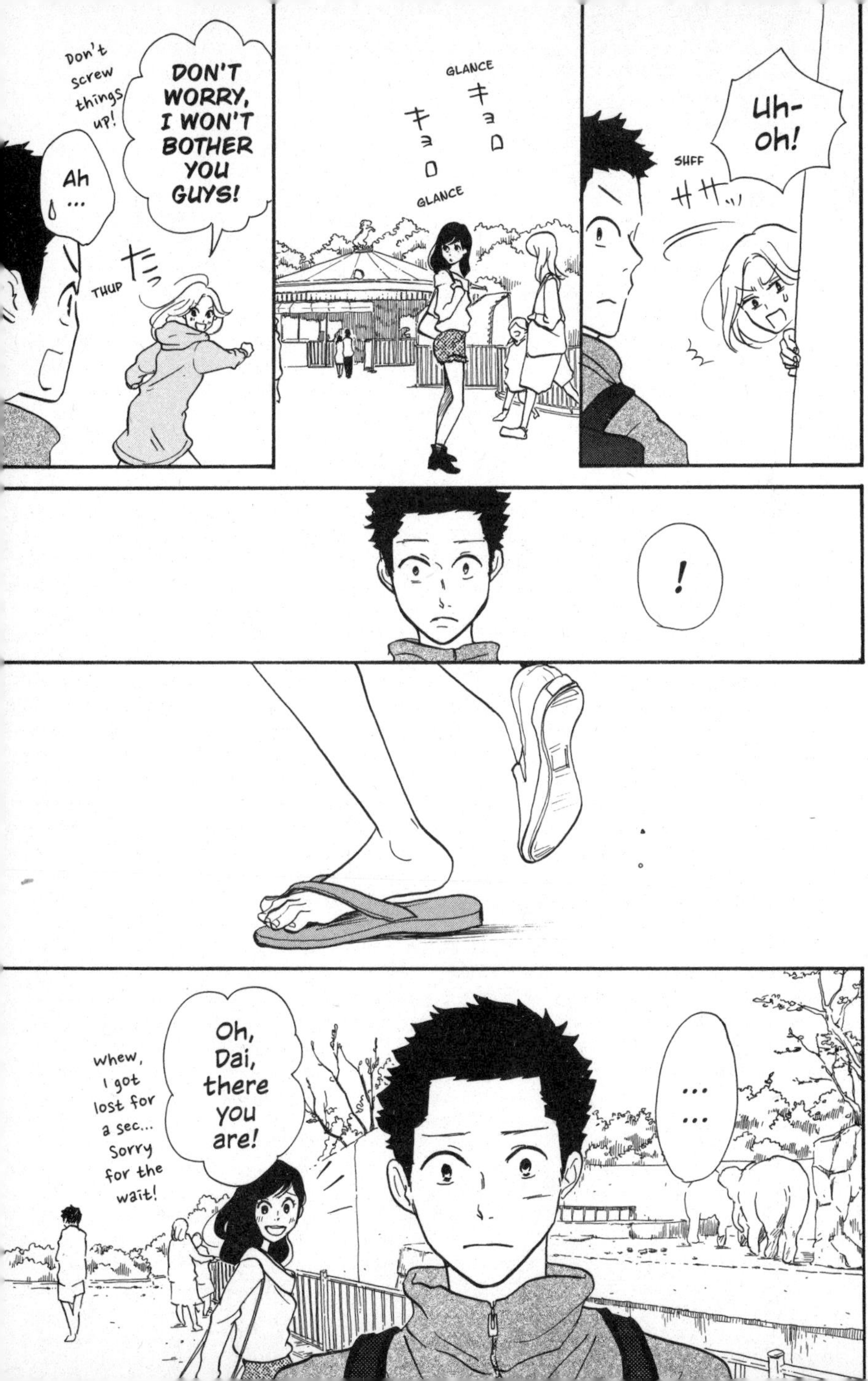
SHUFF
ササッ
Uh-oh!
GLANCE
キョロ
キョロ
GLANCE
DON'T WORRY, I WON'T BOTHER YOU GUYS!
Don't screw things up!
Ah ...
THUP
!
……
……
Oh, Dai, there you are!
whew, I got lost for a sec... Sorry for the wait!

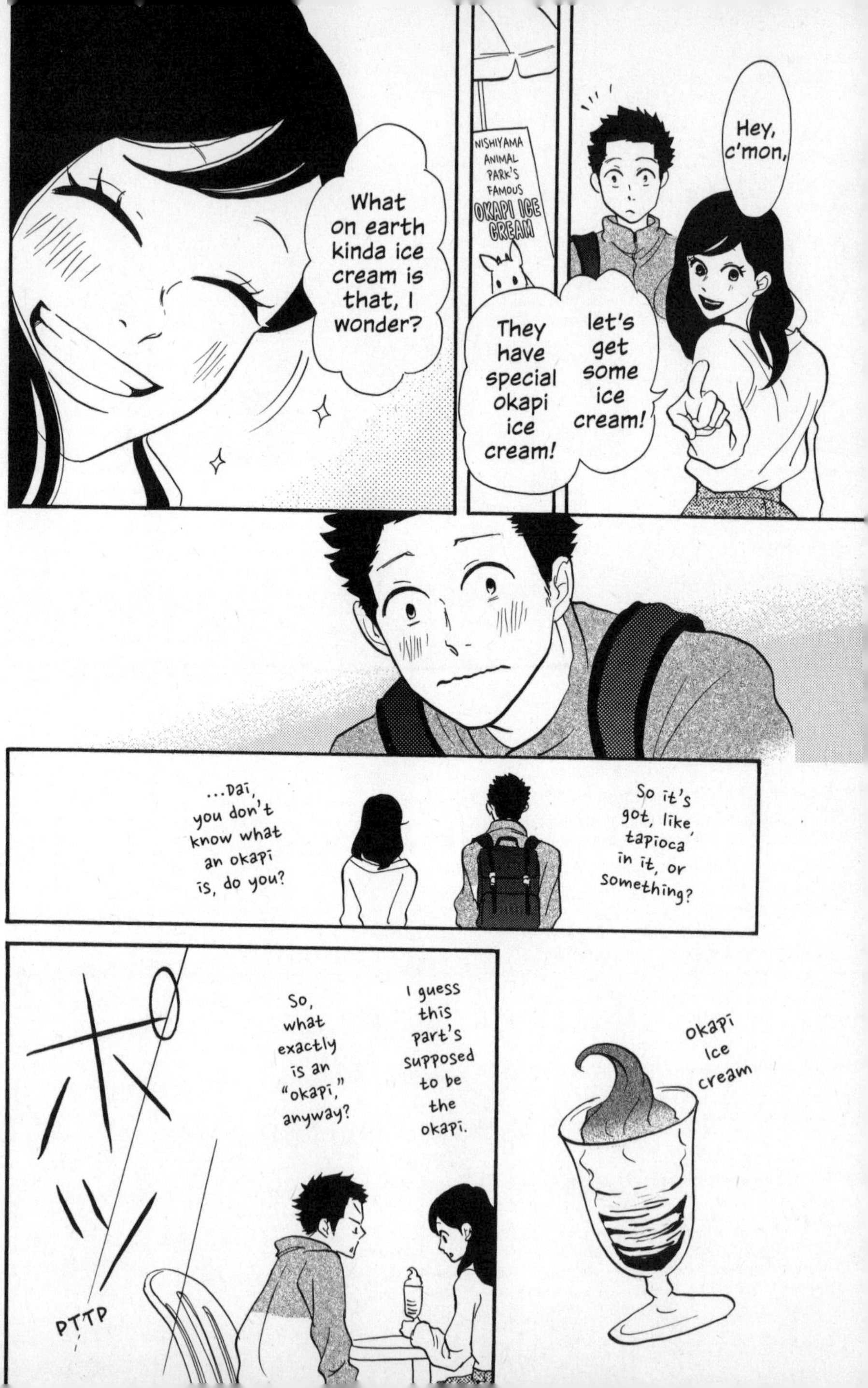
NISHIYAMA ANIMAL PARK'S FAMOUS OKAPI ICE CREAM
Hey, c'mon,
let's get some ice cream!
They have special okapi ice cream!
What on earth kinda ice cream is that, I wonder?
So it's got, like, tapioca in it, or something?
...Dai, you don't know what an okapi is, do you?
Okapi Ice cream
I guess this part's supposed to be the okapi.
So, what exactly is an "okapi," anyway?
PTTP

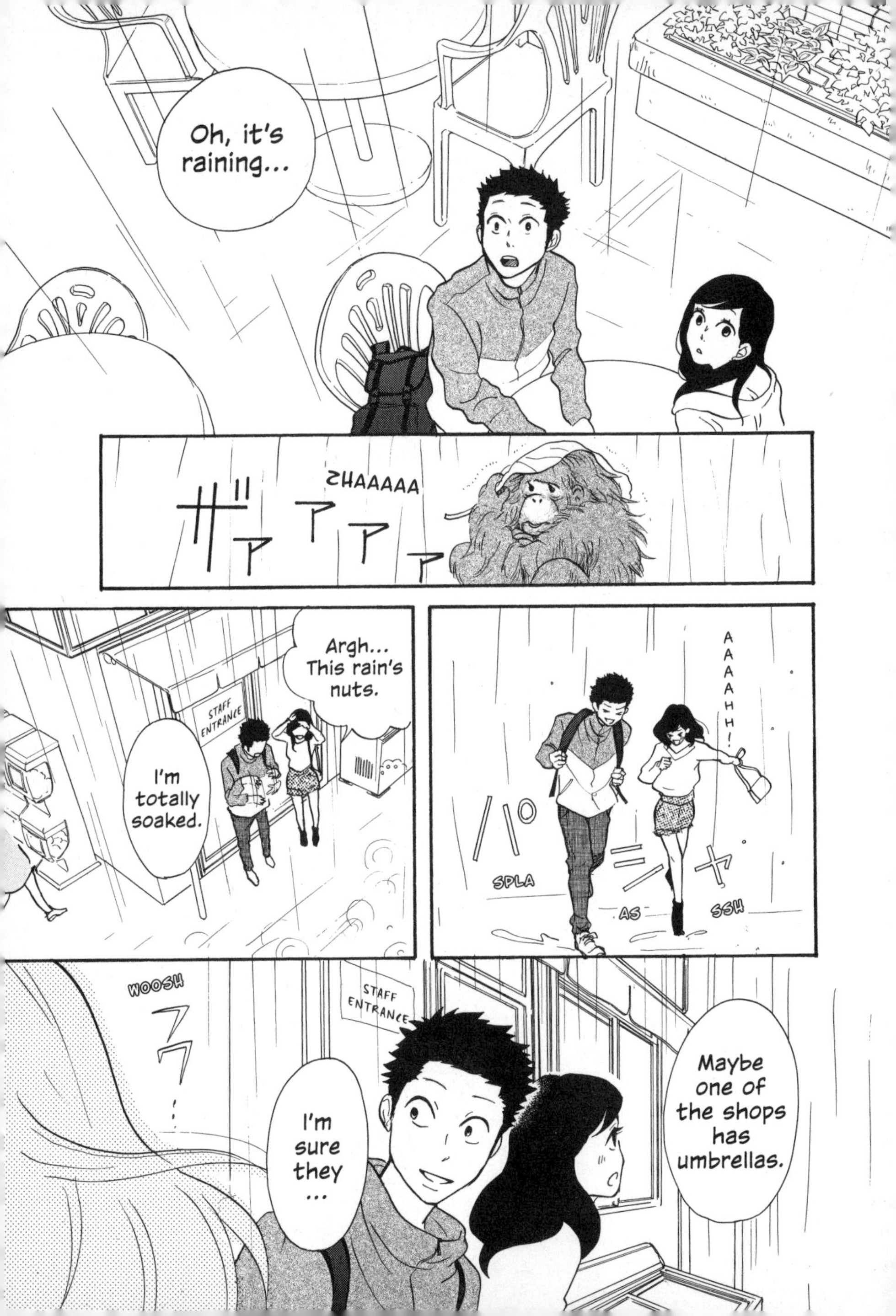
Oh, it's raining...
ZHAAAAA
AAAAAHH!
SPLA
AS
SSH
Argh... This rain's nuts.
I'm totally soaked.
STAFF ENTRANCE
WOOSH
STAFF ENTRANCE
Maybe one of the shops has umbrellas.
I'm sure they ...

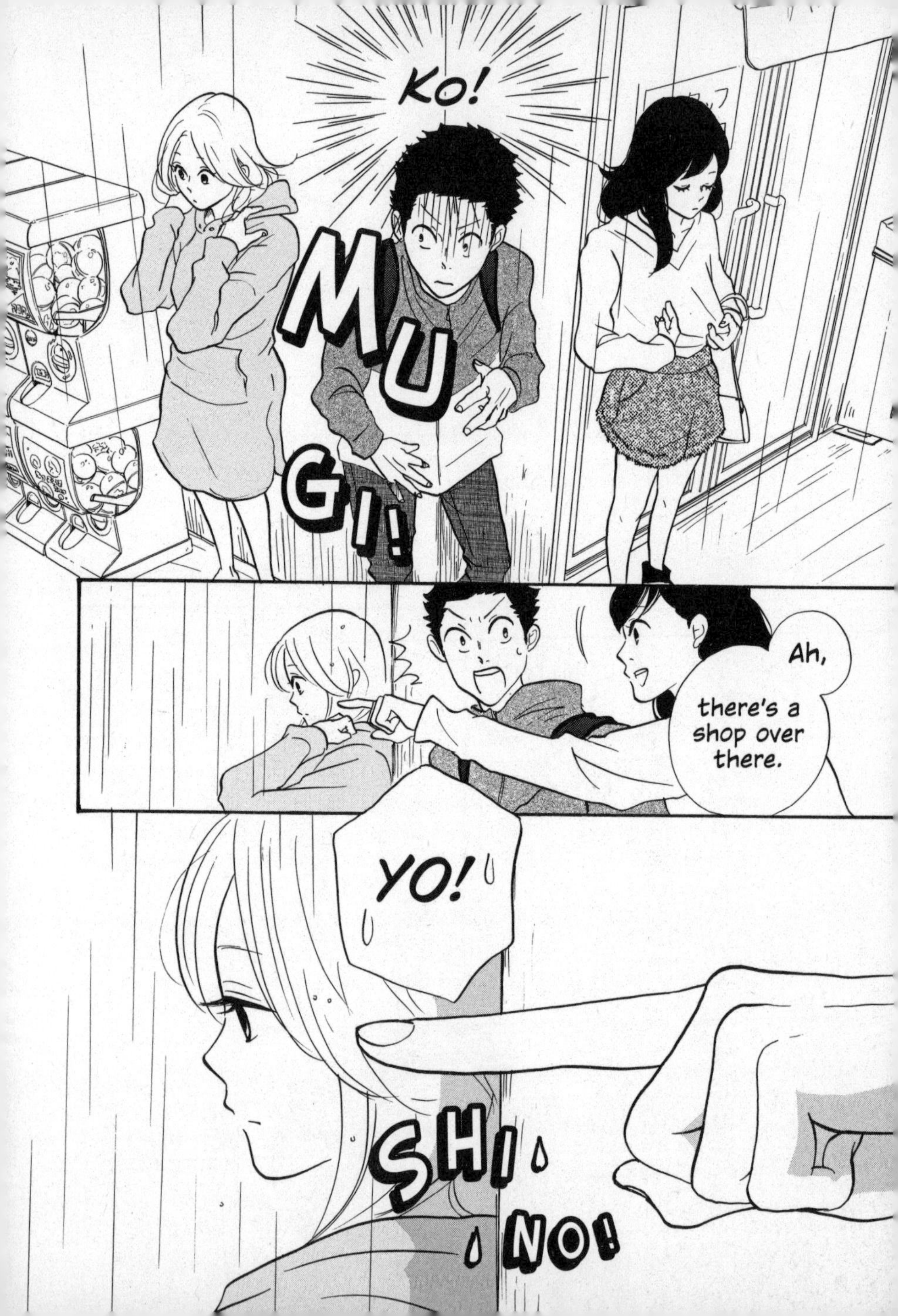
KO!
MU
GI!
Ah, there's a shop over there.
YO!
SHI
NO!

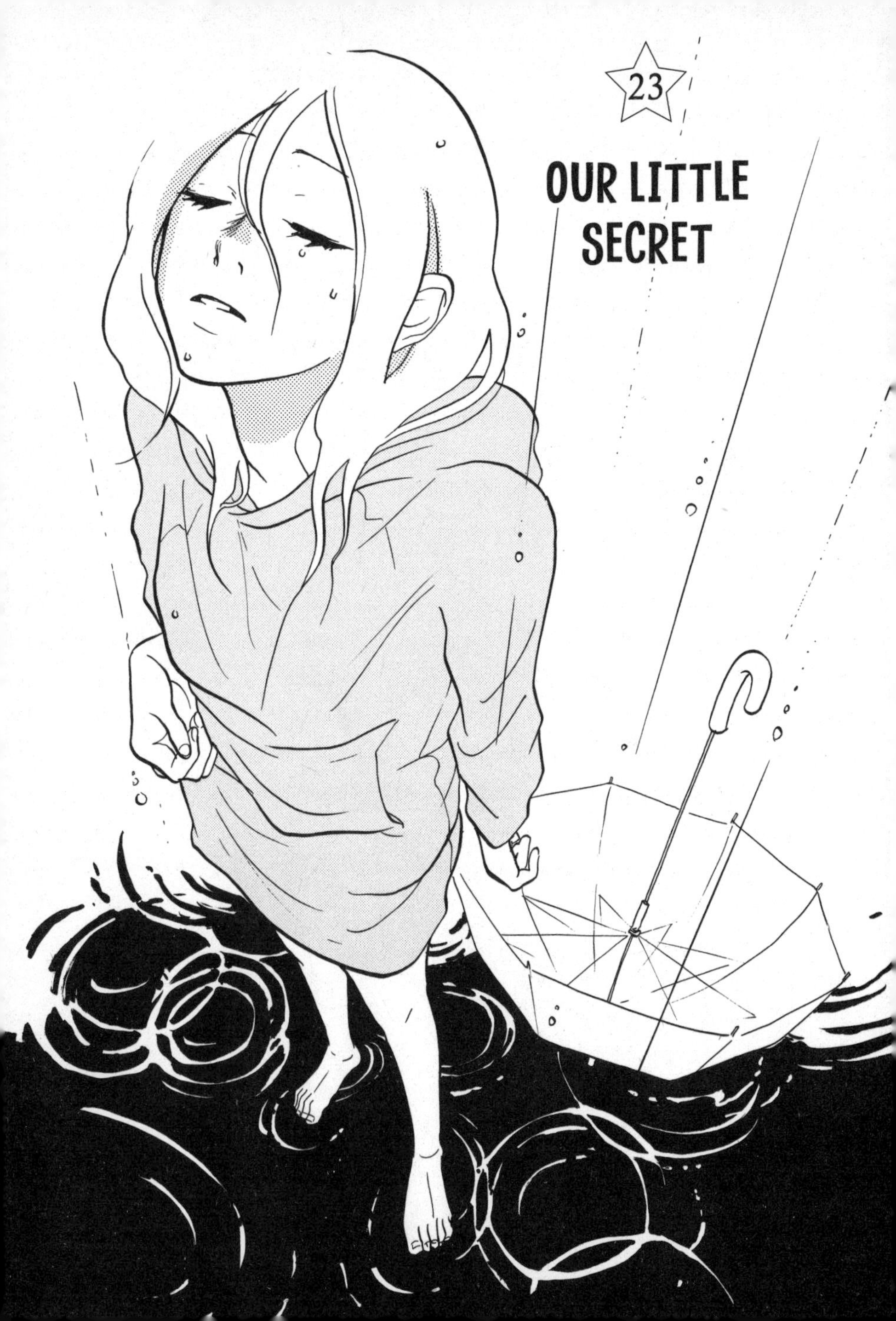
23
OUR LITTLE SECRET

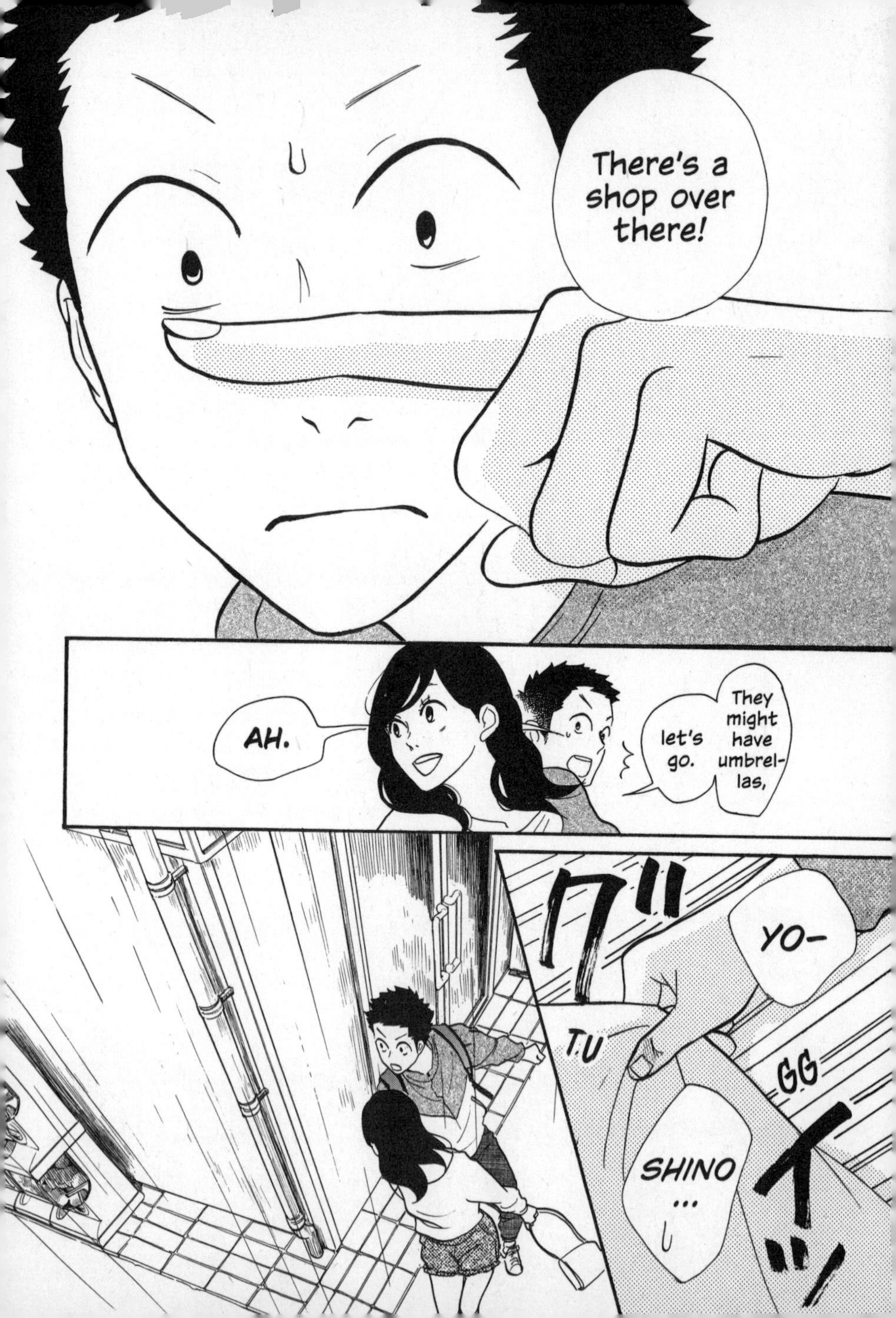
There's a shop over there!
They might have umbrellas, let's go.
AH.
YO-
TUGG
SHINO ...

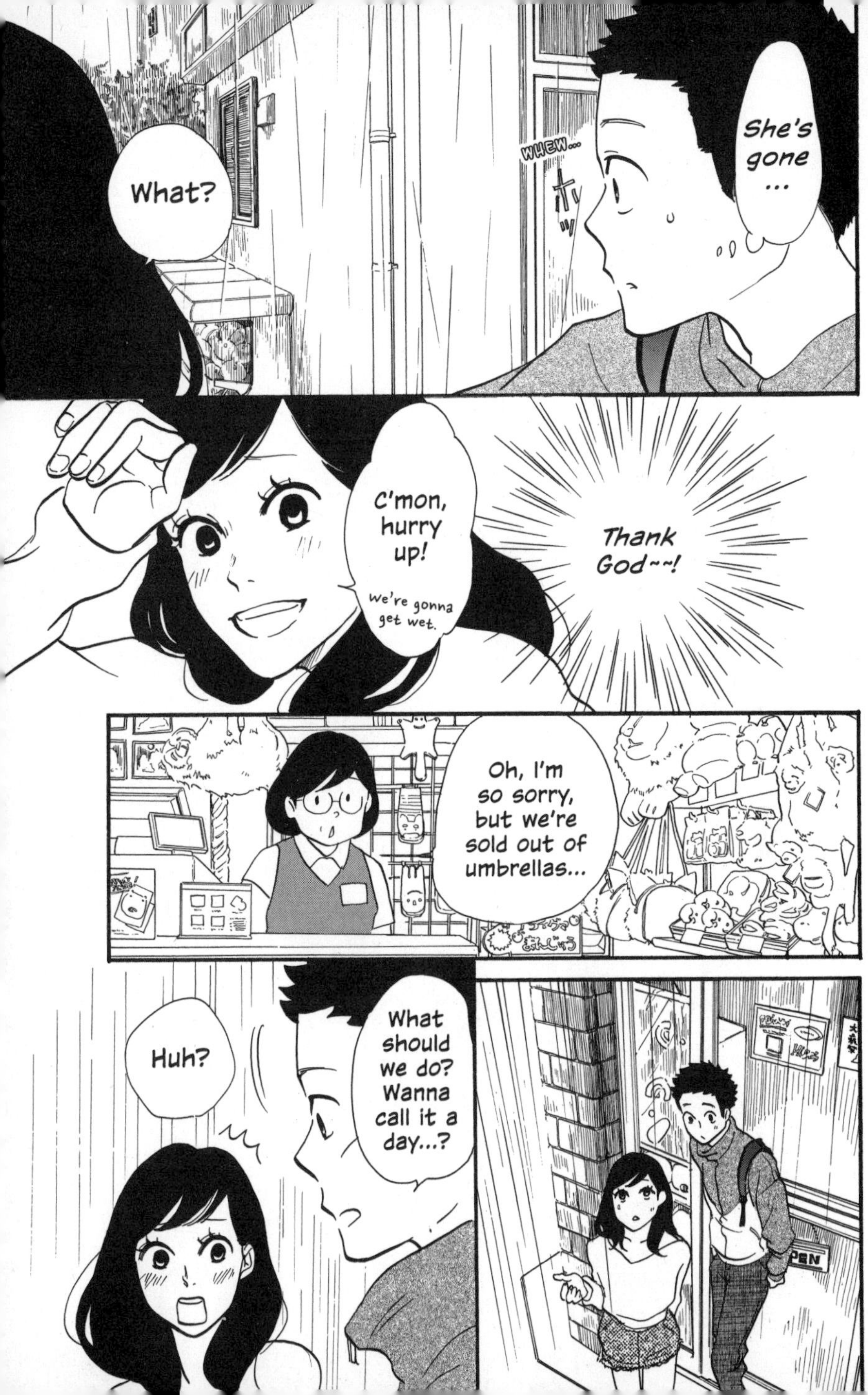
She's gone ...
WHEW...
What?
Thank God~~!
C'mon, hurry up!
We're gonna get wet.
Oh, I'm so sorry, but we're sold out of umbrellas...
What should we do? Wanna call it a day...?
Huh?

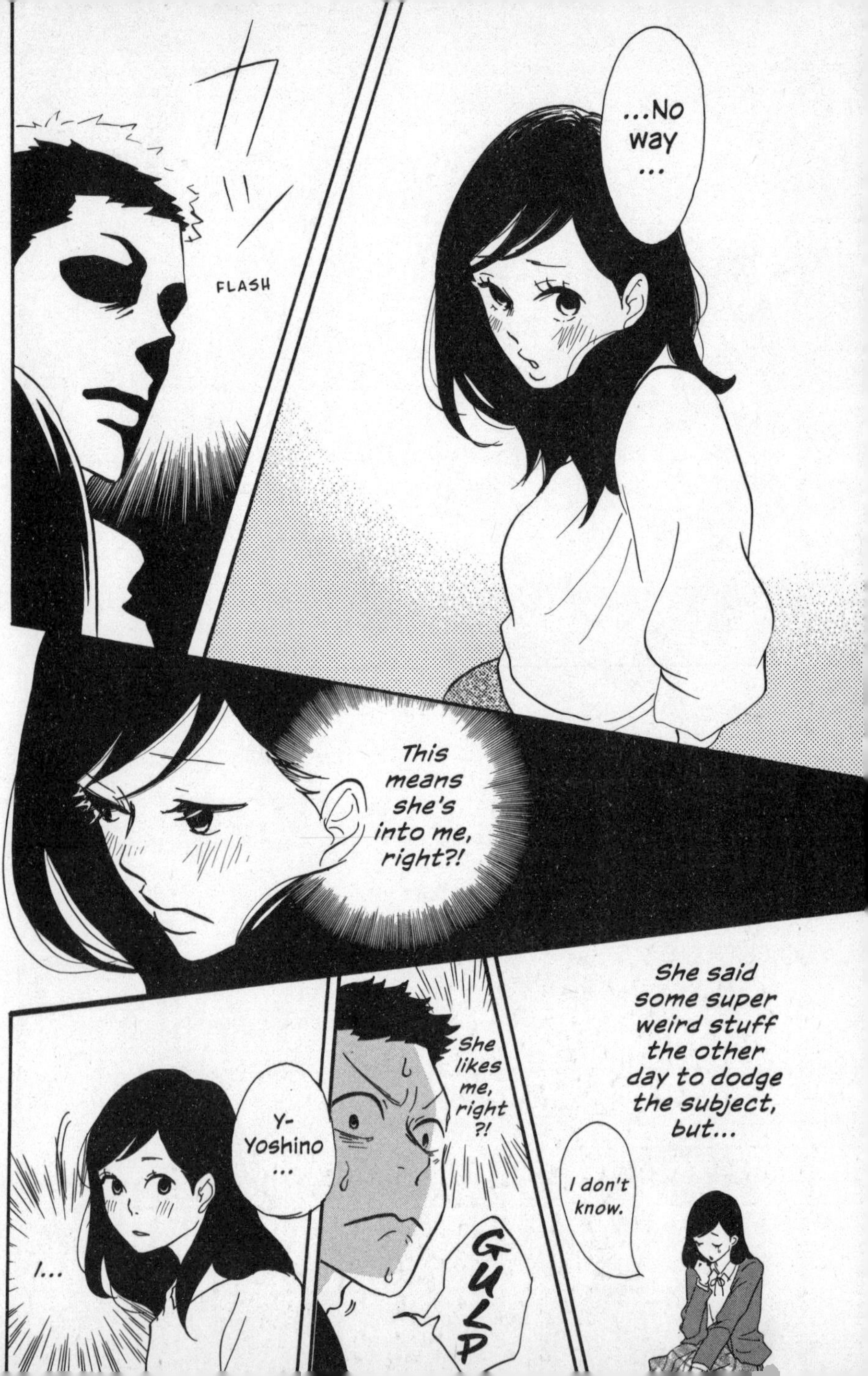
...No way...
FLASH
This means she's into me, right?!
She said some super weird stuff the other day to dodge the subject, but...
I don't know.
She likes me, right?!
GULP
Y-Yoshino...
I...

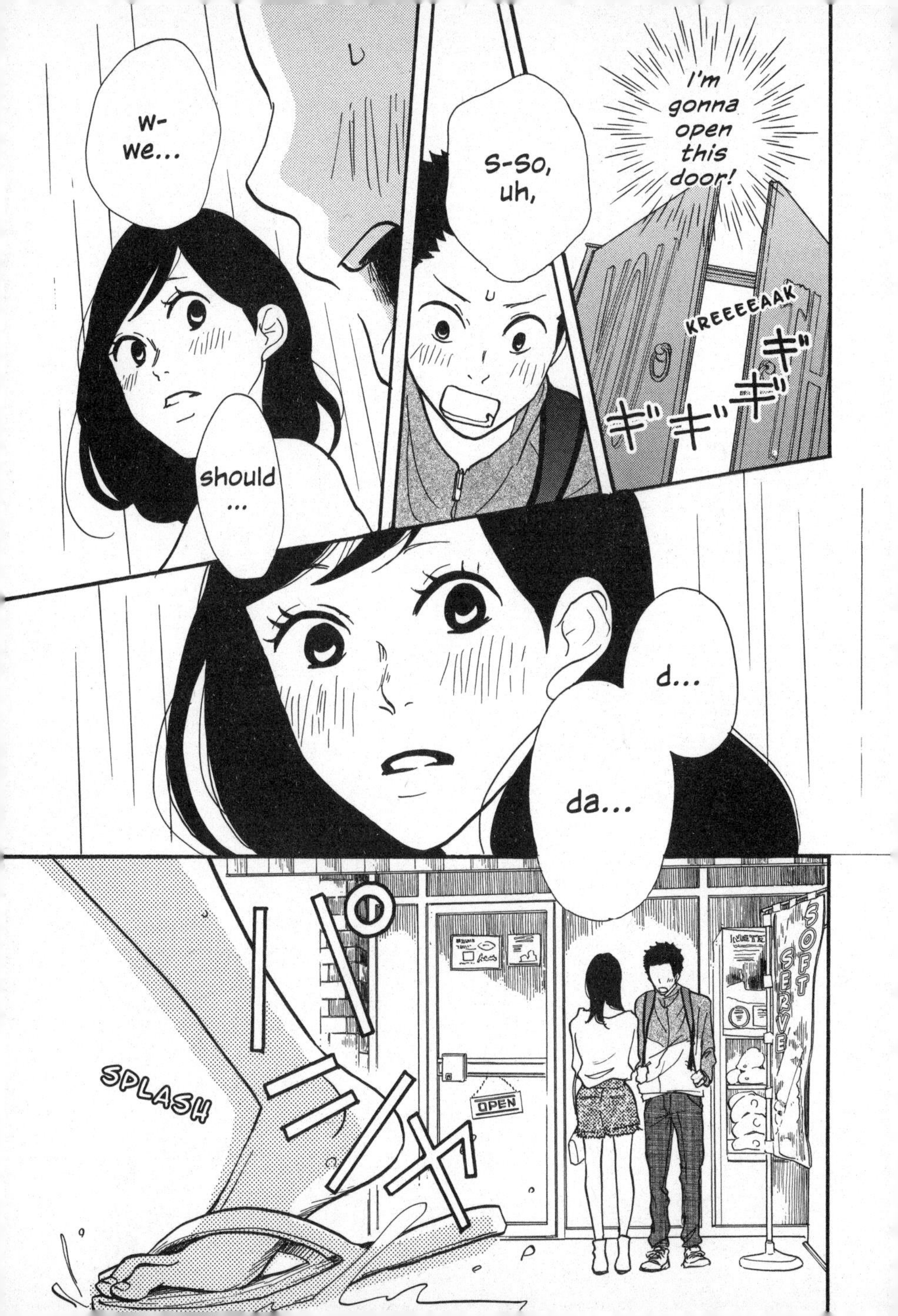
I'm gonna open this door!
KREEEEAAK
ギ
ギギギ
S-So, uh,
w- we...
should ...
d...
da...
SOFT SERVE
OPEN
SPLASH

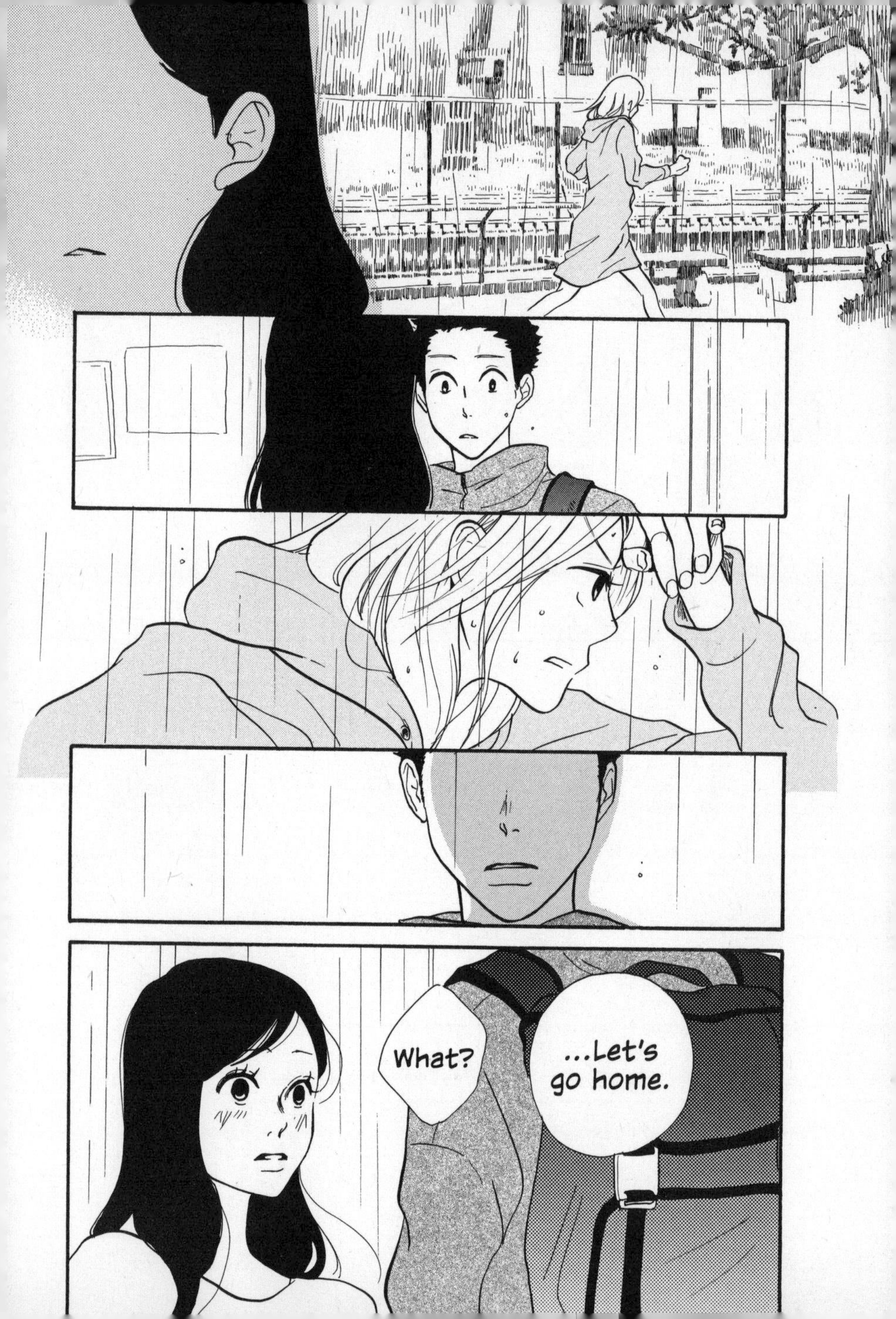
...Let's go home.
What?

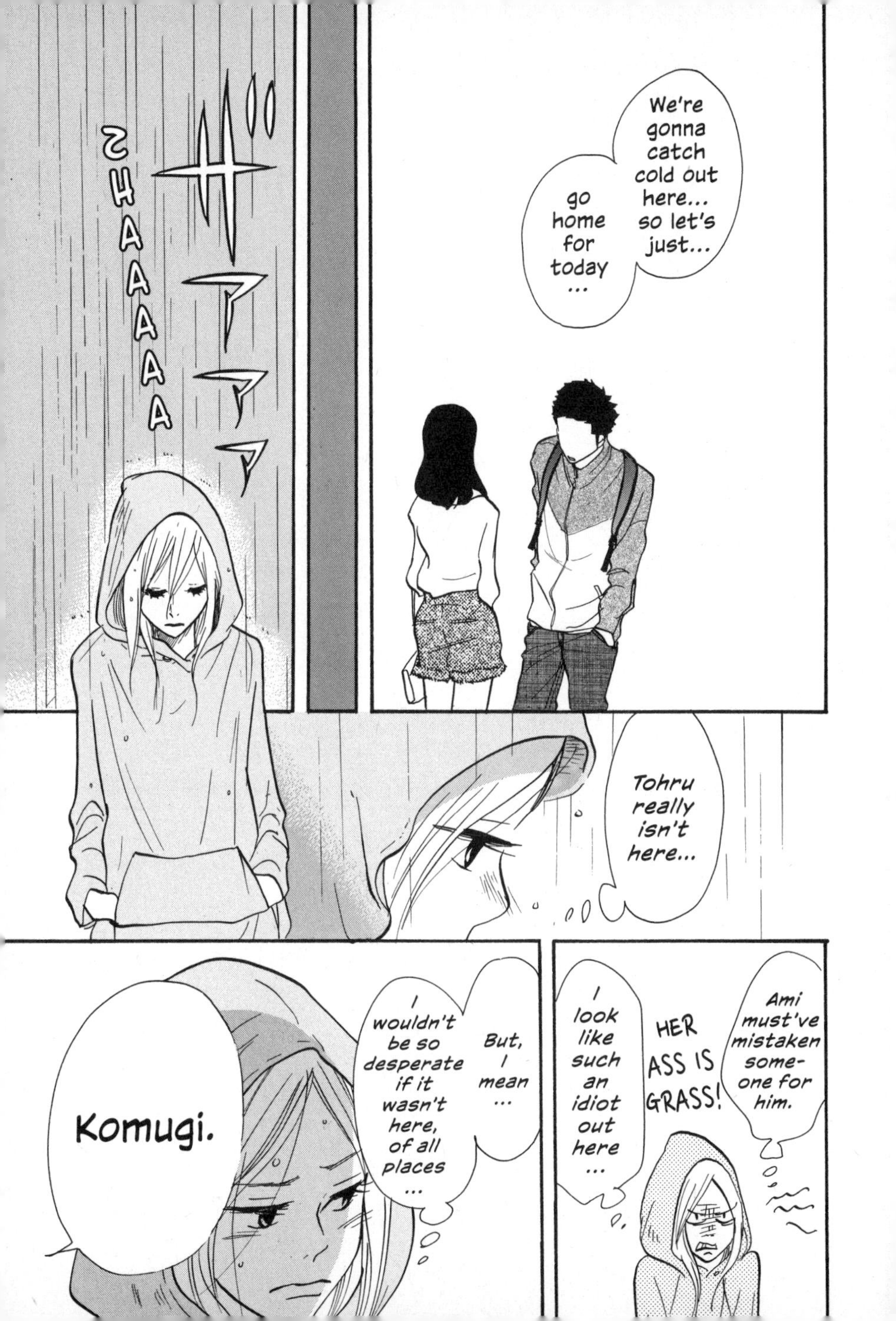
We're gonna catch cold out here... so let's just...
go home for today...
SHAAAAAA
Tohru really isn't here...
Ami must've mistaken someone for him.
HER ASS IS GRASS!
I look like such an idiot out here...
But, I mean...
I wouldn't be so desperate if it wasn't here, of all places...
Komugi.

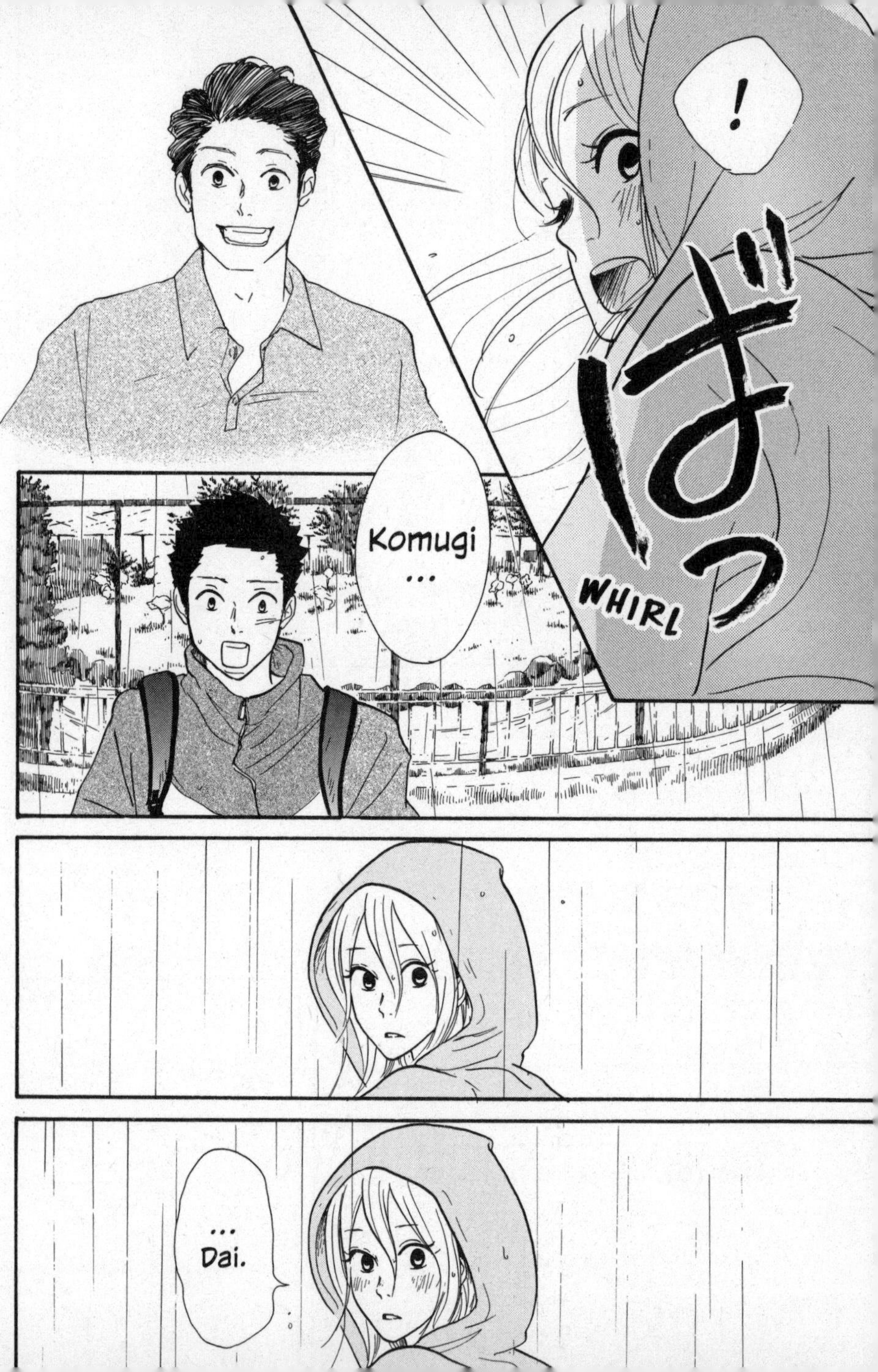
!
ばっ
WHIRL
Komugi ...
... Dai.

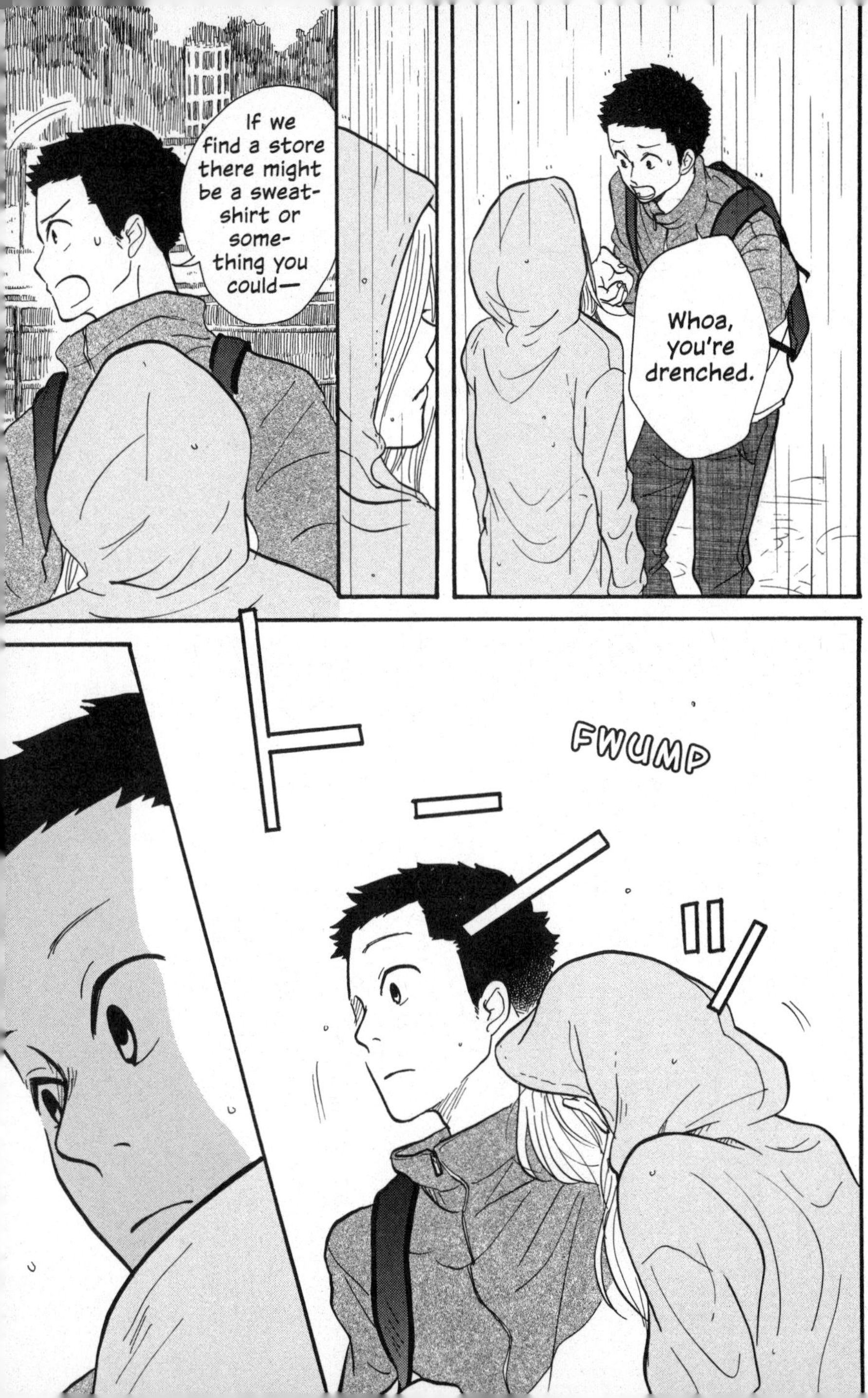
Whoa, you're drenched.
If we find a store there might be a sweat-shirt or some-thing you could—
FWUMP

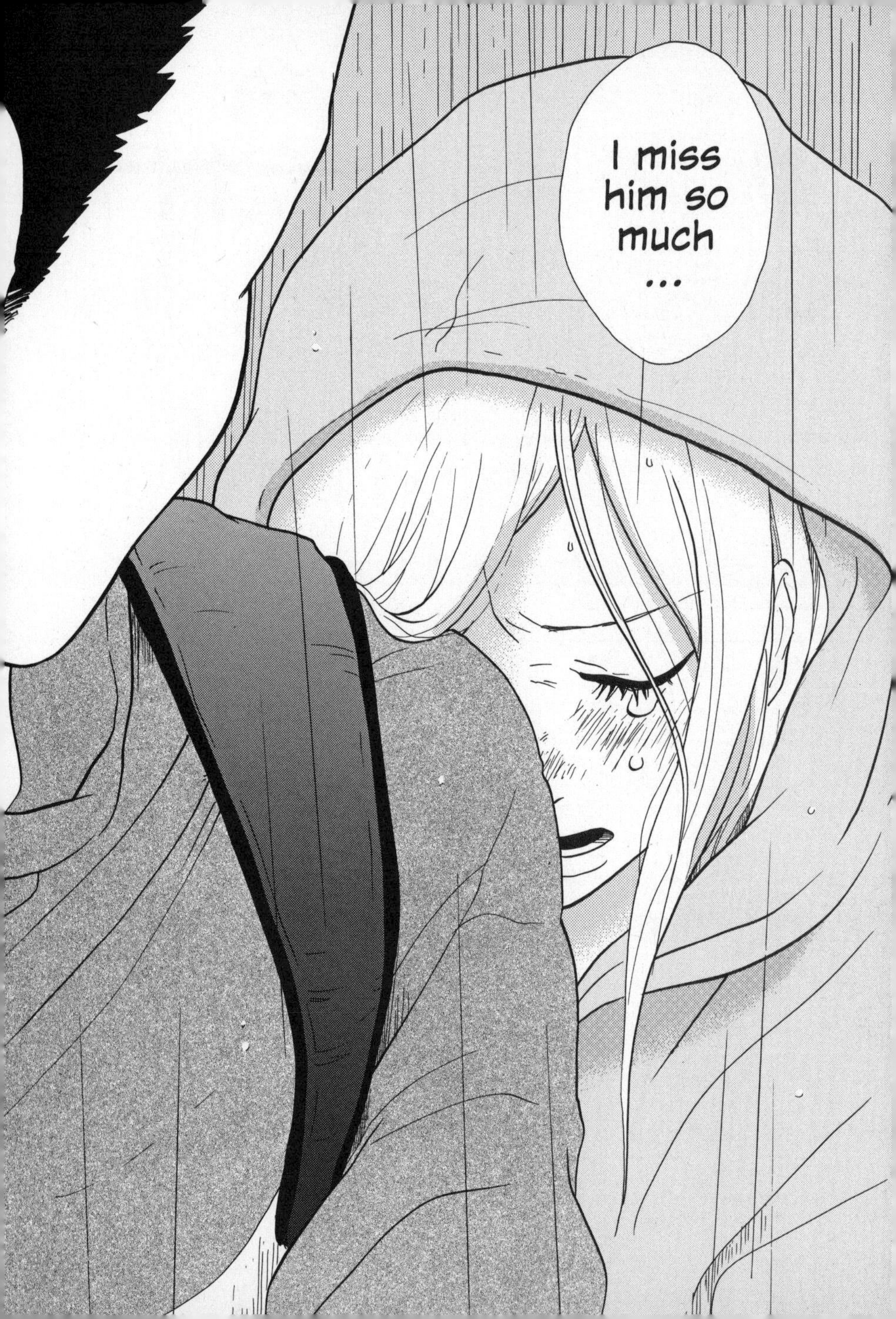
I miss him so much ...

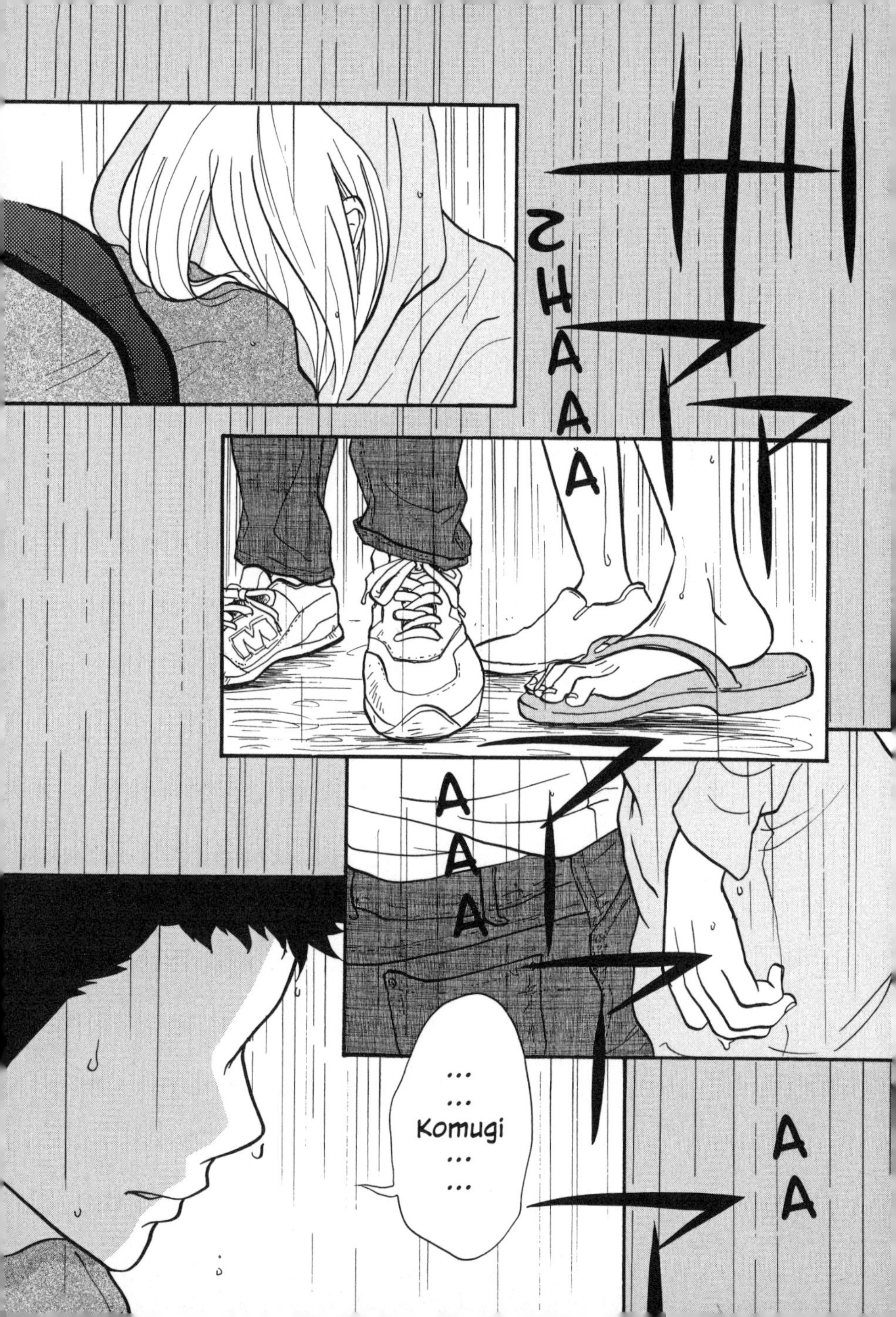
ZHAAAAAAAAA
......
......
Komugi
......
......

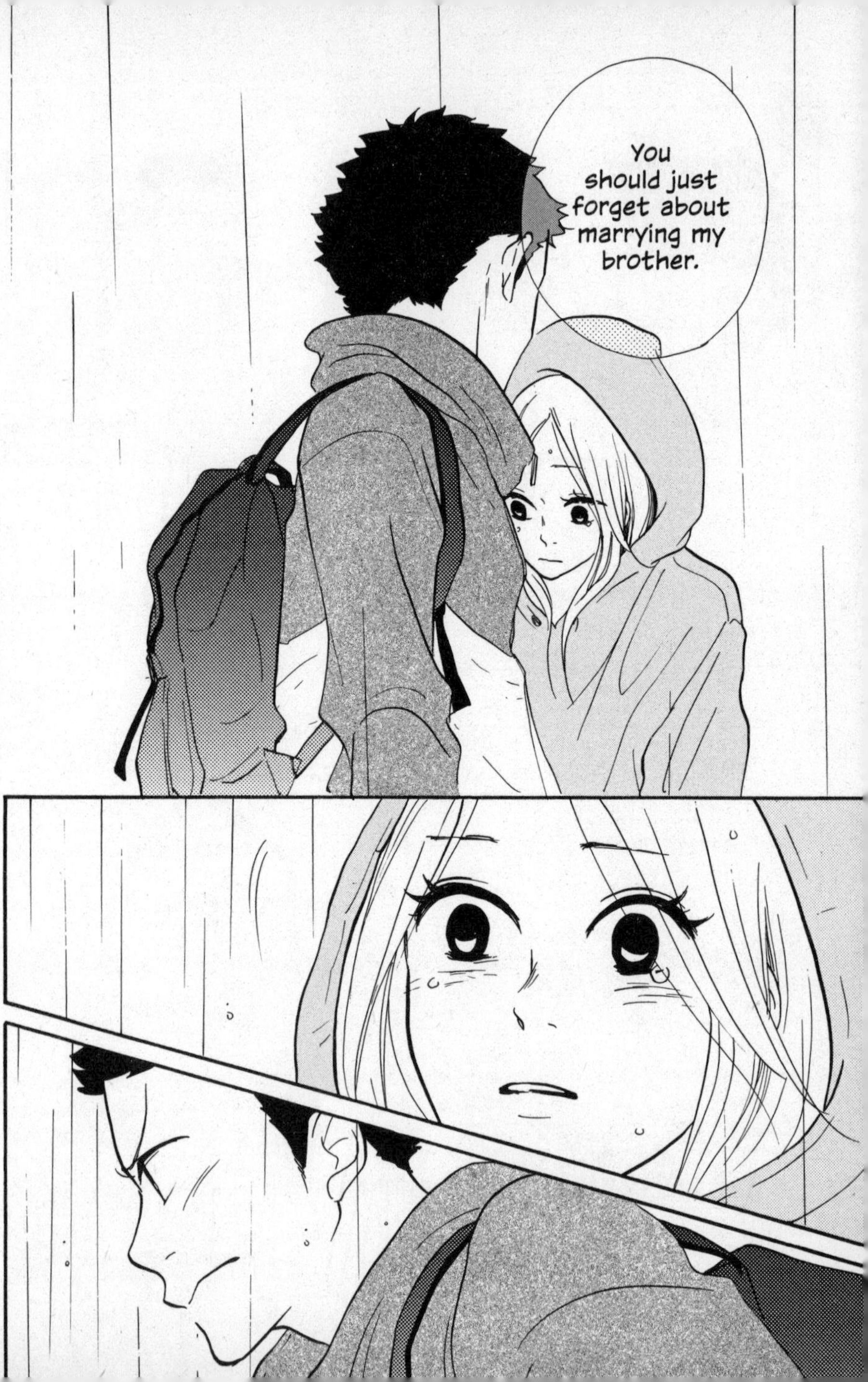
You should just forget about marrying my brother.

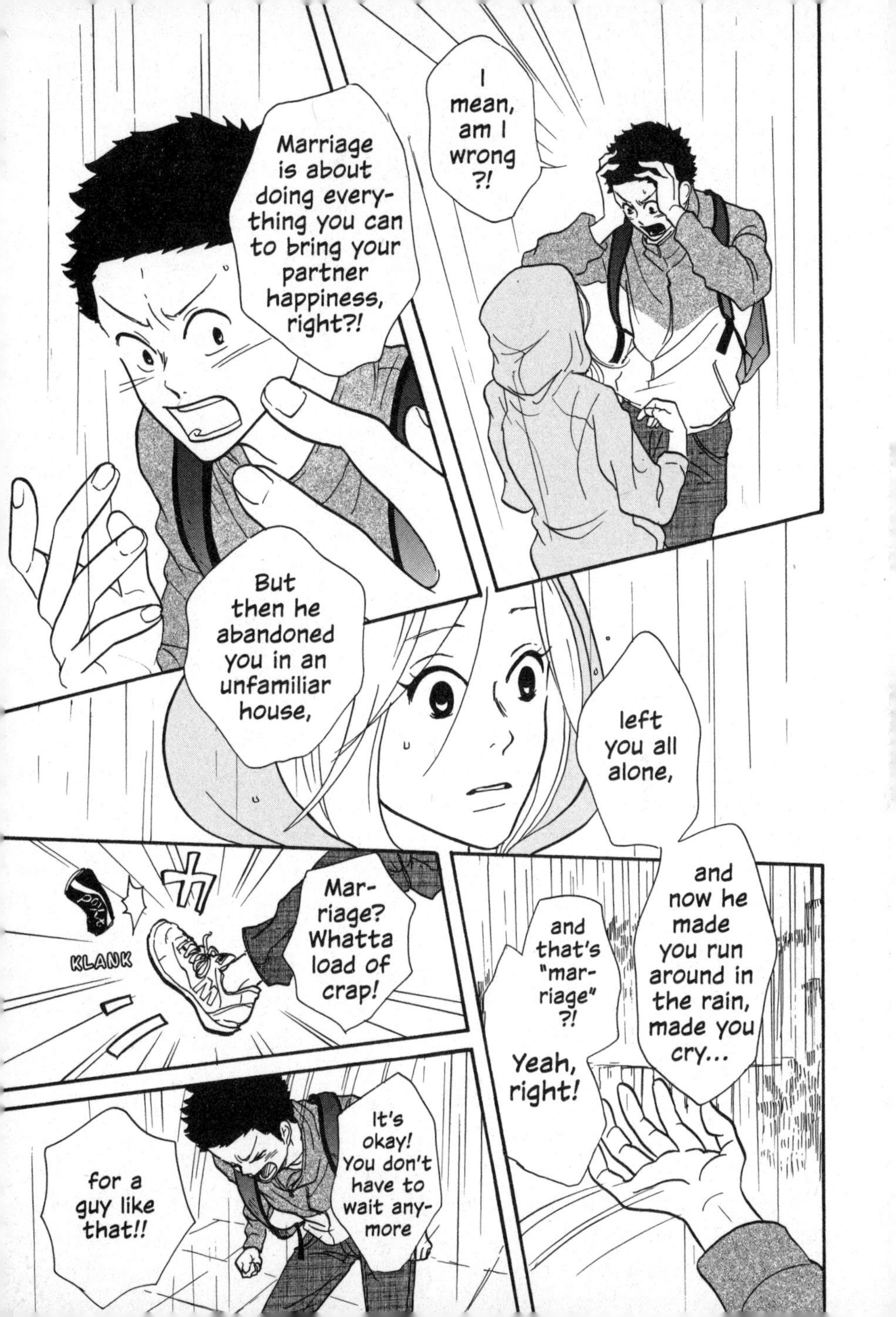
Marriage is about doing every-thing you can to bring your partner happiness, right?!
I mean, am I wrong?!
But then he abandoned you in an unfamiliar house,
left you all alone,
and now he made you run around in the rain, made you cry...
and that's "mar-riage"?!
Yeah, right!
カ
Mar-riage? Whatta load of crap!
KLANK
It's okay! You don't have to wait any-more
for a guy like that!!

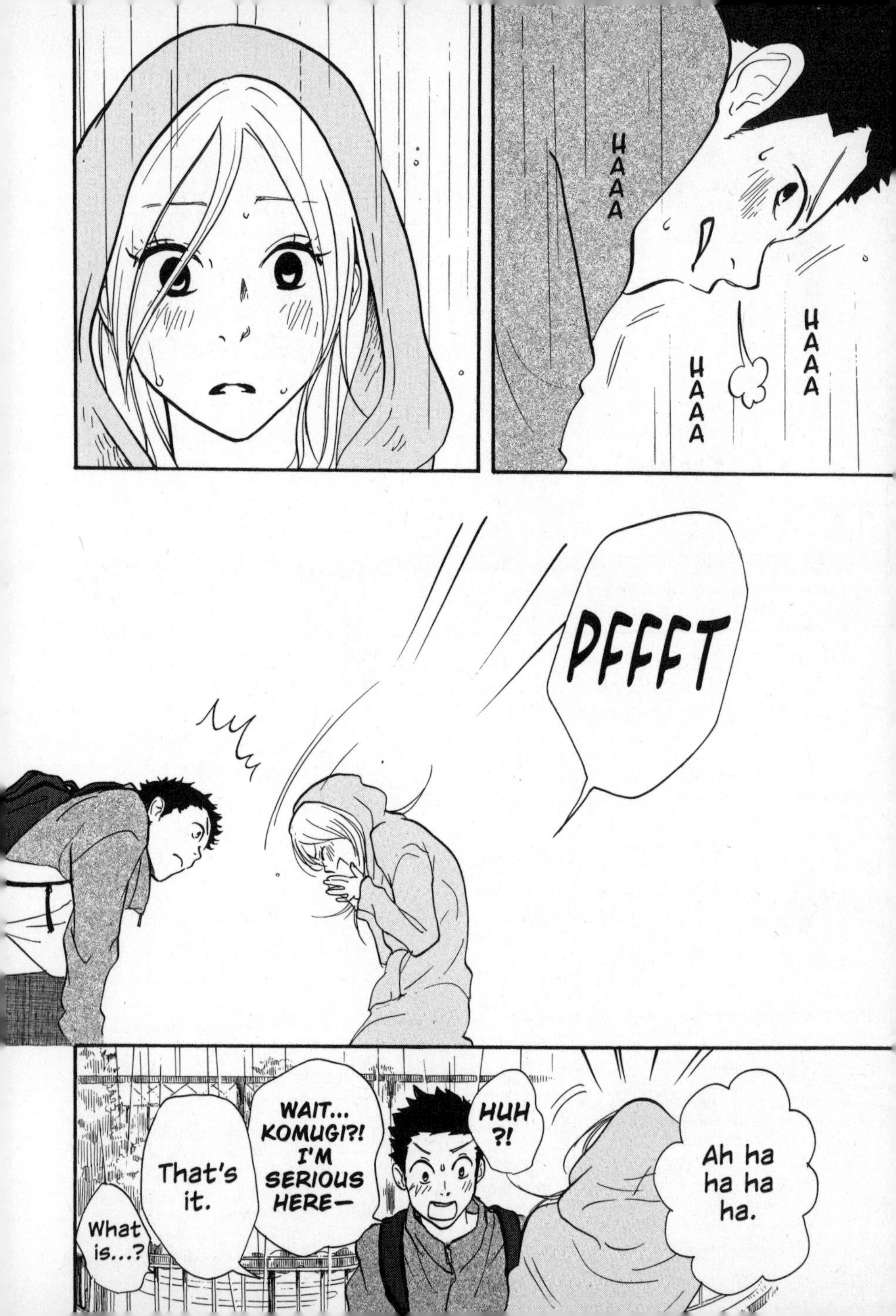
HAAA
HAAA
HAAA
PFFFT
Ah ha ha ha ha.
HUH ?!
WAIT... KOMUGI?! I'M SERIOUS HERE—
That's it.
What is...?

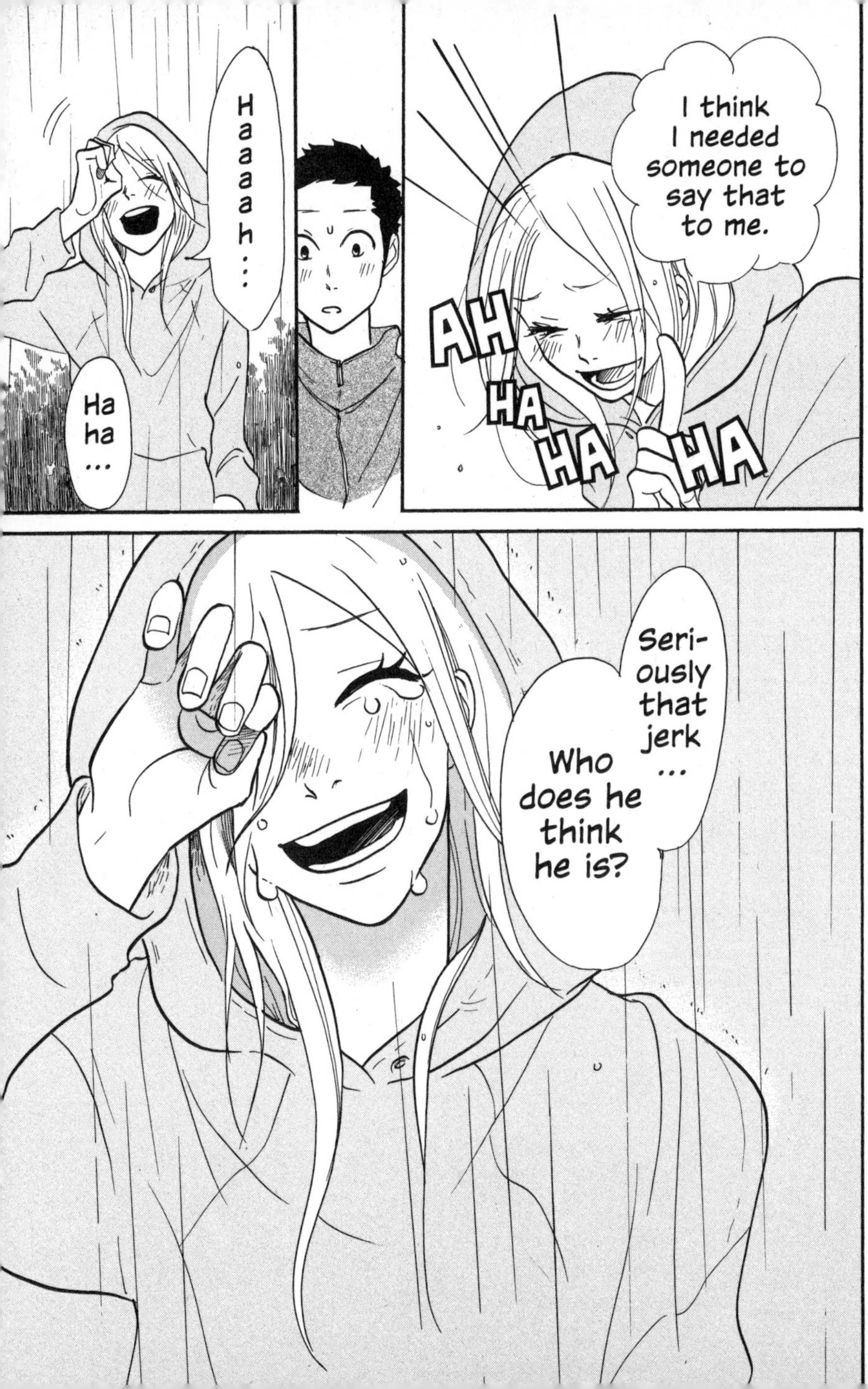
I think I needed someone to say that to me.
AH HA HA HA
Haaaah...
Ha ha...
Seri-ously that jerk...
Who does he think he is?

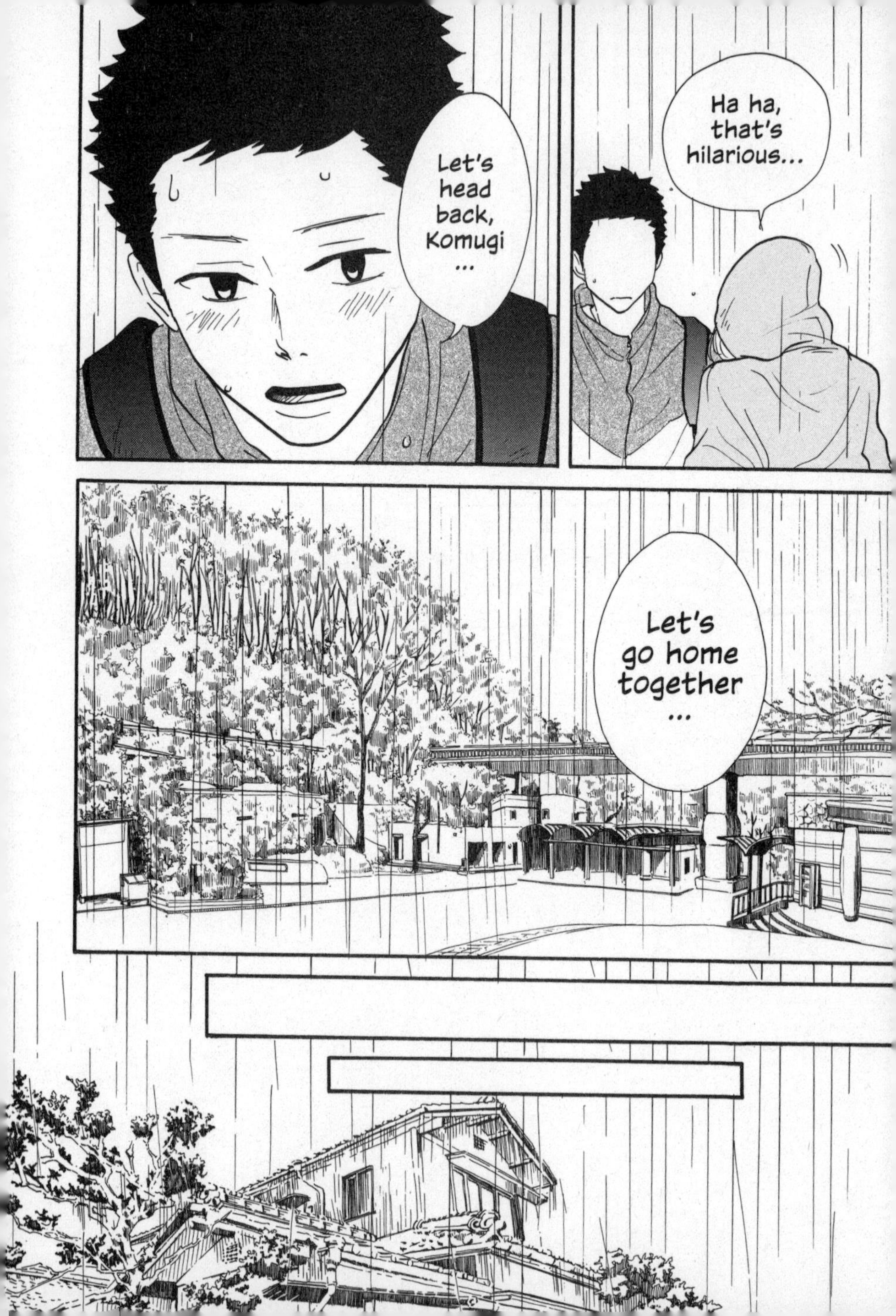
Ha ha, that's hilarious...
Let's head back, Komugi ...
Let's go home together ...

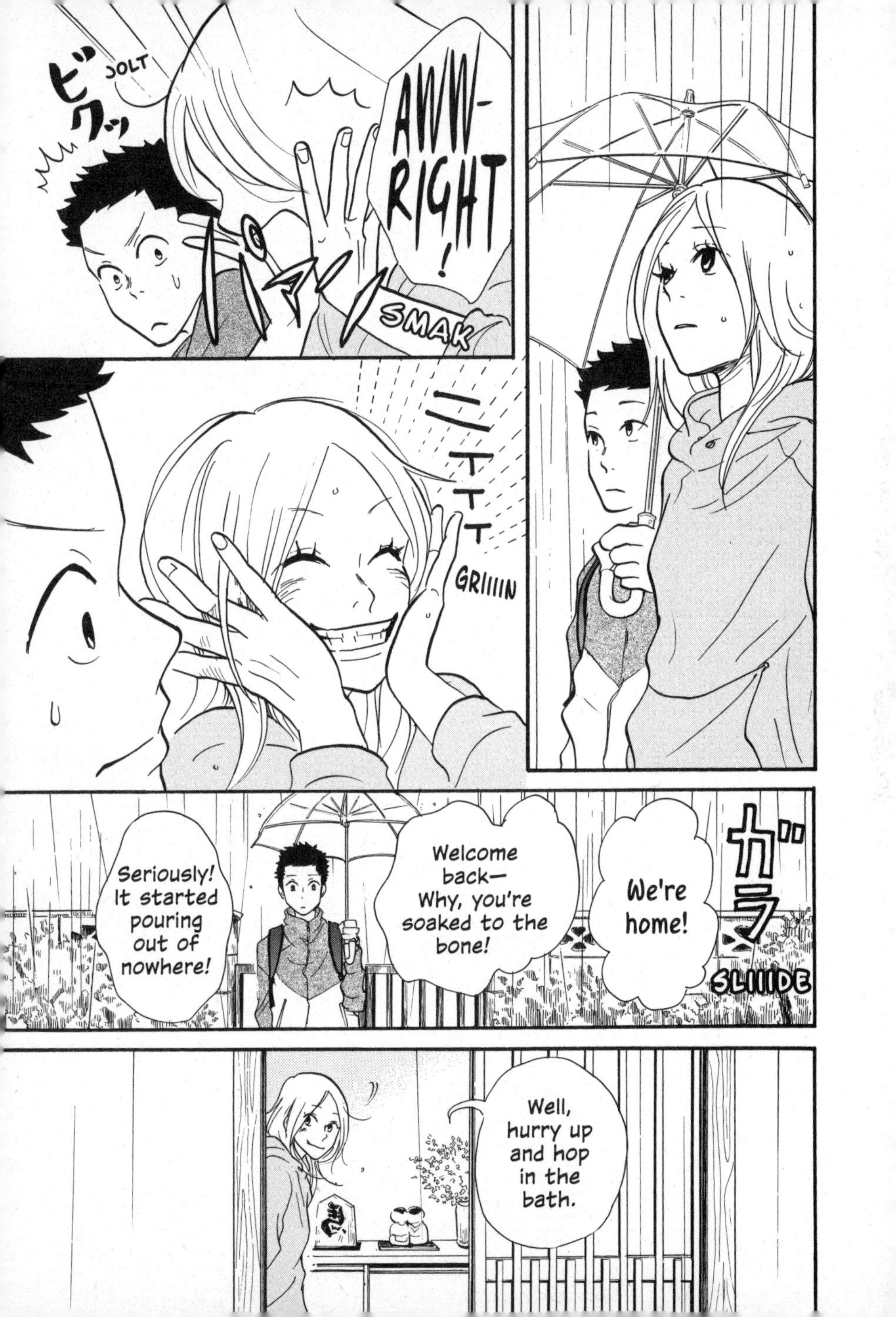
AWW-RIGHT!
SMAK
JOLT
ビクッ
GRIIIIN
ガラ
SLIIIDE
We're home!
Welcome back— Why, you're soaked to the bone!
Seriously! It started pouring out of nowhere!
Well, hurry up and hop in the bath.

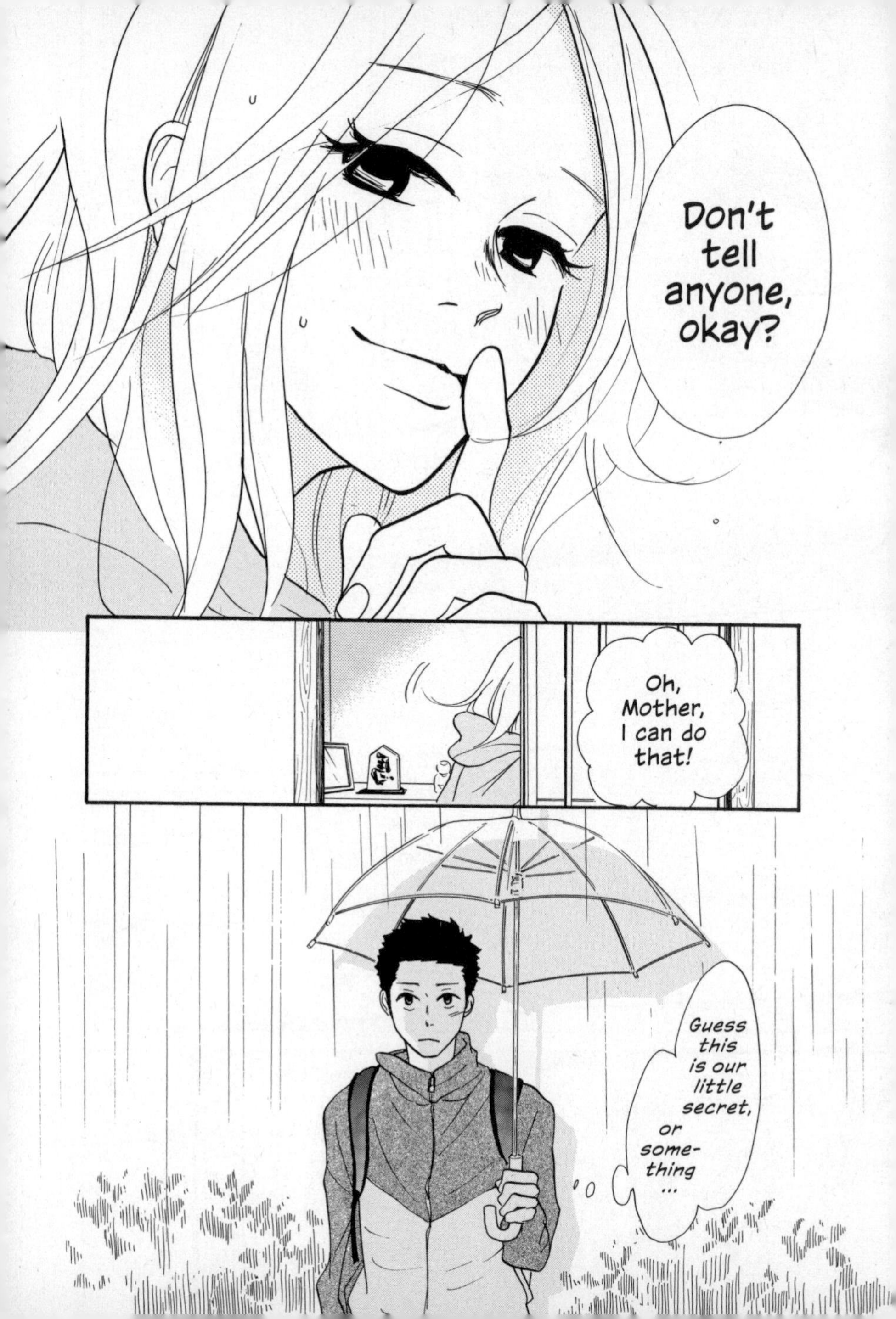
Don't tell anyone, okay?
Oh, Mother, I can do that!
Guess this is our little secret, or some-thing...

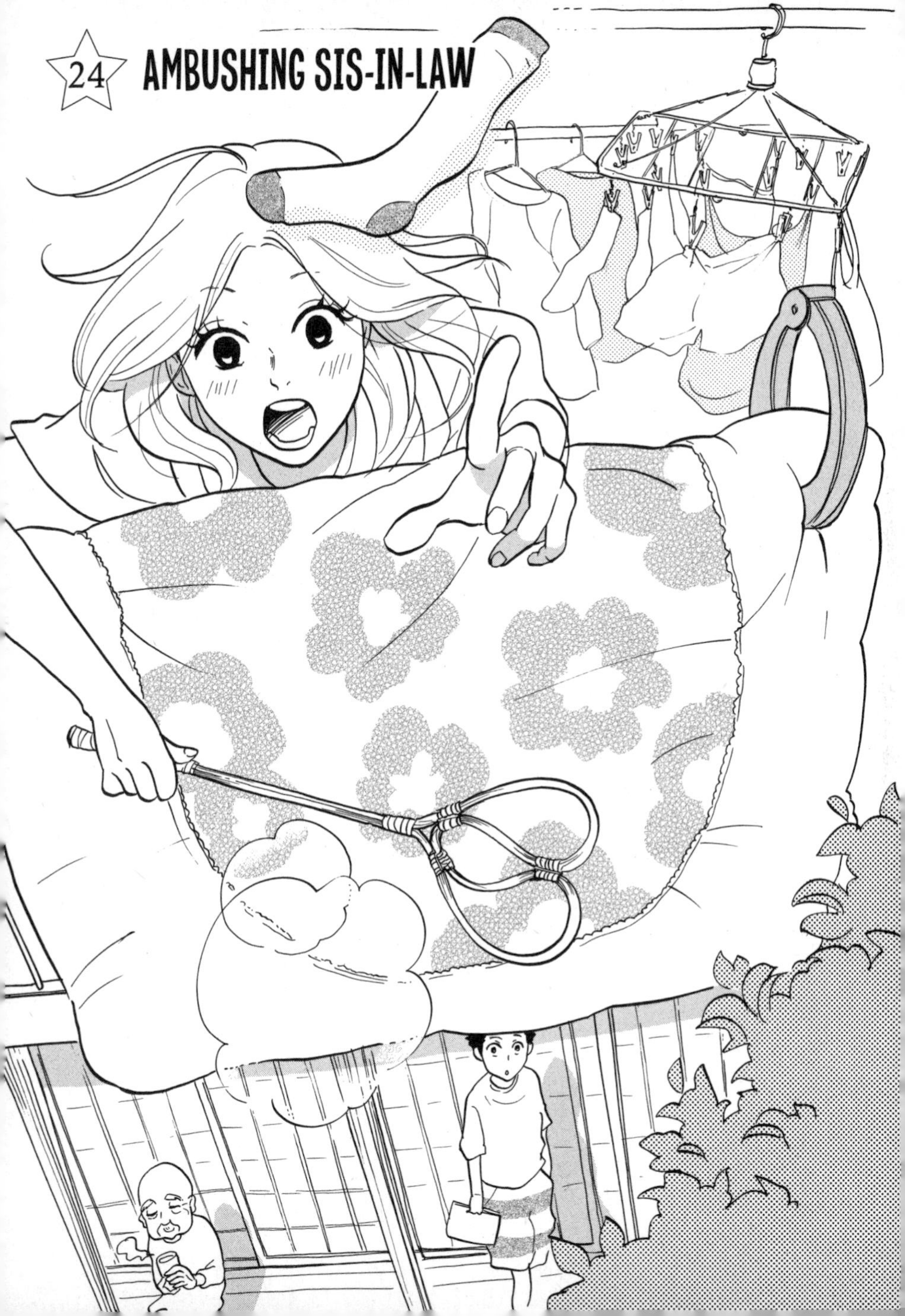
24
AMBUSHING SIS-IN-LAW

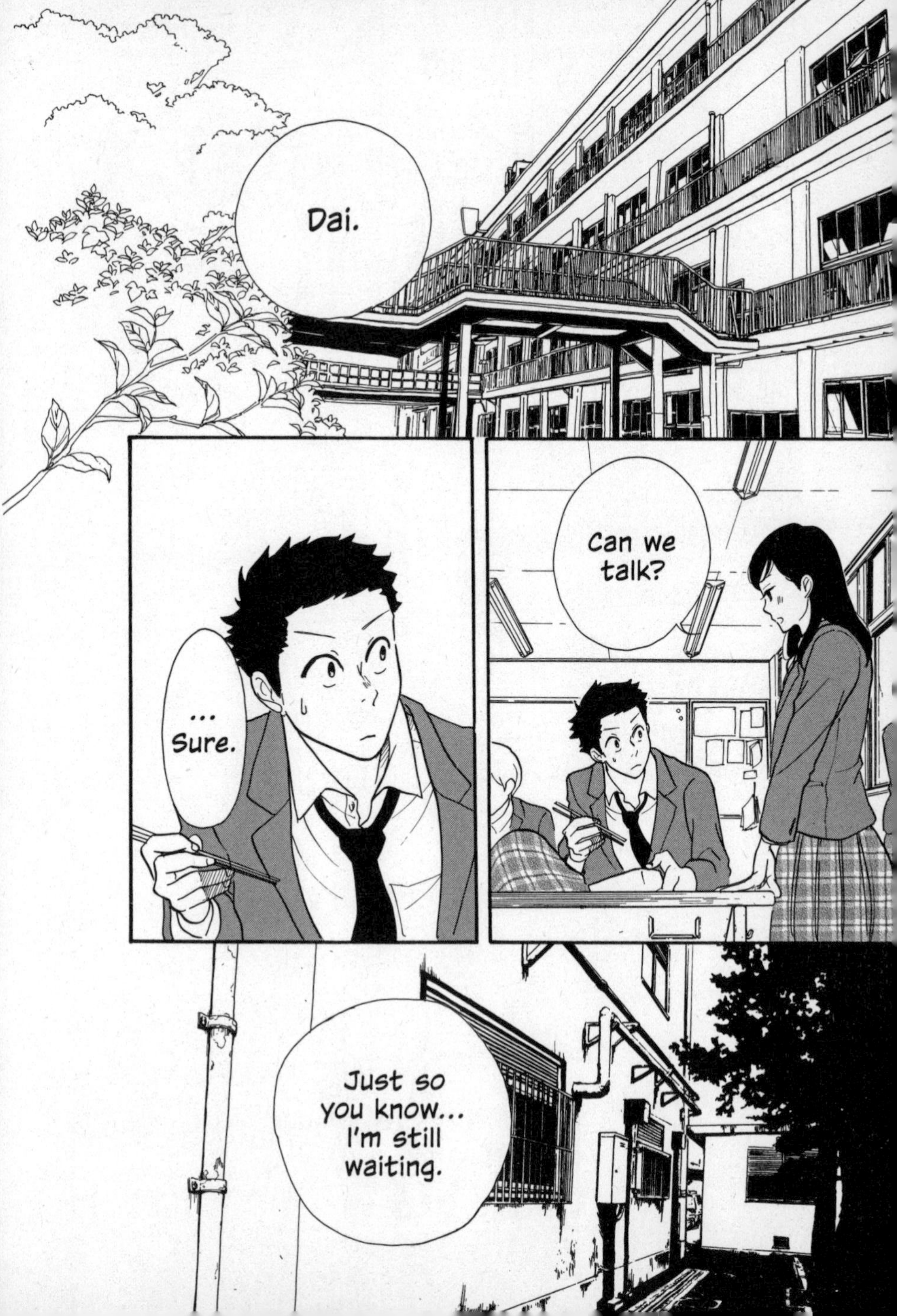
Dai.
Can we talk?
... Sure.
Just so you know... I'm still waiting.

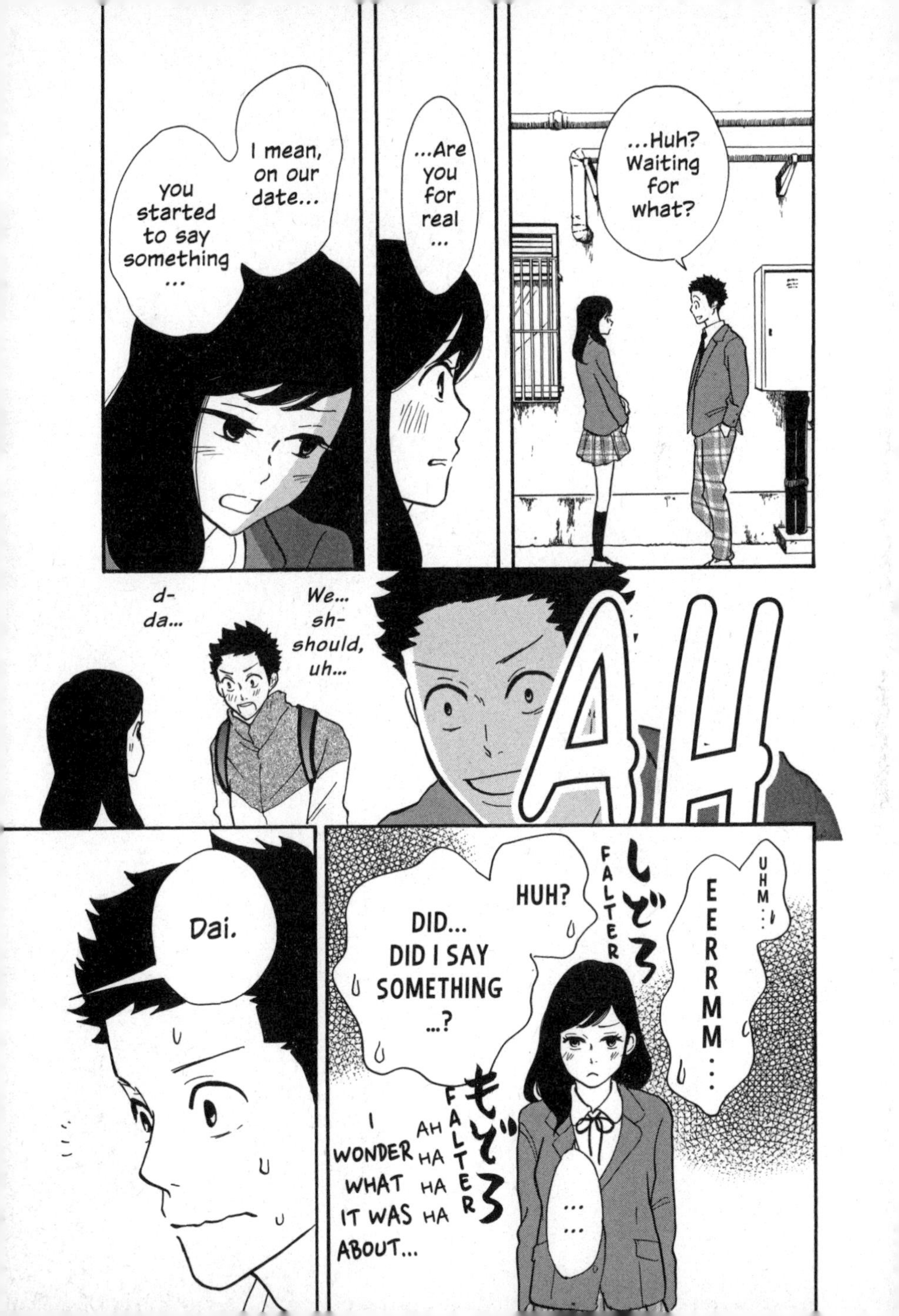
...Huh? Waiting for what?
...Are you for real ...
I mean, on our date... you started to say something ...
AH
We... sh- should, uh...
d- da...
UHM...
EERRMM...
しどろ
FALTER
HUH?
DID... DID I SAY SOMETHING ...?
もどろ
FALTER
AH HA HA HA
I WONDER WHAT IT WAS ABOUT...
... ...
Dai.

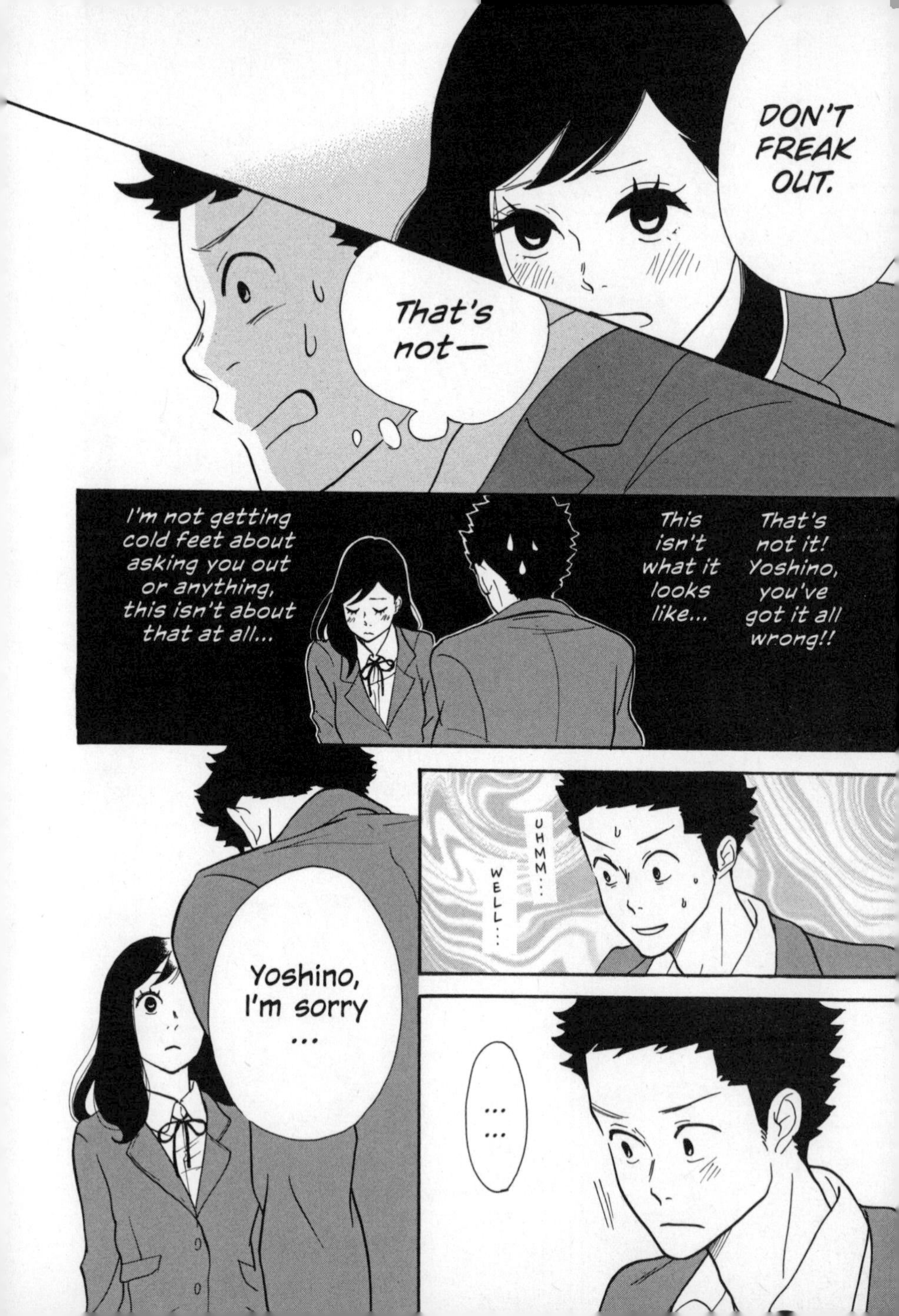
DON'T FREAK OUT.
That's not—
That's not it! Yoshino, you've got it all wrong!!
This isn't what it looks like...
I'm not getting cold feet about asking you out or anything, this isn't about that at all...
UHMM...
WELL...
... ...
Yoshino, I'm sorry ...

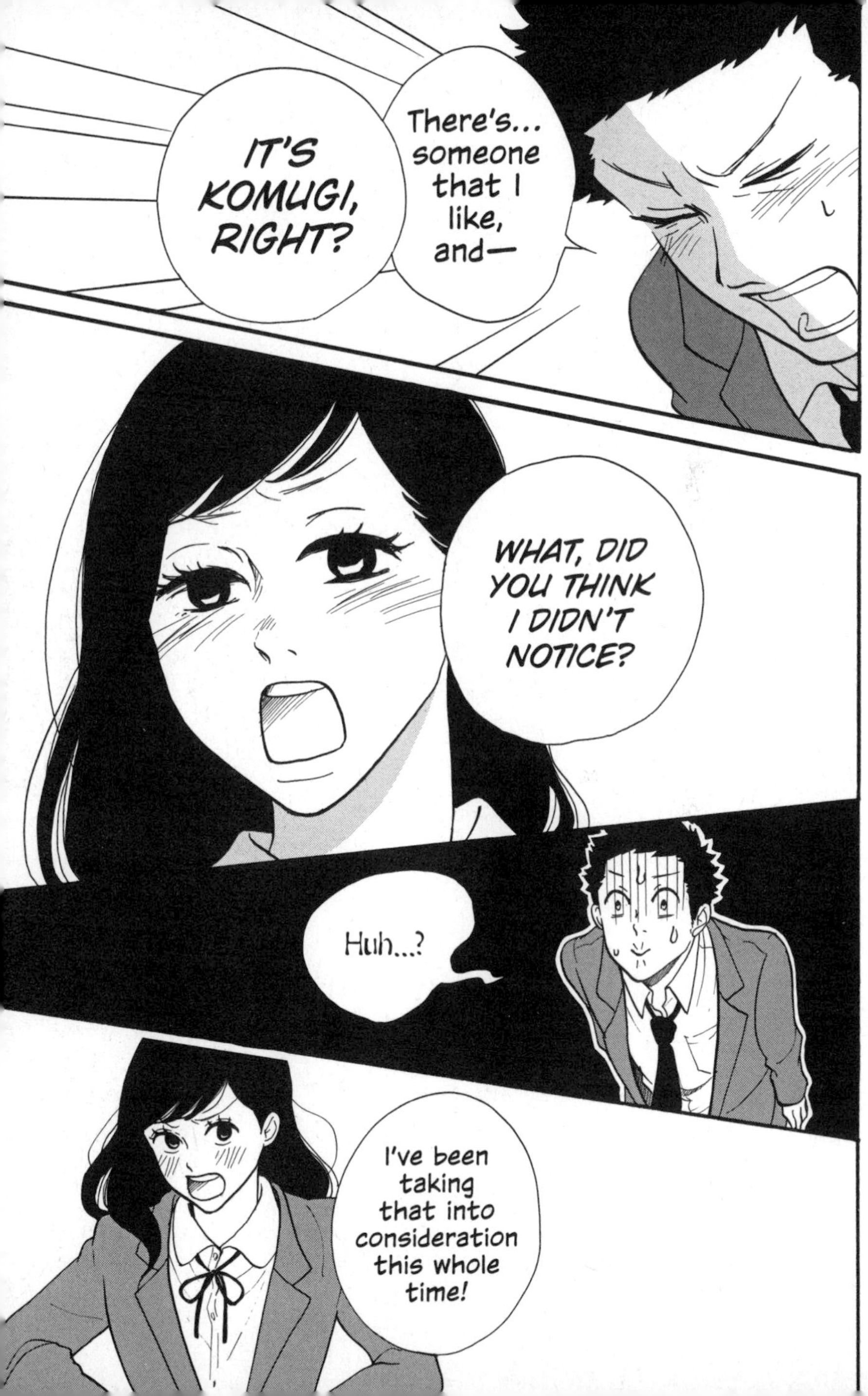
There's... someone that I like, and—
IT'S KOMUGI, RIGHT?
WHAT, DID YOU THINK I DIDN'T NOTICE?
Huh...?
I've been taking that into consideration this whole time!

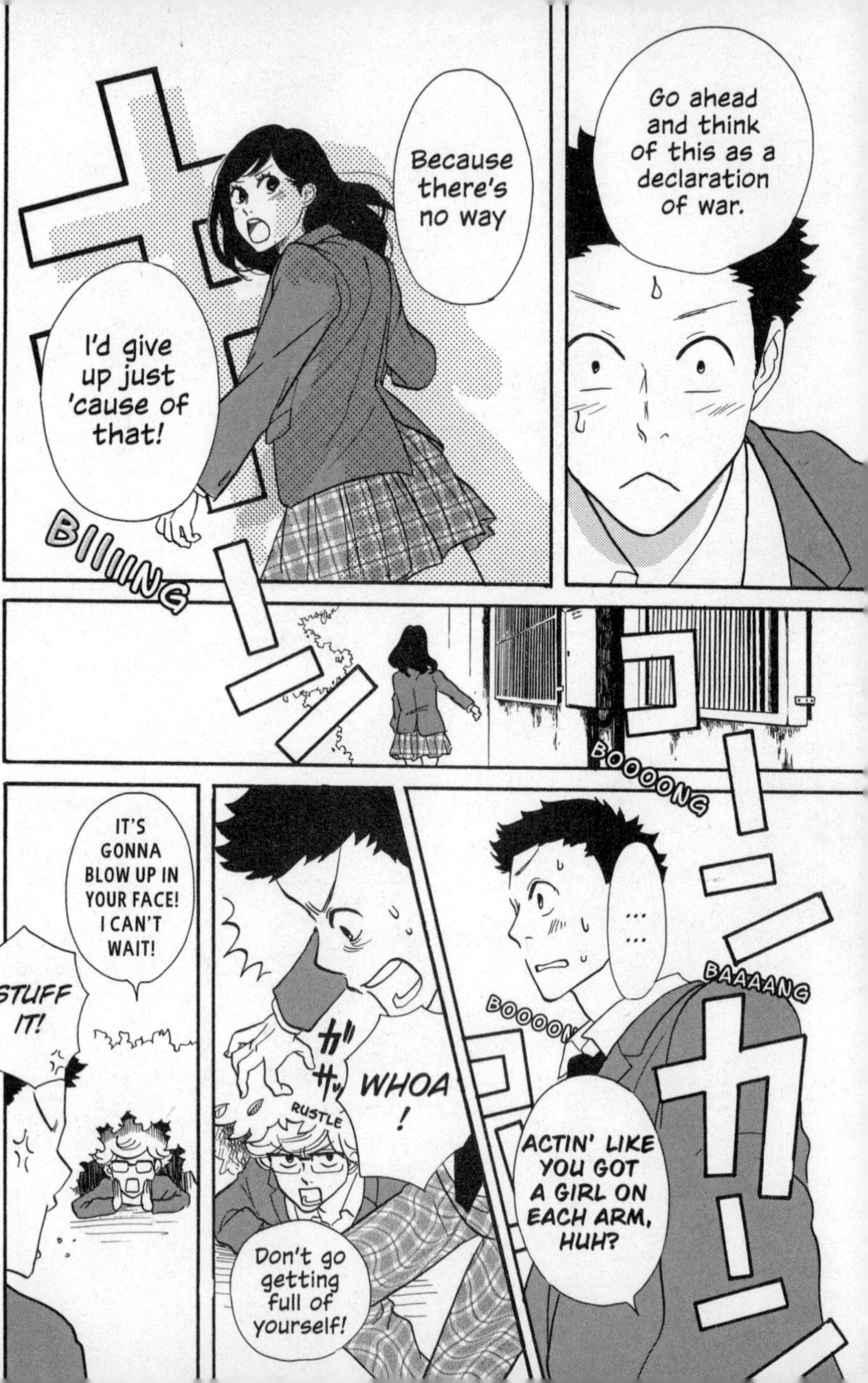
Go ahead and think of this as a declaration of war.
Because there's no way
I'd give up just 'cause of that!
BIIIING
BOOOONG
...
...
BAAAANG
BOOOON
ACTIN' LIKE YOU GOT A GIRL ON EACH ARM, HUH?
WHOA!
RUSTLE
Don't go getting full of yourself!
IT'S GONNA BLOW UP IN YOUR FACE! I CAN'T WAIT!
STUFF IT!

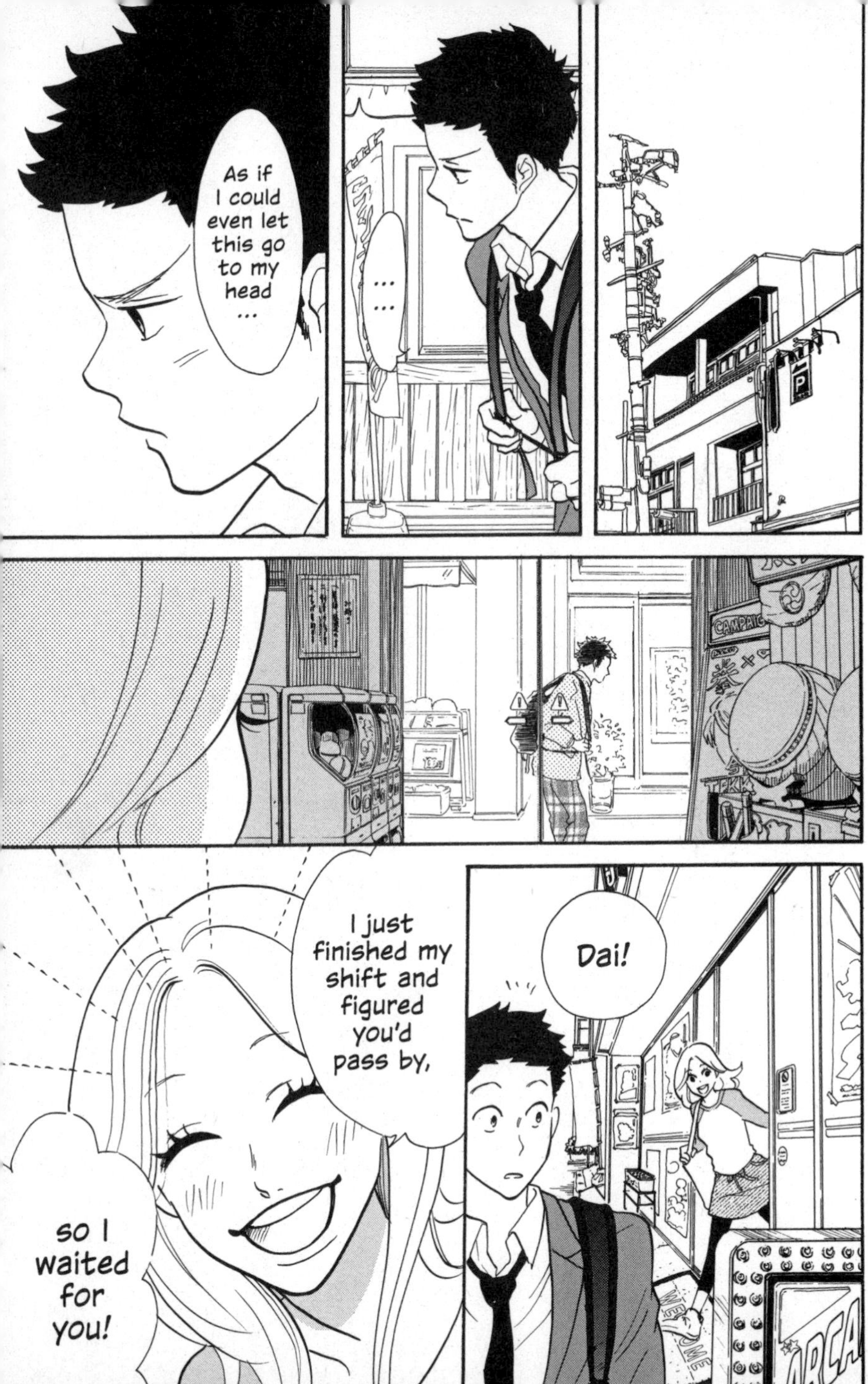
… …
As if I could even let this go to my head …
Dai!
I just finished my shift and figured you'd pass by,
so I waited for you!

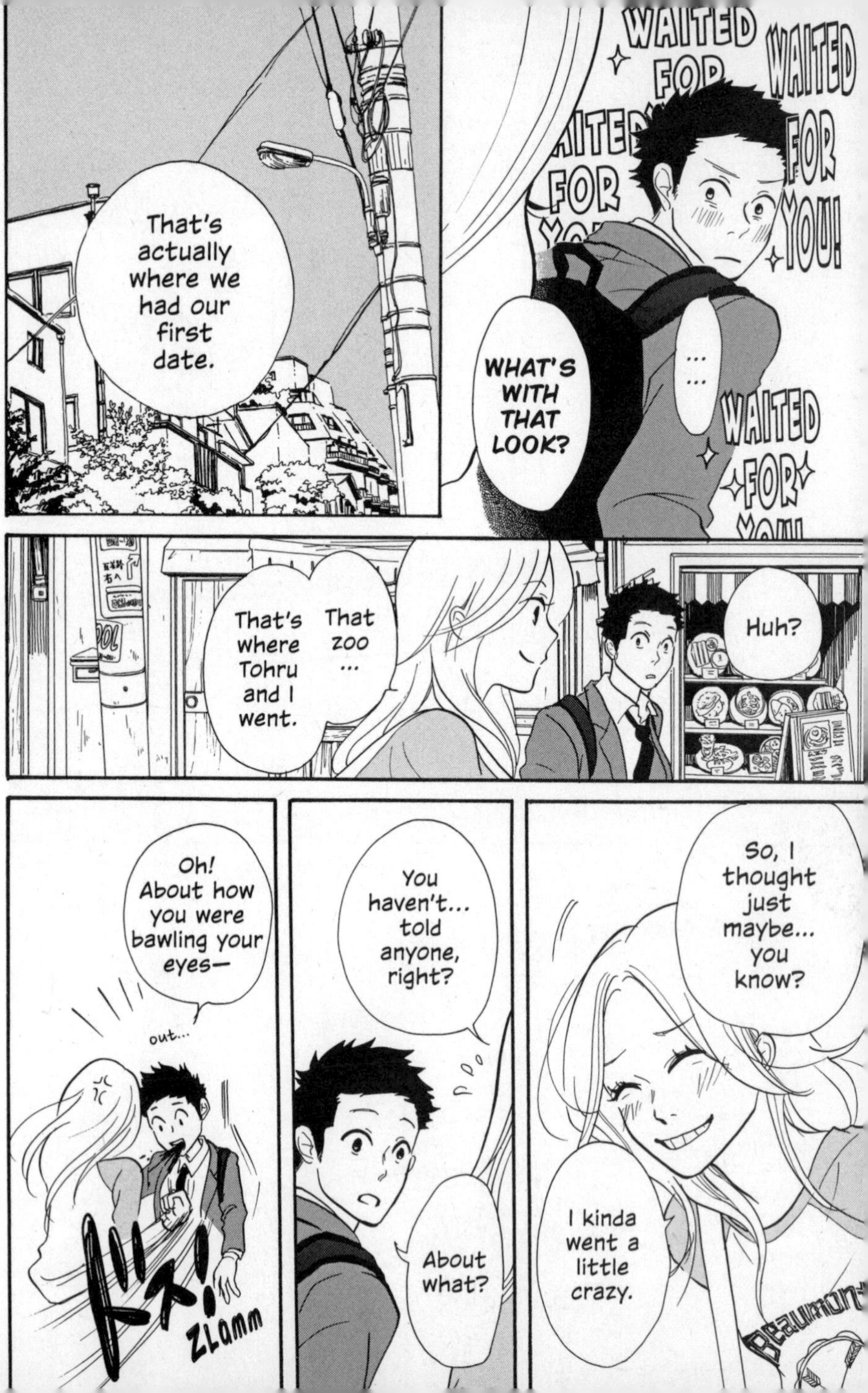
WAITED FOR YOU!
WAITED FOR YOU!
WAITED FOR
……
WHAT'S WITH THAT LOOK?
That's actually where we had our first date.
Huh?
That zoo…
That's where Tohru and I went.
So, I thought just maybe… you know?
I kinda went a little crazy.
You haven't… told anyone, right?
About what?
Oh! About how you were bawling your eyes—
out…
ZLAMM

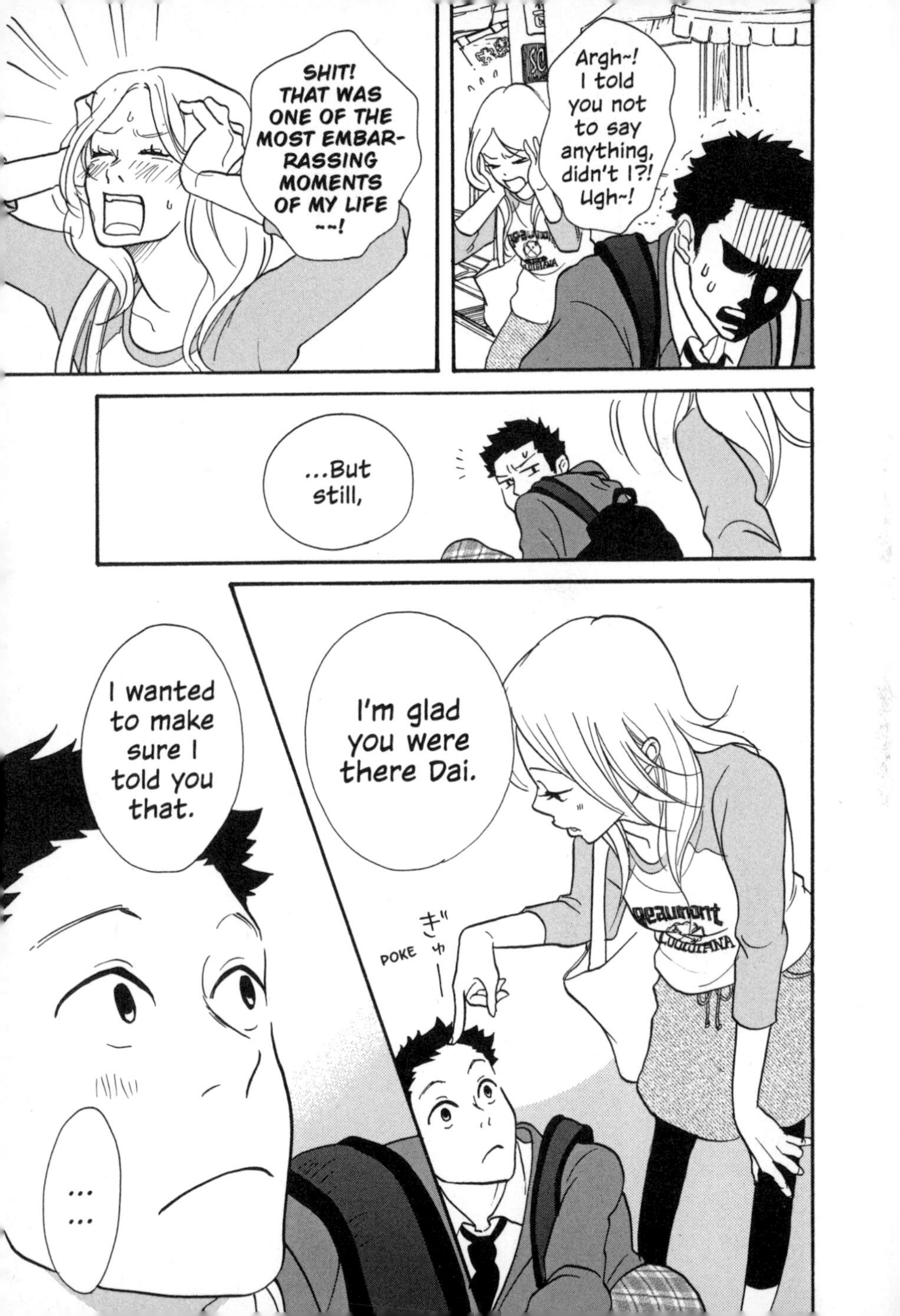
Argh~! I told you not to say anything, didn't I?! Ugh~!
SHIT! THAT WAS ONE OF THE MOST EMBAR-RASSING MOMENTS OF MY LIFE ~~!
...But still,
I'm glad you were there Dai.
POKE
ぎゅー
I wanted to make sure I told you that.
......

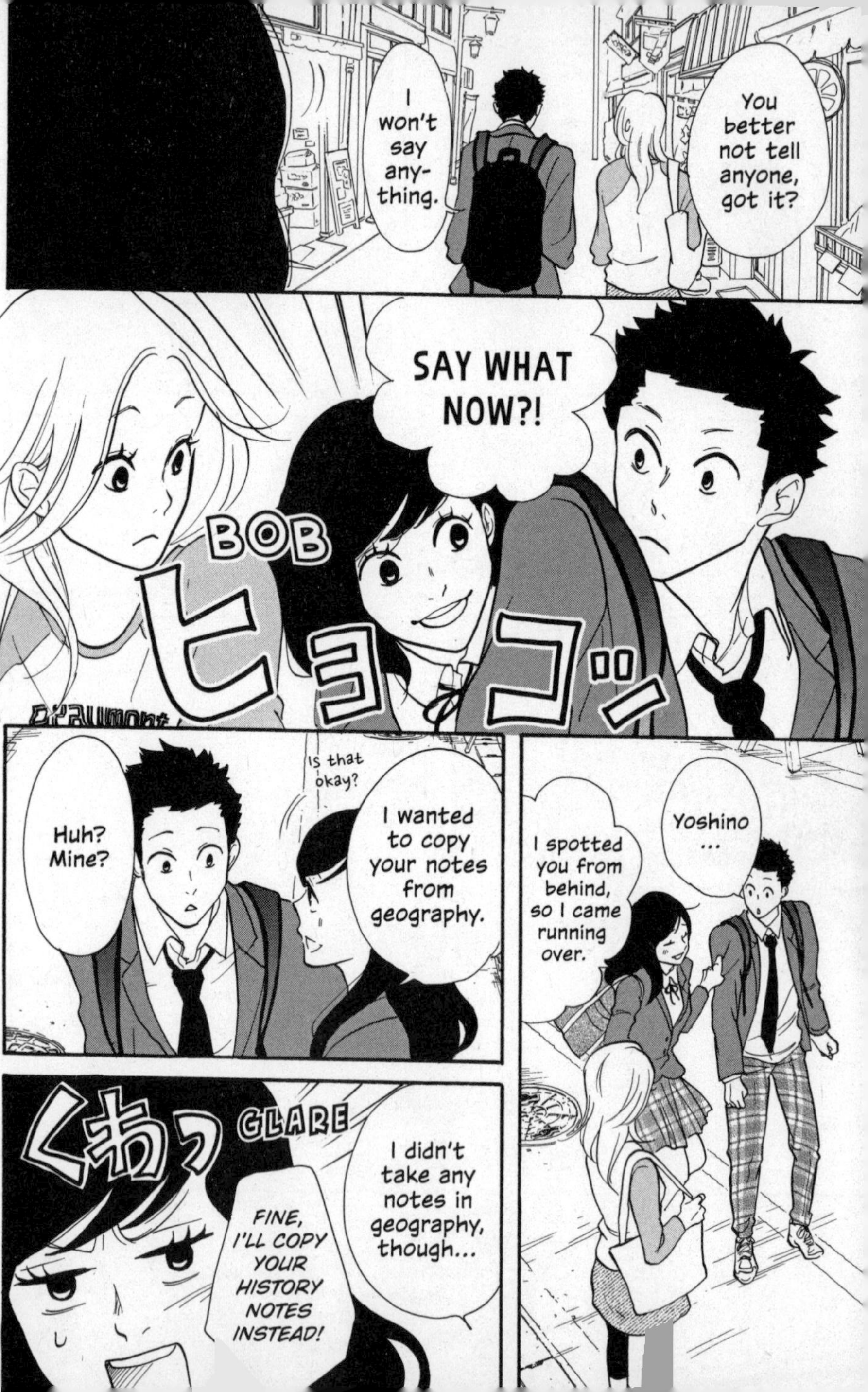
You better not tell anyone, got it?
I won't say any-thing.
SAY WHAT NOW?!
BOB
ヒョコッ
Yoshino...
I spotted you from behind, so I came running over.
I wanted to copy your notes from geography.
Is that okay?
Huh? Mine?
I didn't take any notes in geography, though...
くあっ
GLARE
FINE, I'LL COPY YOUR HISTORY NOTES INSTEAD!

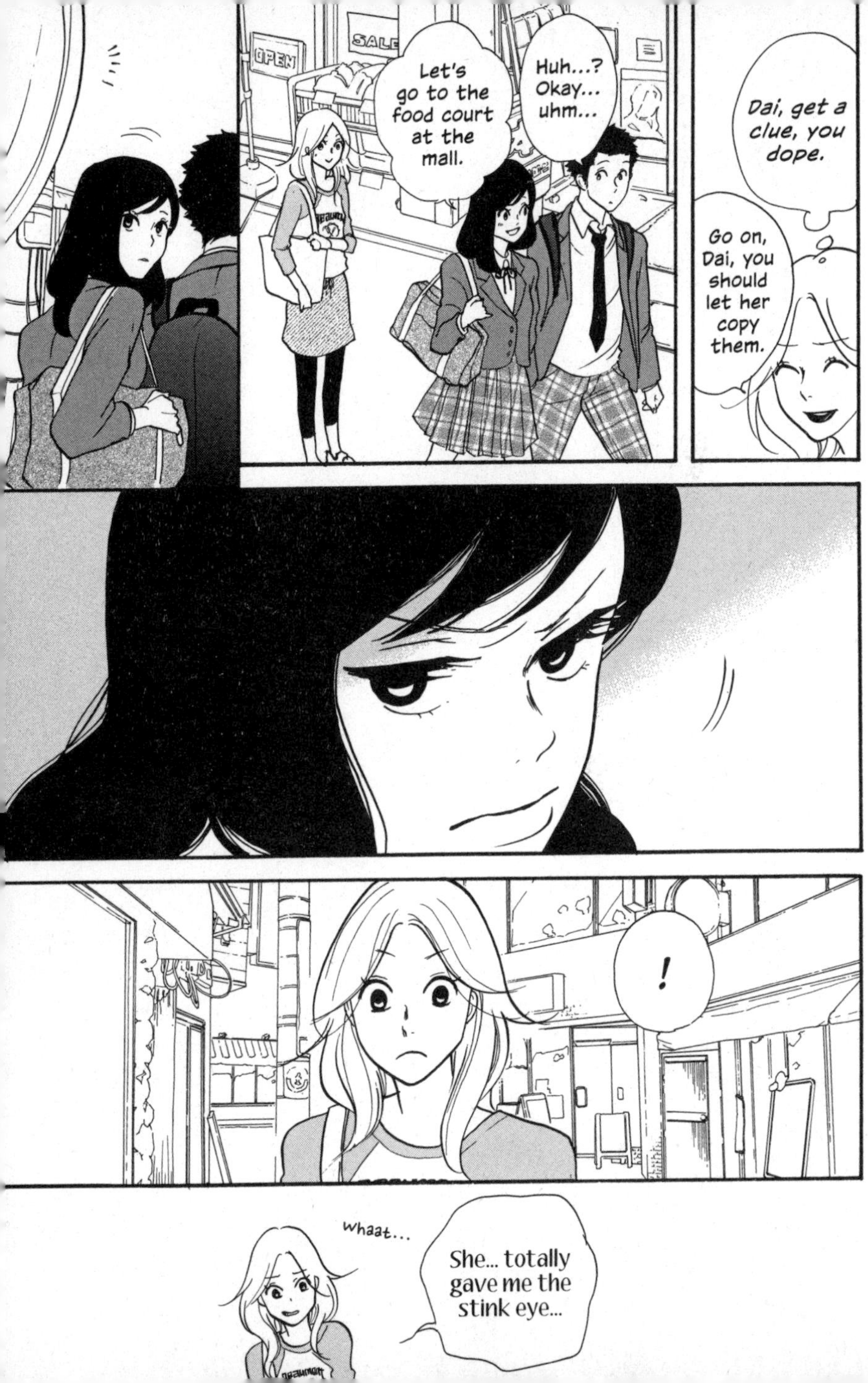
Dai, get a clue, you dope.
Go on, Dai, you should let her copy them.
Huh...? Okay... uhm...
Let's go to the food court at the mall.
!
Whaat...
She... totally gave me the stink eye...

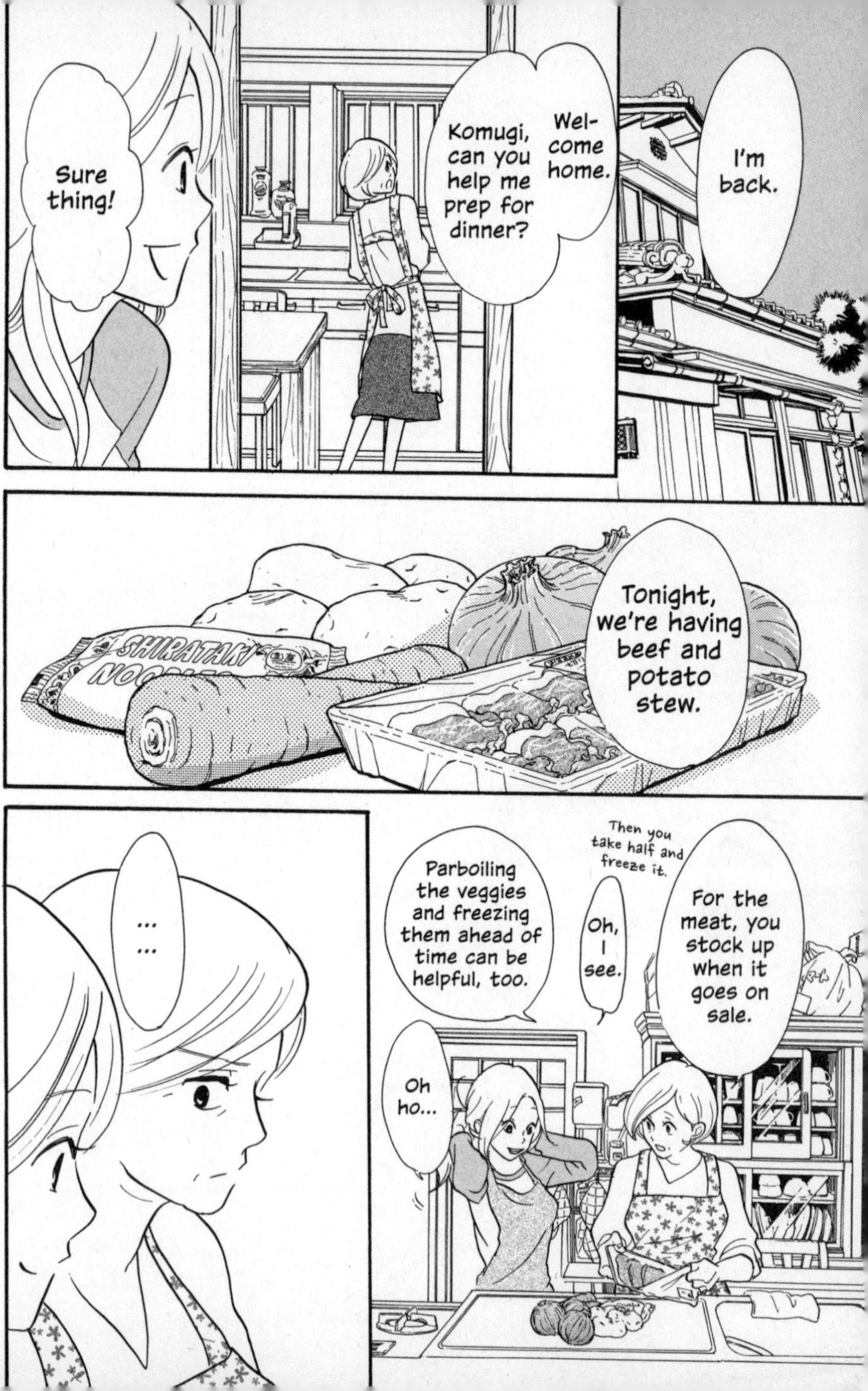
I'm back.
Wel-come home.
Komugi, can you help me prep for dinner?
Sure thing!
Tonight, we're having beef and potato stew.
SHIRATAKI
For the meat, you stock up when it goes on sale.
Then you take half and freeze it.
Oh, I see.
Parboiling the veggies and freezing them ahead of time can be helpful, too.
Oh ho...
... ...

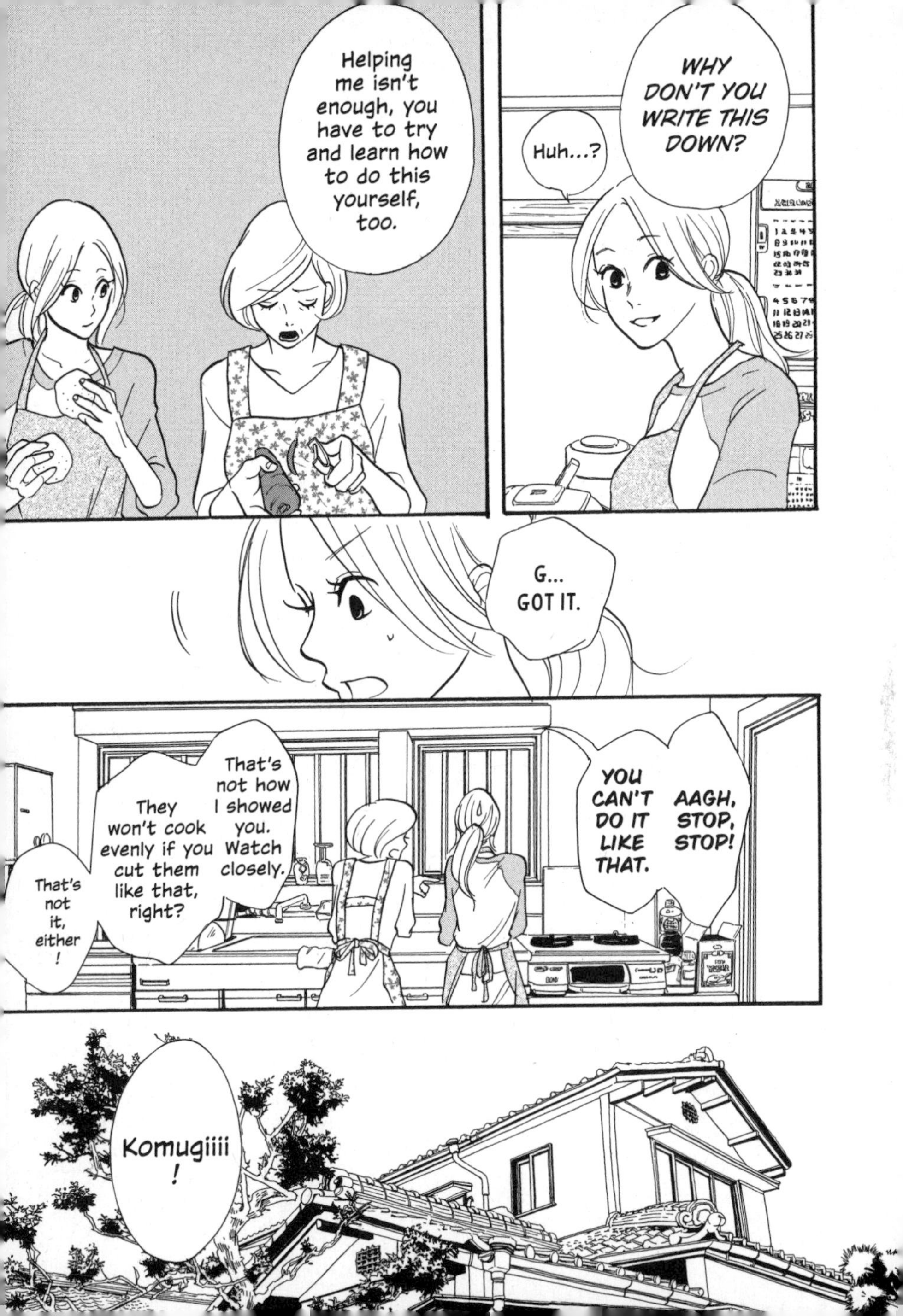
WHY DON'T YOU WRITE THIS DOWN?
Huh...?
Helping me isn't enough, you have to try and learn how to do this yourself, too.
G... GOT IT.
AAGH, STOP, STOP!
YOU CAN'T DO IT LIKE THAT.
That's not how I showed you. Watch closely.
They won't cook evenly if you cut them like that, right?
That's not it, either!
Komugiiii!

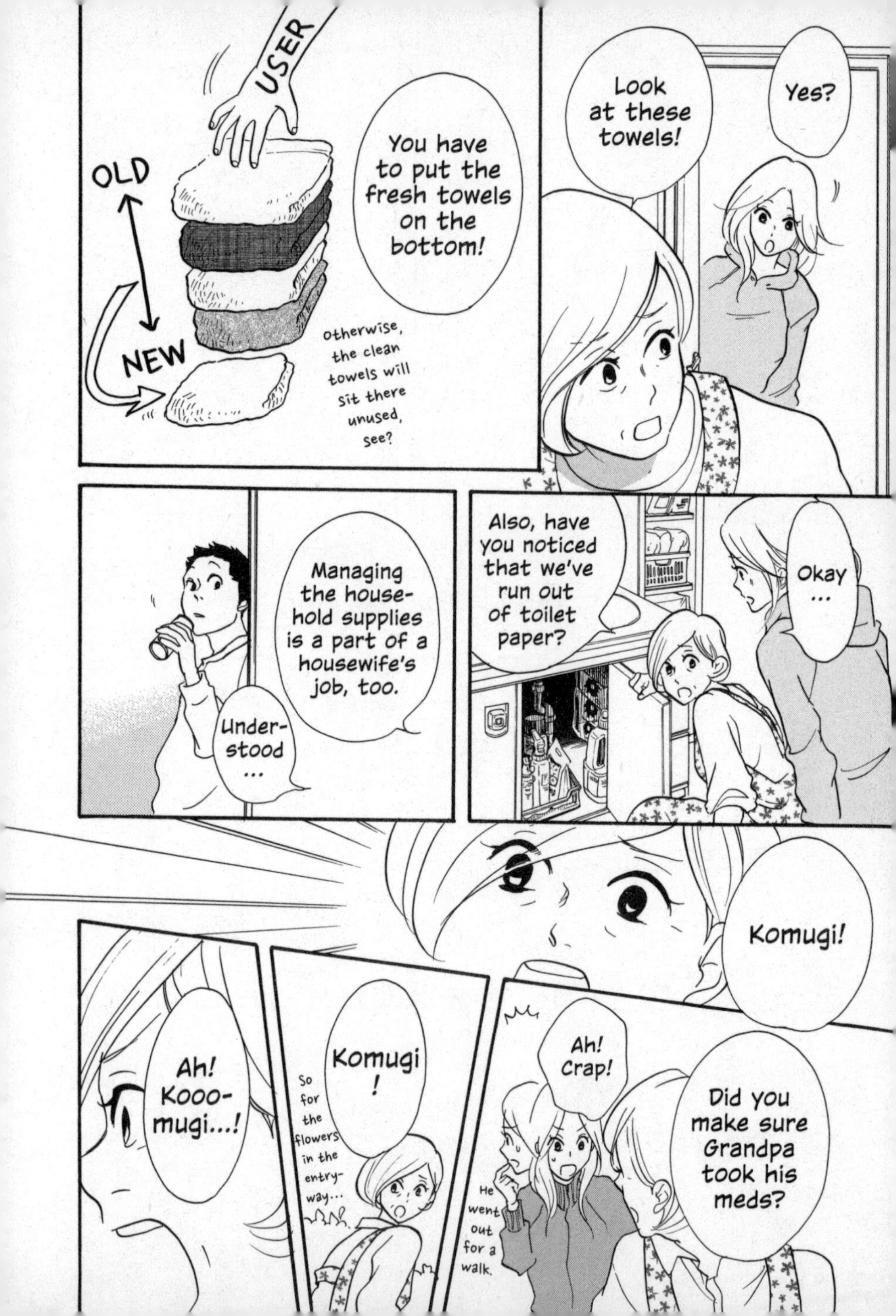

Yes?
Look at these towels!
USER
OLD
NEW
You have to put the fresh towels on the bottom!
Otherwise, the clean towels will sit there unused, see?
Okay ...
Also, have you noticed that we've run out of toilet paper?
Managing the household supplies is a part of a housewife's job, too.
Under-stood ...
Komugi!
Did you make sure Grandpa took his meds?
Ah! Crap!
He went out for a walk.
Komugi!
So for the flowers in the entry-way...
Ah! Kooo-mugi...!

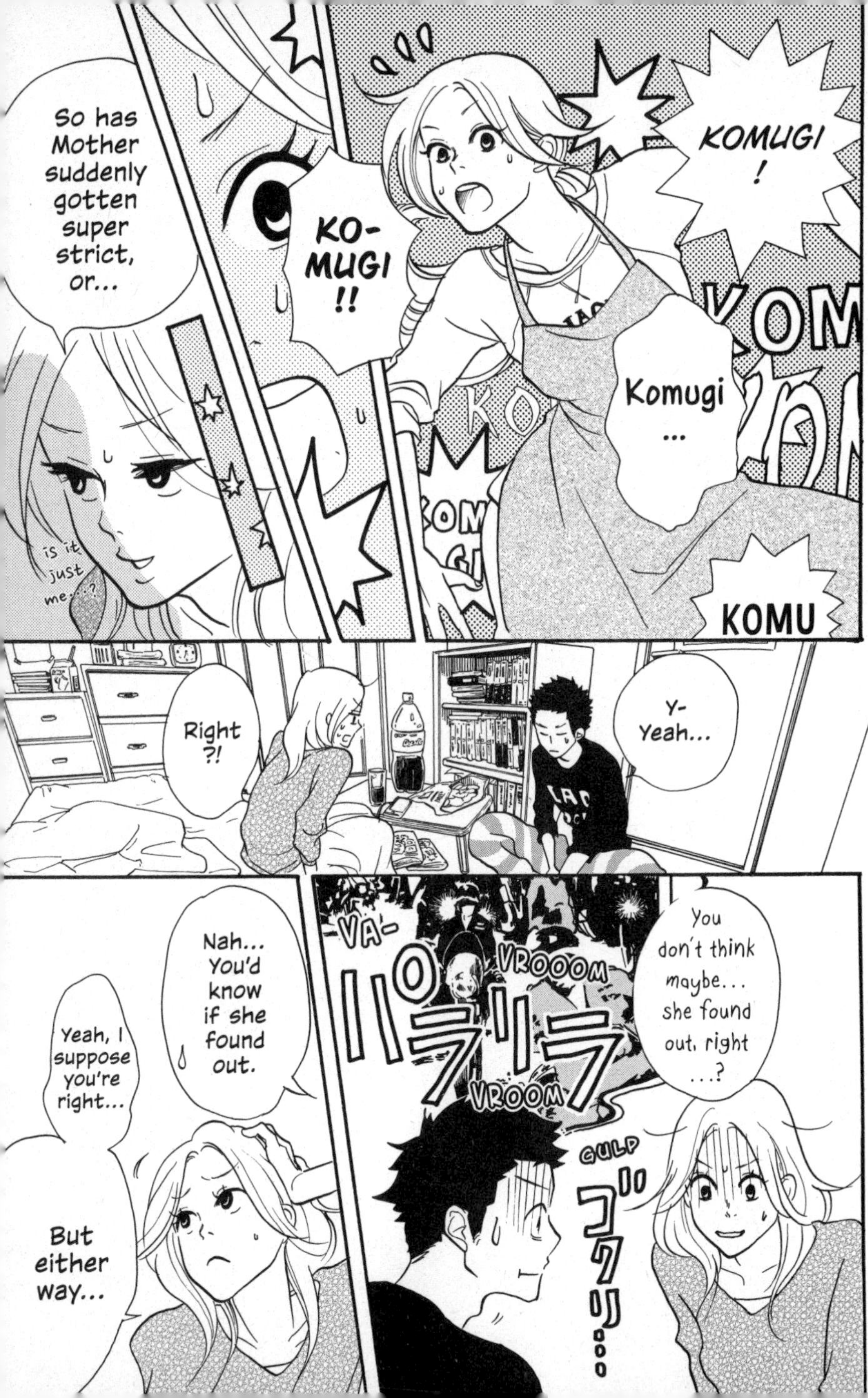
KOMUGI!
Komugi...
KOMU
KO-MUGI!!
So has Mother suddenly gotten super strict, or...
is it just me...?
Y-Yeah...
Right?!
You don't think maybe... she found out, right...?
GULP
VA-
VROOOM
VROOM
Nah... You'd know if she found out.
Yeah, I suppose you're right...
But either way...

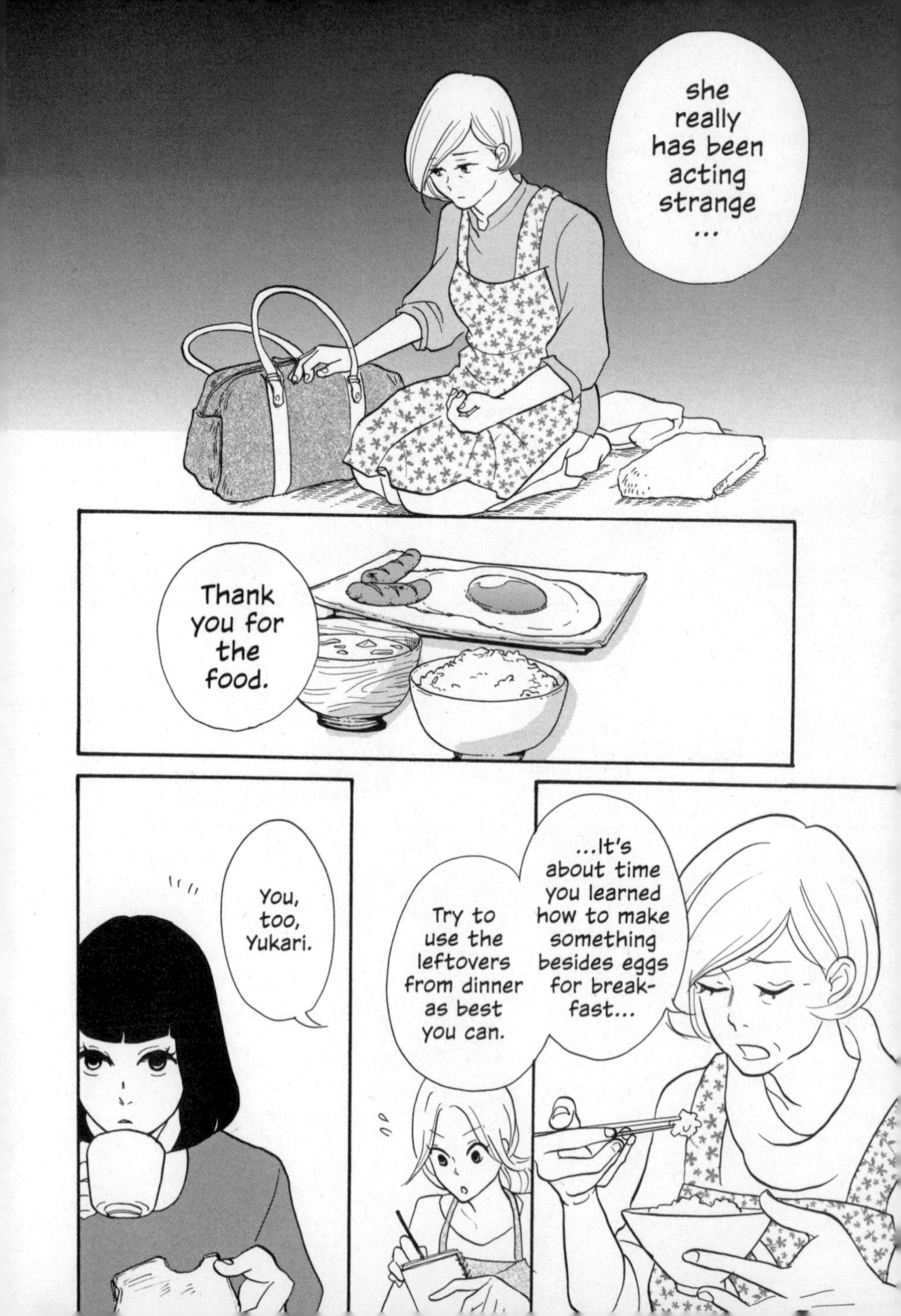

she really has been acting strange ...
Thank you for the food.
...It's about time you learned how to make something besides eggs for break-fast...
Try to use the leftovers from dinner as best you can.
You, too, Yukari.

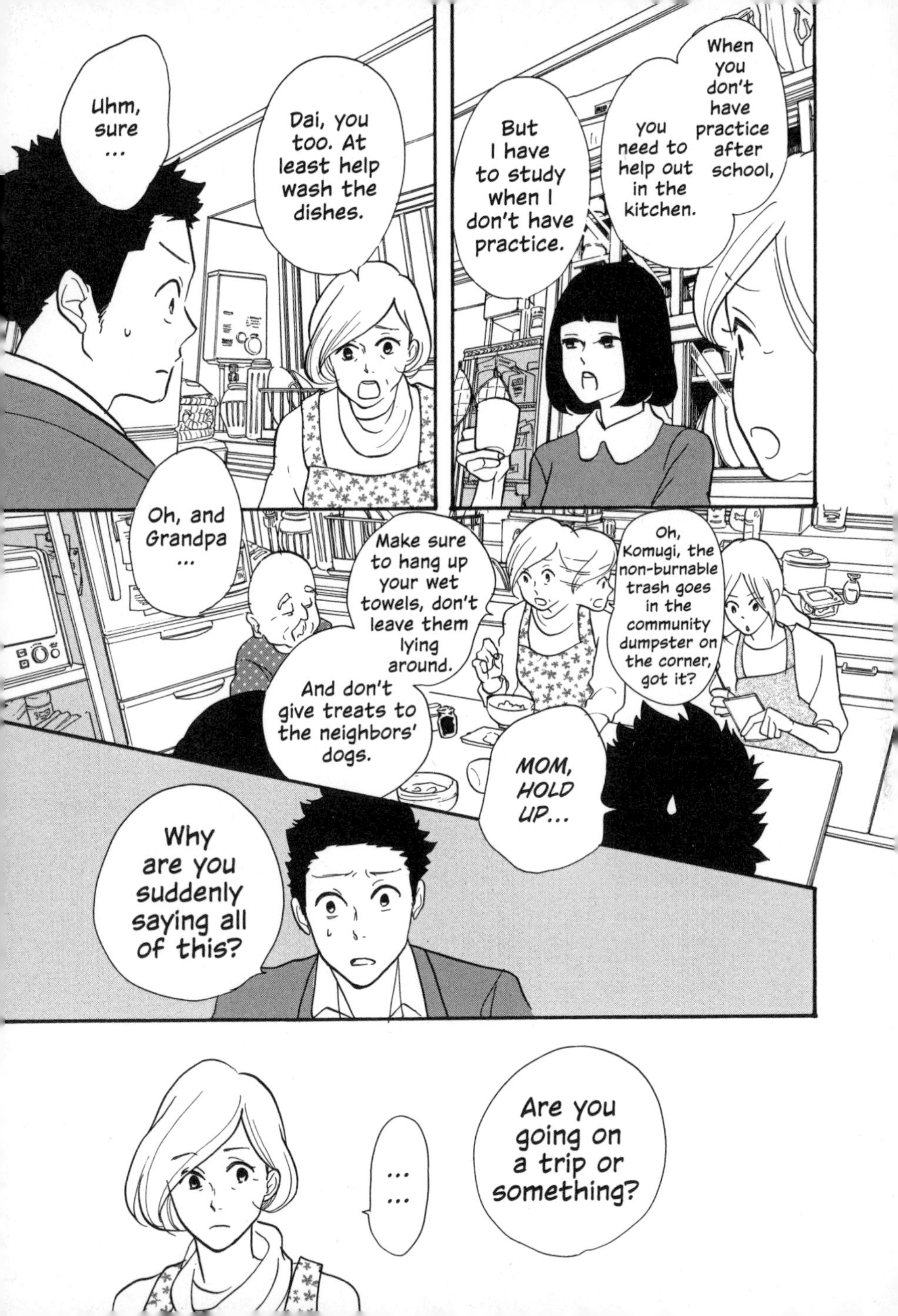
When you don't have practice after school, you need to help out in the kitchen.
But I have to study when I don't have practice.
Dai, you too. At least help wash the dishes.
Uhm, sure ...
Oh, Komugi, the non-burnable trash goes in the community dumpster on the corner, got it?
Oh, and Grandpa ...
Make sure to hang up your wet towels, don't leave them lying around.
And don't give treats to the neighbors' dogs.
MOM, HOLD UP...
Why are you suddenly saying all of this?
Are you going on a trip or something?
... ...

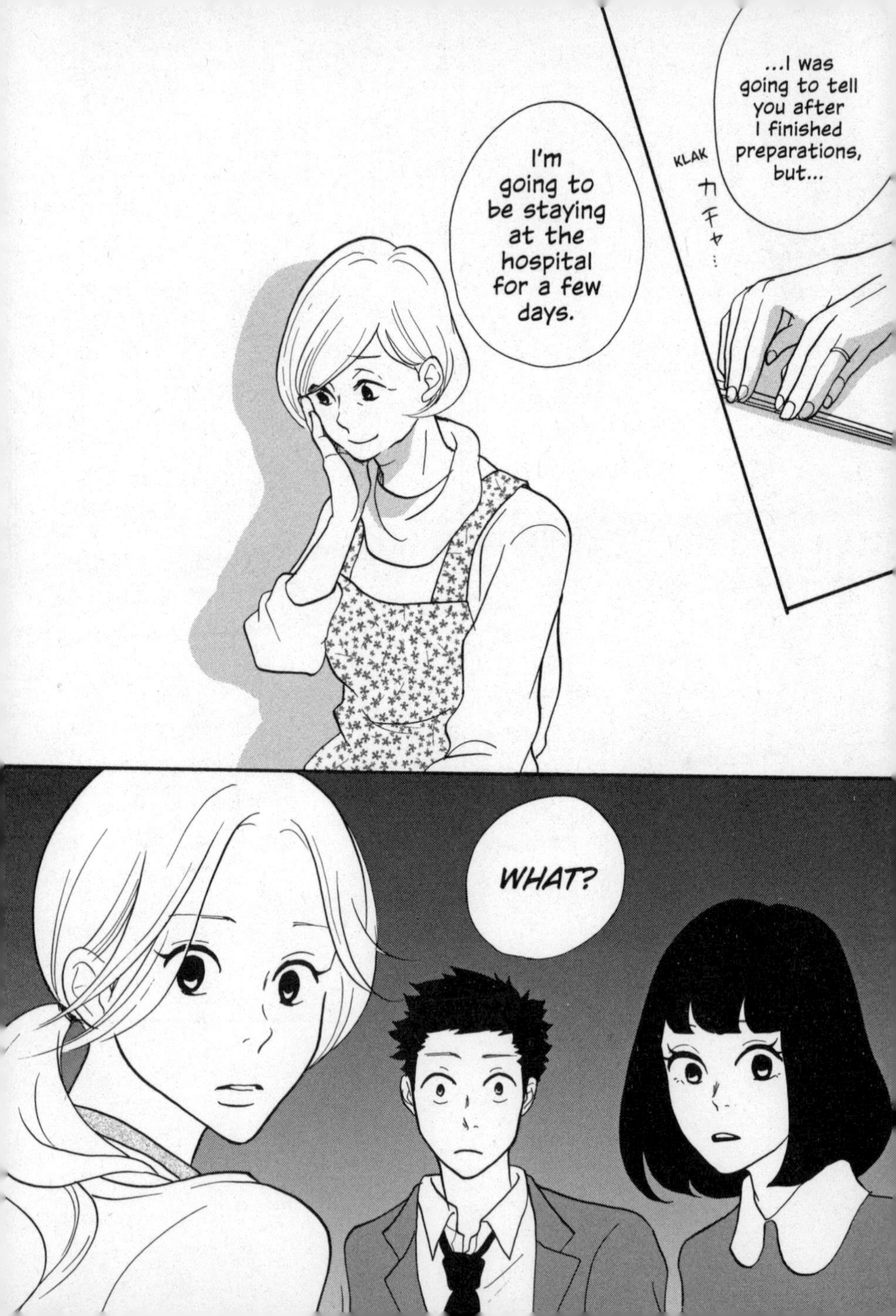
...I was going to tell you after I finished preparations, but...
KLAK
カチャ…
I'm going to be staying at the hospital for a few days.
WHAT?

25 THE INVISIBLE MAN

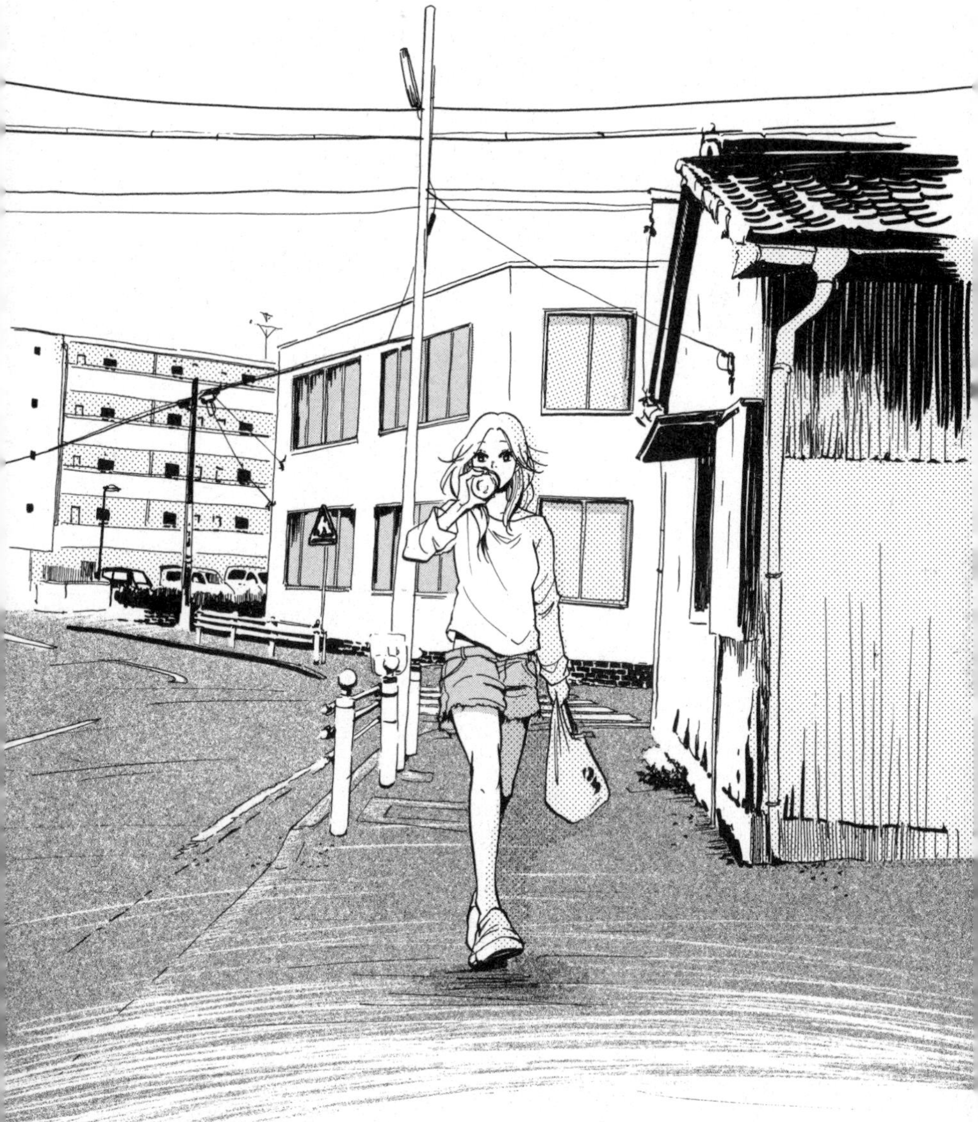

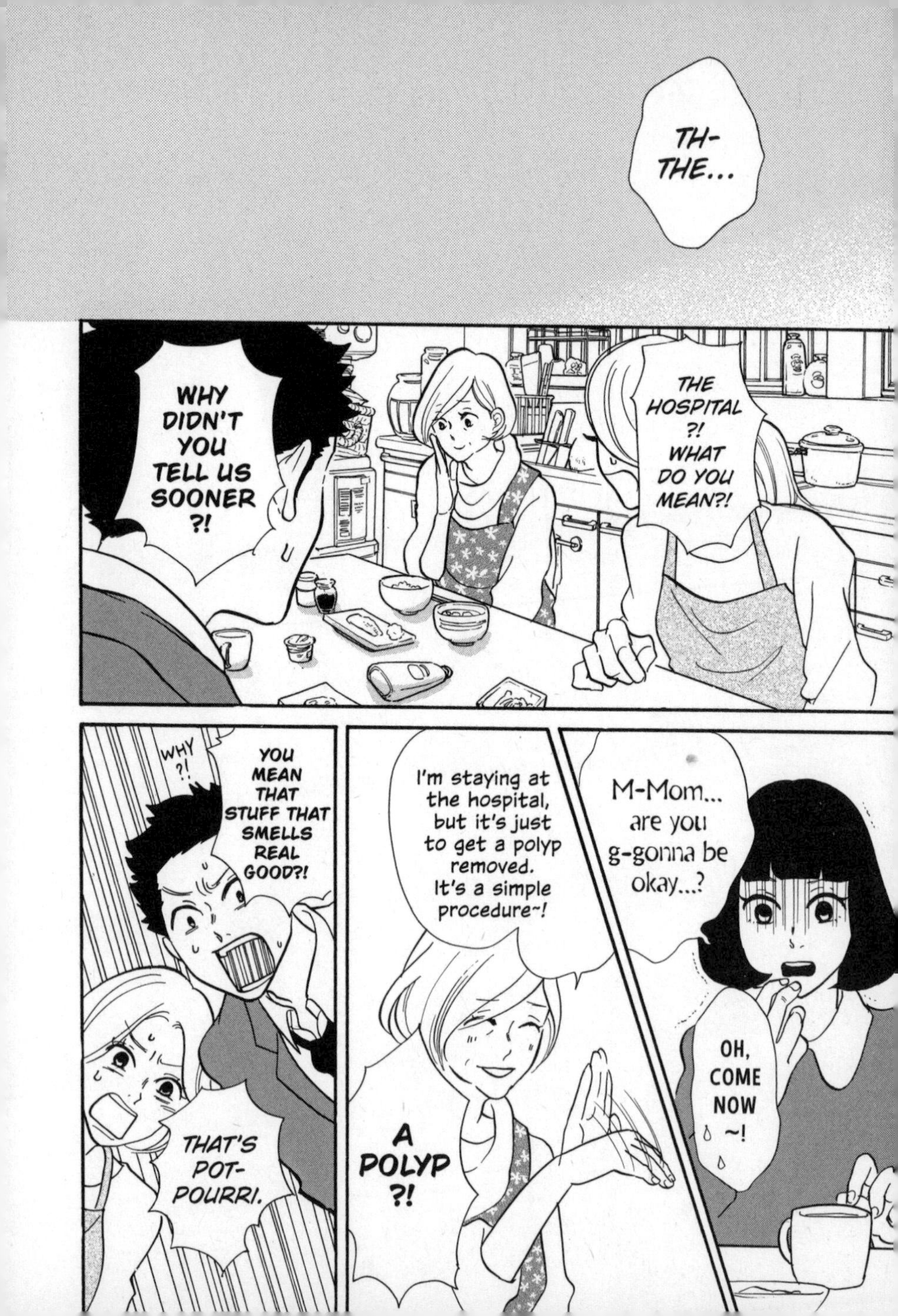
TH- THE...
THE HOSPITAL ?! WHAT DO YOU MEAN?!
WHY DIDN'T YOU TELL US SOONER ?!
M-Mom... are you g-gonna be okay...?
OH, COME NOW ~!
I'm staying at the hospital, but it's just to get a polyp removed. It's a simple procedure~!
A POLYP ?!
WHY ?!
YOU MEAN THAT STUFF THAT SMELLS REAL GOOD?!
THAT'S POT-POURRI.

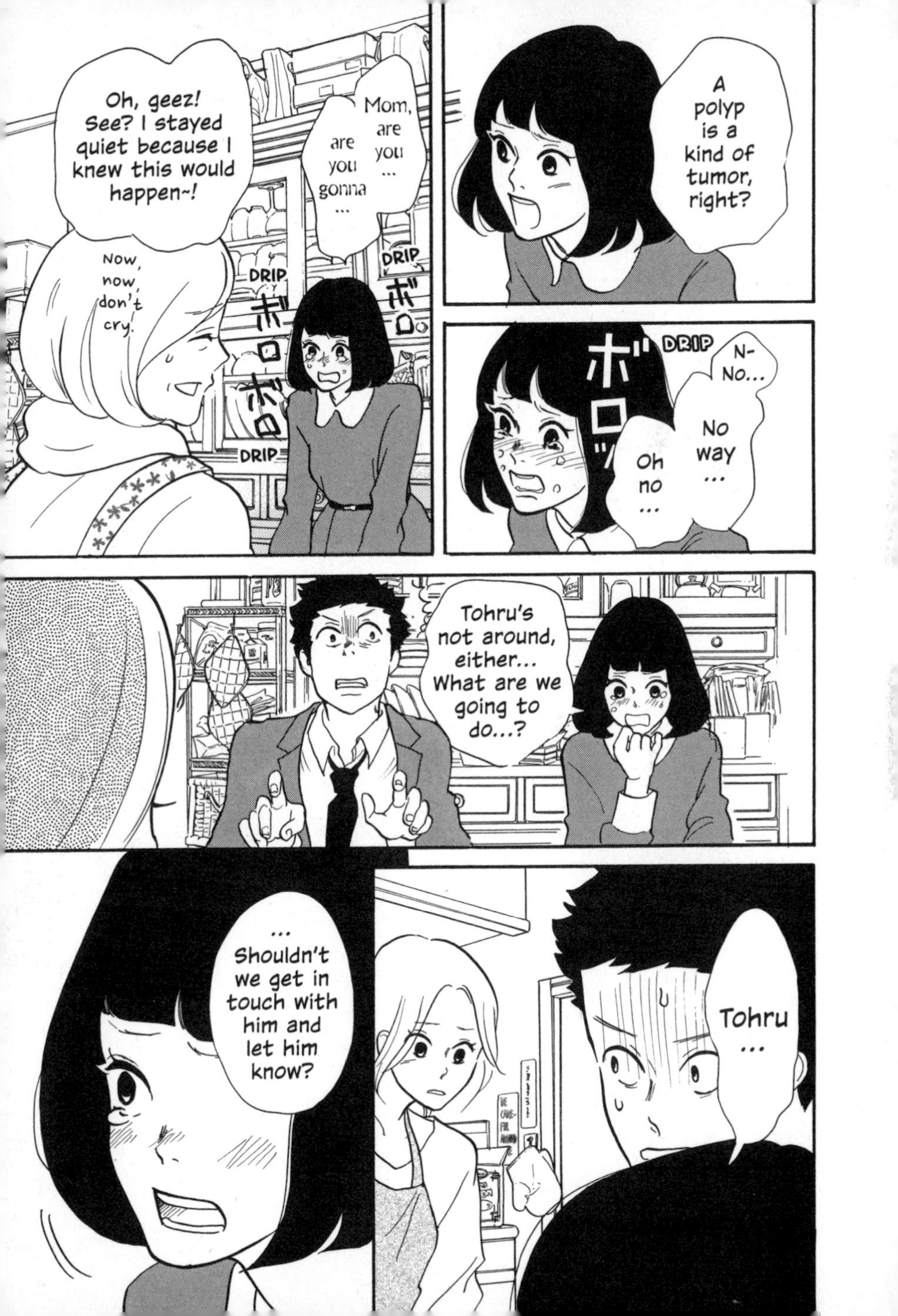
A polyp is a kind of tumor, right?
DRIP
ボロ
N-No...
No way ...
Oh no ...
Mom, are you ...
are you gonna ...
DRIP
ボロ
Oh, geez! See? I stayed quiet because I knew this would happen~!
DRIP
ボロボロ
DRIP
Now, now, don't cry.
Tohru's not around, either... What are we going to do...?
Tohru ...
... Shouldn't we get in touch with him and let him know?

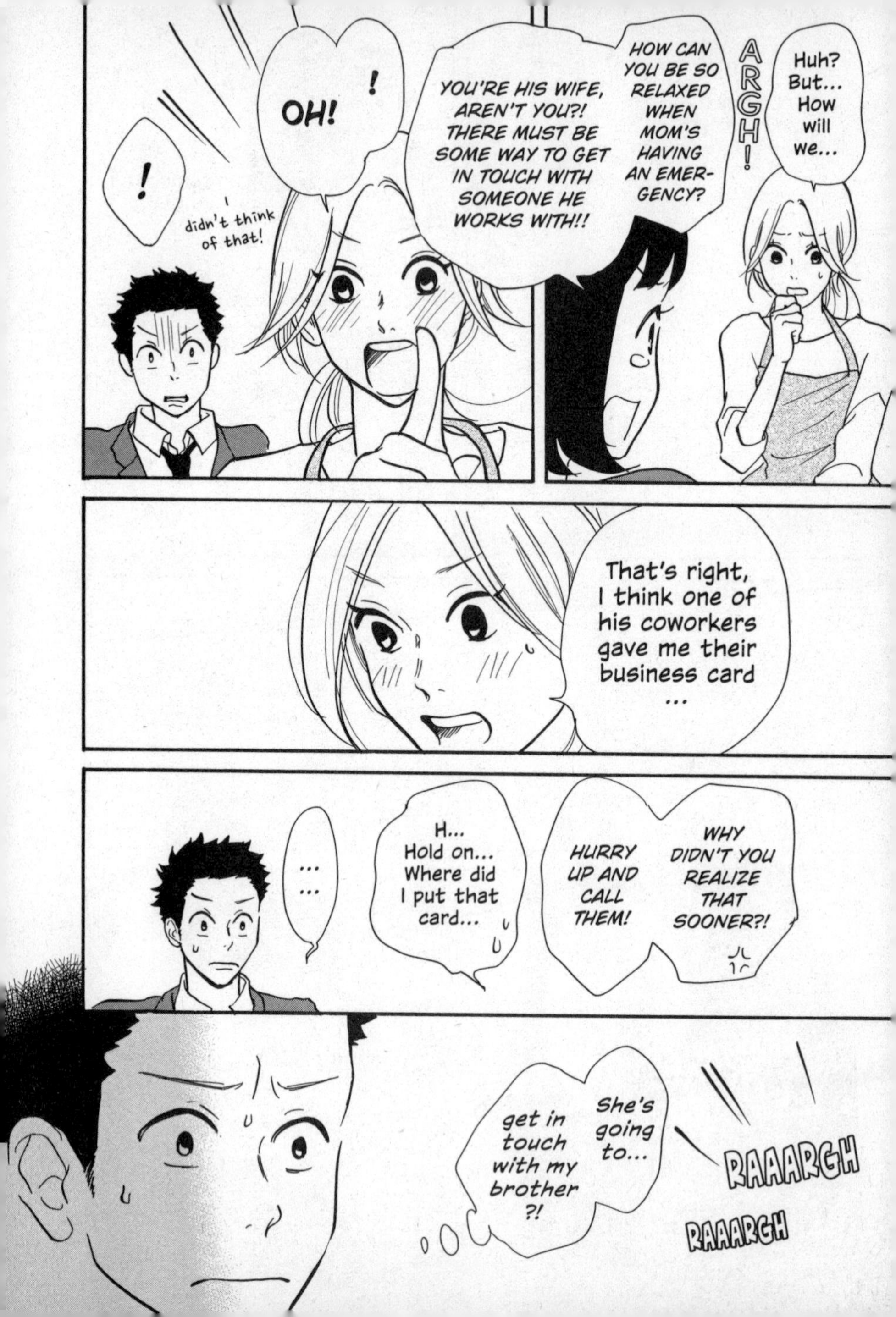
Huh? But... How will we...
ARGH!
HOW CAN YOU BE SO RELAXED WHEN MOM'S HAVING AN EMERGENCY?
YOU'RE HIS WIFE, AREN'T YOU?! THERE MUST BE SOME WAY TO GET IN TOUCH WITH SOMEONE HE WORKS WITH!!
!
OH!
!
I didn't think of that!
That's right, I think one of his coworkers gave me their business card ...
WHY DIDN'T YOU REALIZE THAT SOONER?!
HURRY UP AND CALL THEM!
H... Hold on... Where did I put that card...
... ...
RAAARGH
RAAARGH
She's going to... get in touch with my brother?!

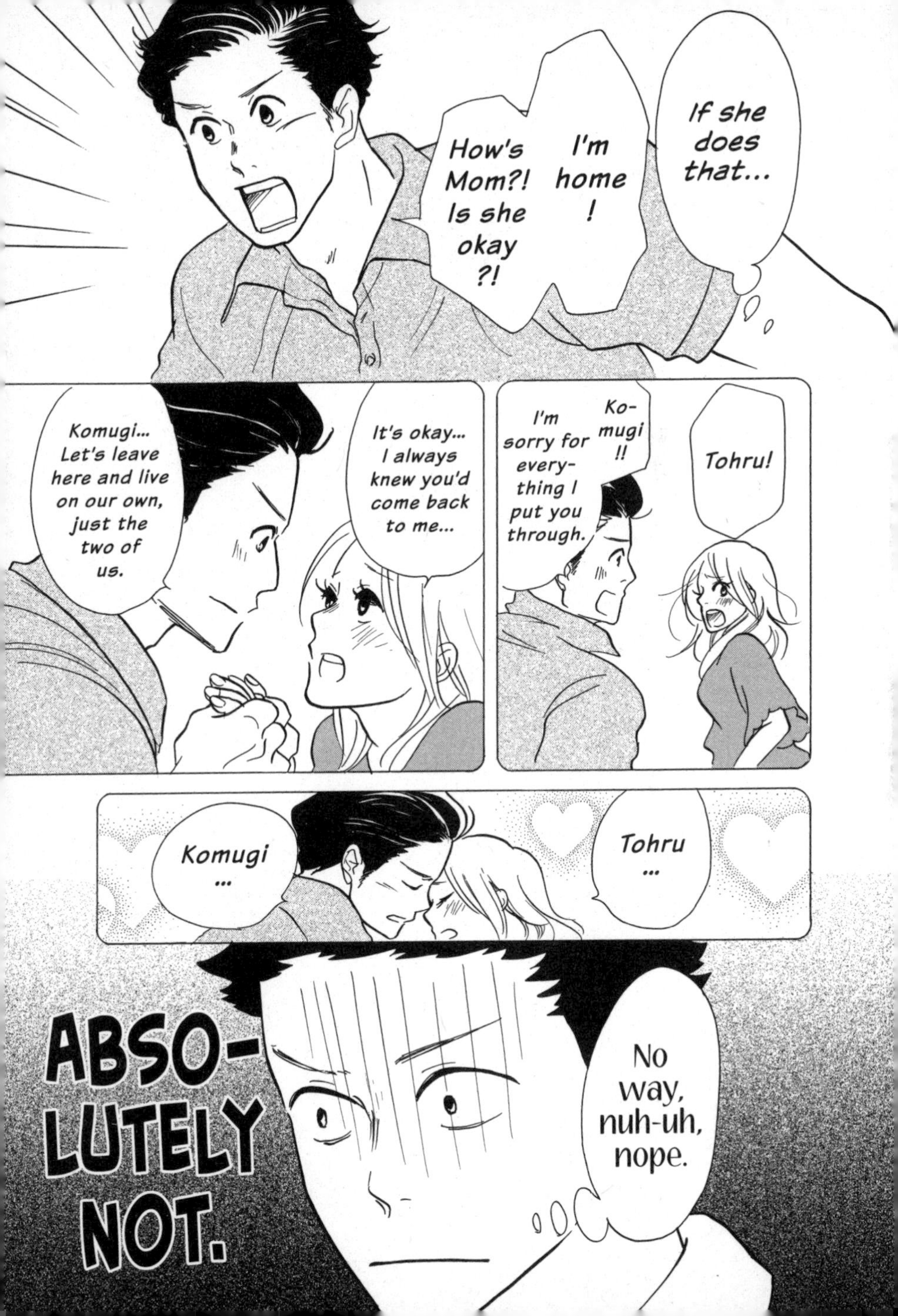
If she does that...
I'm home!
How's Mom?! Is she okay?!
Tohru!
Ko-mugi!!
I'm sorry for every-thing I put you through.
It's okay... I always knew you'd come back to me...
Komugi... Let's leave here and live on our own, just the two of us.
Tohru...
Komugi...
No way, nuh-uh, nope.
ABSO-LUTELY NOT.

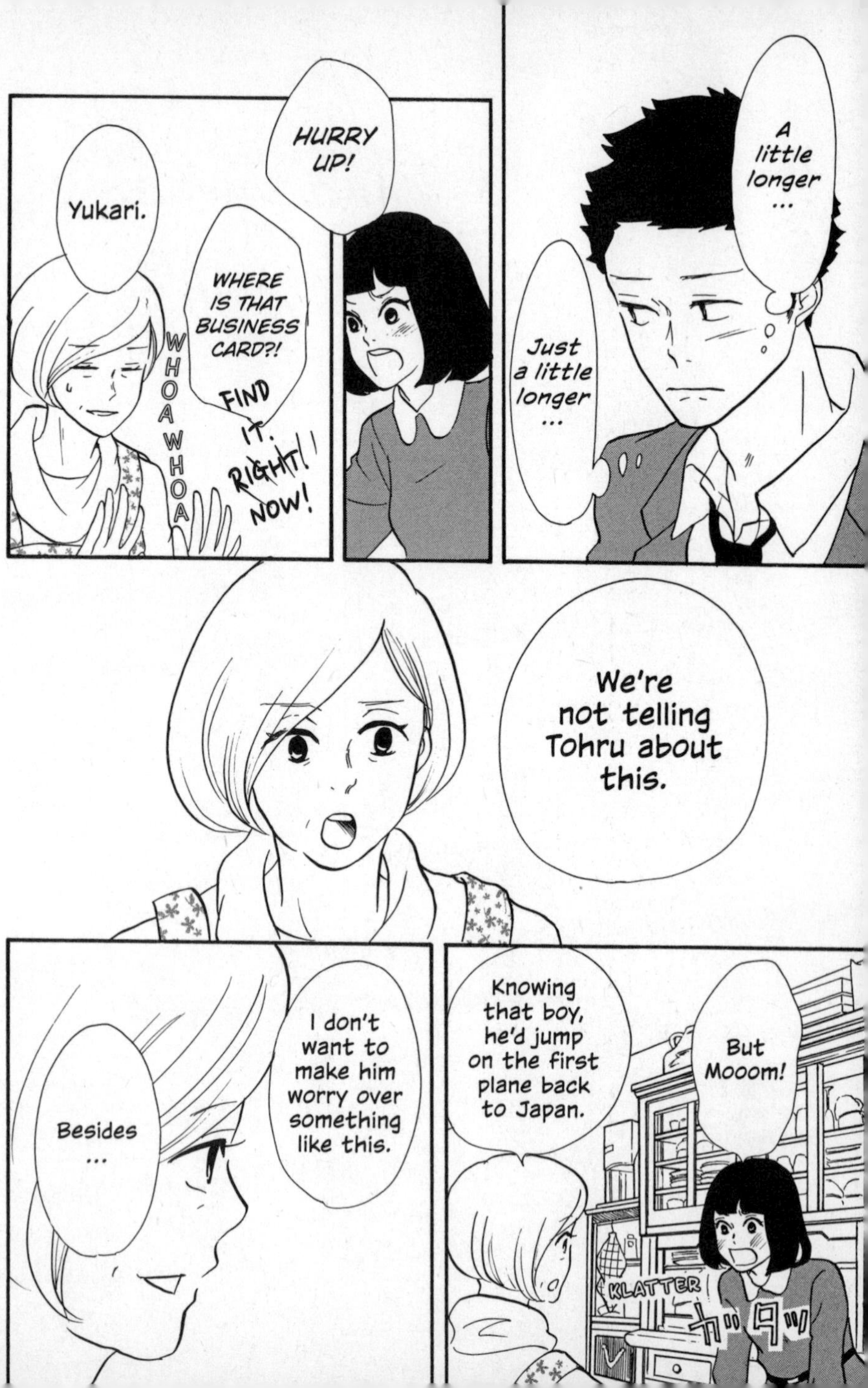
A little longer ...
Just a little longer ...
HURRY UP!
WHERE IS THAT BUSINESS CARD?!
FIND IT. RIGHT NOW!
WHOA WHOA
Yukari.
We're not telling Tohru about this.
But Mooom!
KLATTER
カタッ
Knowing that boy, he'd jump on the first plane back to Japan.
I don't want to make him worry over something like this.
Besides ...

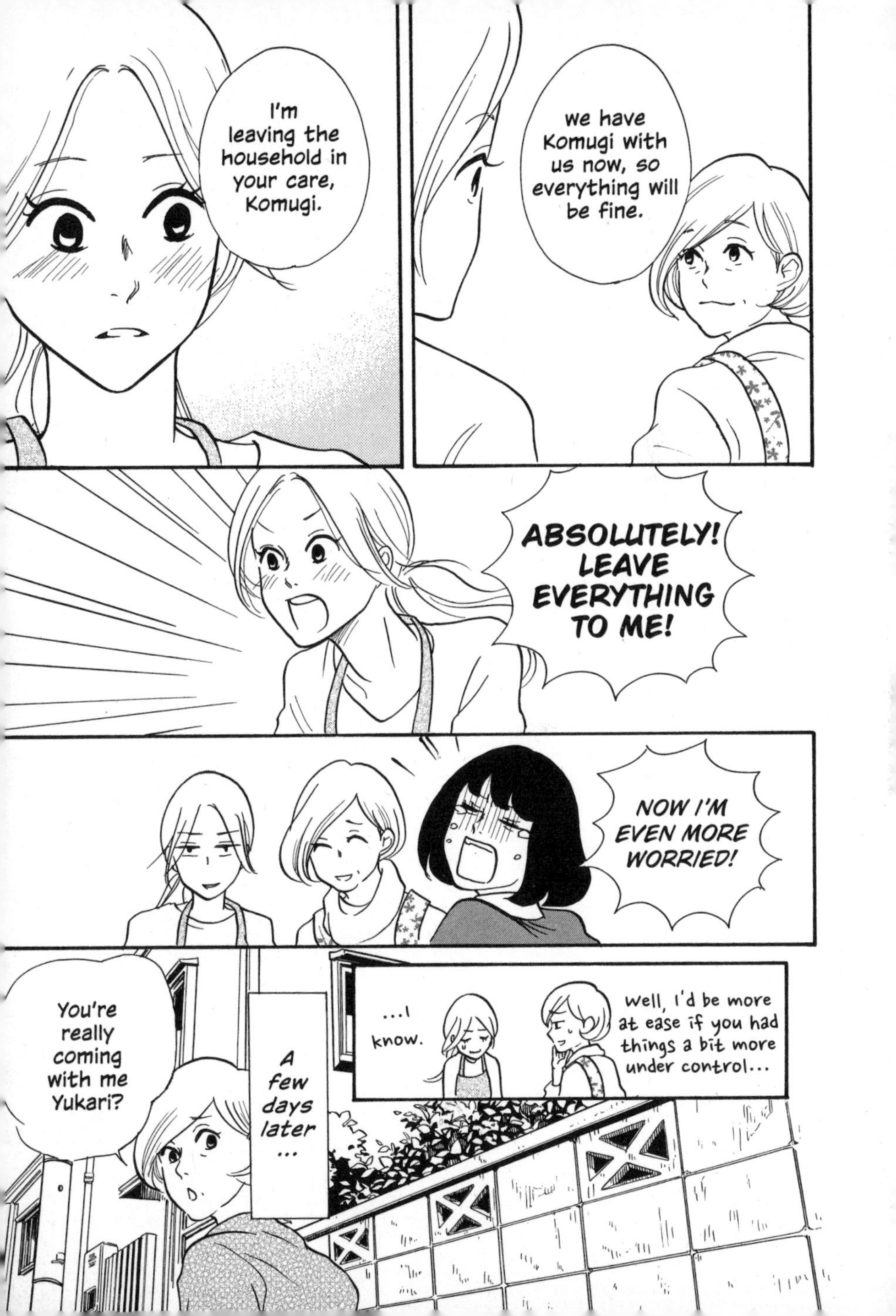
we have Komugi with us now, so everything will be fine.
I'm leaving the household in your care, Komugi.
ABSOLUTELY! LEAVE EVERYTHING TO ME!
NOW I'M EVEN MORE WORRIED!
Well, I'd be more at ease if you had things a bit more under control...
...I know.
A few days later...
You're really coming with me Yukari?

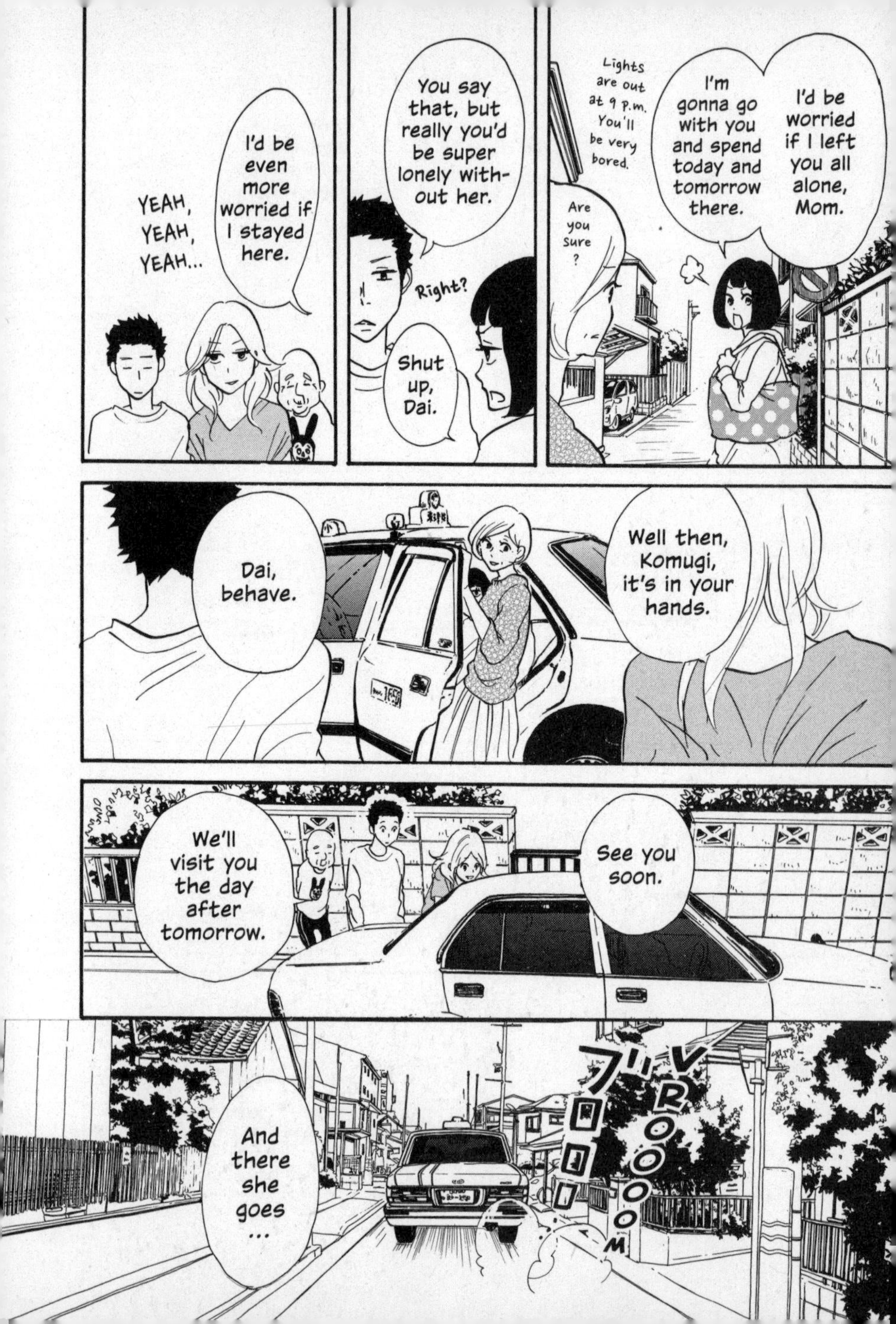
I'd be worried if I left you all alone, Mom.
I'm gonna go with you and spend today and tomorrow there.
Lights are out at 9 p.m. You'll be very bored.
Are you sure?
You say that, but really you'd be super lonely without her.
Right?
Shut up, Dai.
I'd be even more worried if I stayed here.
YEAH, YEAH, YEAH...
Well then, Komugi, it's in your hands.
Dai, behave.
See you soon.
We'll visit you the day after tomorrow.
VROOOOOOM
And there she goes...

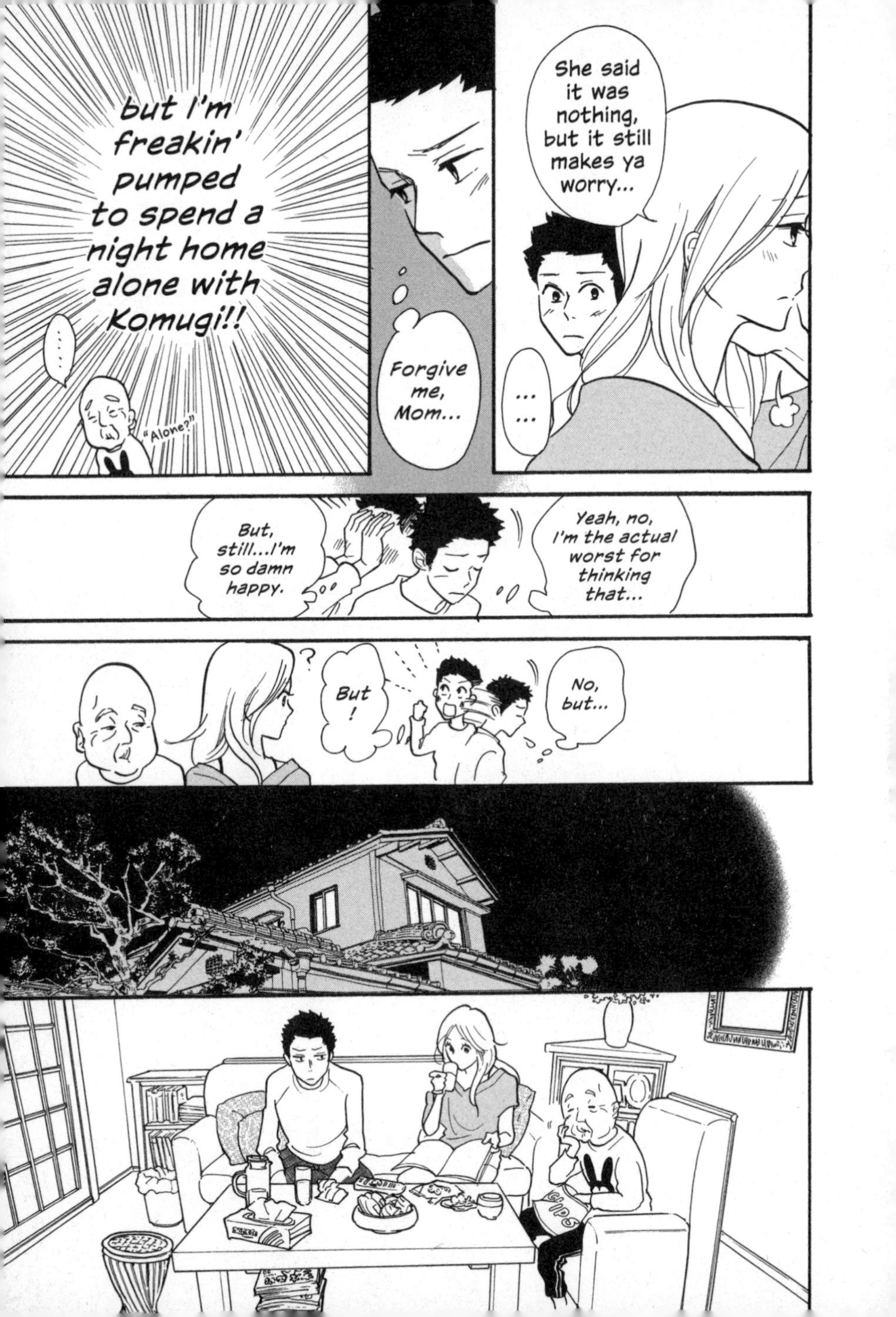
She said it was nothing, but it still makes ya worry...
... ...
Forgive me, Mom...
but I'm freakin' pumped to spend a night home alone with Komugi!!
......
"Alone?"
Yeah, no, I'm the actual worst for thinking that...
But, still...I'm so damn happy.
No, but...
But!
?

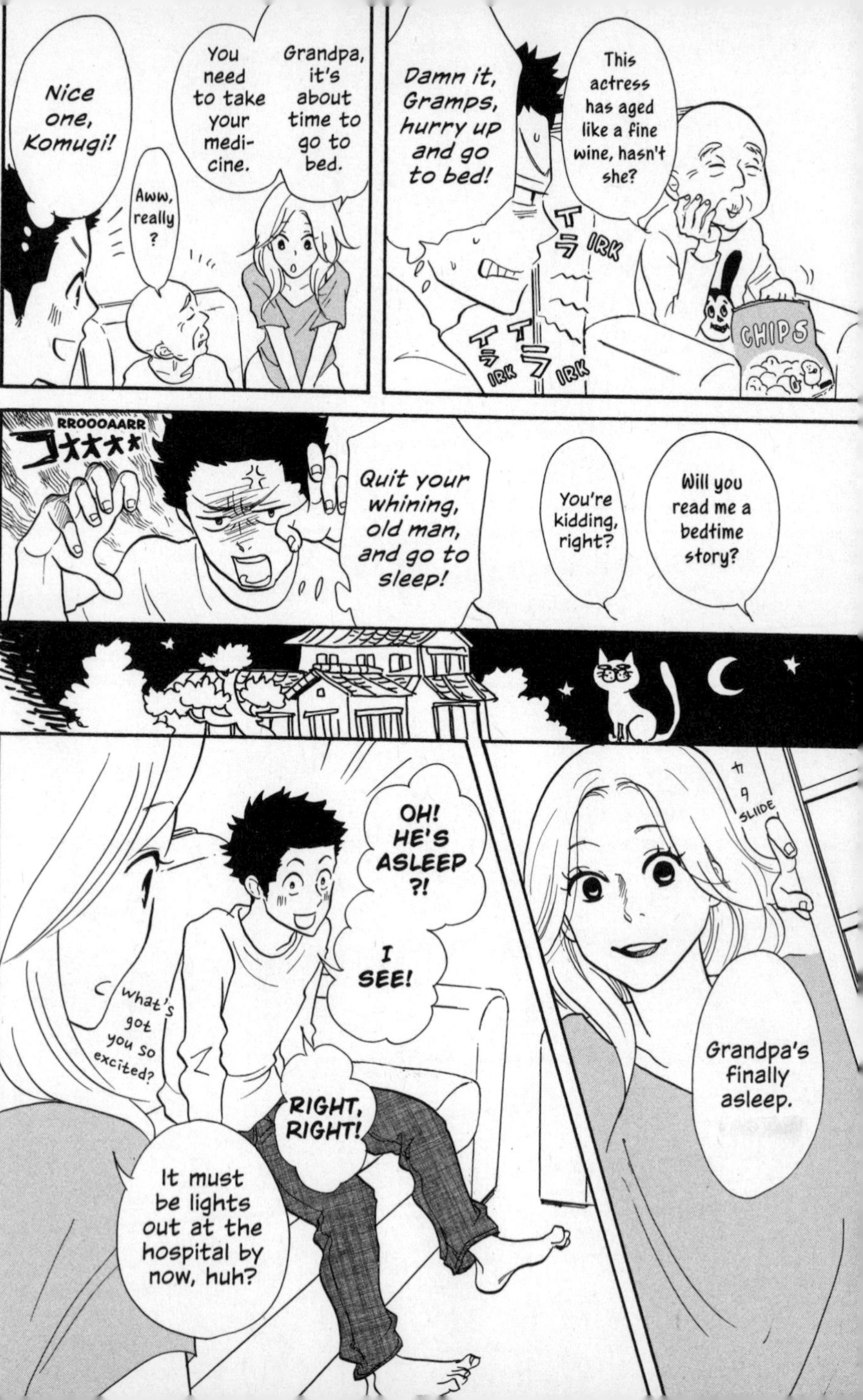

This actress has aged like a fine wine, hasn't she?
IRK
IRK
IRK
Damn it, Gramps, hurry up and go to bed!
Grandpa, it's about time to go to bed.
You need to take your medi-cine.
Aww, really?
Nice one, Komugi!
Will you read me a bedtime story?
You're kidding, right?
Quit your whining, old man, and go to sleep!
RROOOAARR
SLIIDE
Grandpa's finally asleep.
OH! HE'S ASLEEP?!
I SEE!
What's got you so excited?
RIGHT, RIGHT!
It must be lights out at the hospital by now, huh?

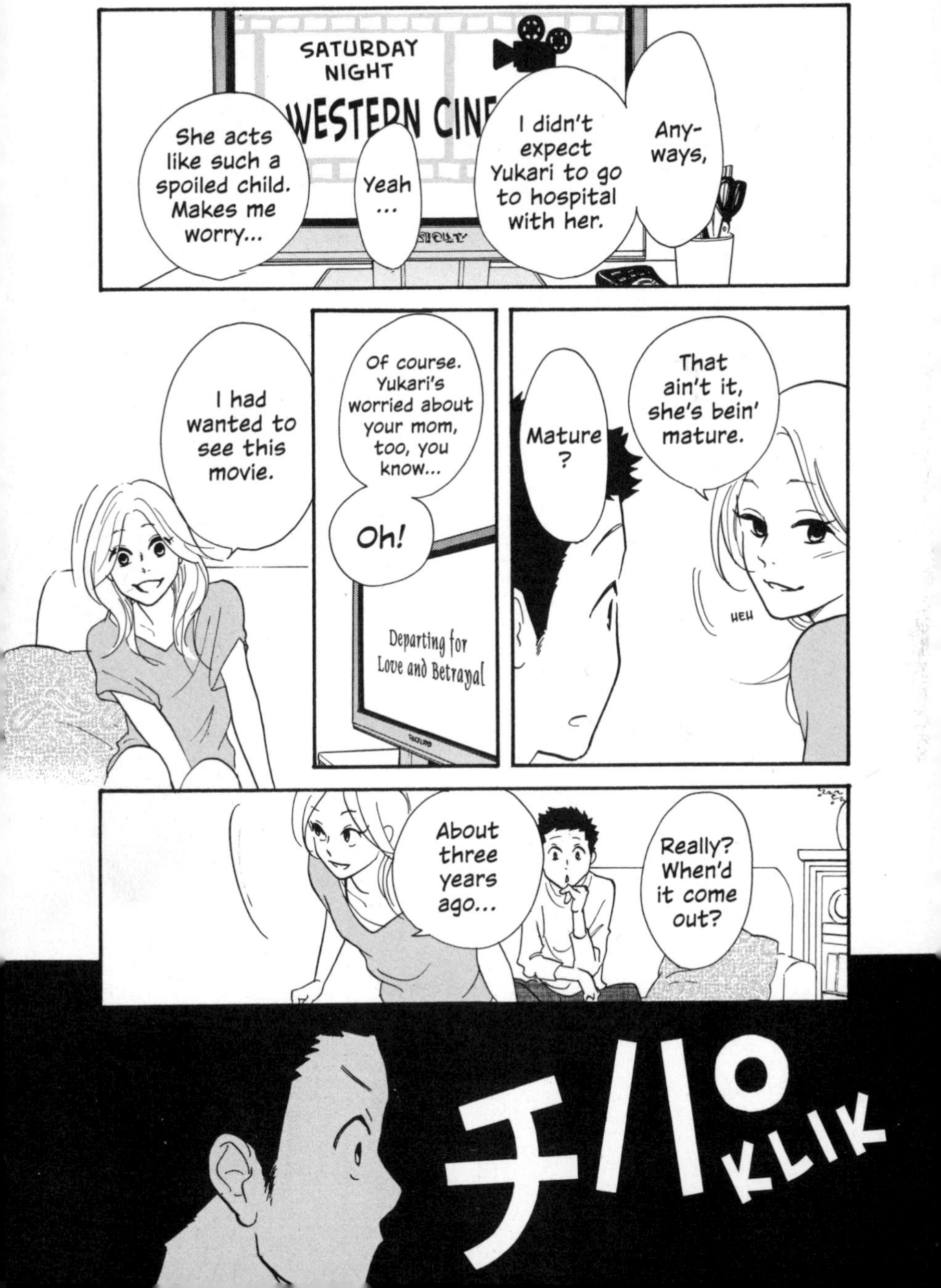
SATURDAY NIGHT
WESTERN CINE
Any- ways,
I didn't expect Yukari to go to hospital with her.
Yeah ...
She acts like such a spoiled child. Makes me worry...
That ain't it, she's bein' mature.
Mature ?
HEH
Of course. Yukari's worried about your mom, too, you know...
Oh!
Departing for Love and Betrayal
I had wanted to see this movie.
Really? When'd it come out?
About three years ago...
チパ
KLIK

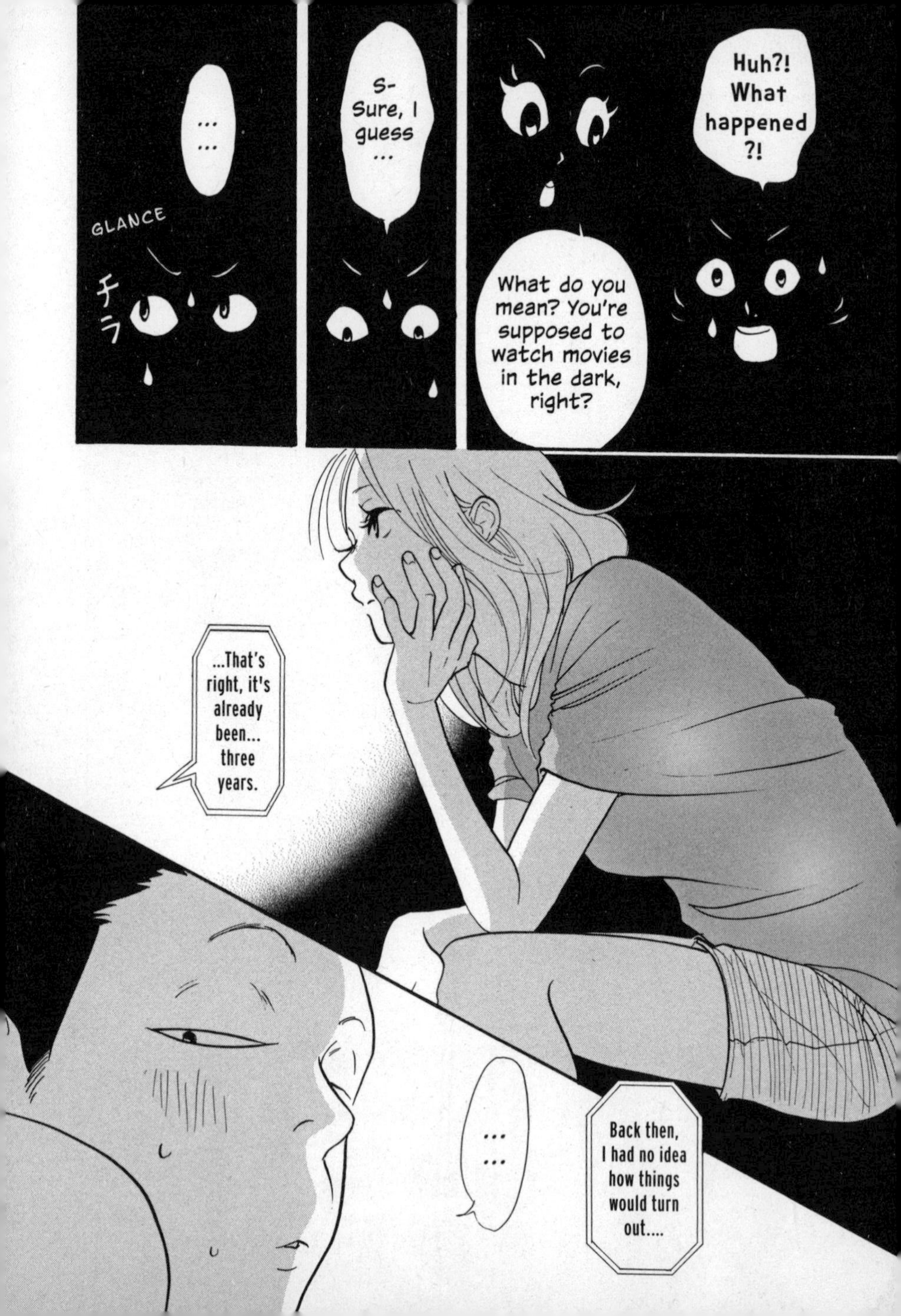

Huh?! What happened?!
What do you mean? You're supposed to watch movies in the dark, right?
S- Sure, I guess ...
... ...
GLANCE
チラ
...That's right, it's already been... three years.
Back then, I had no idea how things would turn out....
... ...

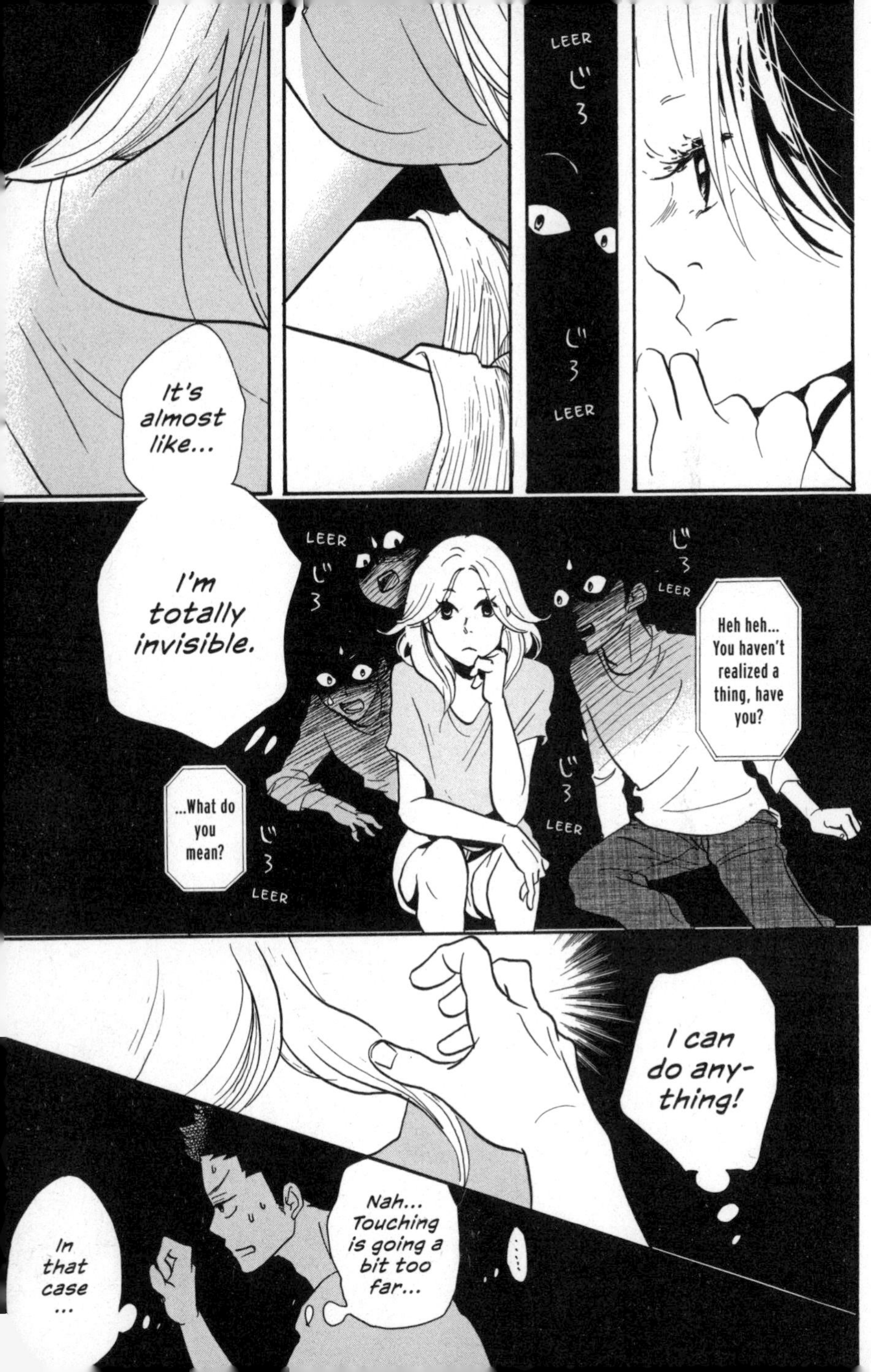
LEER
じろ
じろ
LEER
It's almost like...
I'm totally invisible.
じろ
LEER
Heh heh... You haven't realized a thing, have you?
LEER
じろ
じろ
LEER
じろ
LEER
...What do you mean?
I can do any-thing!
...
Nah... Touching is going a bit too far...
In that case...

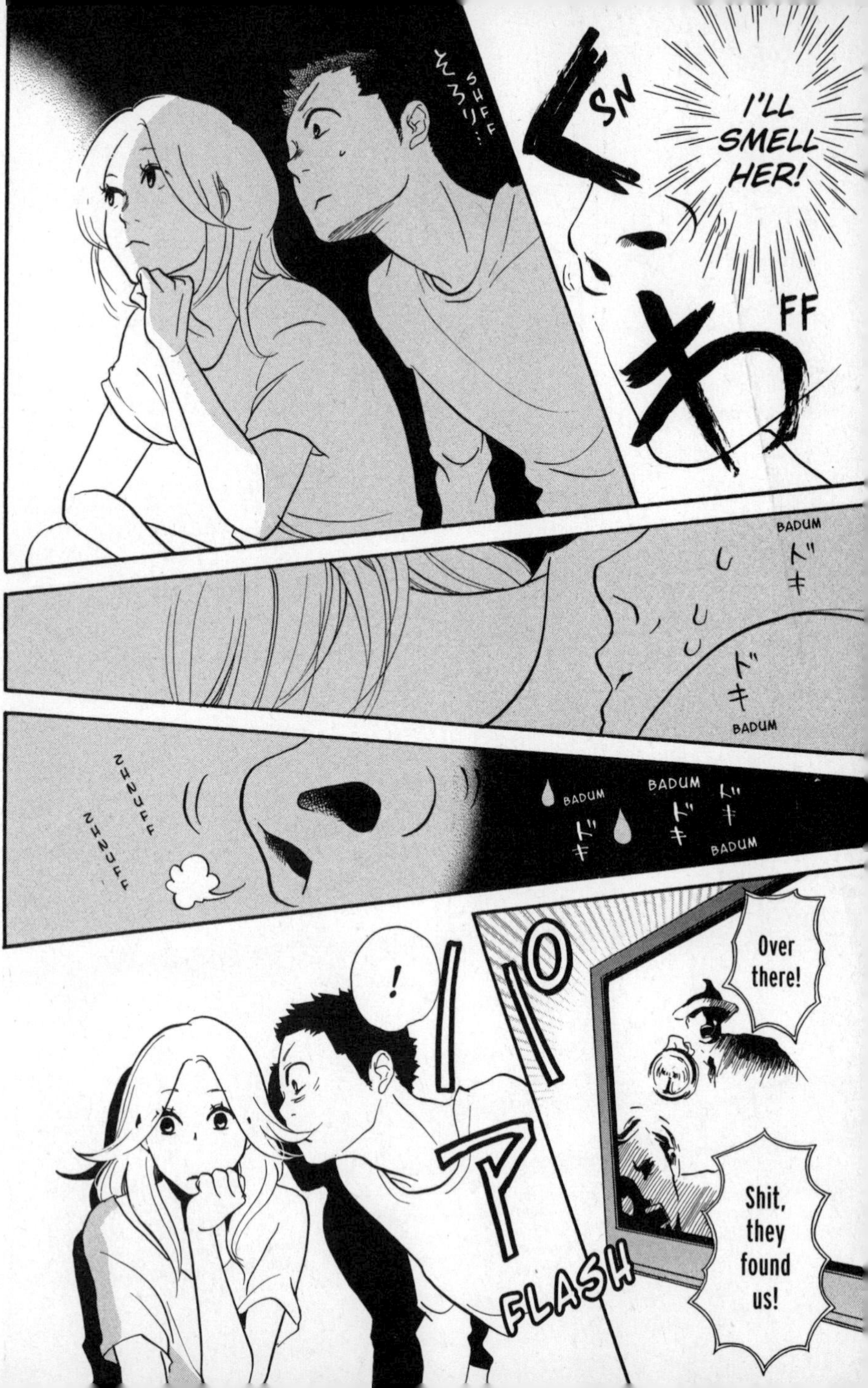

I'LL SMELL HER!
SN
FF
SHUFF
そろり…
BADUM
ドキ
ドキ
BADUM
BADUM
ドキ
BADUM
ドキ
BADUM
ドキ
ZHNUFF
ZHNUFF
Over there!
Shit, they found us!
!
FLASH

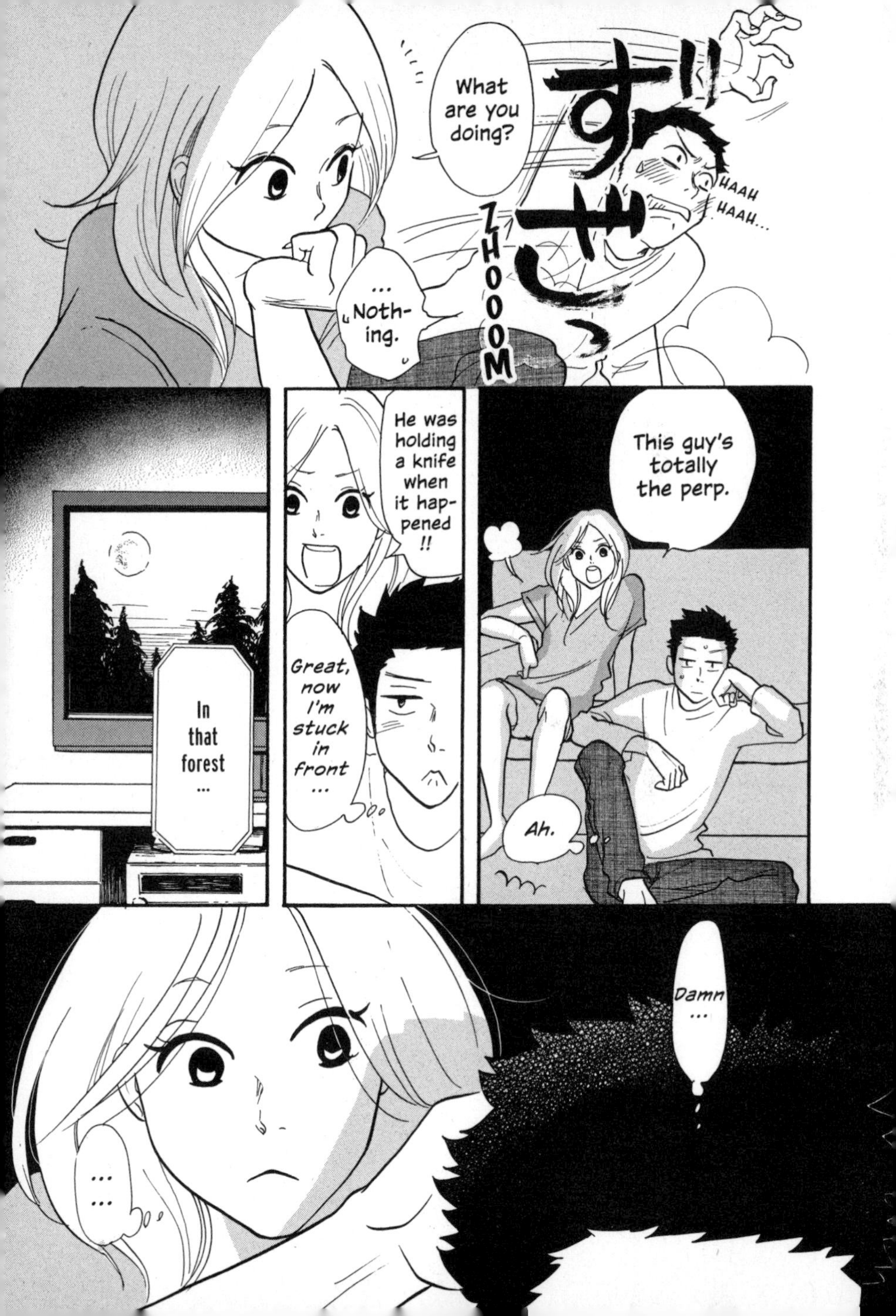
HAAH HAAH...
ZHOOOM
What are you doing?
...Nothing.
This guy's totally the perp.
Ah.
He was holding a knife when it happened!!
Great, now I'm stuck in front...
In that forest...
Damn...
......

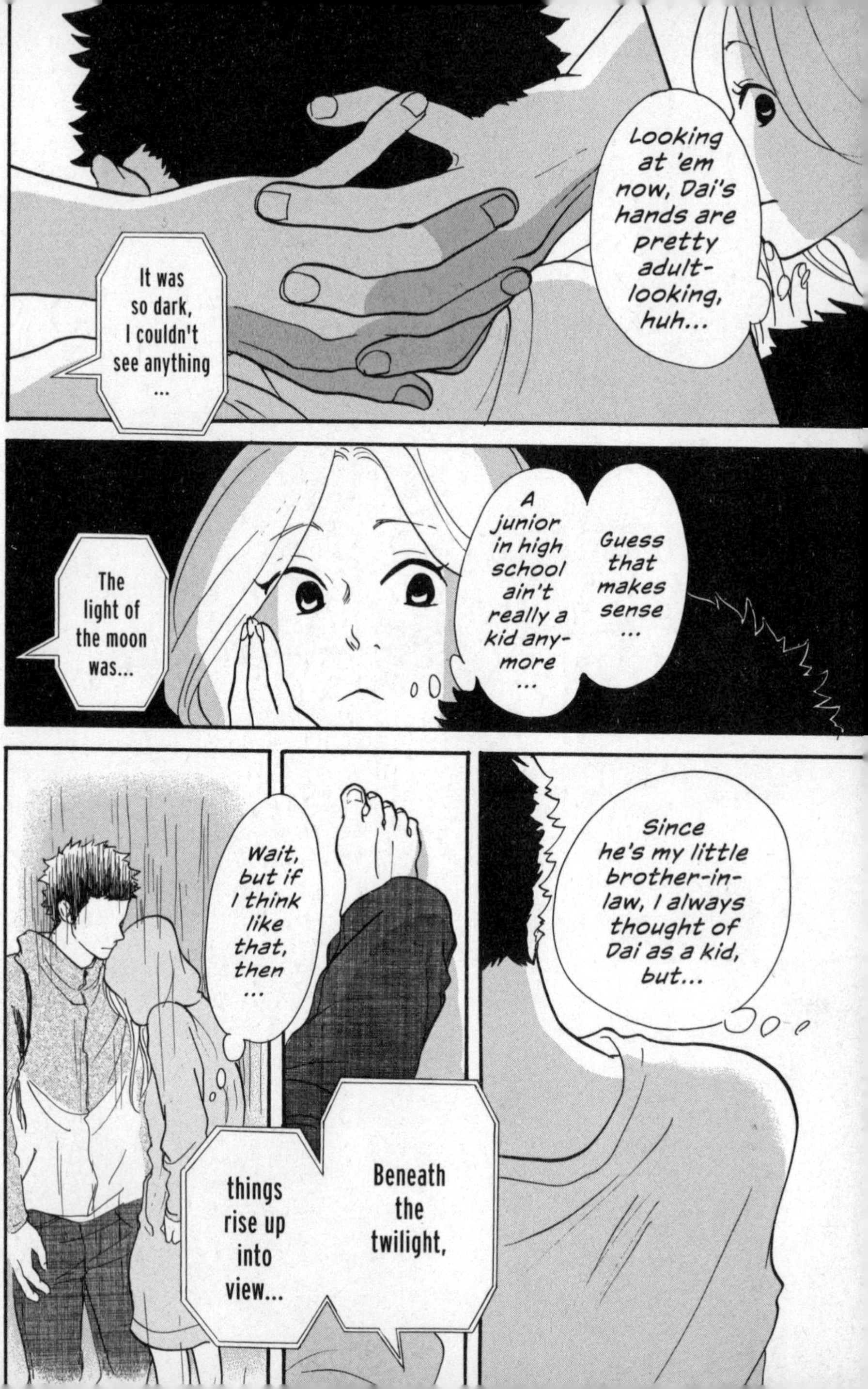
Looking at 'em now, Dai's hands are pretty adult-looking, huh...
It was so dark, I couldn't see anything ...
Guess that makes sense ...
A junior in high school ain't really a kid any-more ...
The light of the moon was...
Since he's my little brother-in-law, I always thought of Dai as a kid, but...
Wait, but if I think like that, then ...
Beneath the twilight,
things rise up into view...

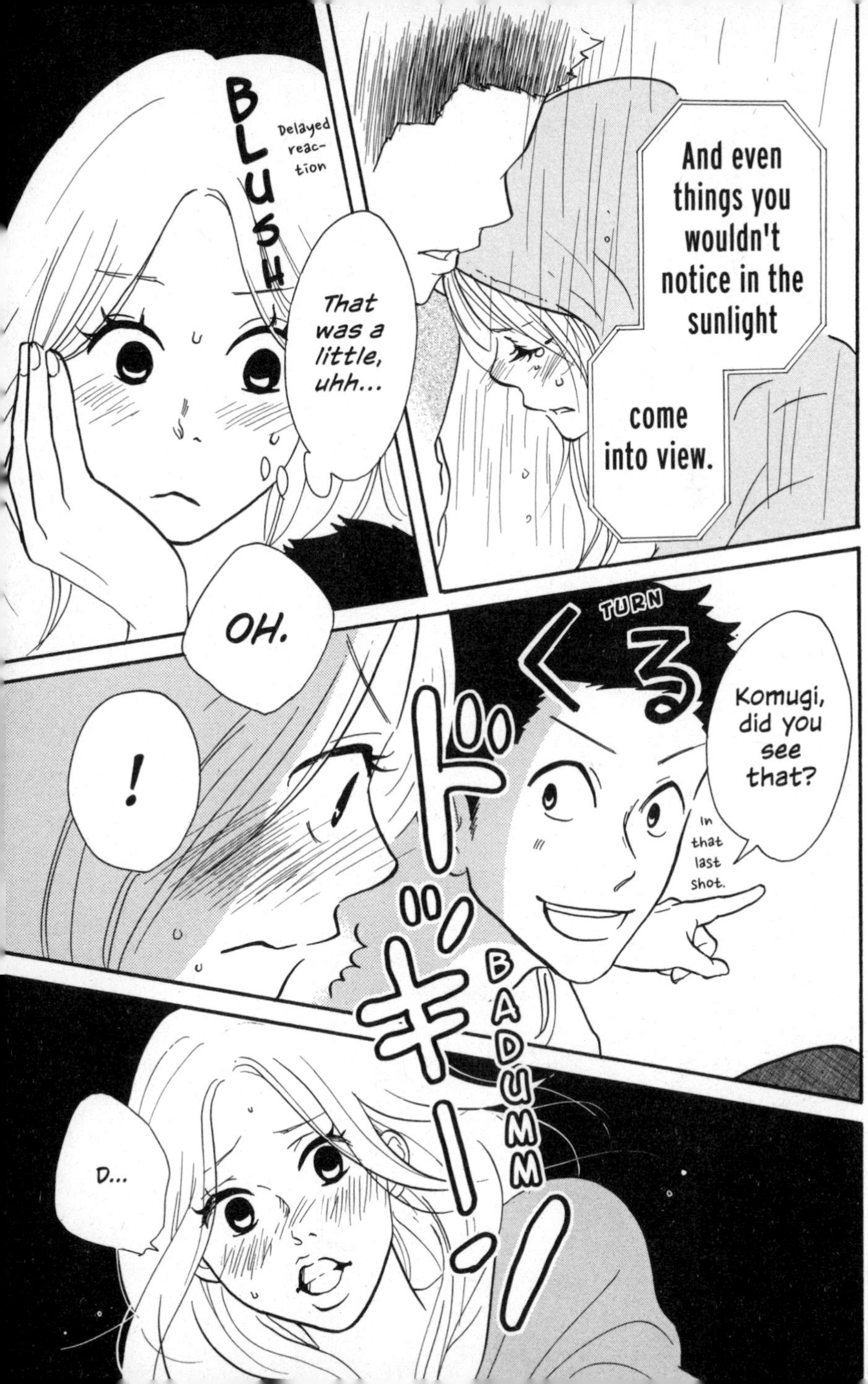
And even things you wouldn't notice in the sunlight
come into view.
BLUSH
Delayed reaction
That was a little, uhh...
OH.
TURN
くる
Komugi, did you see that?
In that last shot.
!
ドッキーン
BADUMM
D...

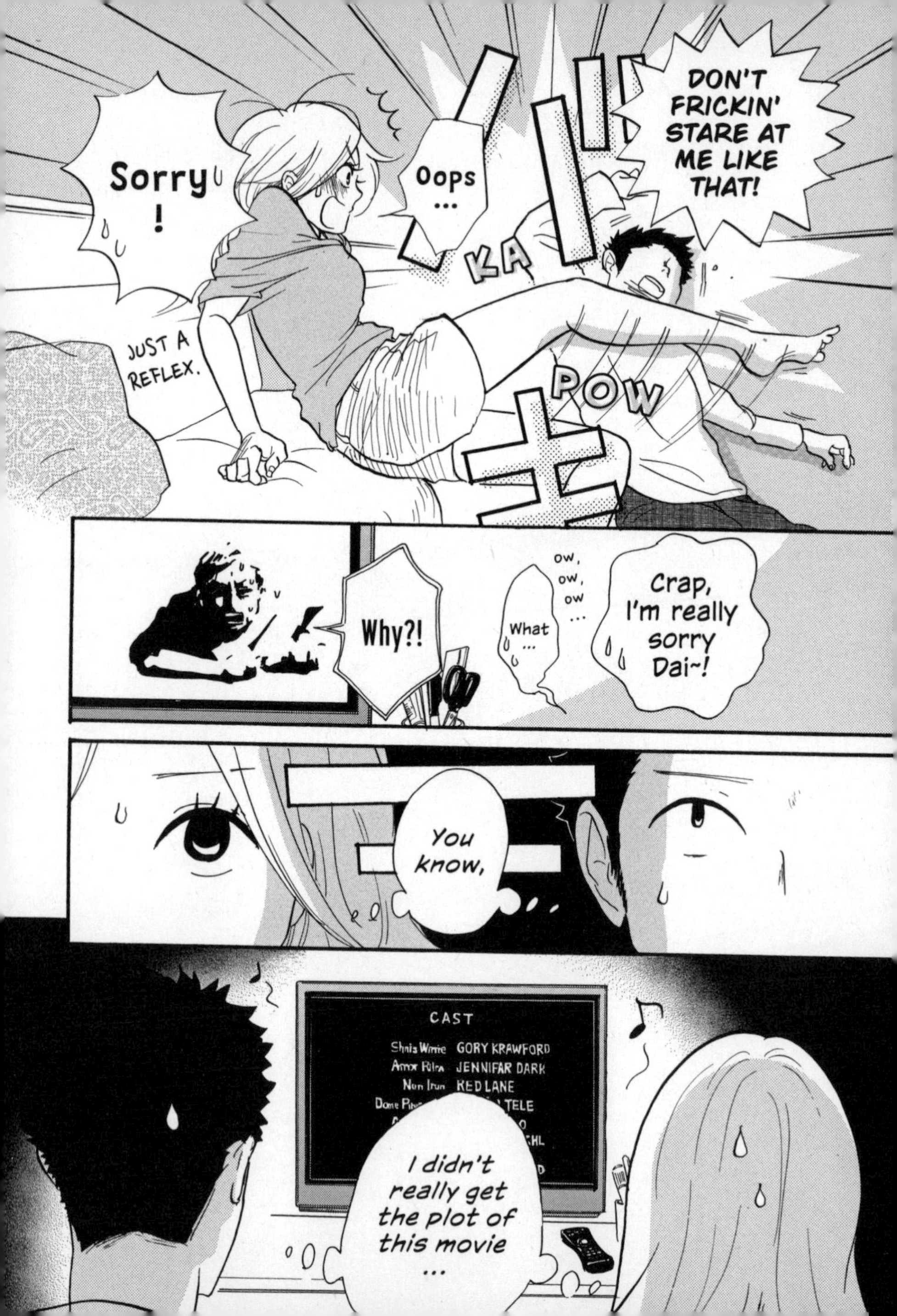
DON'T FRICKIN' STARE AT ME LIKE THAT!
KA
POW
Oops ...
Sorry!
JUST A REFLEX.
Crap, I'm really sorry Dai~!
ow, ow, ow ...
What ...
Why?!
You know,
CAST
GORY KRAWFORD
JENNIFAR DARK
RED LANE
I didn't really get the plot of this movie ...

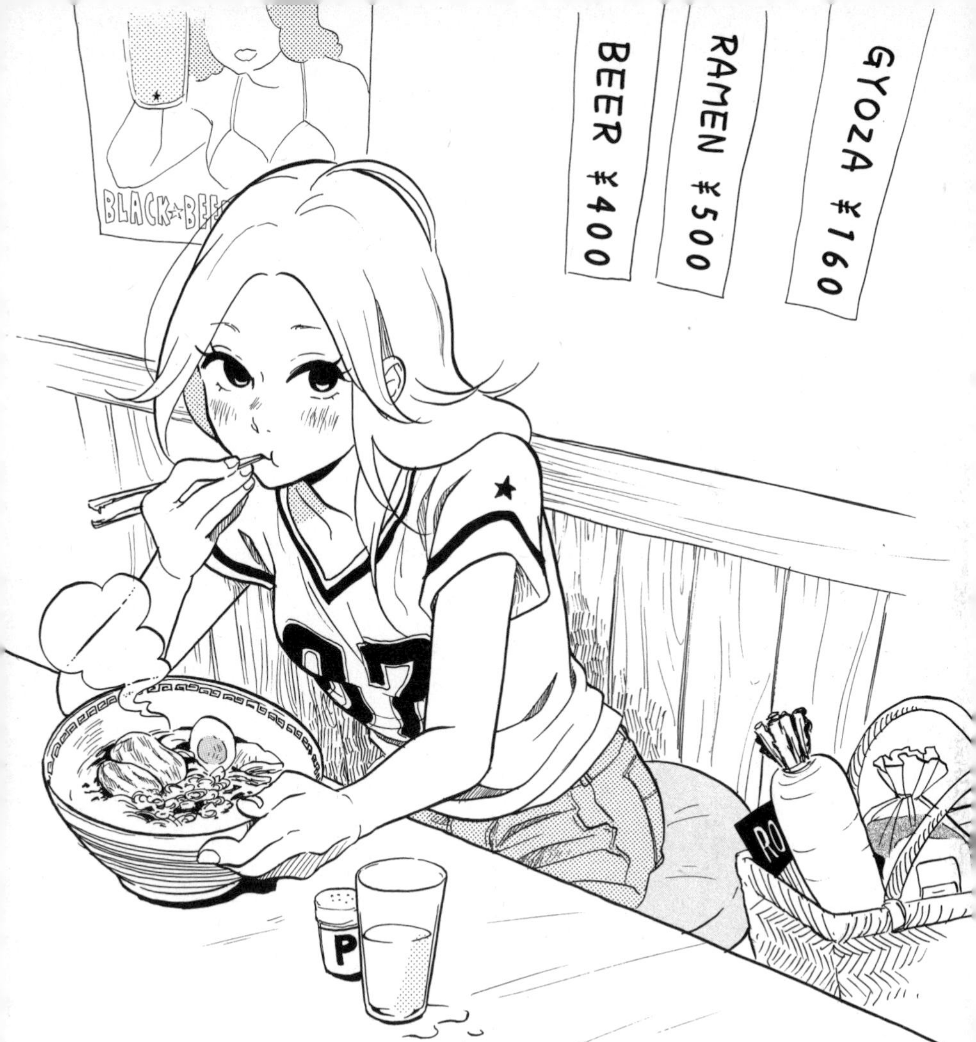
GYOZA ¥160
RAMEN ¥500
BEER ¥400
BLACK☆

26 WIVES AND LADDERS

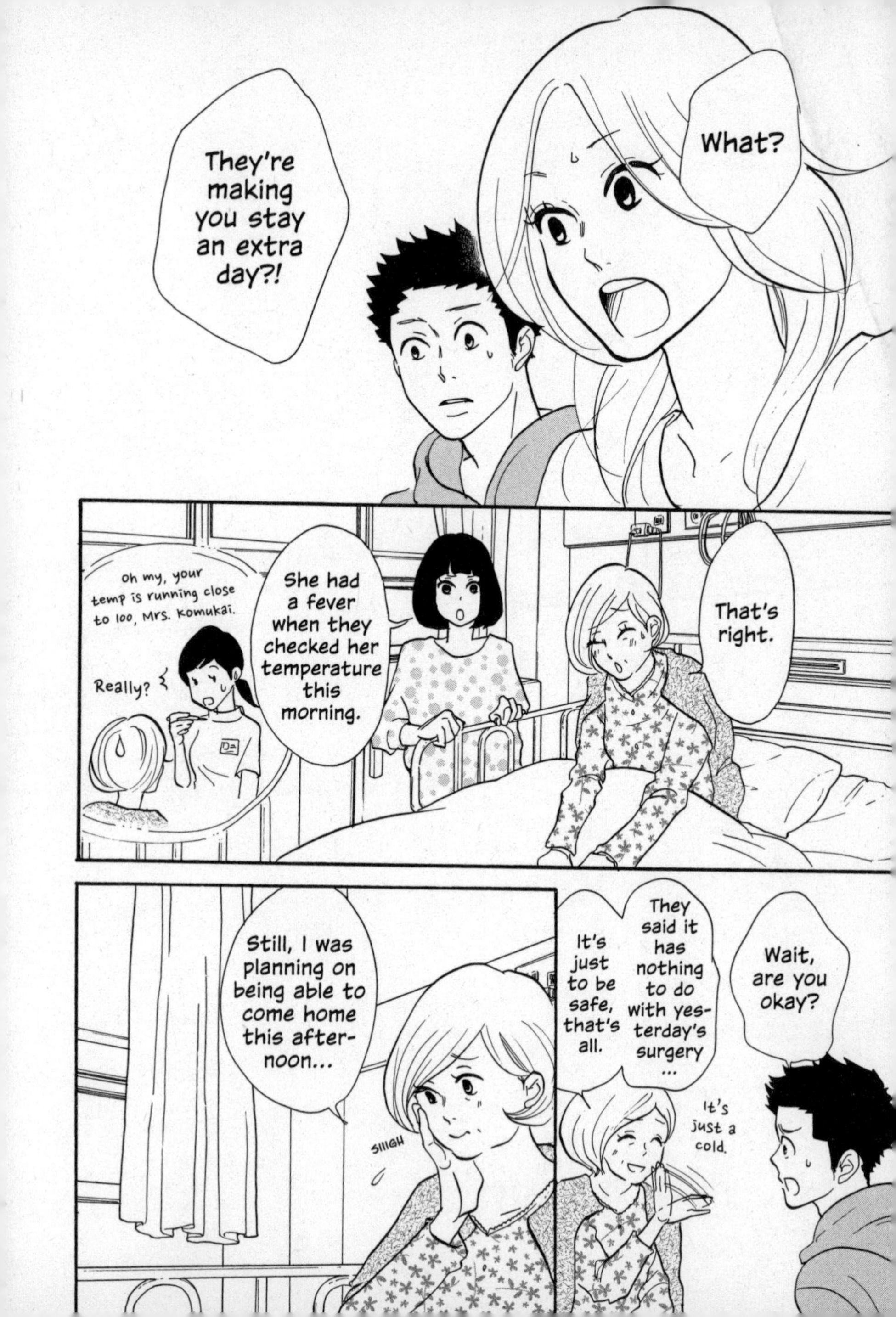
What?
They're making you stay an extra day?!
That's right.
She had a fever when they checked her temperature this morning.
Oh my, your temp is running close to 100, Mrs. Komukai.
Really?
Wait, are you okay?
They said it has nothing to do with yesterday's surgery...
It's just to be safe, that's all.
It's just a cold.
Still, I was planning on being able to come home this afternoon...
SIIIGH

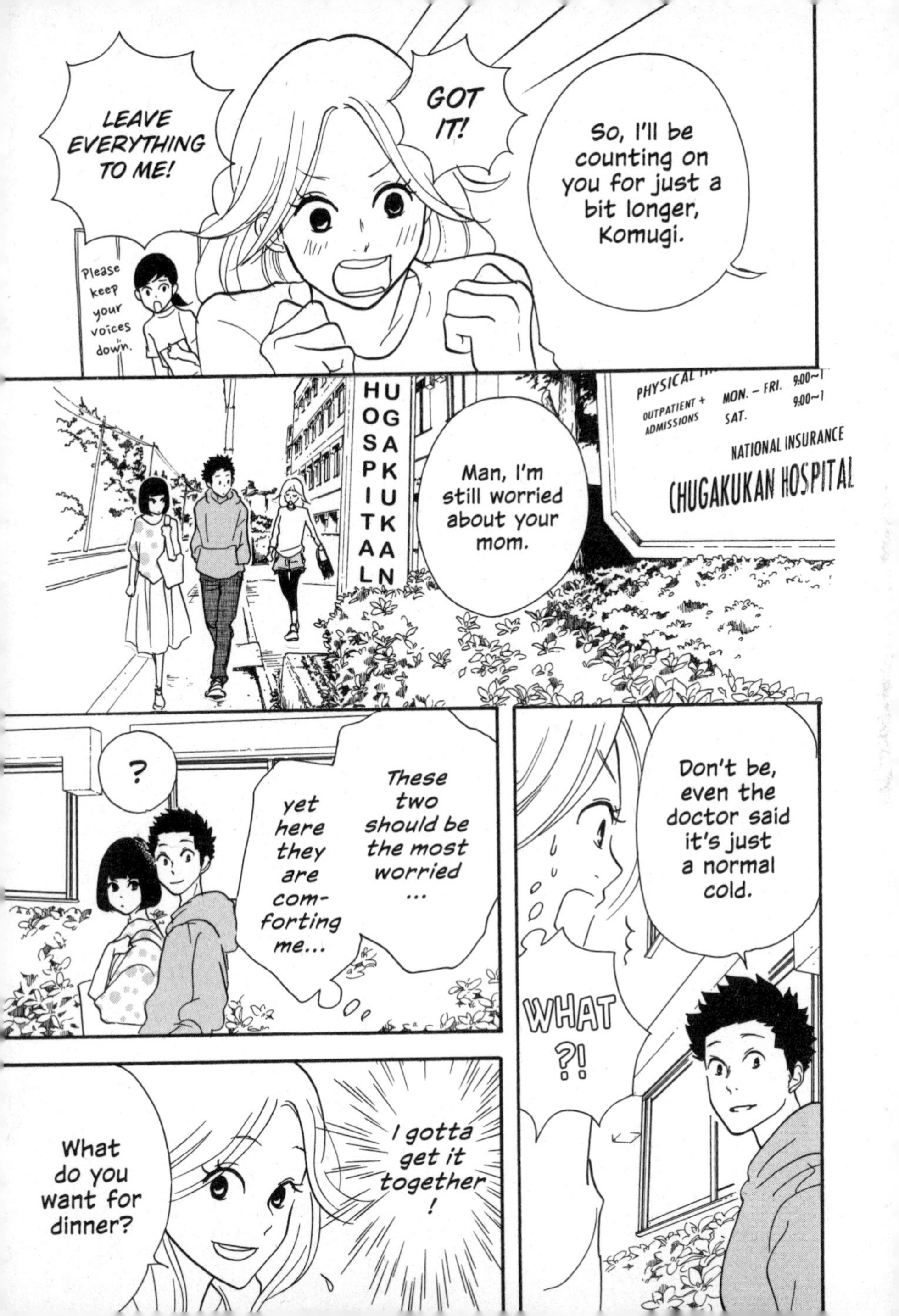
So, I'll be counting on you for just a bit longer, Komugi.
GOT IT!
LEAVE EVERYTHING TO ME!
Please keep your voices down.
PHYSICAL
OUTPATIENT + ADMISSIONS MON. – FRI. 9:00~1
SAT. 9:00~1
NATIONAL INSURANCE
CHUGAKUKAN HOSPITAL
Man, I'm still worried about your mom.
HOSPITAL
Don't be, even the doctor said it's just a normal cold.
WHAT?!
These two should be the most worried...
yet here they are com-forting me...
?
I gotta get it together!
What do you want for dinner?

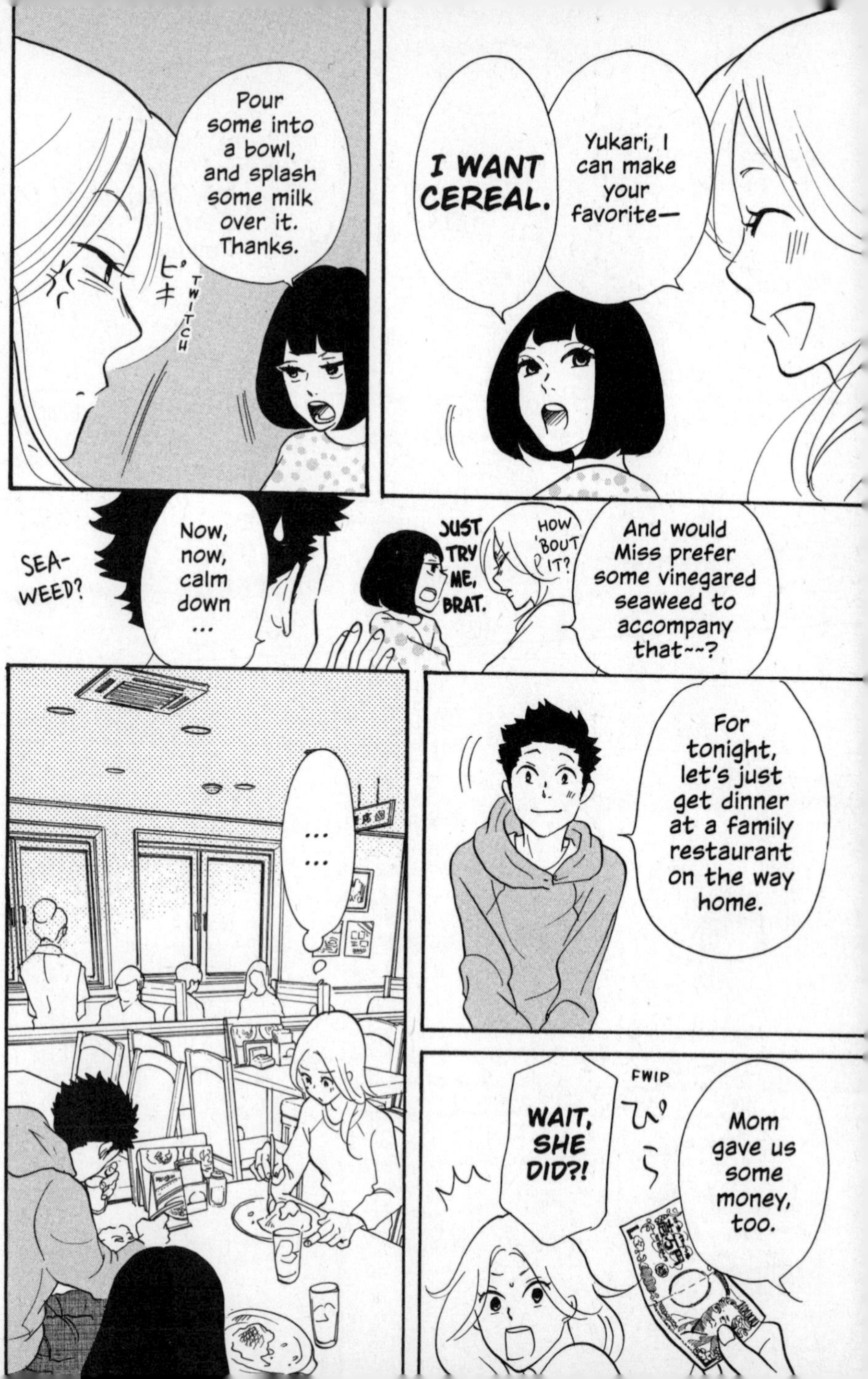
Yukari, I can make your favorite—
I WANT CEREAL.
Pour some into a bowl, and splash some milk over it. Thanks.
ピキ
TWITCH
And would Miss prefer some vinegared seaweed to accompany that~~?
HOW 'BOUT IT?
JUST TRY ME, BRAT.
Now, now, calm down ...
SEA-WEED?
For tonight, let's just get dinner at a family restaurant on the way home.
Mom gave us some money, too.
FWIP
ぴら
WAIT, SHE DID?!
... ...

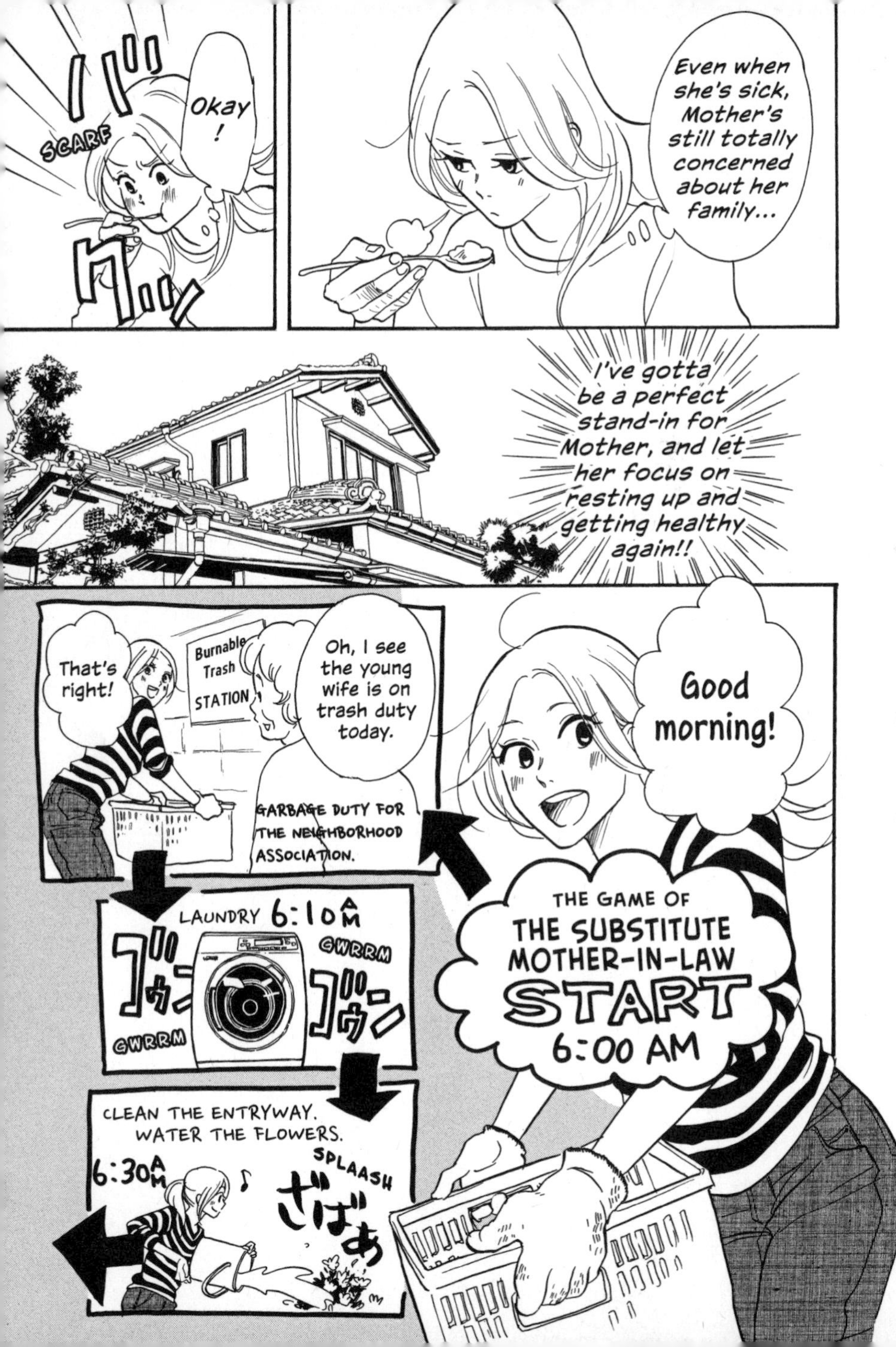
Even when she's sick, Mother's still totally concerned about her family...
SCARF
Okay!
I've gotta be a perfect stand-in for Mother, and let her focus on resting up and getting healthy again!!
Good morning!
THE GAME OF
THE SUBSTITUTE MOTHER-IN-LAW
START
6:00 AM
Oh, I see the young wife is on trash duty today.
That's right!
Burnable Trash STATION
GARBAGE DUTY FOR THE NEIGHBORHOOD ASSOCIATION.
LAUNDRY 6:10 AM
GWRRM
GWRRM
CLEAN THE ENTRYWAY.
WATER THE FLOWERS.
6:30 AM
SPLAASH
ざばあ

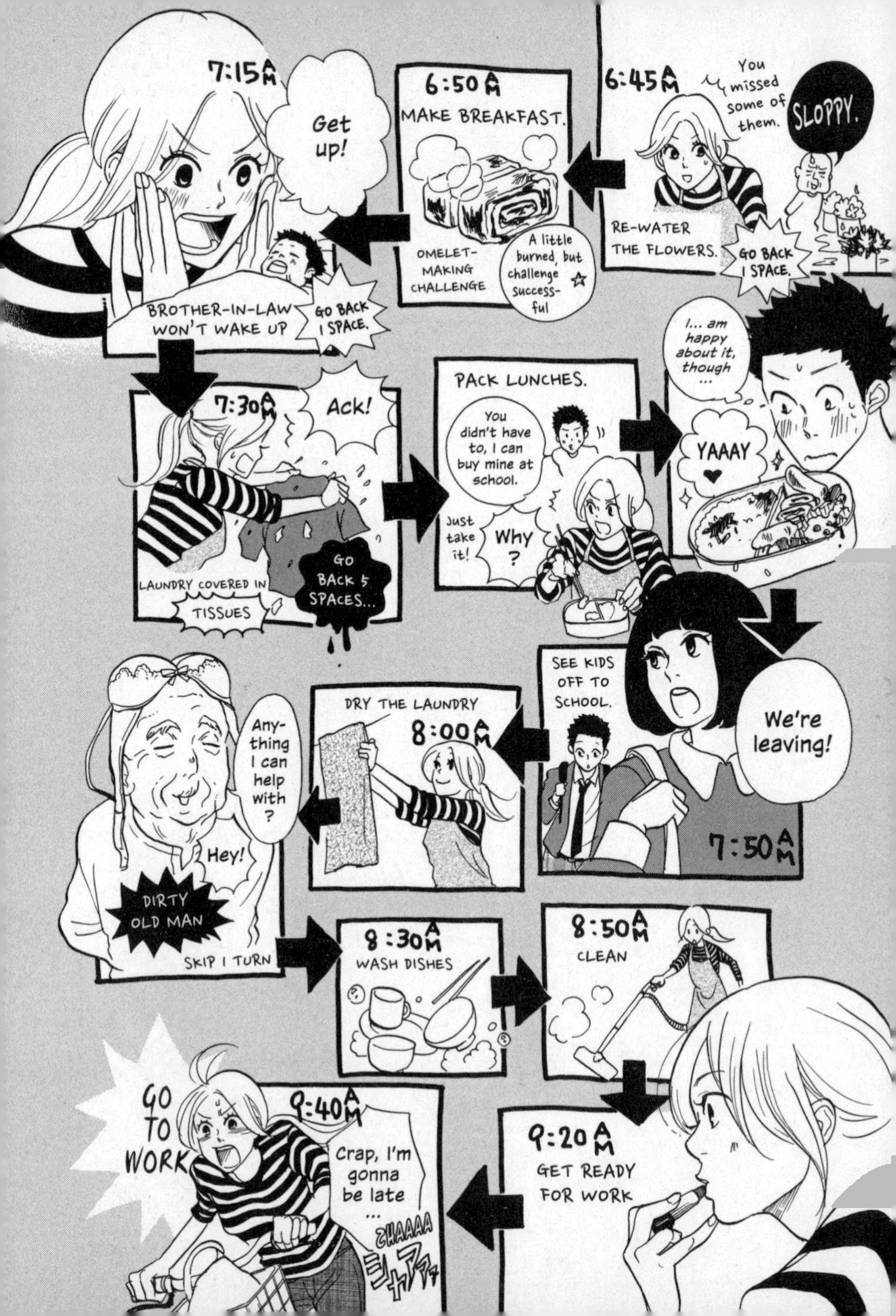
6:45 AM
You missed some of them.
SLOPPY.
RE-WATER THE FLOWERS.
GO BACK 1 SPACE.
6:50 AM
MAKE BREAKFAST.
OMELET-MAKING CHALLENGE
A little burned, but challenge successful ☆
7:15 AM
Get up!
BROTHER-IN-LAW WON'T WAKE UP
GO BACK 1 SPACE.
7:30 AM
Ack!
LAUNDRY COVERED IN TISSUES
GO BACK 5 SPACES...
PACK LUNCHES.
You didn't have to, I can buy mine at school.
Why?
Just take it!
YAAAY ♥
I... am happy about it, though...
We're leaving!
SEE KIDS OFF TO SCHOOL.
7:50 AM
DRY THE LAUNDRY
8:00 AM
Anything I can help with?
Hey!
DIRTY OLD MAN
SKIP 1 TURN
8:30 AM
WASH DISHES
8:50 AM
CLEAN
9:20 AM
GET READY FOR WORK
9:40 AM
GO TO WORK
Crap, I'm gonna be late...
SHAAAA

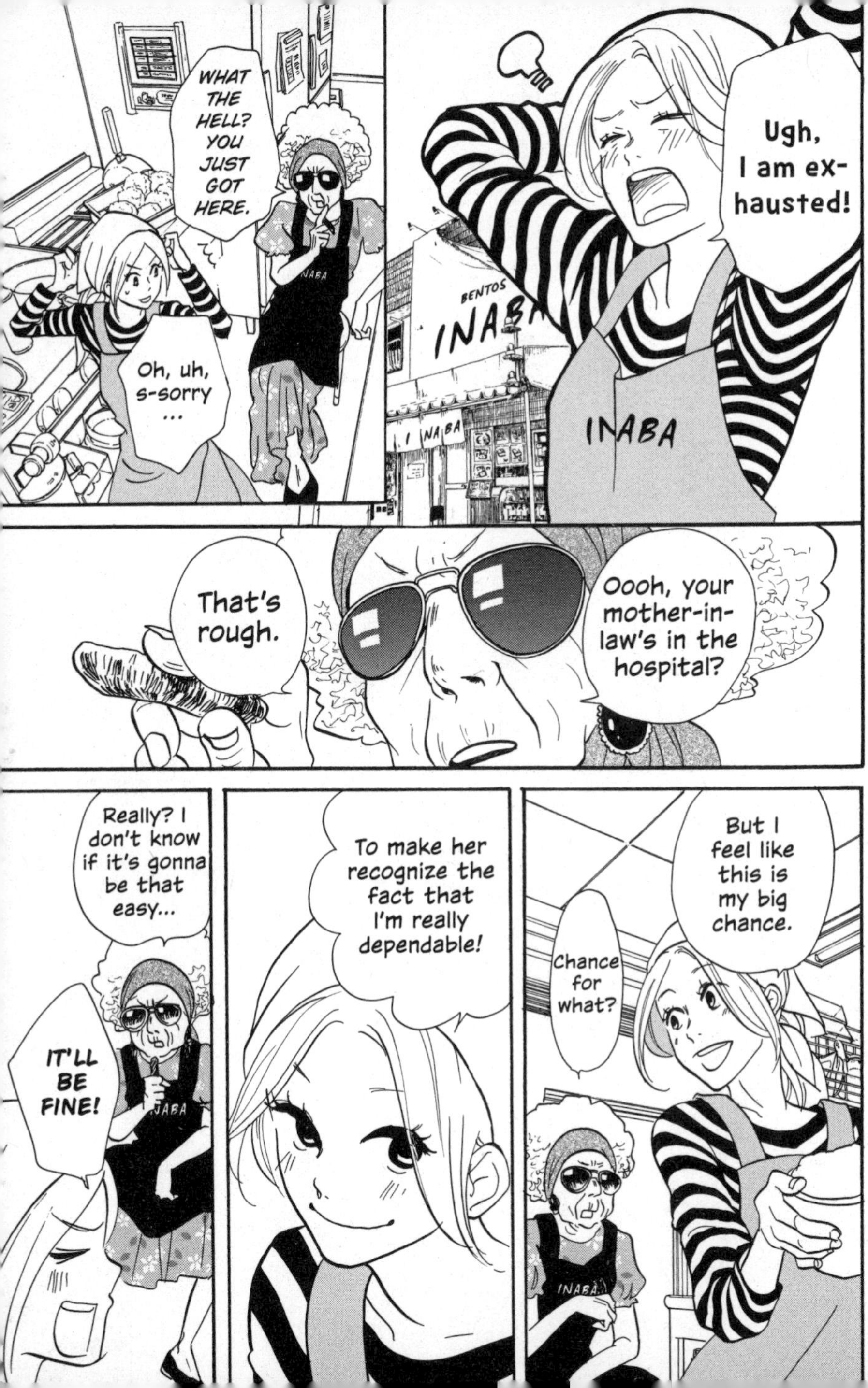
Ugh, I am exhausted!
INABA
BENTOS INABA
WHAT THE HELL? YOU JUST GOT HERE.
Oh, uh, s-sorry ...
INABA
Oooh, your mother-in-law's in the hospital?
That's rough.
But I feel like this is my big chance.
Chance for what?
INABA
To make her recognize the fact that I'm really dependable!
Really? I don't know if it's gonna be that easy...
IT'LL BE FINE!
INABA

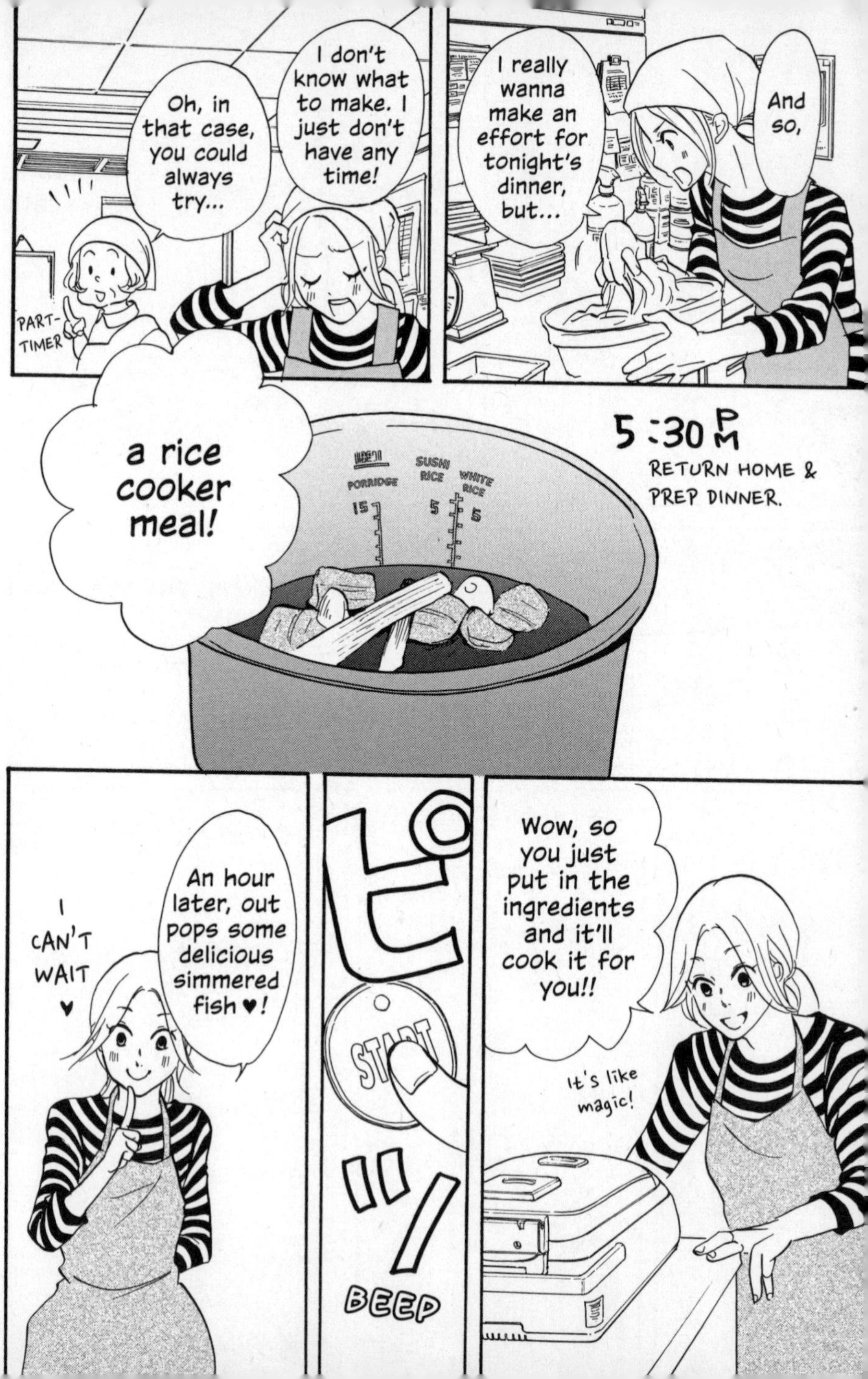

And so,
I really wanna make an effort for tonight's dinner, but...
I don't know what to make. I just don't have any time!
Oh, in that case, you could always try...
PART-TIMER
5:30 PM
RETURN HOME & PREP DINNER.
a rice cooker meal!
SUSHI RICE
WHITE RICE
PORRIDGE
15
5
5
Wow, so you just put in the ingredients and it'll cook it for you!!
It's like magic!
START
BEEP
An hour later, out pops some delicious simmered fish ♥!
I CAN'T WAIT ♥

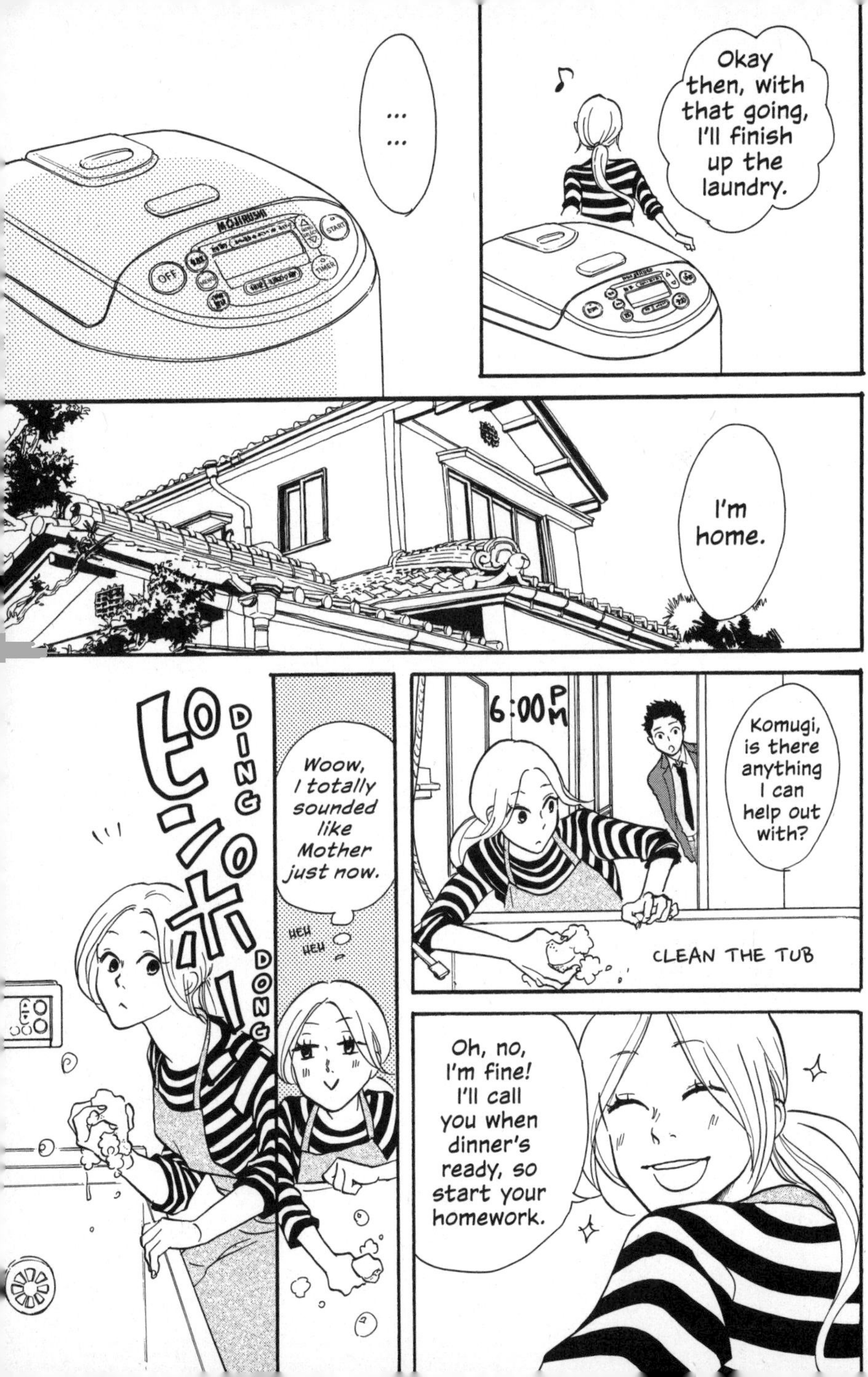
Okay then, with that going, I'll finish up the laundry.
……
I'm home.
6:00 PM
Komugi, is there anything I can help out with?
CLEAN THE TUB
Oh, no, I'm fine! I'll call you when dinner's ready, so start your homework.
DING
DONG
Woow, I totally sounded like Mother just now.
HEH HEH

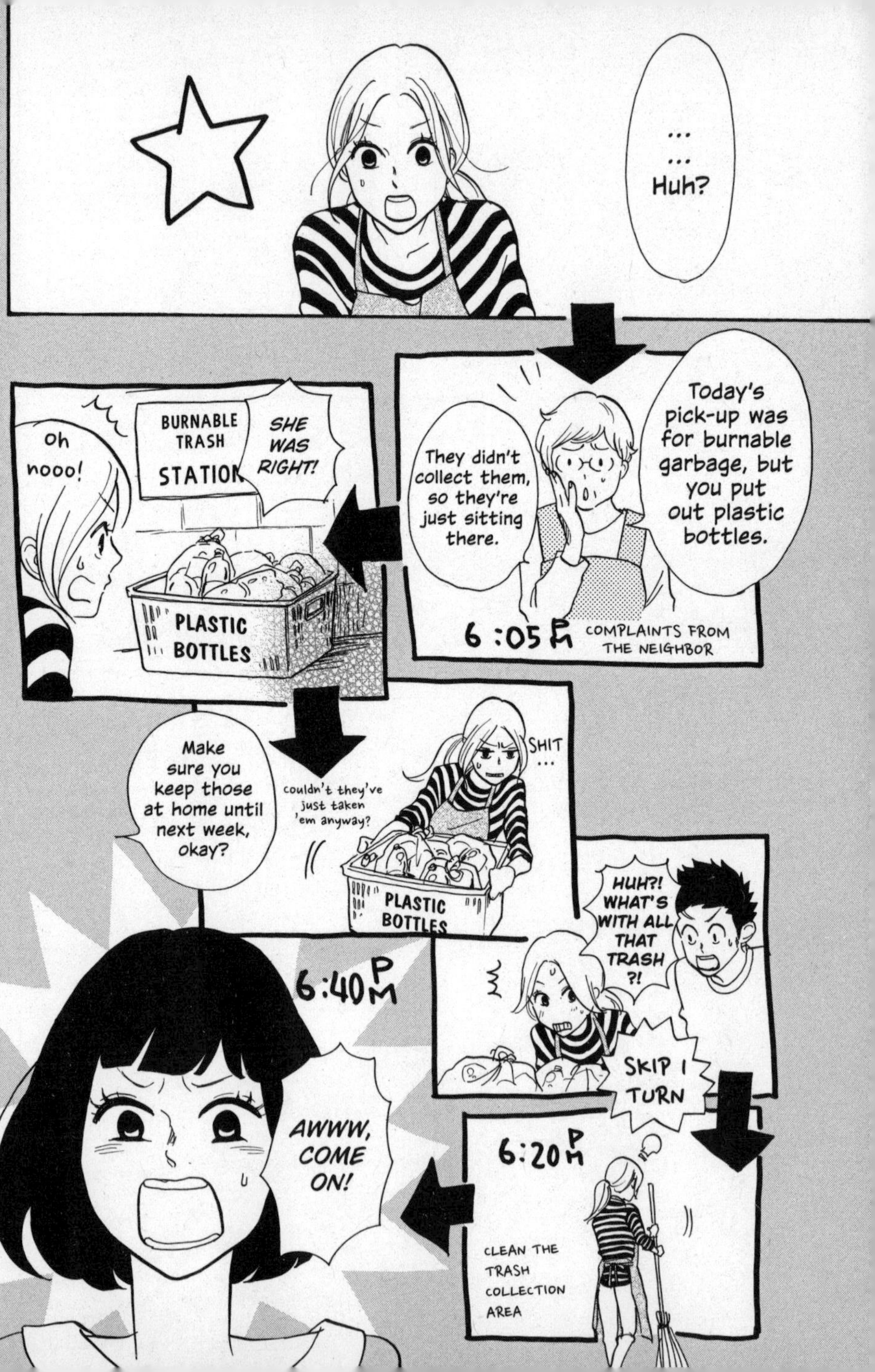
… … Huh?
Today's pick-up was for burnable garbage, but you put out plastic bottles.
They didn't collect them, so they're just sitting there.
6:05 PM
COMPLAINTS FROM THE NEIGHBOR
SHE WAS RIGHT!
BURNABLE TRASH STATION
Oh nooo!
PLASTIC BOTTLES
SHIT …
couldn't they've just taken 'em anyway?
PLASTIC BOTTLES
Make sure you keep those at home until next week, okay?
HUH?! WHAT'S WITH ALL THAT TRASH?!
SKIP 1 TURN
6:40 PM
6:20 PM
CLEAN THE TRASH COLLECTION AREA
AWWW, COME ON!

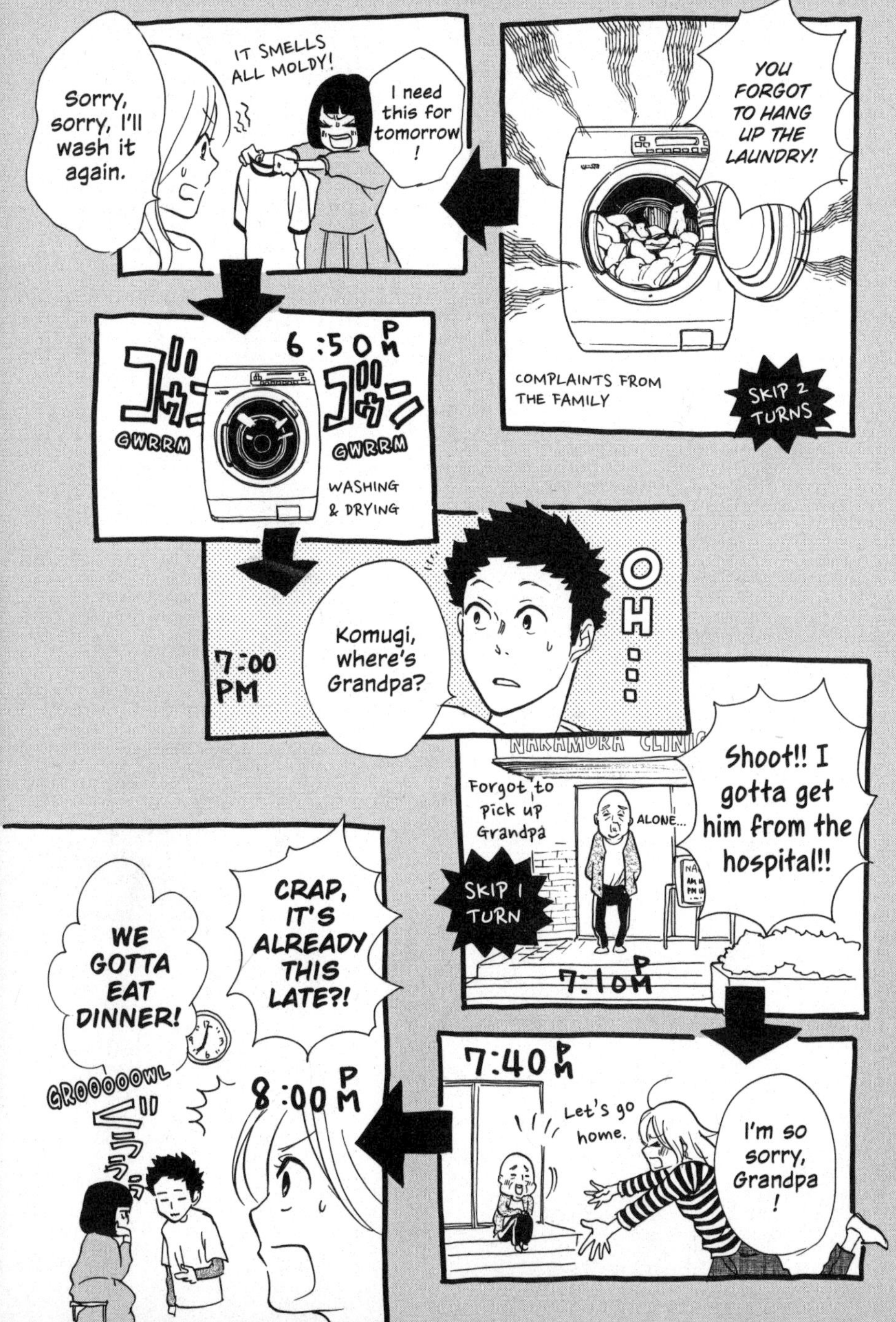

YOU FORGOT TO HANG UP THE LAUNDRY!
COMPLAINTS FROM THE FAMILY
SKIP 2 TURNS
IT SMELLS ALL MOLDY!
I need this for tomorrow!
Sorry, sorry, I'll wash it again.
6:50 PM
GWRRM
GWRRM
WASHING & DRYING
OH...
Komugi, where's Grandpa?
7:00 PM
NAKAMURA CLINIC
Shoot!! I gotta get him from the hospital!!
ALONE...
Forgot to pick up Grandpa
SKIP 1 TURN
7:10 PM
7:40 PM
I'm so sorry, Grandpa!
Let's go home.
8:00 PM
CRAP, IT'S ALREADY THIS LATE?!
WE GOTTA EAT DINNER!
GROOOOOWL

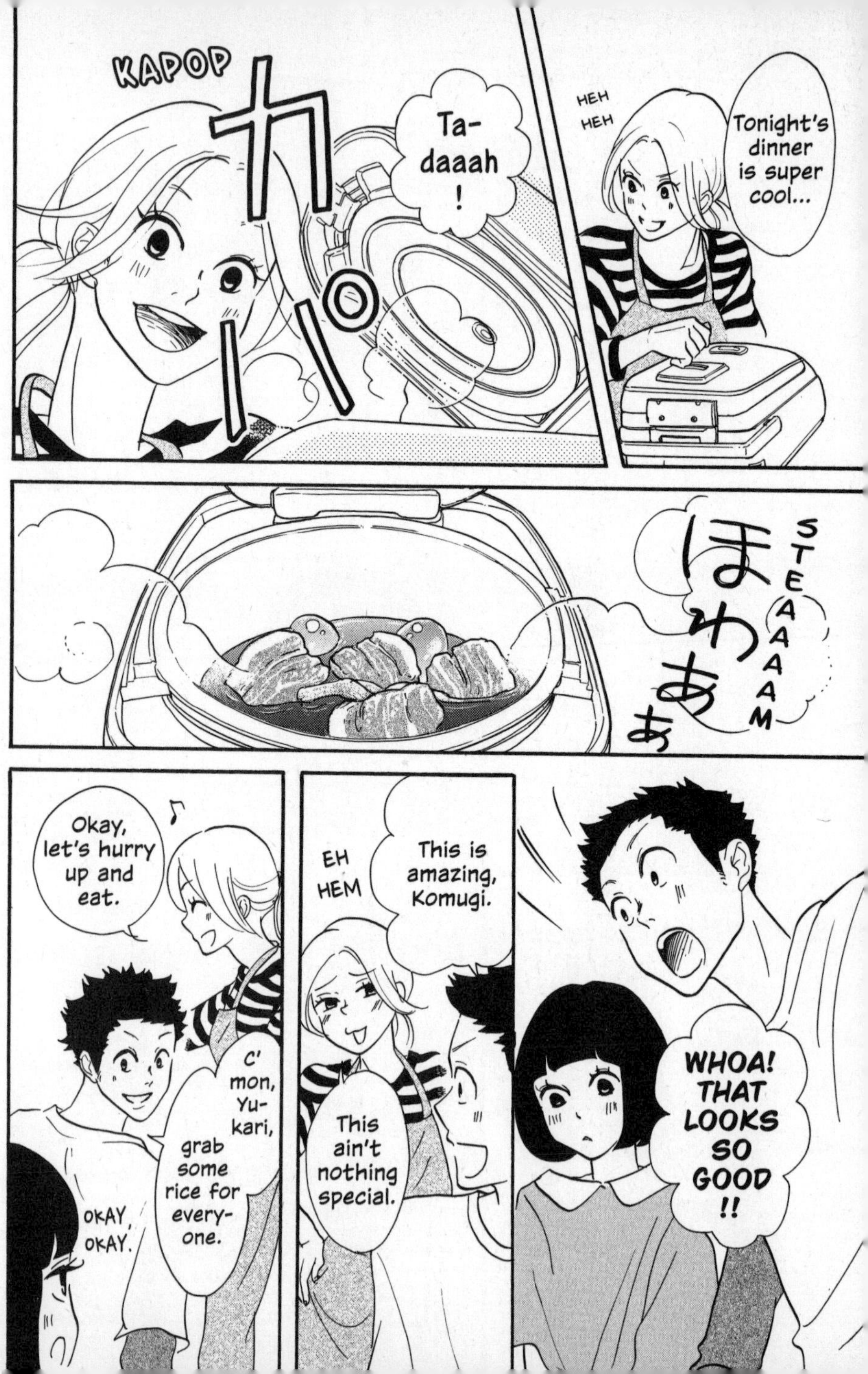
HEH HEH
Tonight's dinner is super cool...
KAPOP
Ta-daaah!
STEAAAAAM
WHOA! THAT LOOKS SO GOOD!!
This is amazing, Komugi.
EH HEM
This ain't nothing special.
Okay, let's hurry up and eat.
C'mon, Yukari, grab some rice for everyone.
OKAY, OKAY.

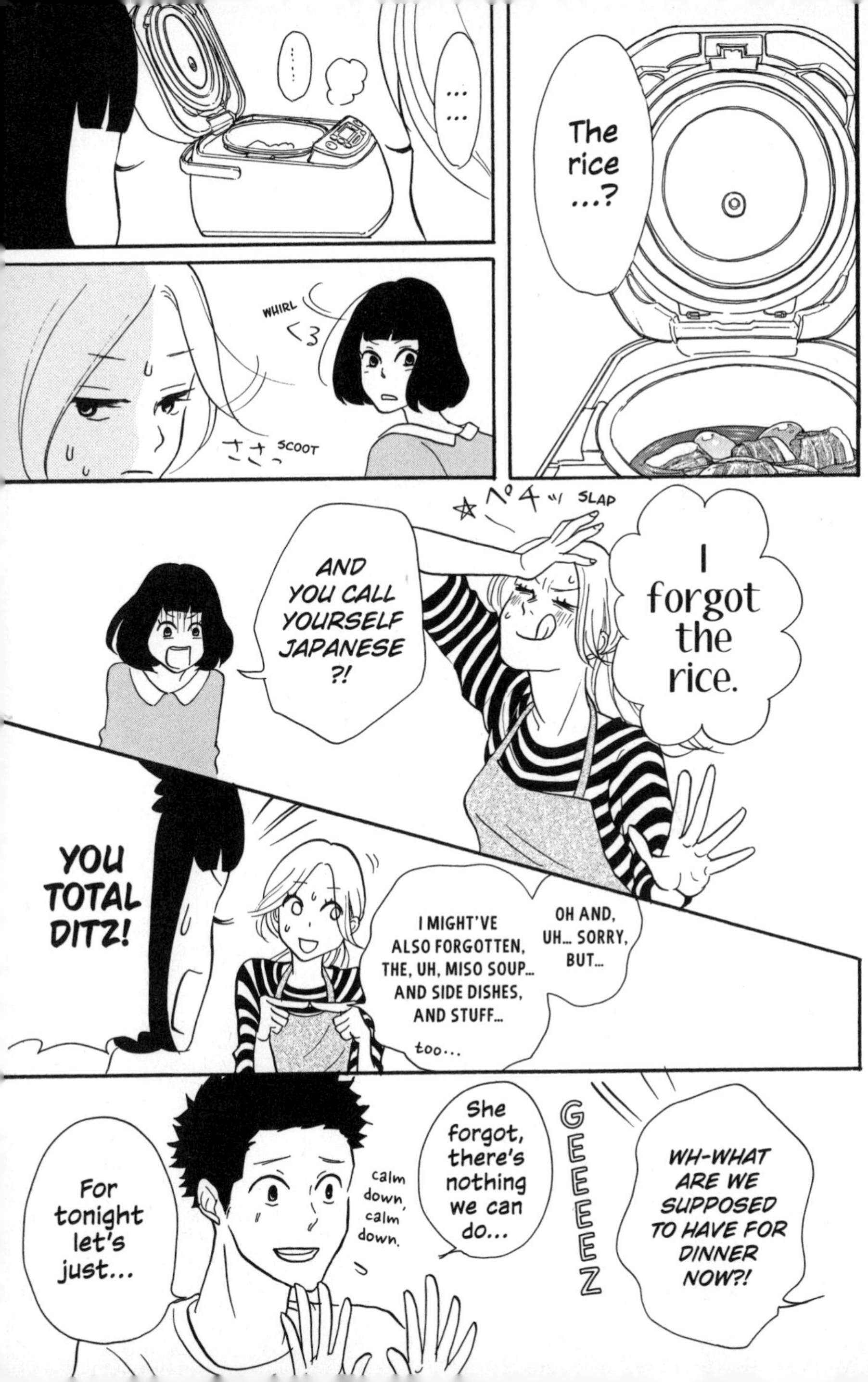

The rice ...?
......
...
...
WHIRL くる
ささっ SCOOT
I forgot the rice.
☆ペチッ SLAP
AND YOU CALL YOURSELF JAPANESE ?!
OH AND, UH... SORRY, BUT...
I MIGHT'VE ALSO FORGOTTEN, THE, UH, MISO SOUP... AND SIDE DISHES, AND STUFF...
too...
YOU TOTAL DITZ!
WH-WHAT ARE WE SUPPOSED TO HAVE FOR DINNER NOW?!
GEEEEZ
She forgot, there's nothing we can do...
calm down, calm down.
For tonight let's just...

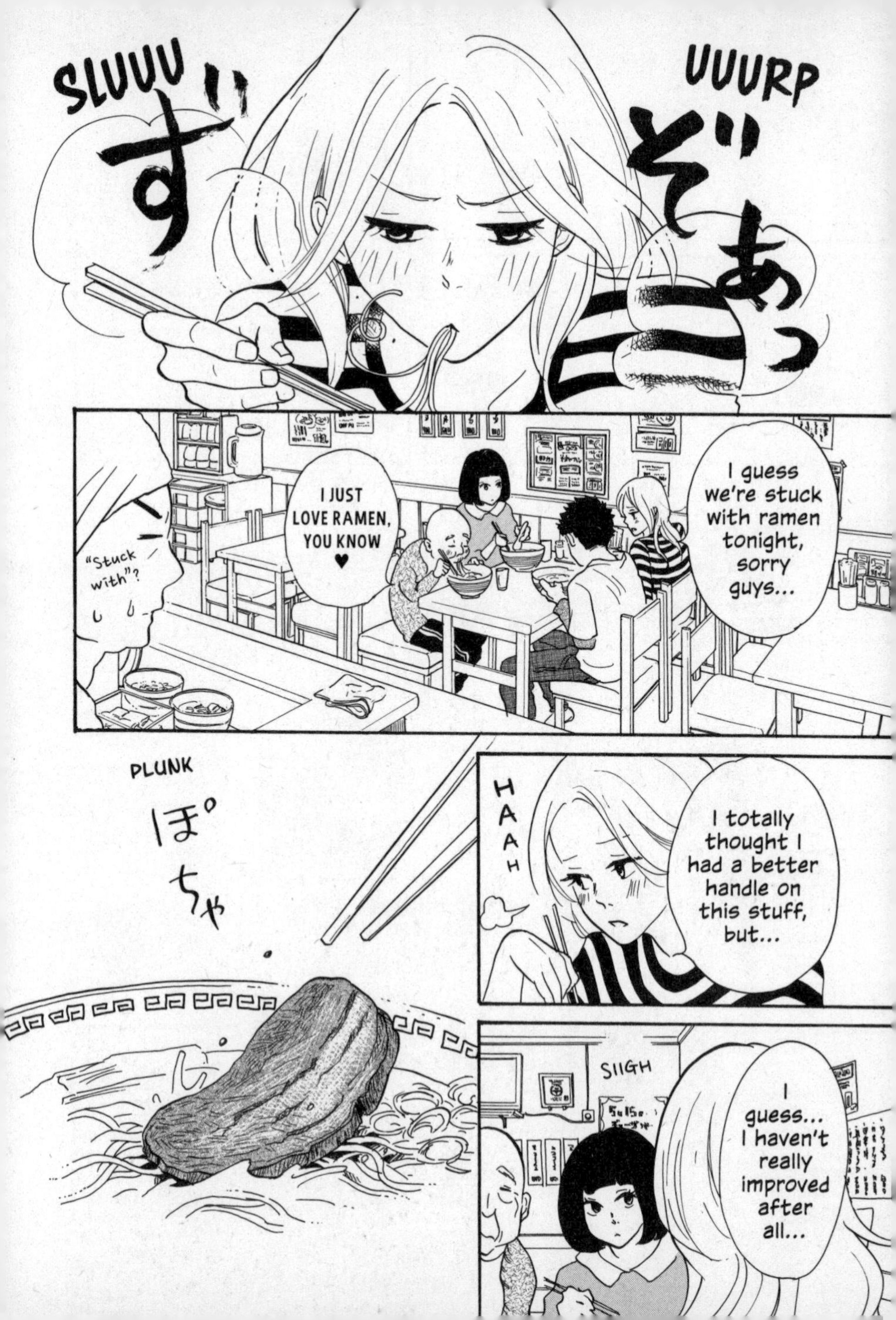

SLUUU
すい
UUURP
ぞあっ
I guess we're stuck with ramen tonight, sorry guys...
I JUST LOVE RAMEN, YOU KNOW ♥
"Stuck with"?
I totally thought I had a better handle on this stuff, but...
HAAH
SIIGH
I guess... I haven't really improved after all...
PLUNK
ぽちゃ

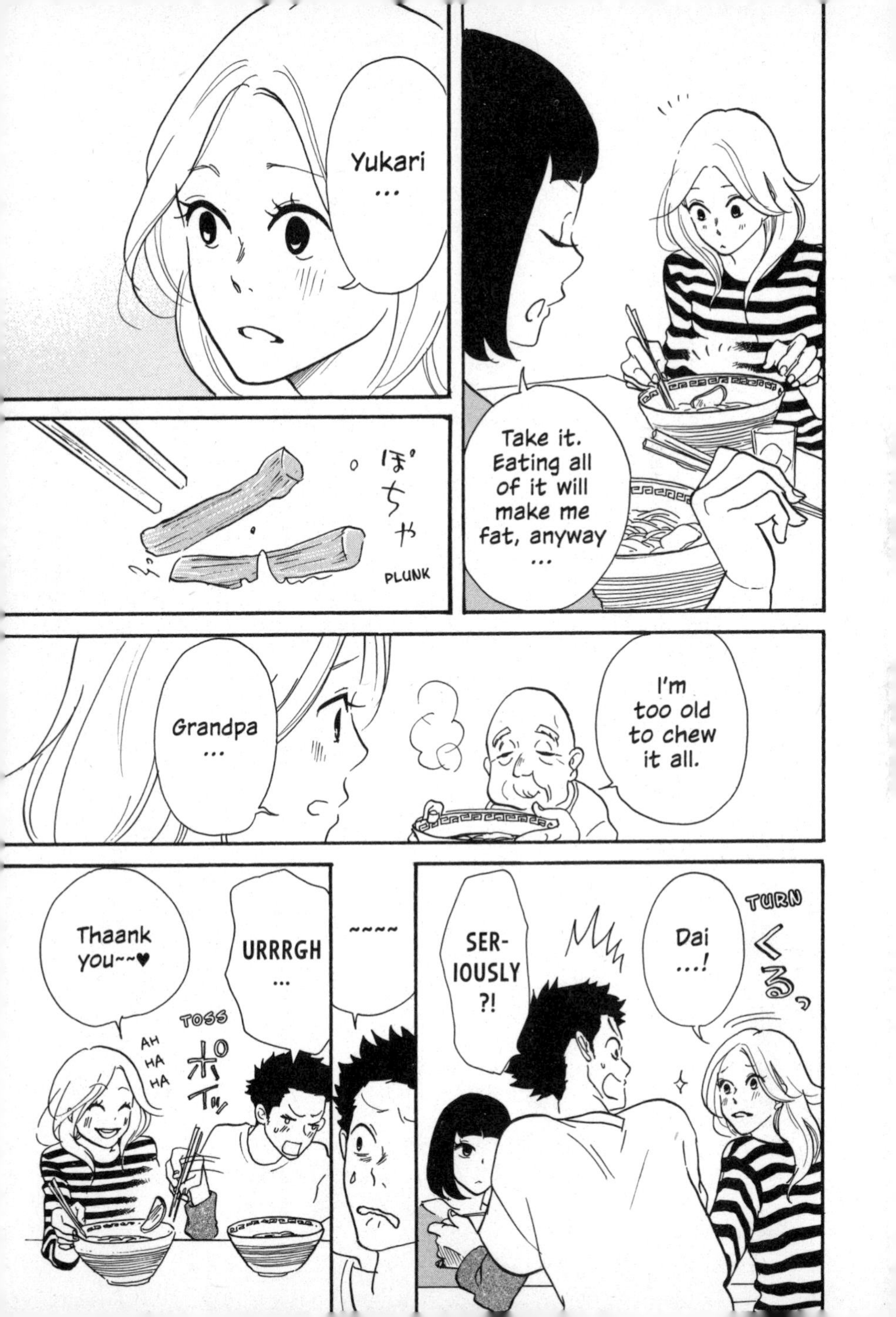
Take it. Eating all of it will make me fat, anyway ...
Yukari ...
ぽちゃ
PLUNK
I'm too old to chew it all.
Grandpa ...
TURN
くるっ
Dai ...!
SER-IOUSLY ?!
~~~~
URRRGH ...
Thaank you~~♥
TOSS
ポイッ
AH HA HA
~~~~

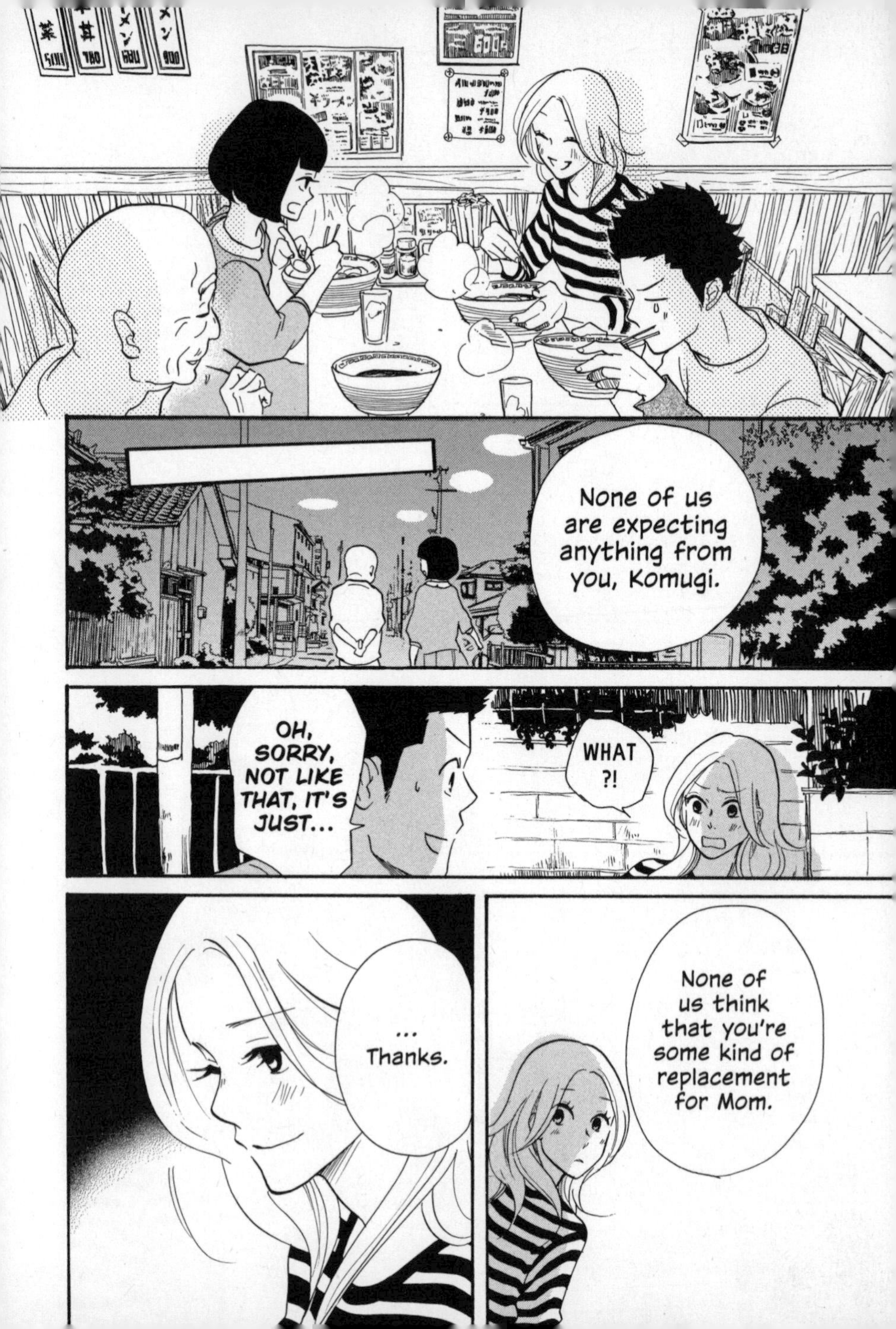
None of us are expecting anything from you, Komugi.
WHAT ?!
OH, SORRY, NOT LIKE THAT, IT'S JUST...
None of us think that you're some kind of replacement for Mom.
... Thanks.

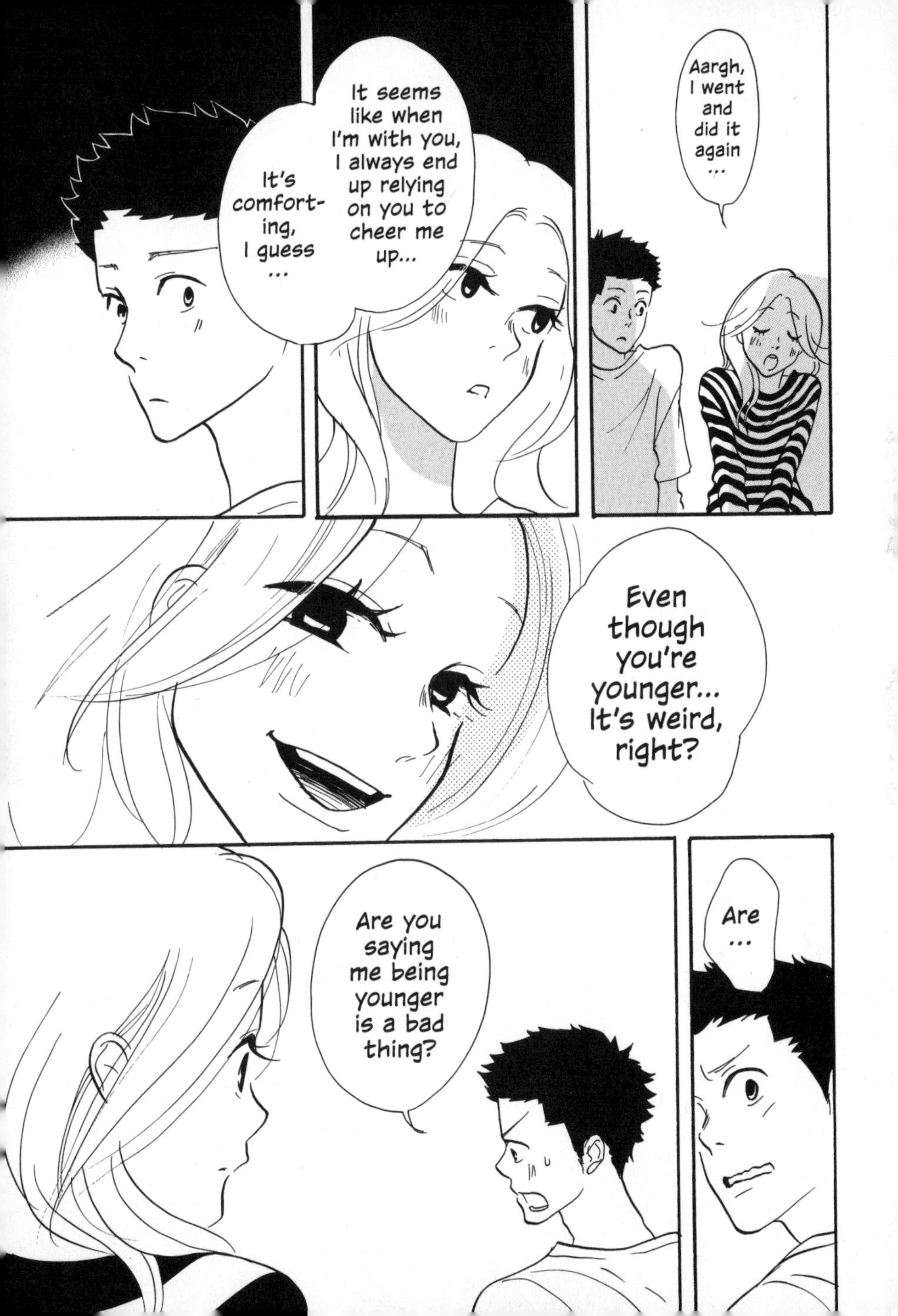
Aargh, I went and did it again ...
It seems like when I'm with you, I always end up relying on you to cheer me up...
It's comforting, I guess ...
Even though you're younger... It's weird, right?
Are ...
Are you saying me being younger is a bad thing?

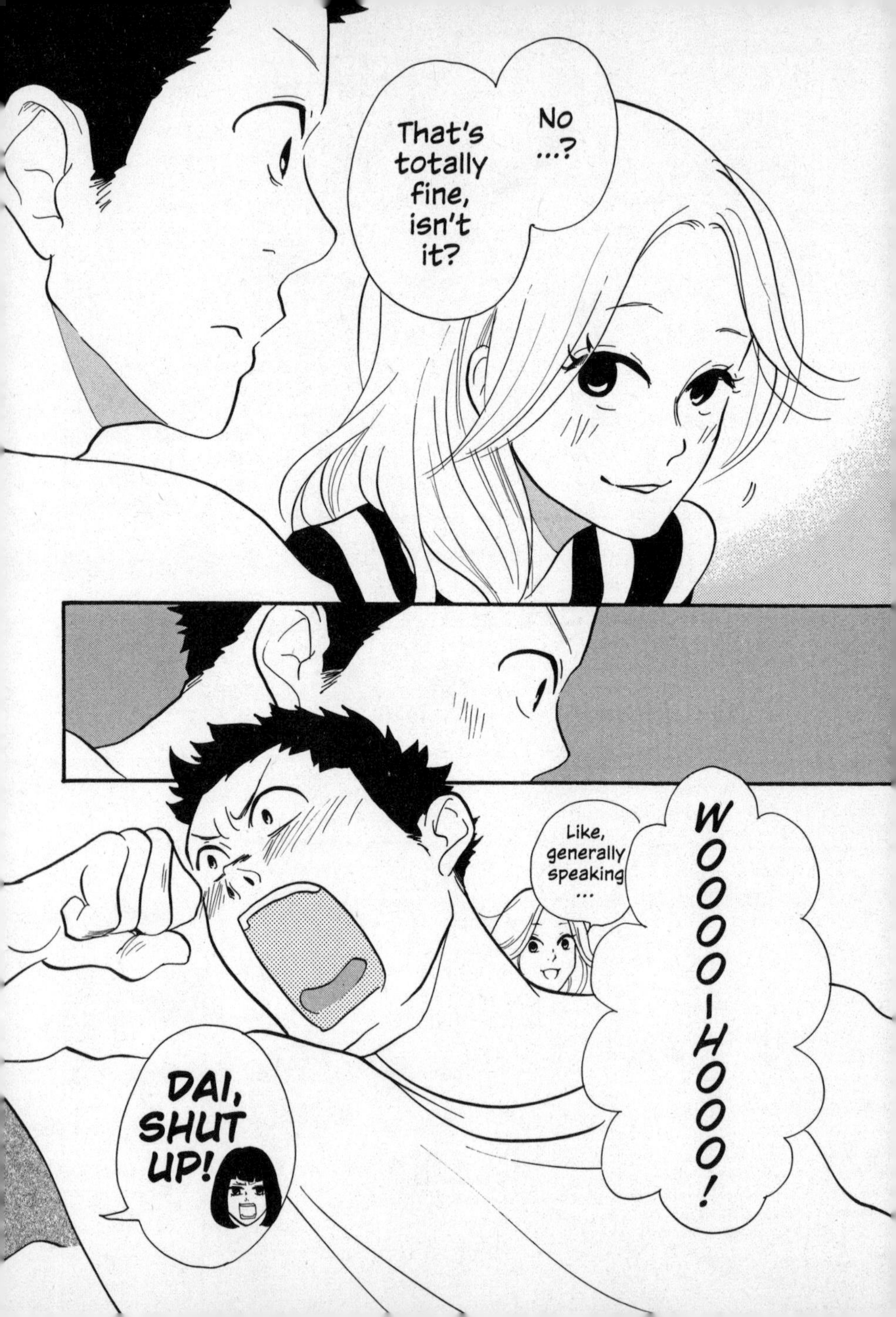
No ...?
That's totally fine, isn't it?
WOOOOO-HOOOO!
Like, generally speaking ...
DAI, SHUT UP!

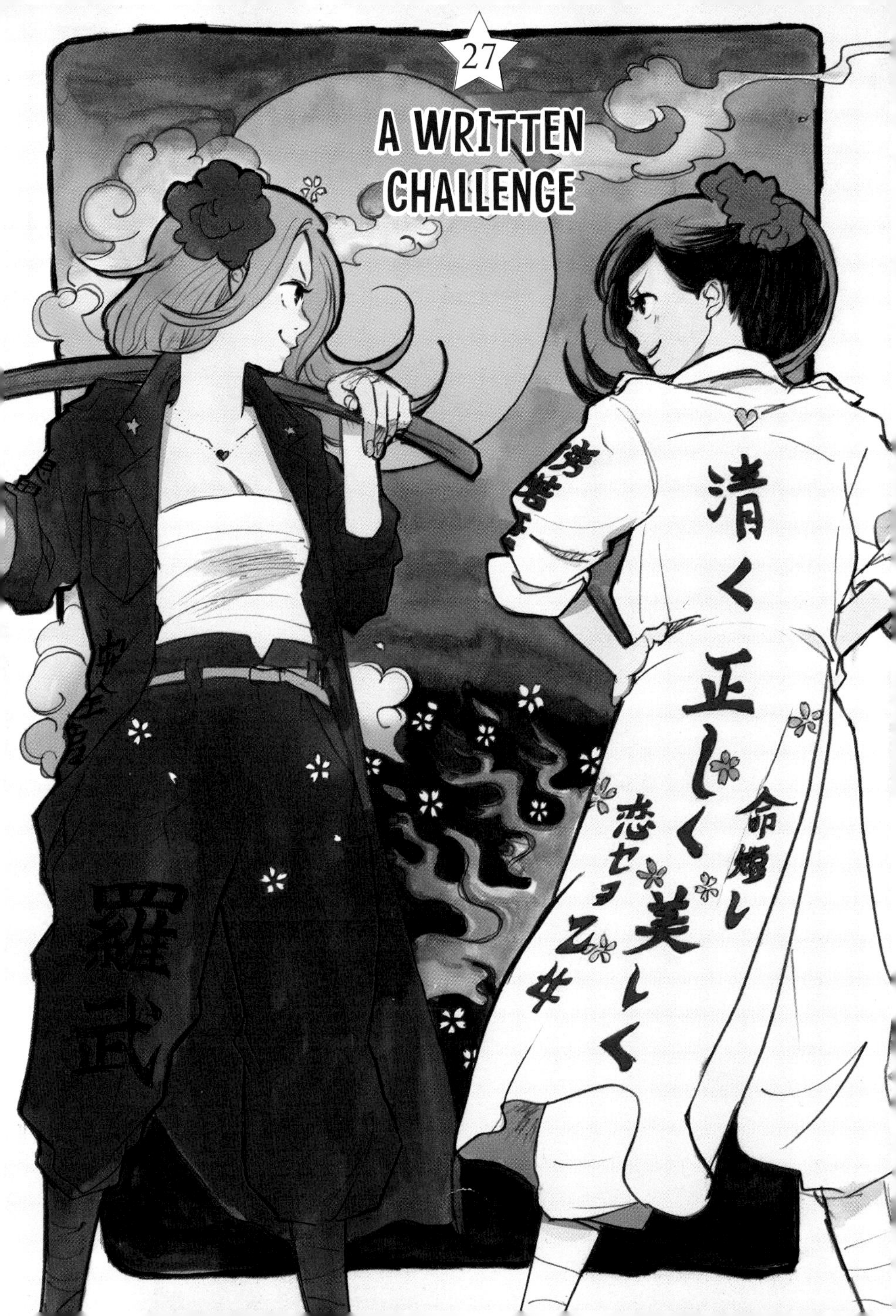
27
A WRITTEN CHALLENGE
清く正しく美しく
命短し恋セヨ乙女
羅武

The Delinquent HOUSEWIFE!

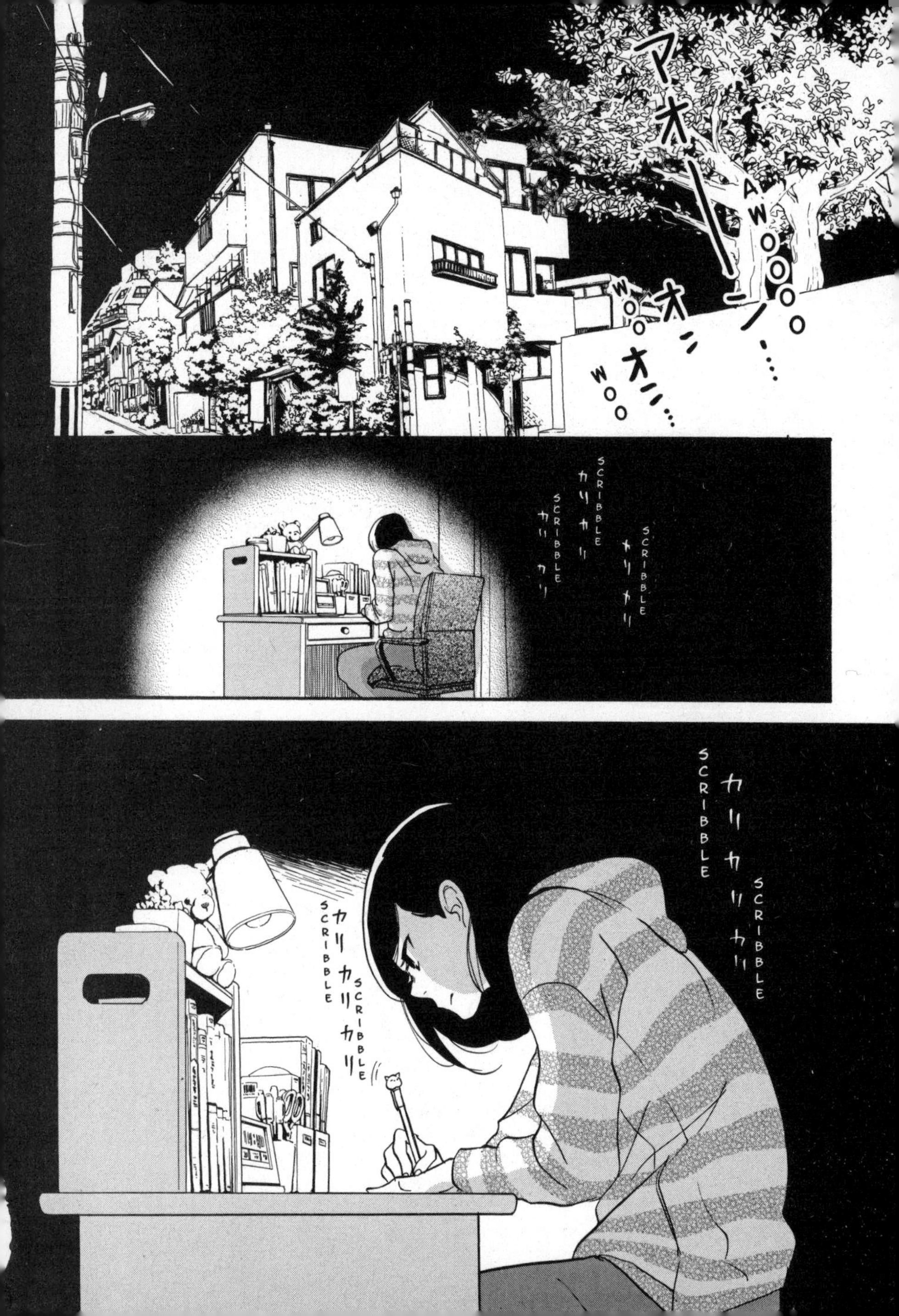

アオーーン…
AWOOOO
オ～ン
WOO
オ～ン…
WOO
カリカリ
SCRIBBLE
カリカリ
SCRIBBLE
カリカリ
SCRIBBLE
カリカリ
SCRIBBLE
カリカリ
SCRIBBLE
カリカリ
SCRIBBLE

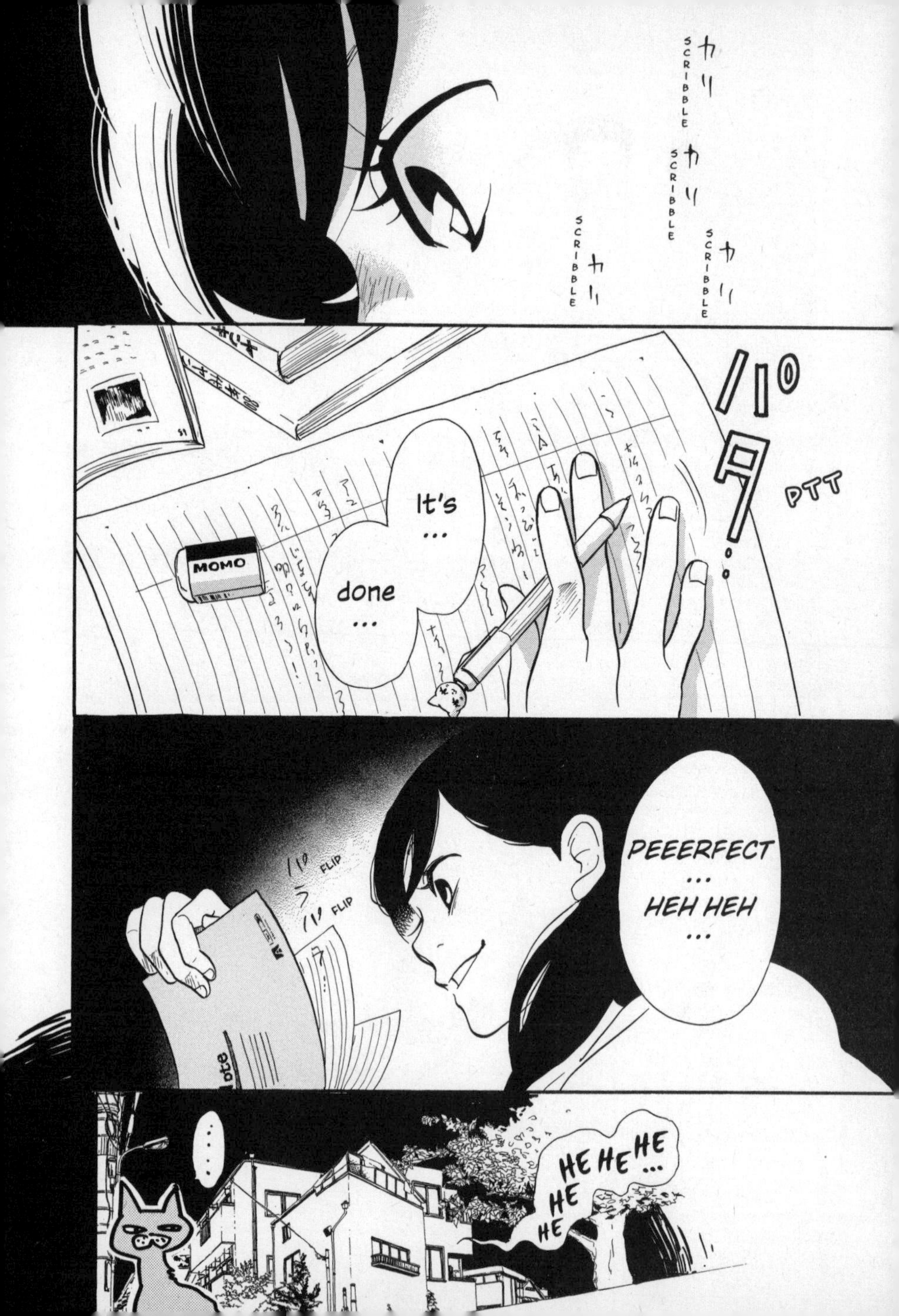
SCRIBBLE
SCRIBBLE
SCRIBBLE
SCRIBBLE
PTT
It's ... done ...
FLIP
FLIP
PEEERFECT ... HEH HEH ...
HE HE HE HE HE ...
...

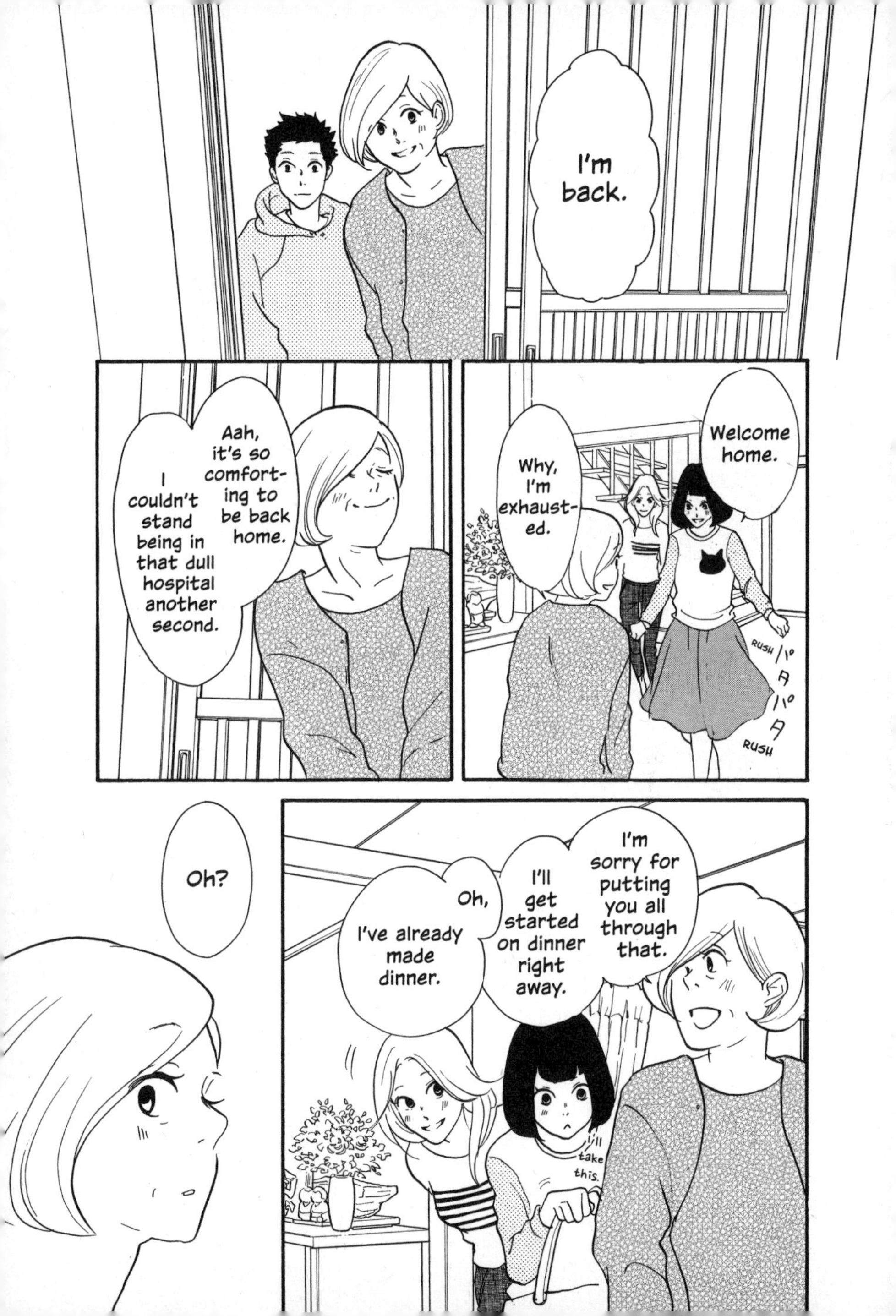
I'm back.
Welcome home.
Why, I'm exhausted.
RUSH パタ パタ RUSH
Aah, it's so comforting to be back home.
I couldn't stand being in that dull hospital another second.
I'm sorry for putting you all through that.
I'll get started on dinner right away.
Oh, I've already made dinner.
I'll take this.
Oh?

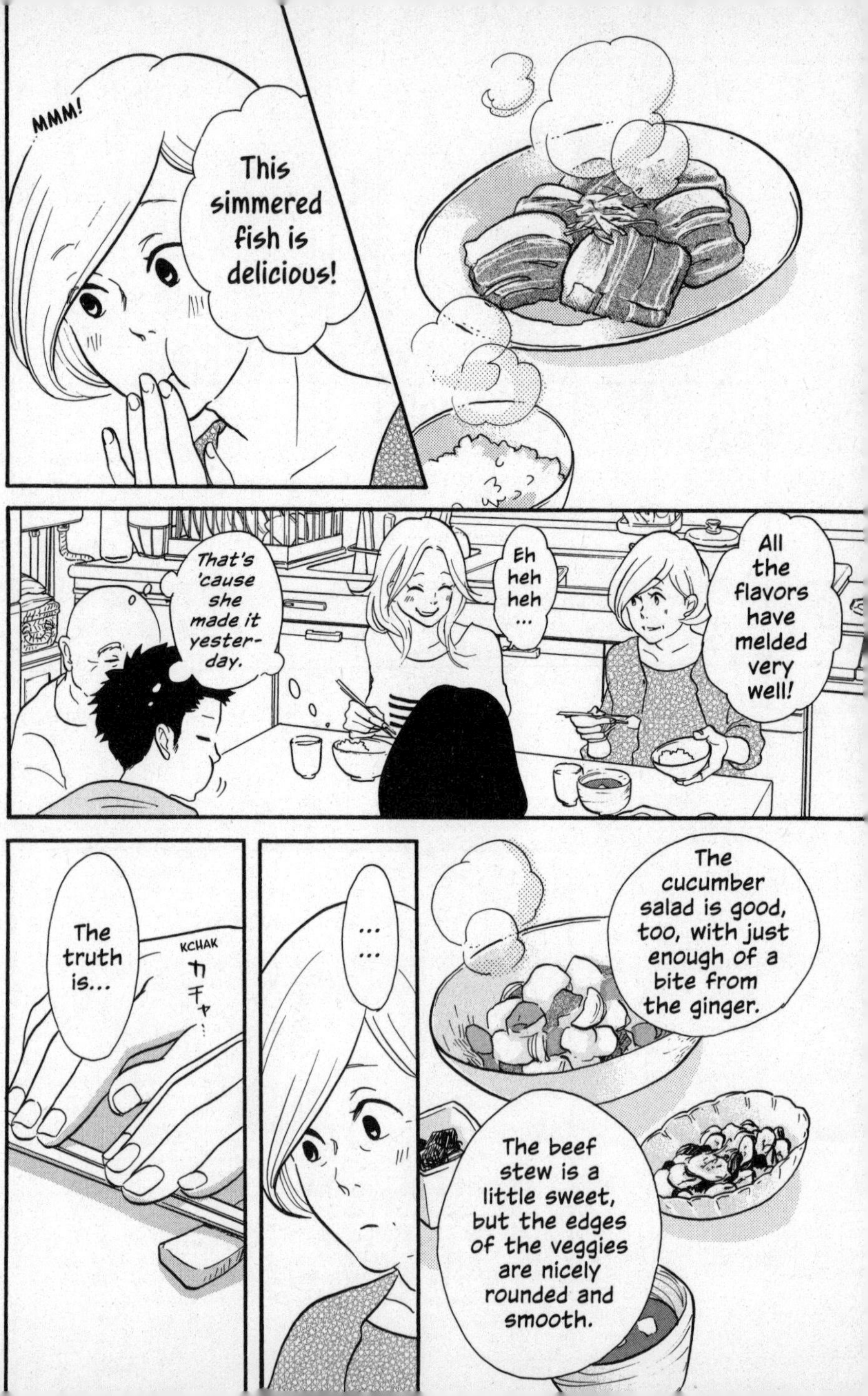
MMM!
This simmered fish is delicious!
All the flavors have melded very well!
Eh heh heh...
That's 'cause she made it yester-day.
The cucumber salad is good, too, with just enough of a bite from the ginger.
The beef stew is a little sweet, but the edges of the veggies are nicely rounded and smooth.
... ...
The truth is...
KCHAK
カチャ…

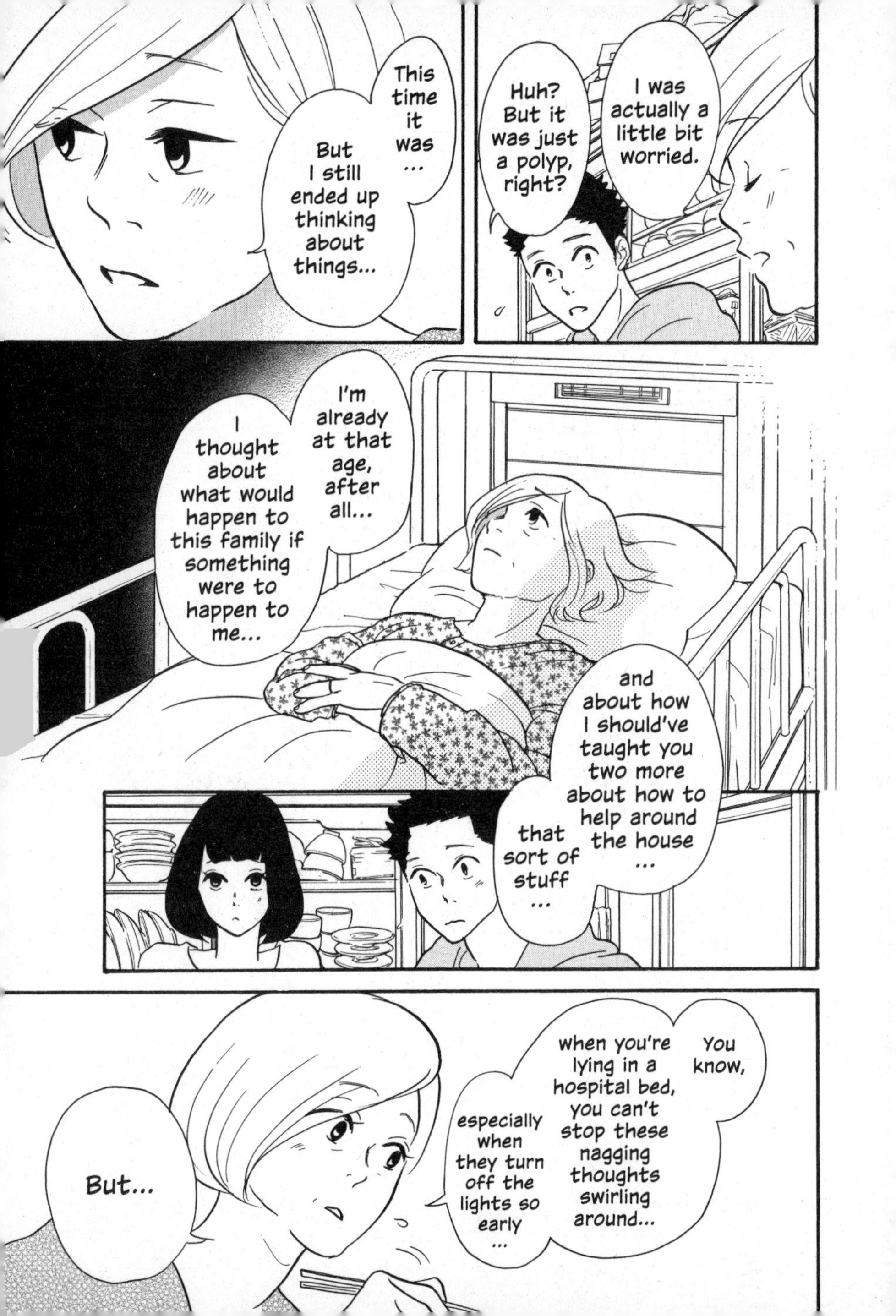
I was actually a little bit worried.
Huh? But it was just a polyp, right?
This time it was...
But I still ended up thinking about things...
I'm already at that age, after all...
I thought about what would happen to this family if something were to happen to me...
and about how I should've taught you two more about how to help around the house...
that sort of stuff...
You know,
when you're lying in a hospital bed, you can't stop these nagging thoughts swirling around...
especially when they turn off the lights so early...
But...

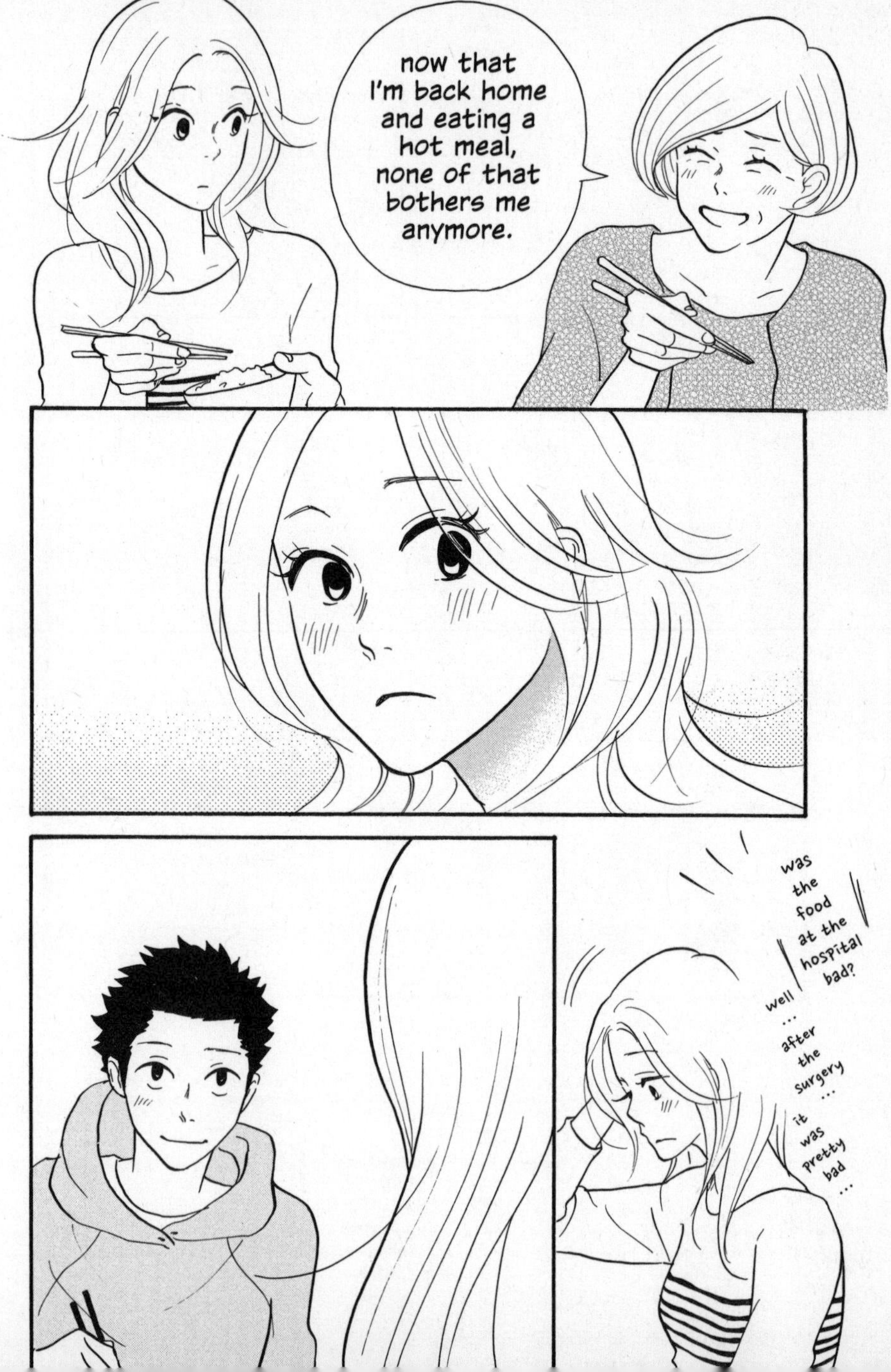
now that I'm back home and eating a hot meal, none of that bothers me anymore.
was the food at the hospital bad?
well... after the surgery... it was pretty bad...

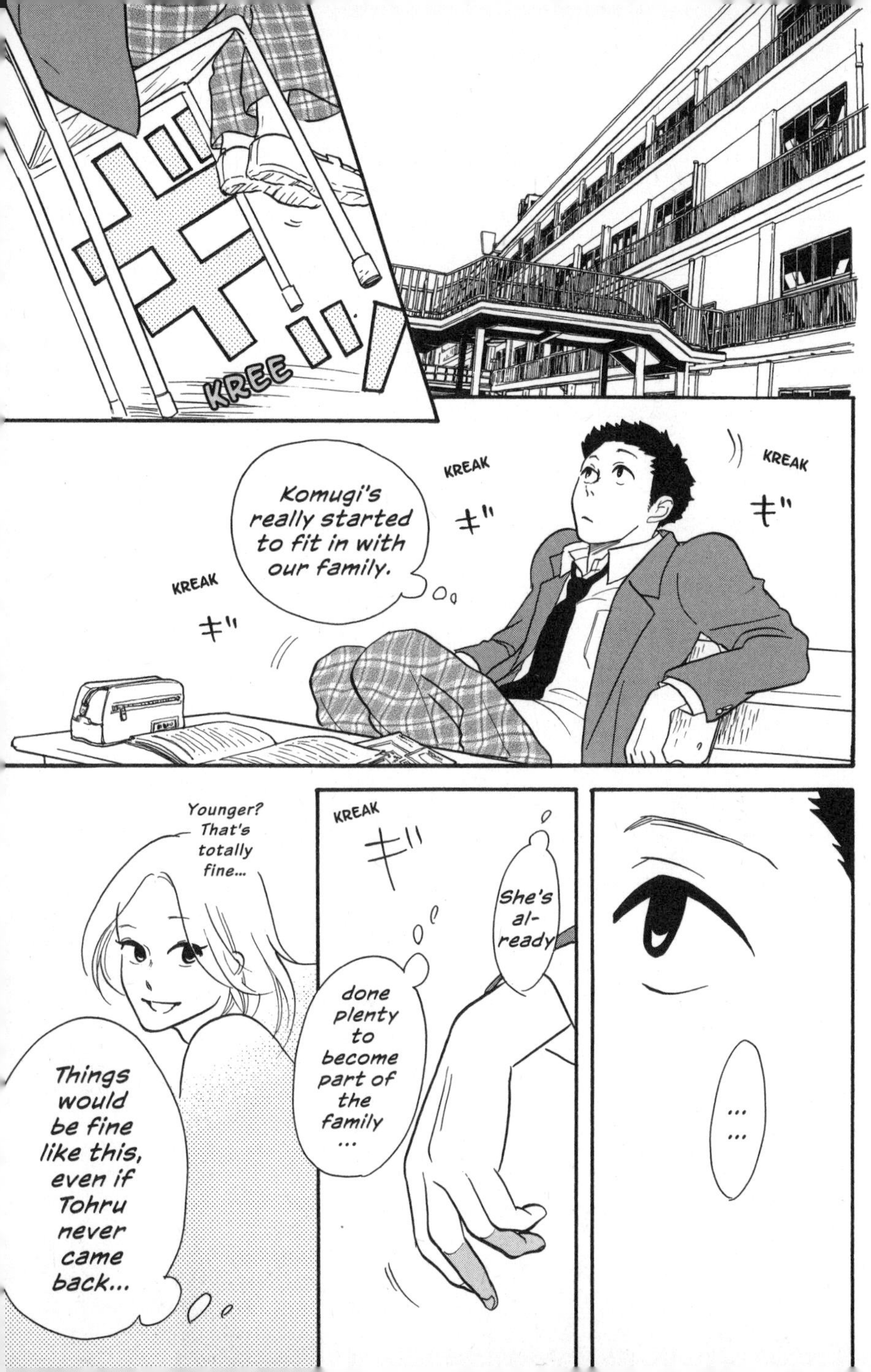
KREE
KREAK
ギ
Komugi's really started to fit in with our family.
KREAK
ギ
KREAK
ギ
……
KREAK
ギ
She's al-ready done plenty to become part of the family…
Younger? That's totally fine...
Things would be fine like this, even if Tohru never came back...

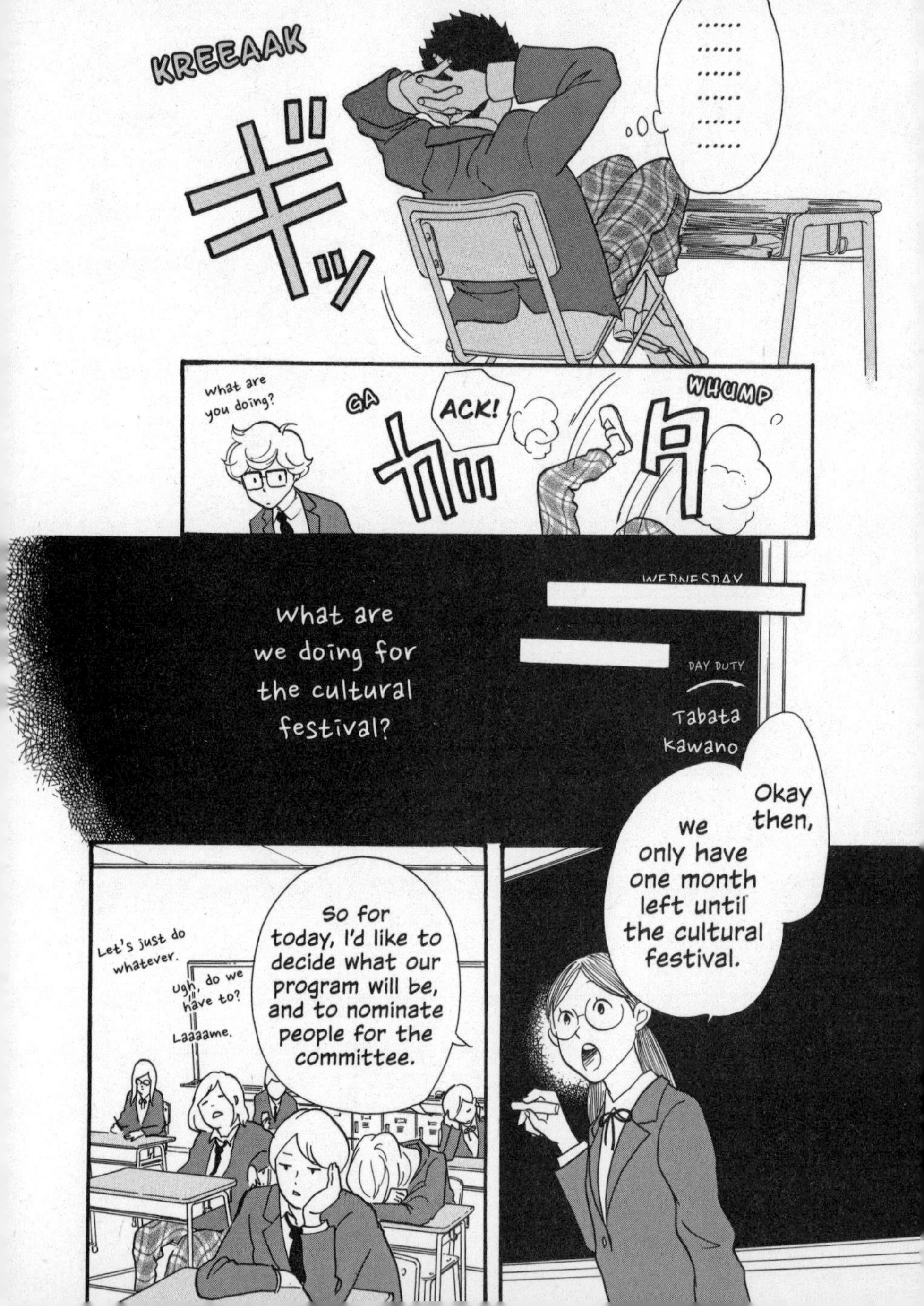
......
......
......
......
......
......
KREEAAK
ギッ
WHUMP
ACK!
GA
ガッ
What are you doing?
WEDNESDAY
DAY DUTY
Tabata
Kawano
What are we doing for the cultural festival?
Okay then, we only have one month left until the cultural festival.
So for today, I'd like to decide what our program will be, and to nominate people for the committee.
Let's just do whatever.
Ugh, do we have to?
Laaaame.

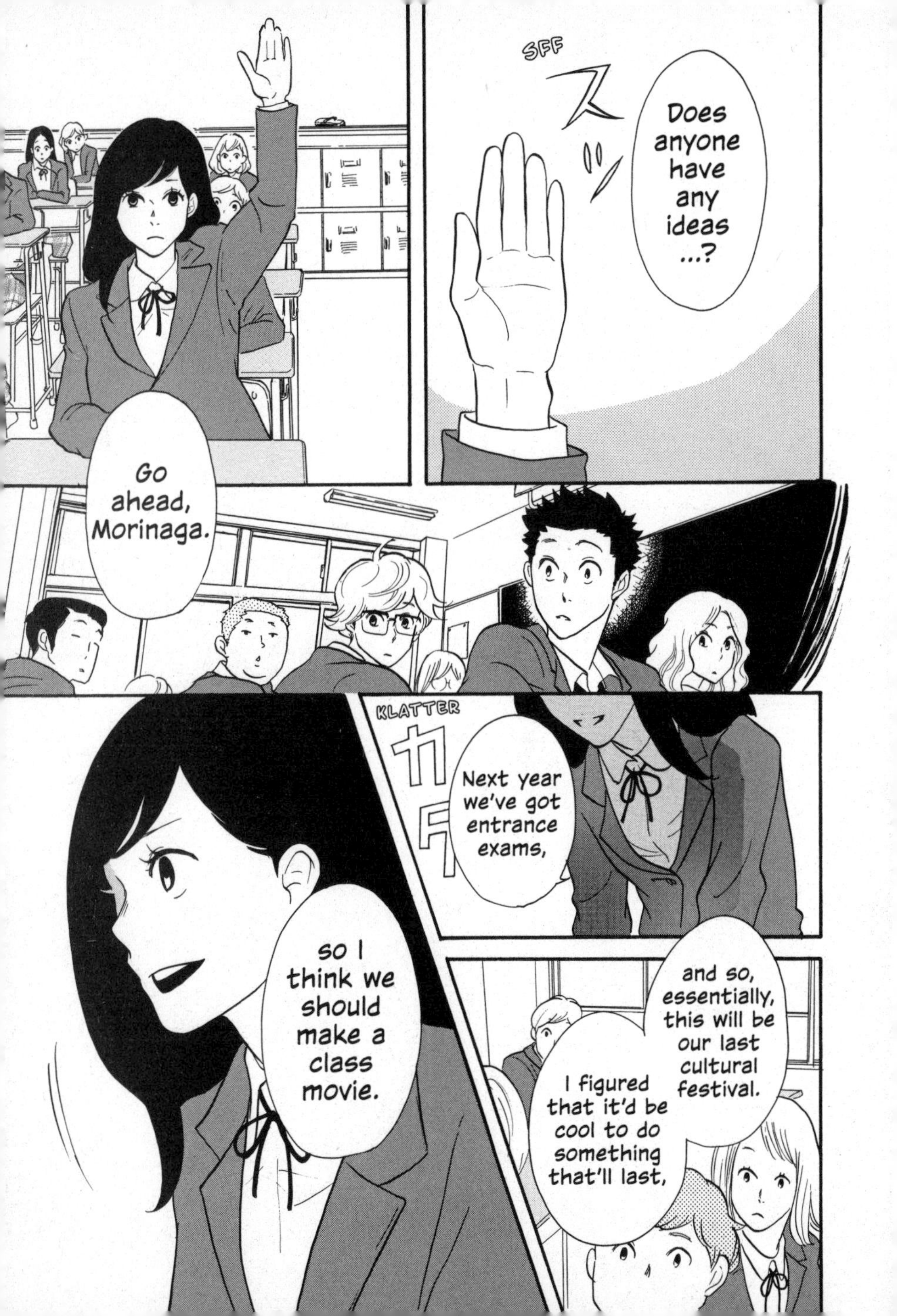
SFF
Does anyone have any ideas ...?
Go ahead, Morinaga.
KLATTER
Next year we've got entrance exams,
and so, essentially, this will be our last cultural festival.
I figured that it'd be cool to do something that'll last,
so I think we should make a class movie.

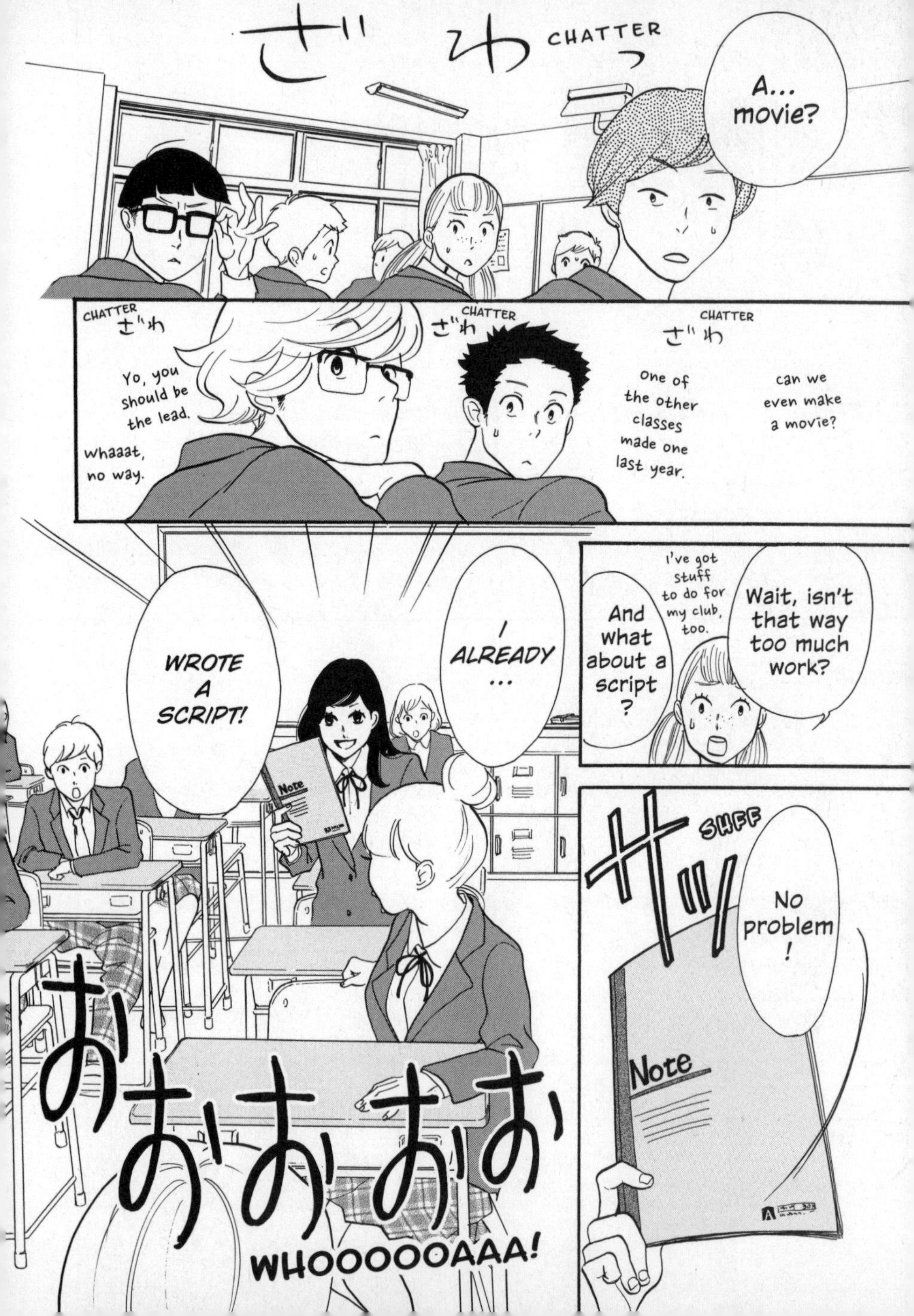
ざわ
CHATTER
A... movie?
can we even make a movie?
One of the other classes made one last year.
CHATTER
ざわ
CHATTER
ざわ
CHATTER
ざわ
Yo, you should be the lead.
Whaaat, no way.
Wait, isn't that way too much work?
I've got stuff to do for my club, too.
And what about a script?
サッ
SHFF
No problem!
Note
I ALREADY...
WROTE A SCRIPT!
Note
おおおお
WHOOOOOAAA!

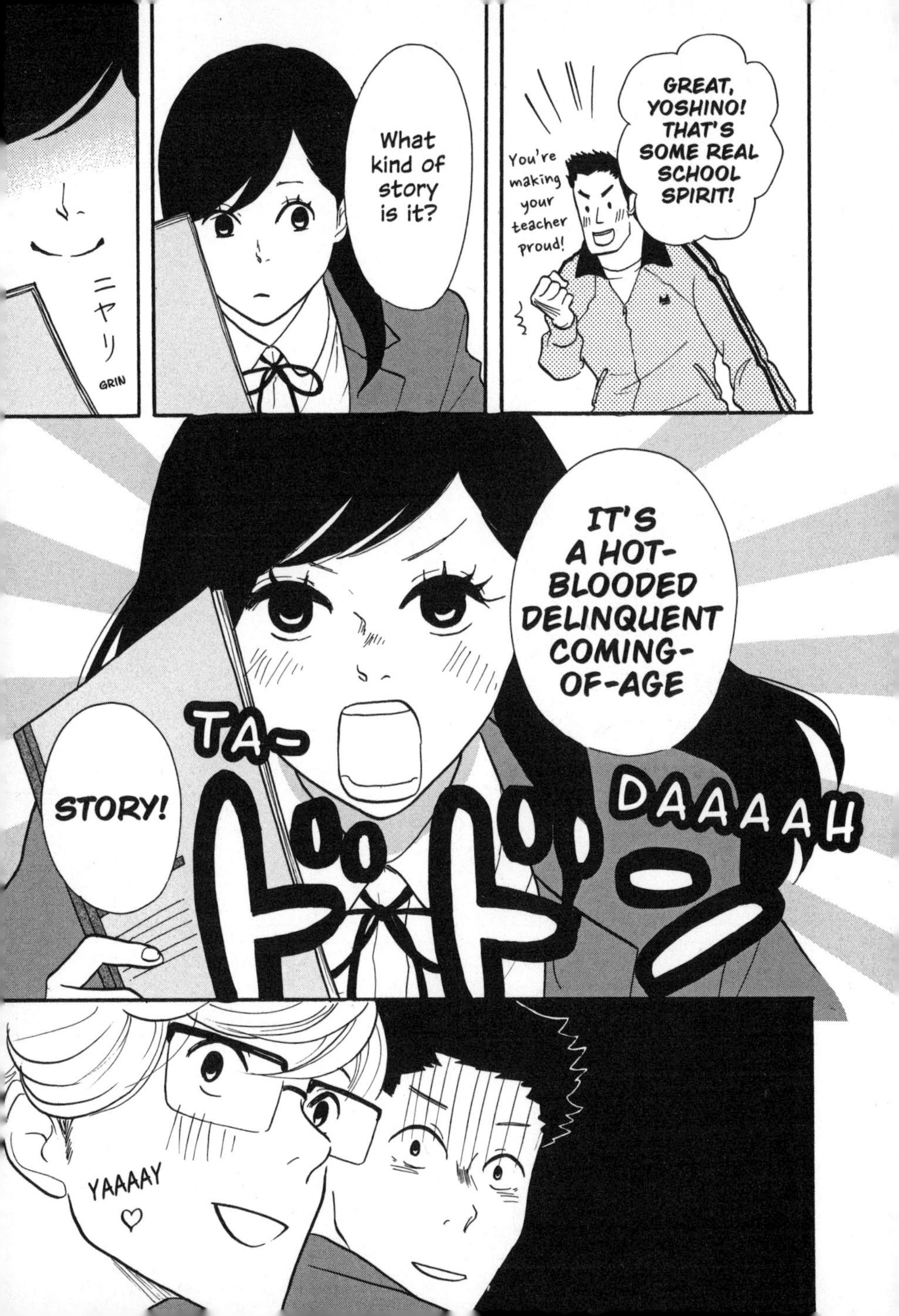
GREAT, YOSHINO! THAT'S SOME REAL SCHOOL SPIRIT!
You're making your teacher proud!
What kind of story is it?
ニヤリ
GRIN
IT'S A HOT-BLOODED DELINQUENT COMING-OF-AGE
TA-
DAAAAAH
STORY!
YAAAAY ♡

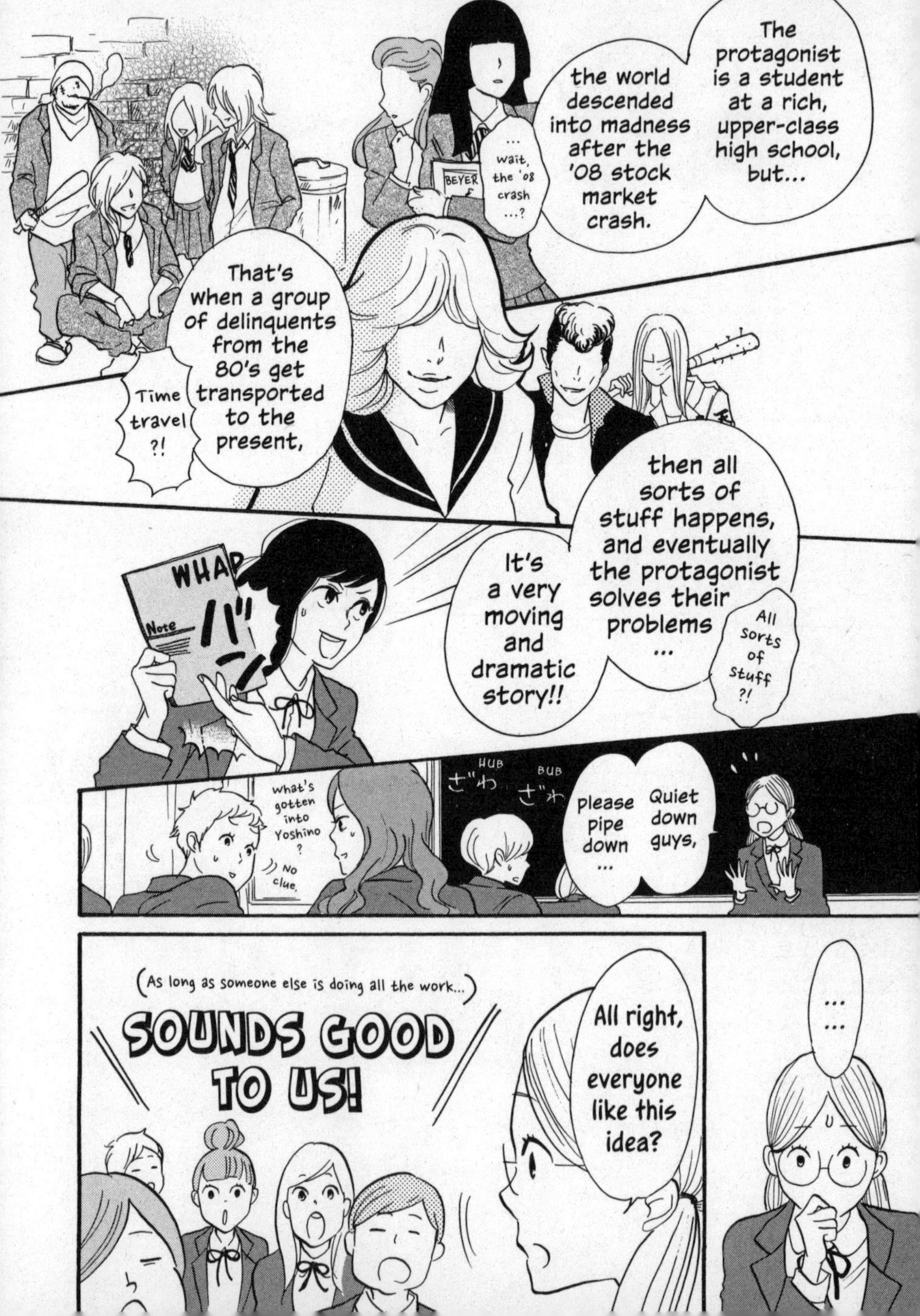
The protagonist is a student at a rich, upper-class high school, but...
the world descended into madness after the '08 stock market crash.
... wait, the '08 crash ...?
BEYER
That's when a group of delinquents from the 80's get transported to the present,
Time travel?!
then all sorts of stuff happens, and eventually the protagonist solves their problems ...
It's a very moving and dramatic story!!
All sorts of stuff?!
WHAP
バ
Note
Quiet down guys,
please pipe down ...
HUB BUB
ざわ ざわ
what's gotten into Yoshino?
No clue.
... ...
All right, does everyone like this idea?
(As long as someone else is doing all the work...)
SOUNDS GOOD TO US!

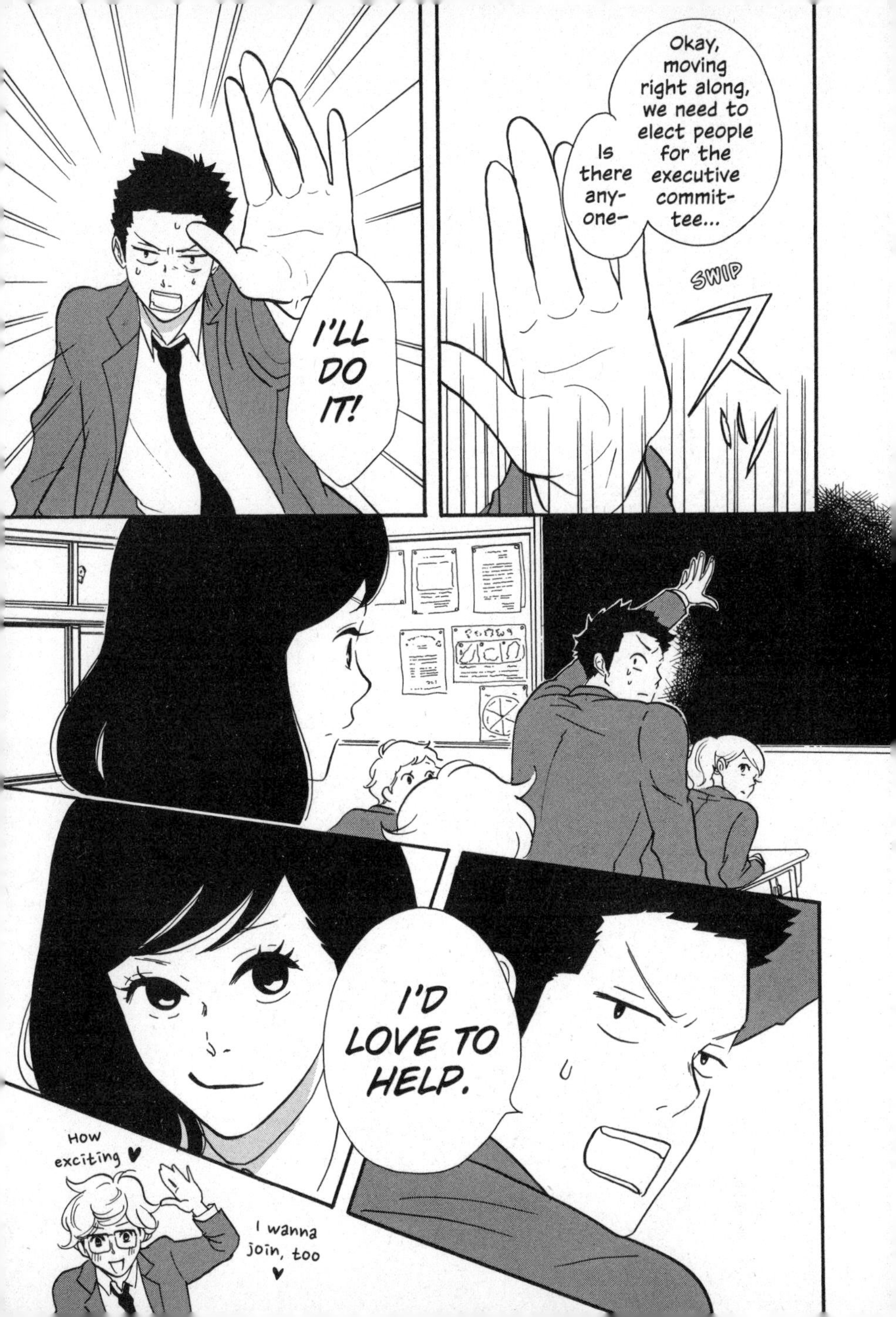
Okay, moving right along, we need to elect people for the executive commit-tee...
Is there any-one-
SWIP
I'LL DO IT!
I'D LOVE TO HELP.
How exciting ♥
I wanna join, too ♥

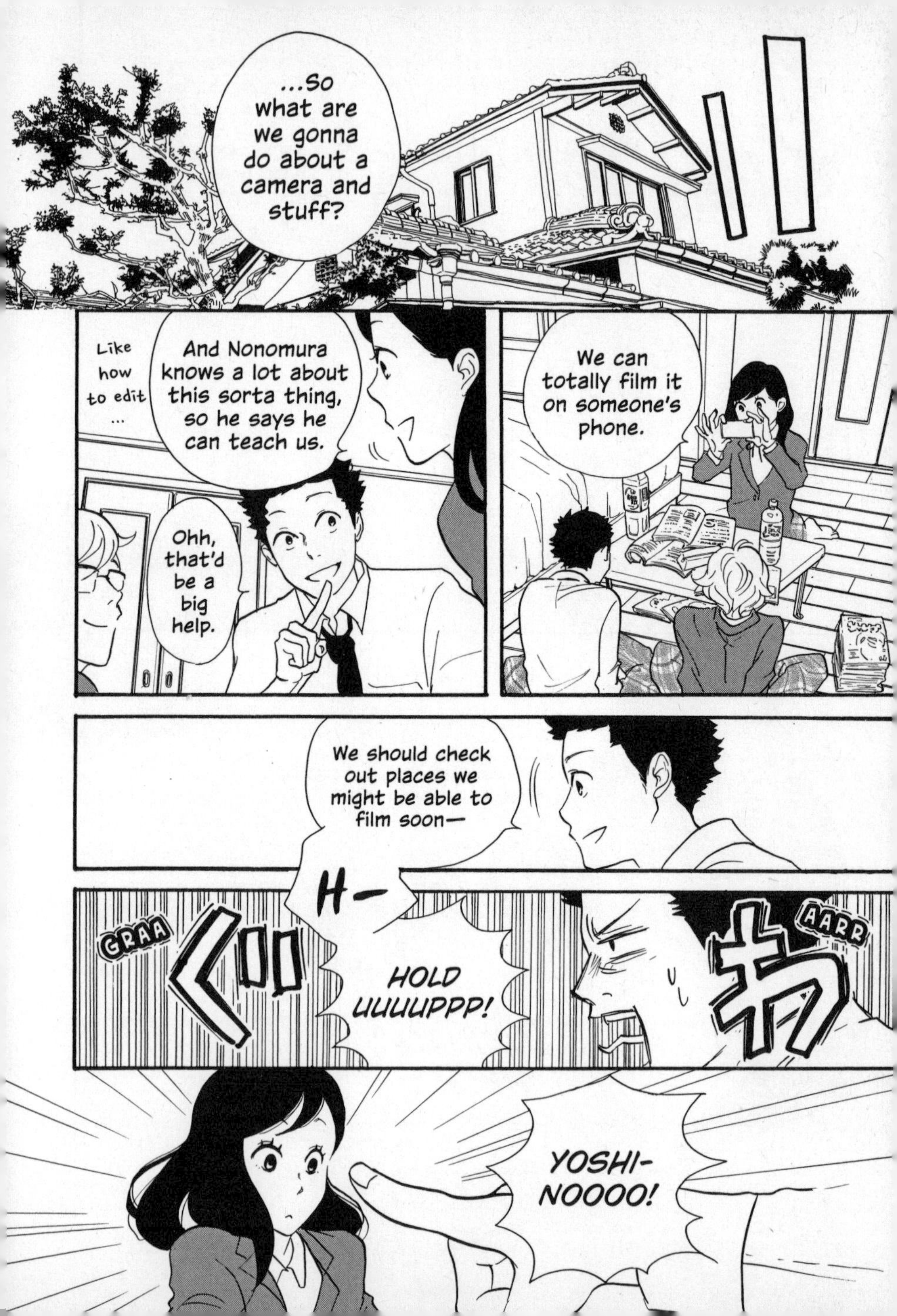
...So what are we gonna do about a camera and stuff?
We can totally film it on someone's phone.
And Nonomura knows a lot about this sorta thing, so he says he can teach us.
Like how to edit ...
Ohh, that'd be a big help.
We should check out places we might be able to film soon—
H—
AARR
GRAA
HOLD UUUUPPP!
YOSHI-NOOOO!

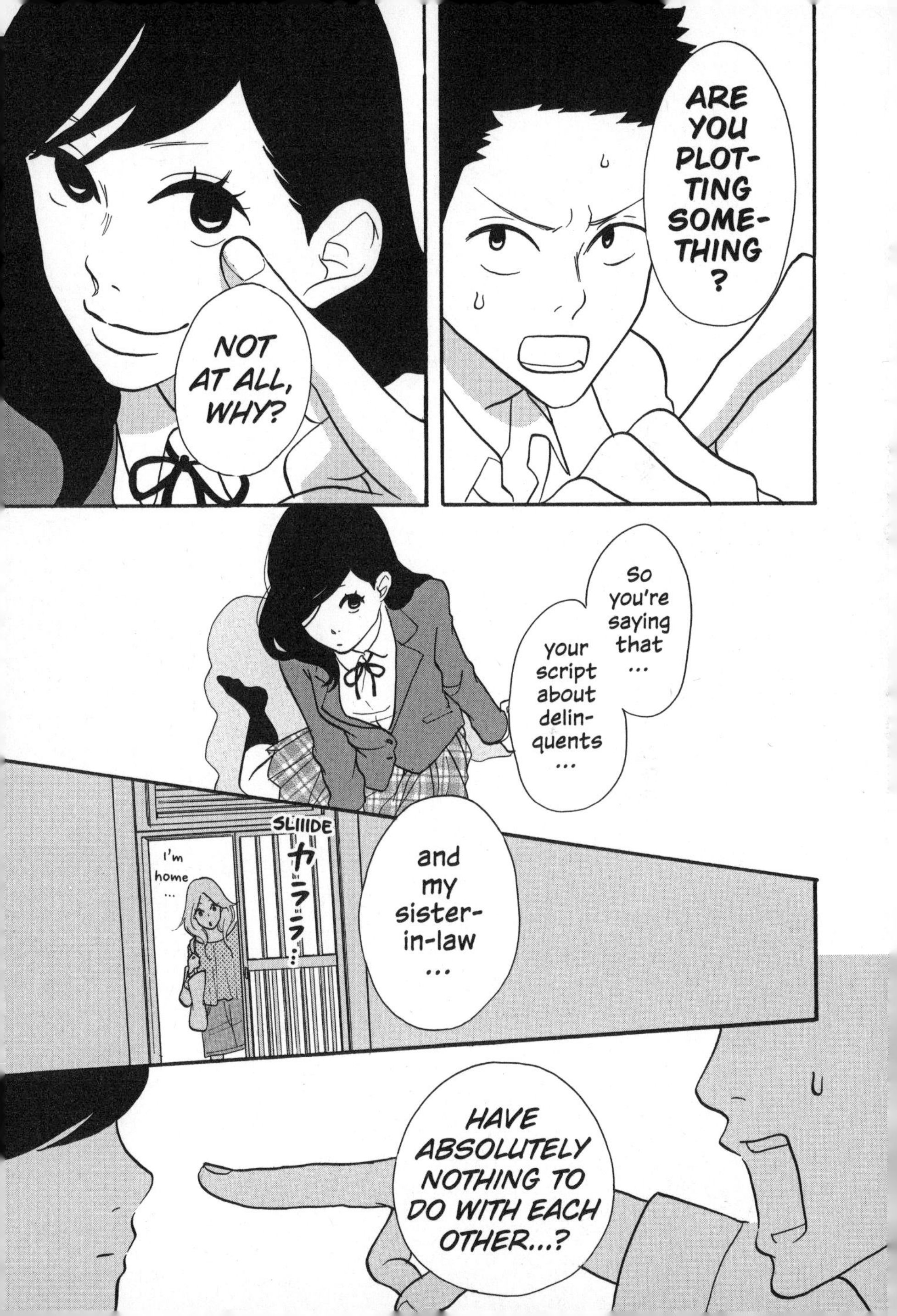
ARE YOU PLOTTING SOMETHING?
NOT AT ALL, WHY?
So you're saying that...
your script about delinquents...
and my sister-in-law...
SLIIIDE
カララ…
I'm home...
HAVE ABSOLUTELY NOTHING TO DO WITH EACH OTHER...?

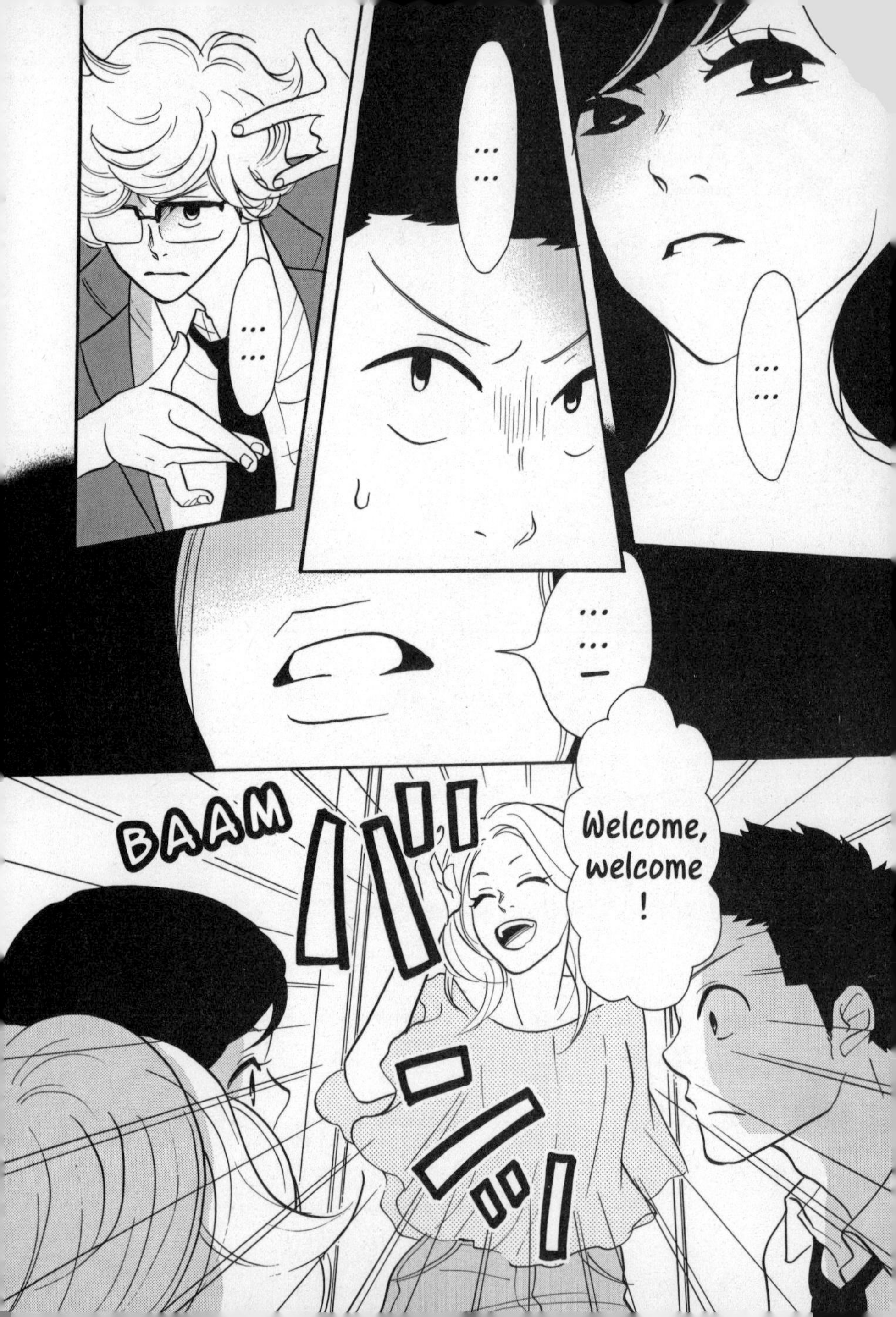
……
……
……
……—
Welcome, welcome!
BAAM

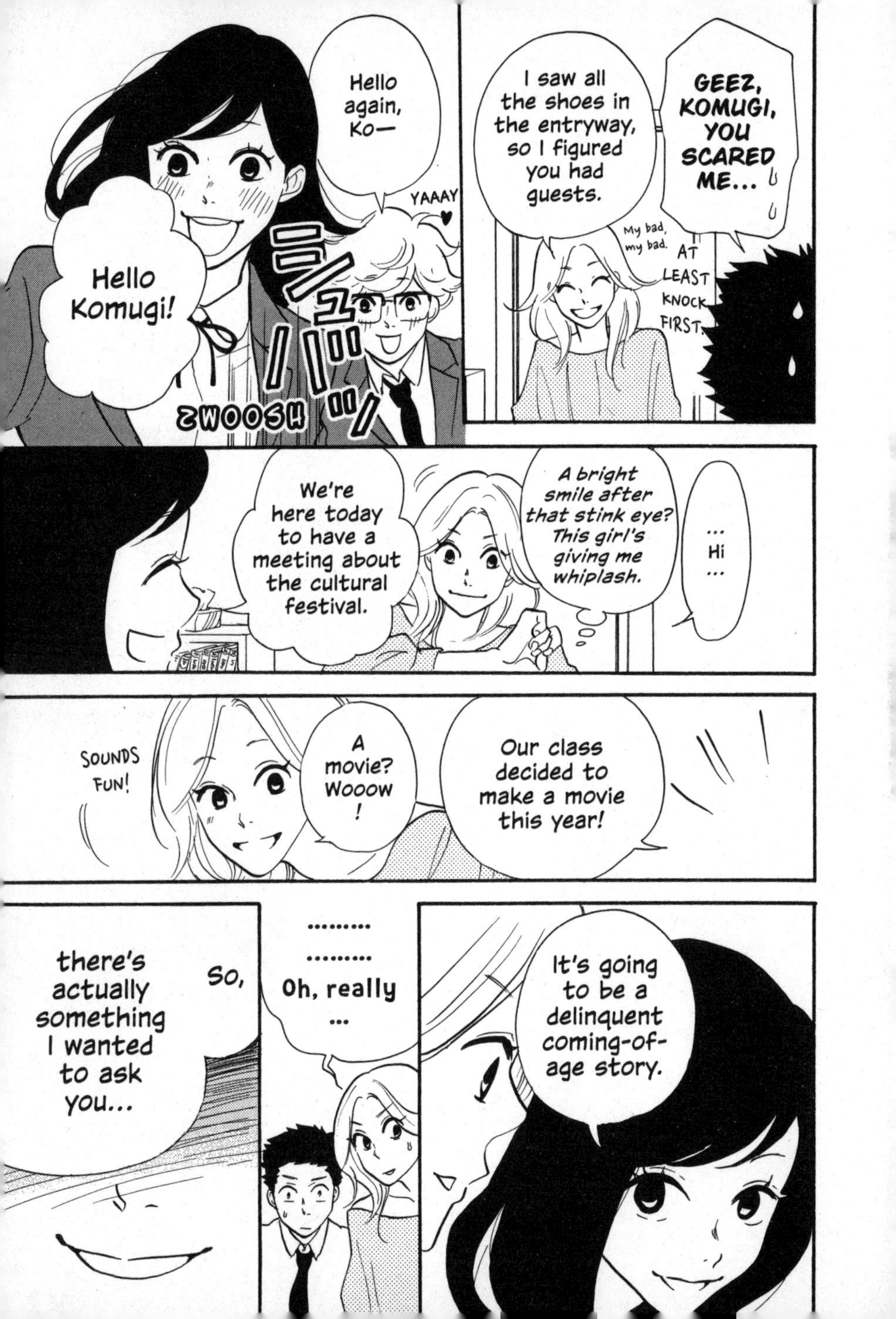
GEEZ, KOMUGI, YOU SCARED ME...
I saw all the shoes in the entryway, so I figured you had guests.
My bad, my bad.
AT LEAST KNOCK FIRST.
Hello again, Ko—
YAAAY ♥
Hello Komugi!
SWOOSH
...Hi...
A bright smile after that stink eye? This girl's giving me whiplash.
We're here today to have a meeting about the cultural festival.
Our class decided to make a movie this year!
A movie? Wooow!
SOUNDS FUN!
It's going to be a delinquent coming-of-age story.
.... Oh, really...
So,
there's actually something I wanted to ask you...

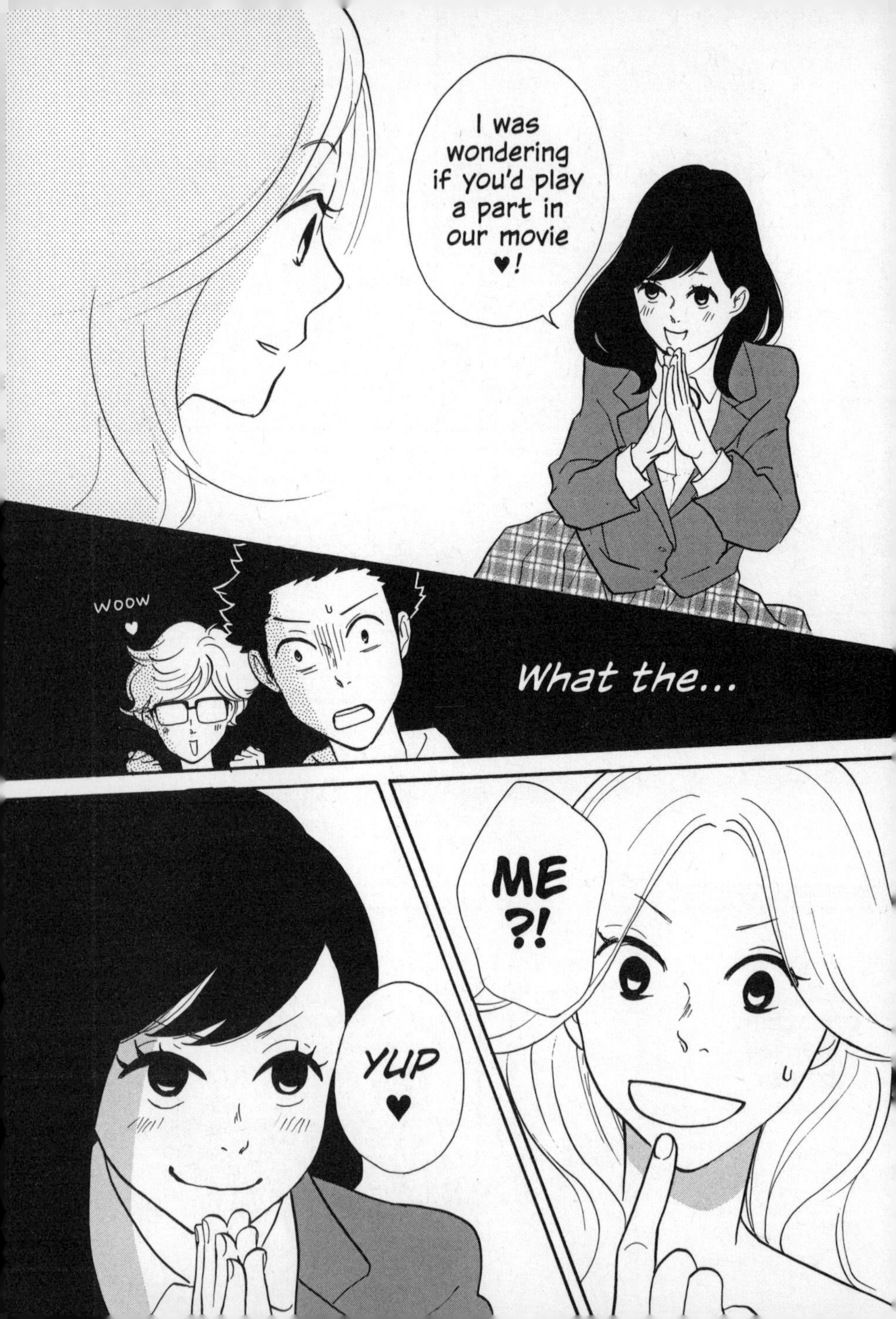
I was wondering if you'd play a part in our movie ♥!
What the...
WOOW ♥
ME ?!
YUP ♥

28
A DANGEROUS OFFER

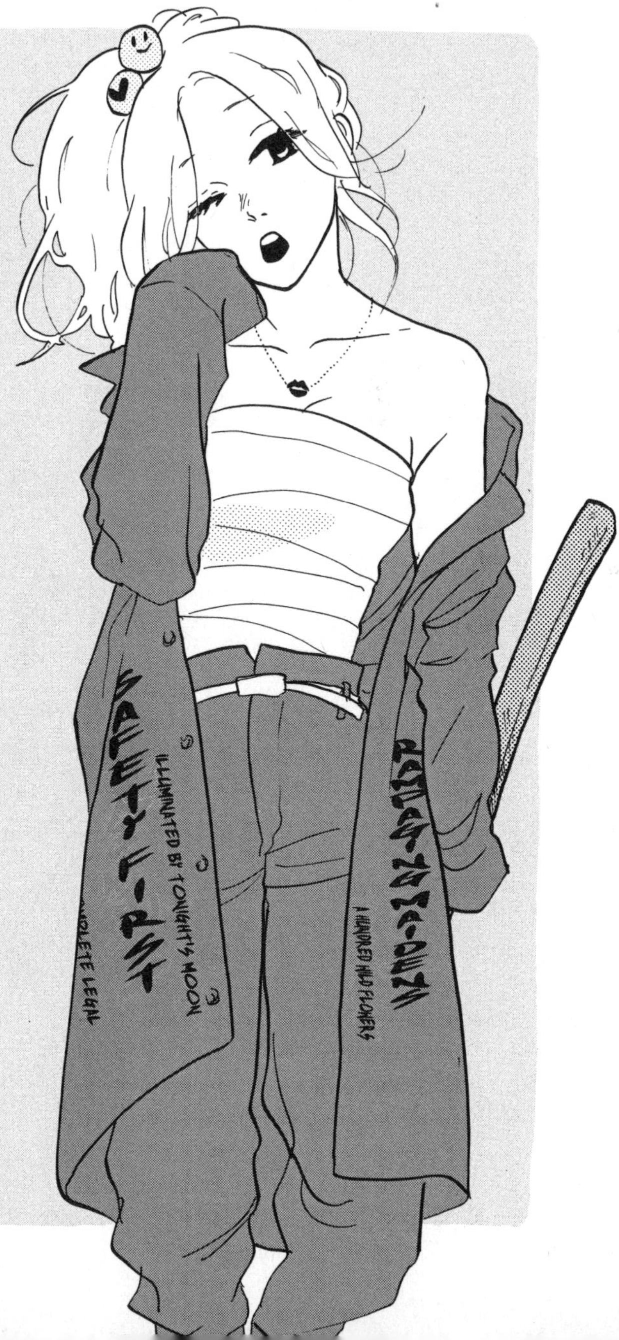
ILLUMINATED BY TONIGHT'S MOON
A HUNDRED WILD FLOWERS

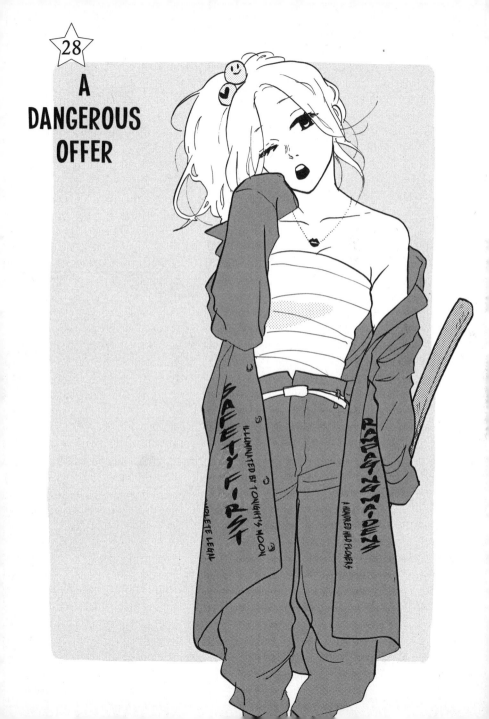

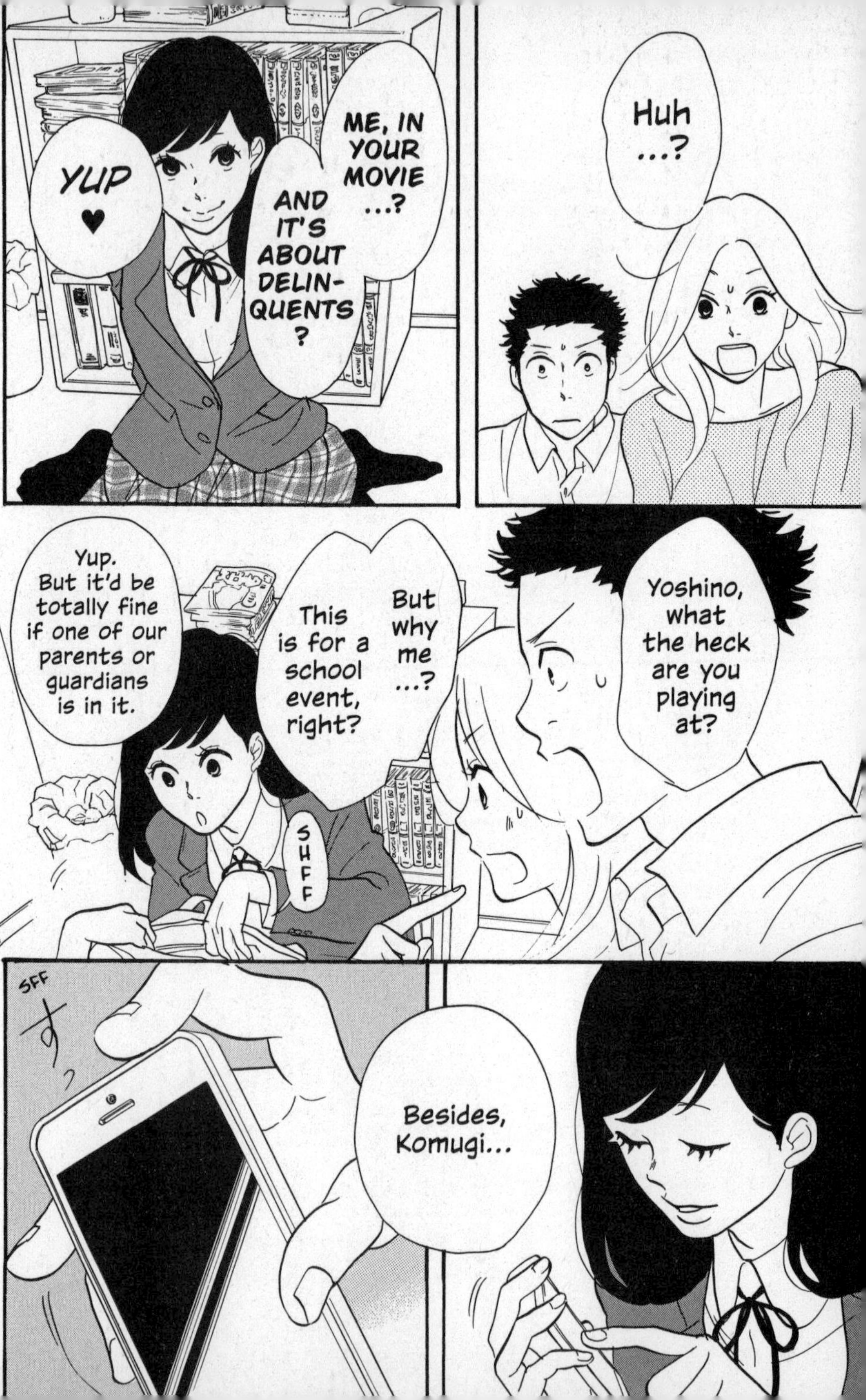
Huh ...?
ME, IN YOUR MOVIE ...?
AND IT'S ABOUT DELIN-QUENTS?
YUP ♥
Yoshino, what the heck are you playing at?
But why me ...?
This is for a school event, right?
SHFF
Yup. But it'd be totally fine if one of our parents or guardians is in it.
Besides, Komugi...
SFF

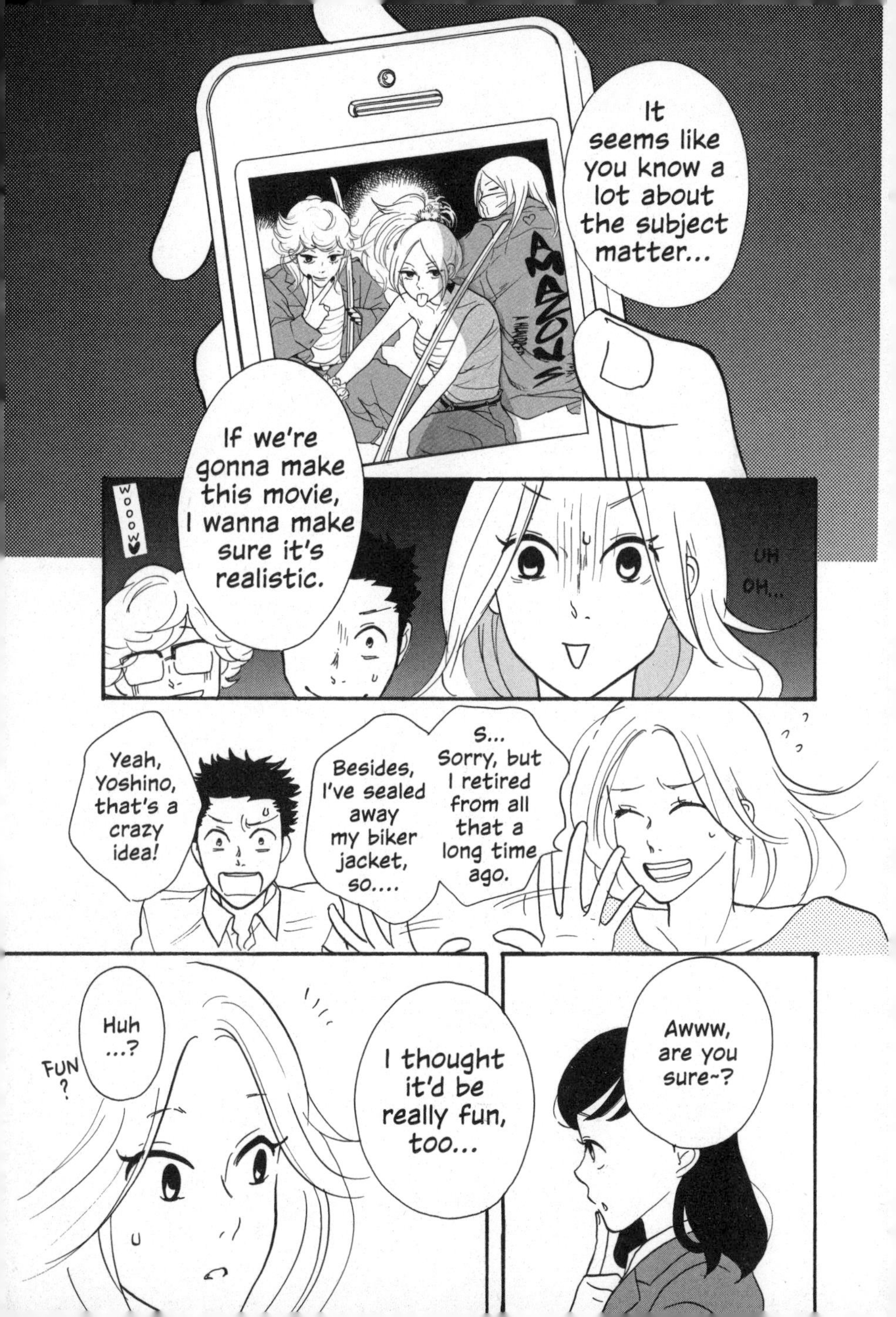
It seems like you know a lot about the subject matter...
If we're gonna make this movie, I wanna make sure it's realistic.
UH OH...
WOOOW♥
S... Sorry, but I retired from all that a long time ago.
Besides, I've sealed away my biker jacket, so....
Yeah, Yoshino, that's a crazy idea!
Awww, are you sure~?
I thought it'd be really fun, too...
Huh ...?
FUN ?

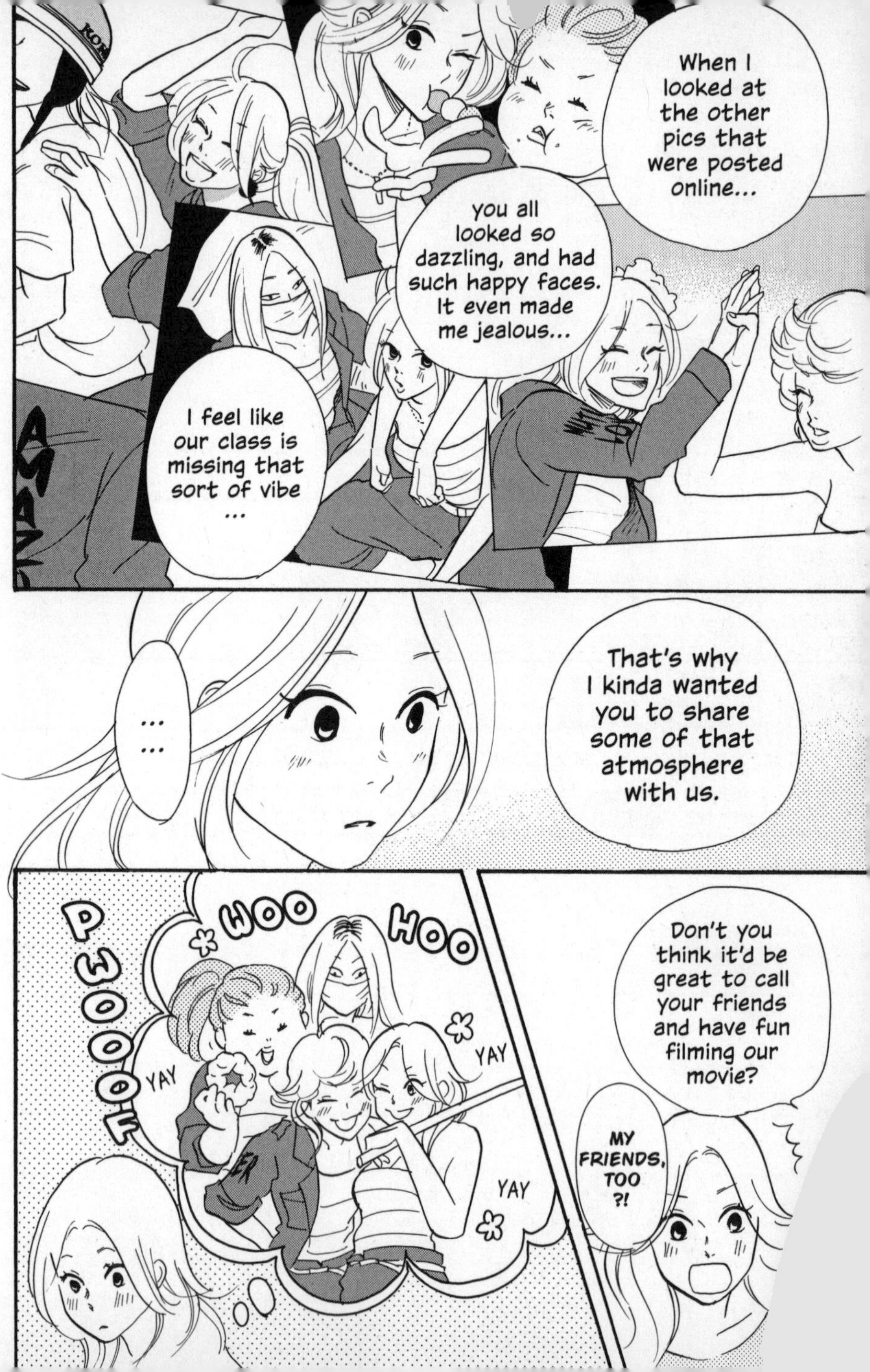
When I looked at the other pics that were posted online...
you all looked so dazzling, and had such happy faces. It even made me jealous...
I feel like our class is missing that sort of vibe ...
That's why I kinda wanted you to share some of that atmosphere with us.
... ...
Don't you think it'd be great to call your friends and have fun filming our movie?
MY FRIENDS, TOO ?!
WOO HOO
PWOOOF
YAY
YAY
YAY

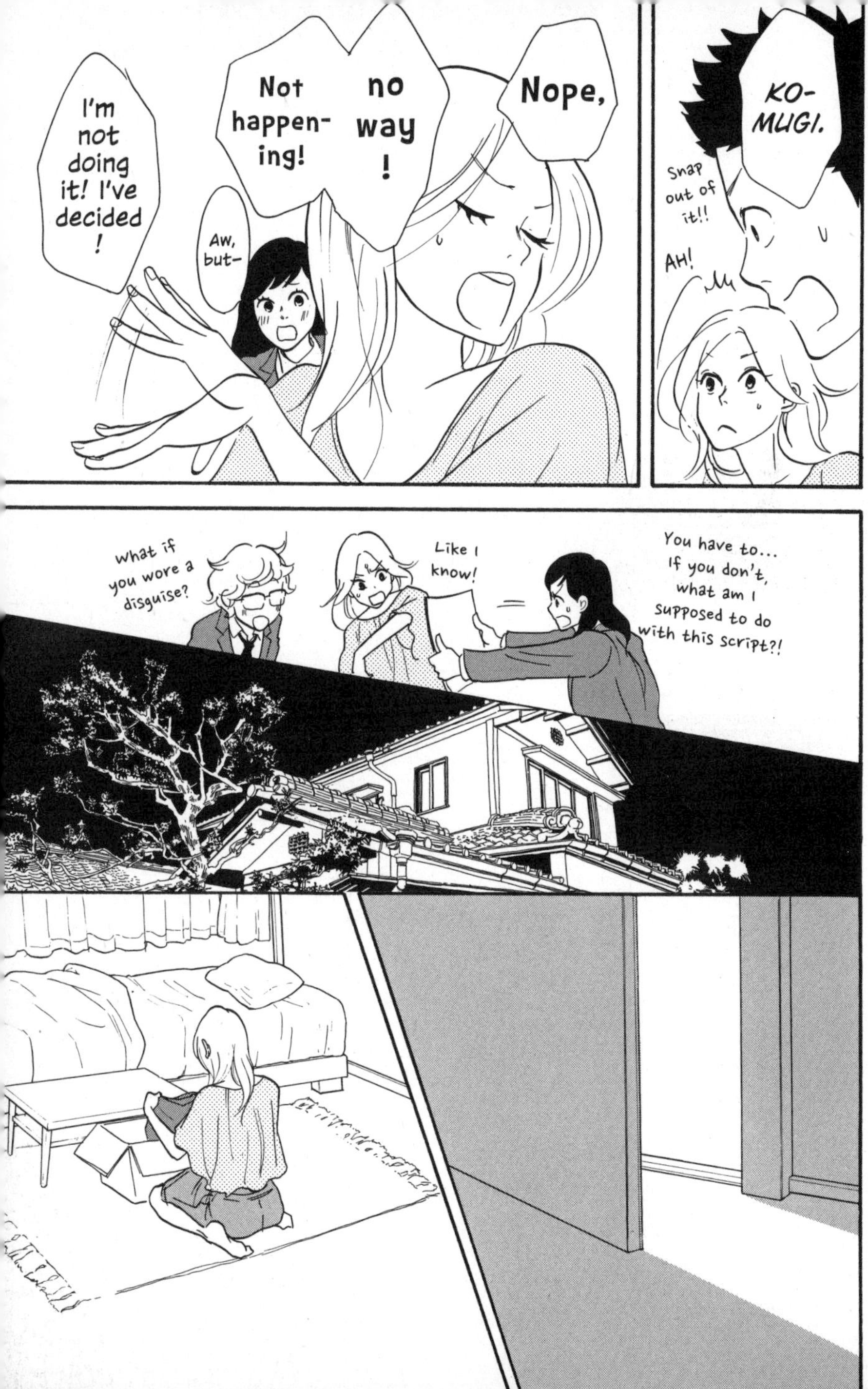
KO-MUGI.
Snap out of it!!
AH!
Nope,
no way!
Not happening!
I'm not doing it! I've decided!
Aw, but-
You have to... If you don't, what am I supposed to do with this script?!
Like I know!
What if you wore a disguise?

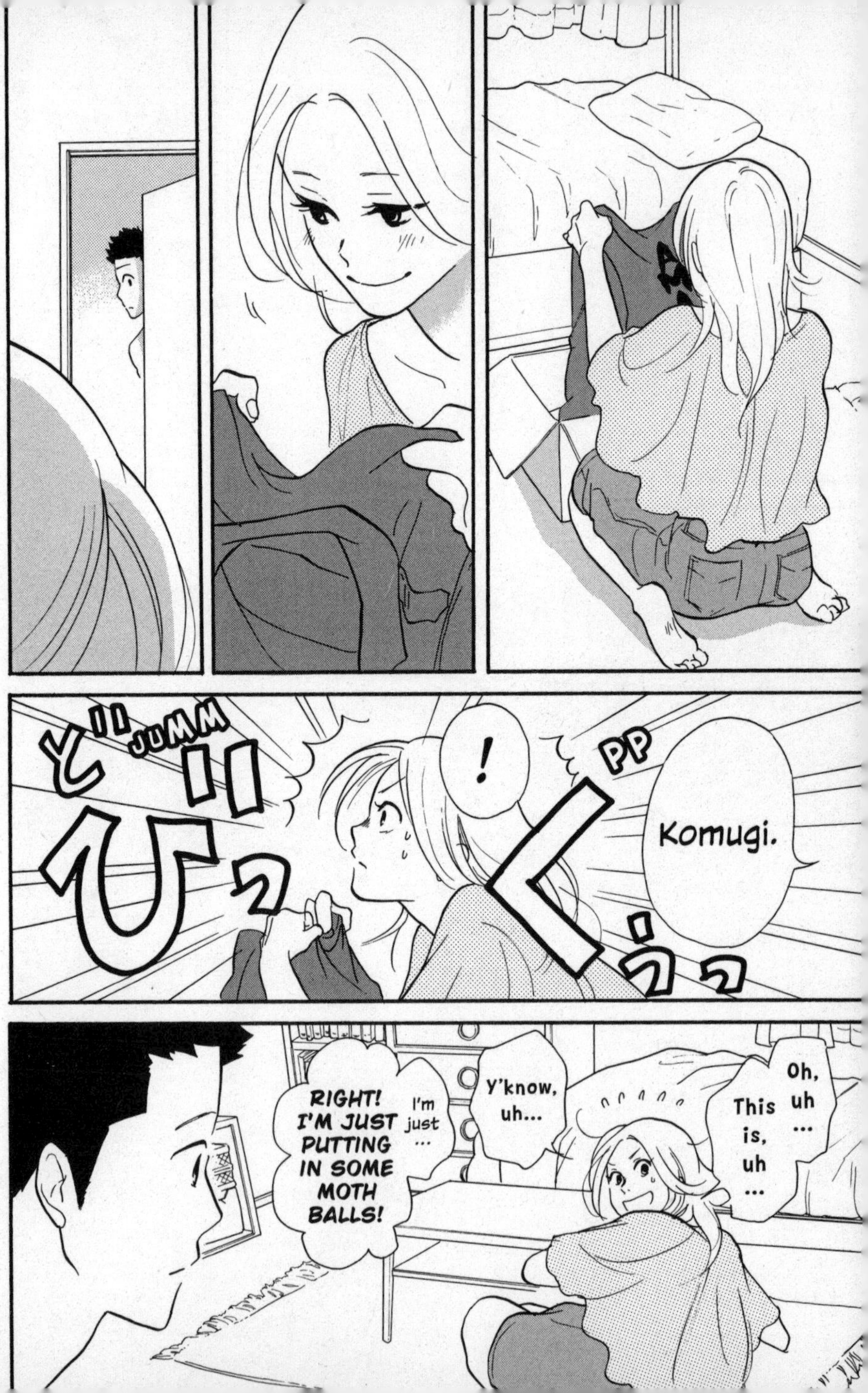
Komugi.
PP
!
JUMM
Oh, uh ...
This is, uh ...
Y'know, uh...
I'm just ...
RIGHT! I'M JUST PUTTING IN SOME MOTH BALLS!

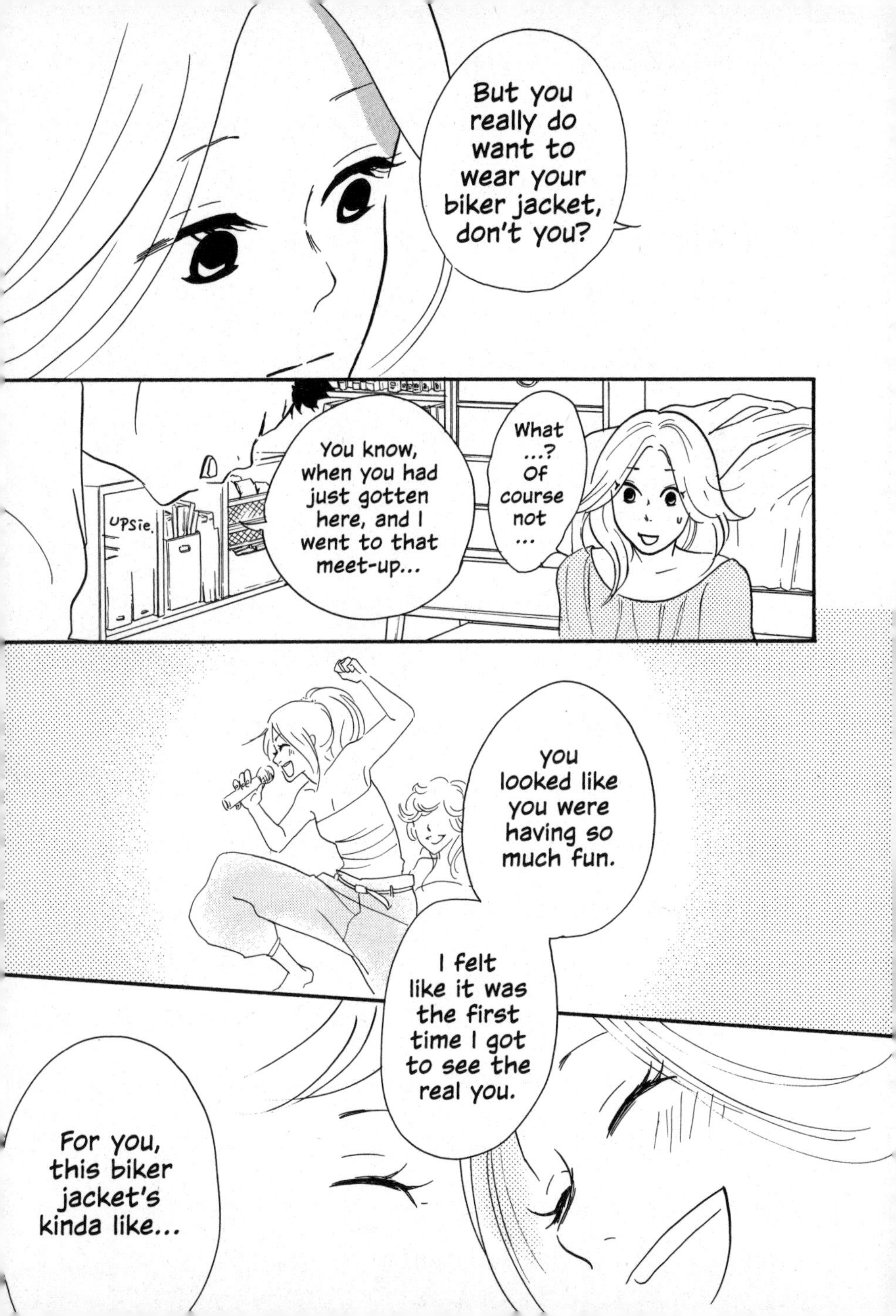
But you really do want to wear your biker jacket, don't you?
What ...? Of course not ...
You know, when you had just gotten here, and I went to that meet-up...
UPSie.
you looked like you were having so much fun.
I felt like it was the first time I got to see the real you.
For you, this biker jacket's kinda like...

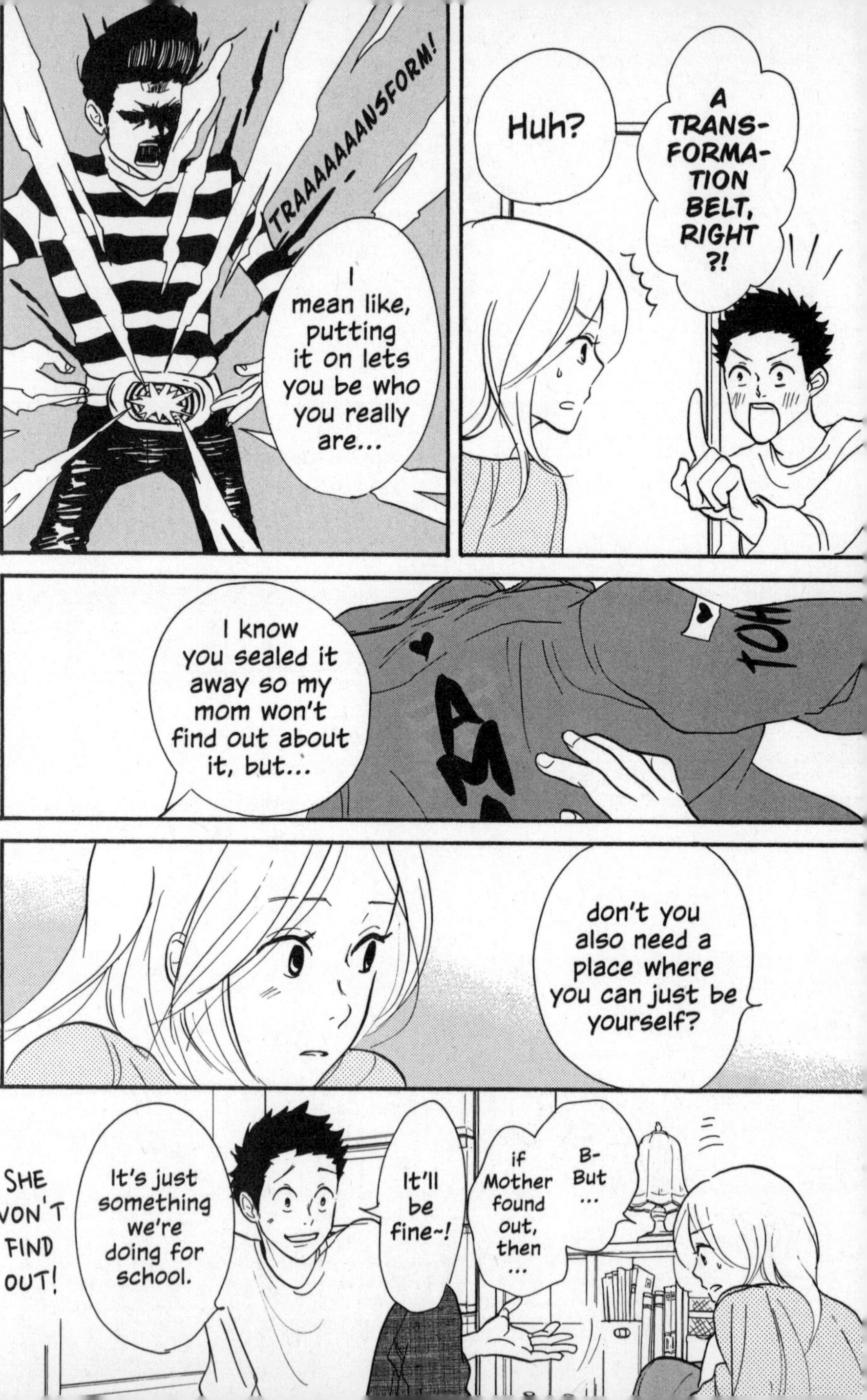
A TRANSFORMATION BELT, RIGHT?!
Huh?
TRAAAAAAANSFORM!
I mean like, putting it on lets you be who you really are...
I know you sealed it away so my mom won't find out about it, but...
don't you also need a place where you can just be yourself?
B-But...
if Mother found out, then...
It'll be fine~!
It's just something we're doing for school.
SHE WON'T FIND OUT!

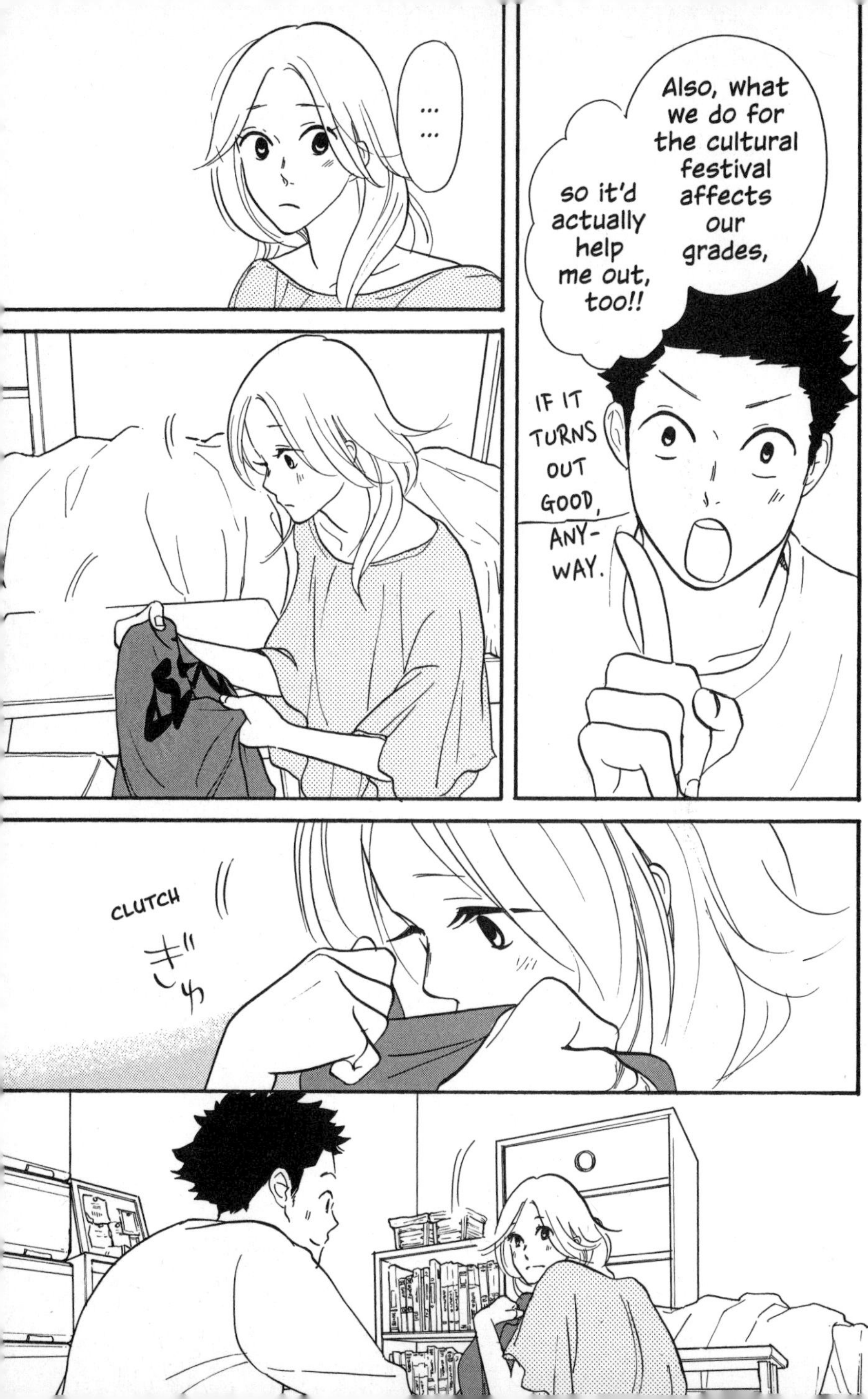
Also, what we do for the cultural festival affects our grades,
so it'd actually help me out, too!!
IF IT TURNS OUT GOOD, ANY-WAY.
……
……
CLUTCH
ぎゅ

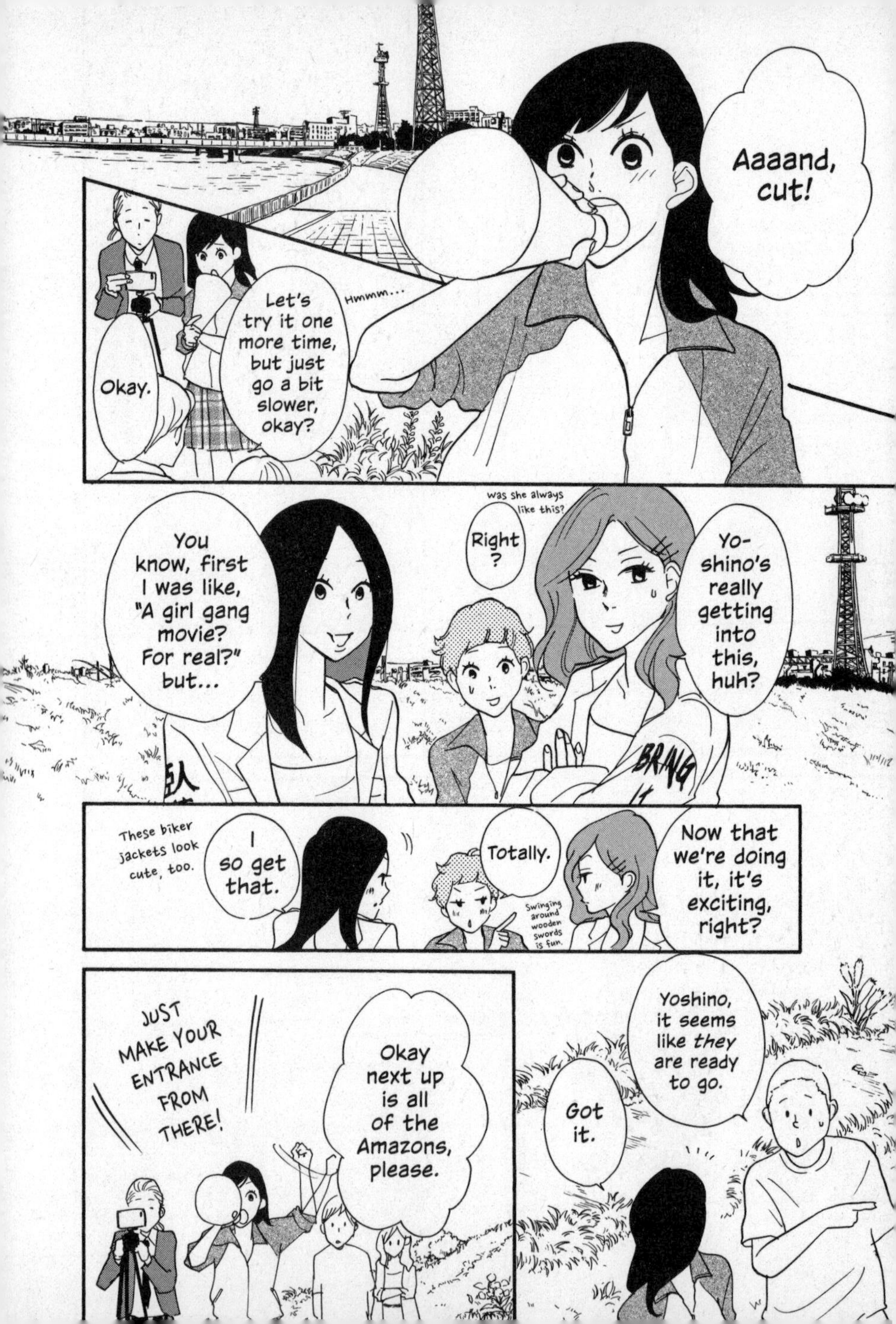
Aaaand, cut!
Hmmm...
Let's try it one more time, but just go a bit slower, okay?
Okay.
Yo-shino's really getting into this, huh?
Right?
was she always like this?
You know, first I was like, "A girl gang movie? For real?" but...
Now that we're doing it, it's exciting, right?
Swinging around wooden swords is fun.
Totally.
I so get that.
These biker jackets look cute, too.
Yoshino, it seems like *they* are ready to go.
Got it.
Okay next up is all of the Amazons, please.
JUST MAKE YOUR ENTRANCE FROM THERE!

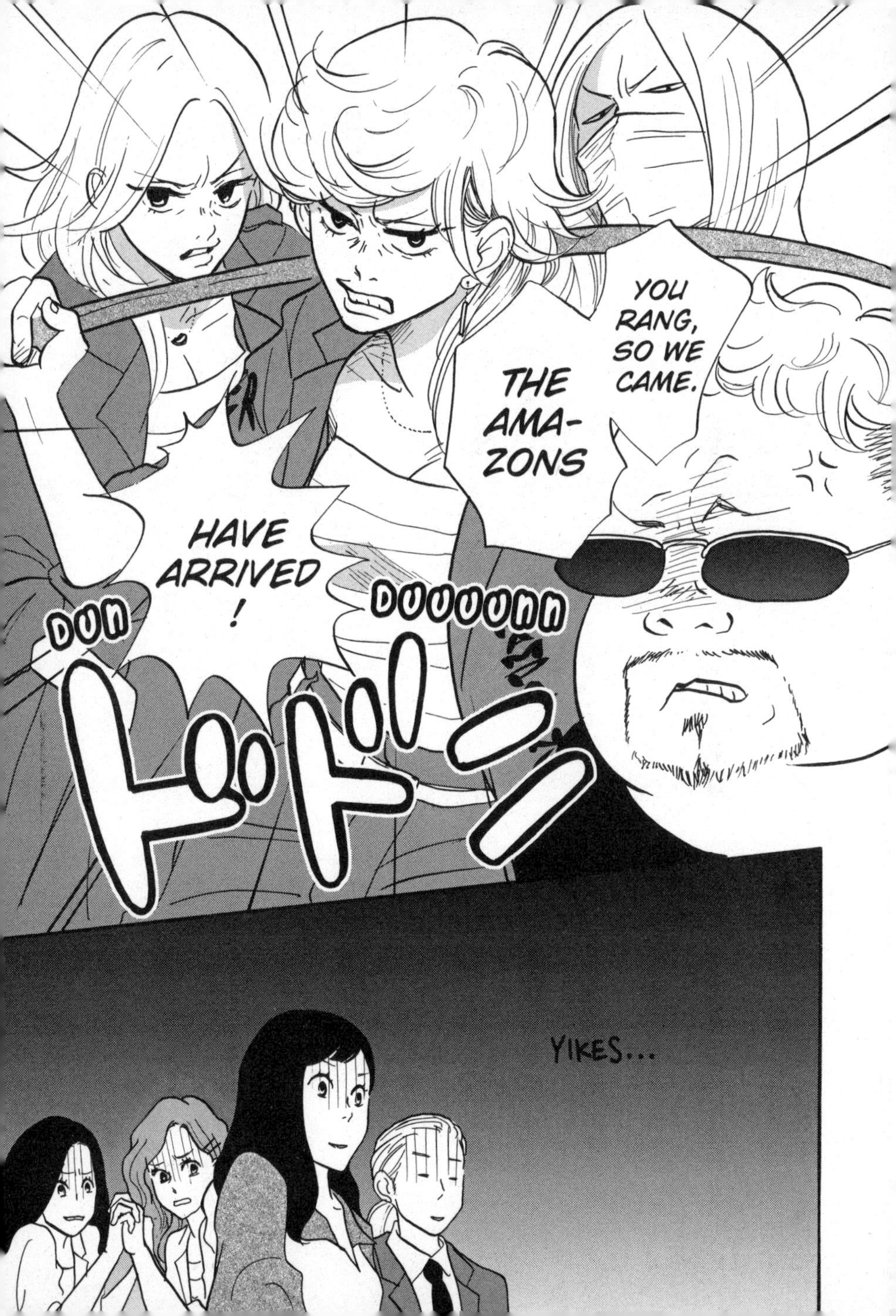
YOU RANG, SO WE CAME.
THE AMAZONS
HAVE ARRIVED!
DUUUUUNN
DUN
ドドーン
YIKES...

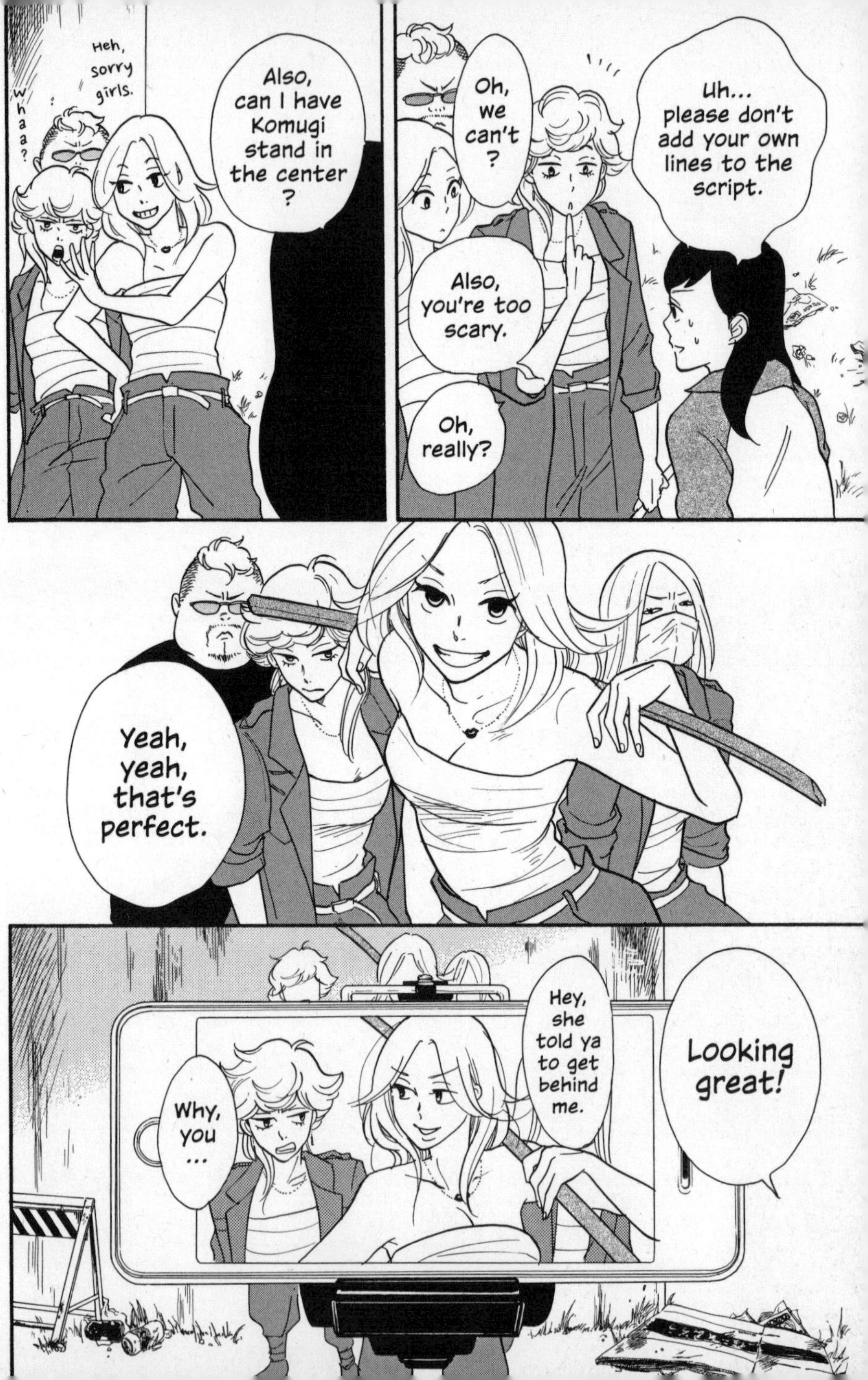
Uh... please don't add your own lines to the script.
Oh, we can't?
Also, you're too scary.
Oh, really?
Also, can I have Komugi stand in the center?
Heh, sorry girls.
Whaa?
Yeah, yeah, that's perfect.
Looking great!
Hey, she told ya to get behind me.
Why, you...

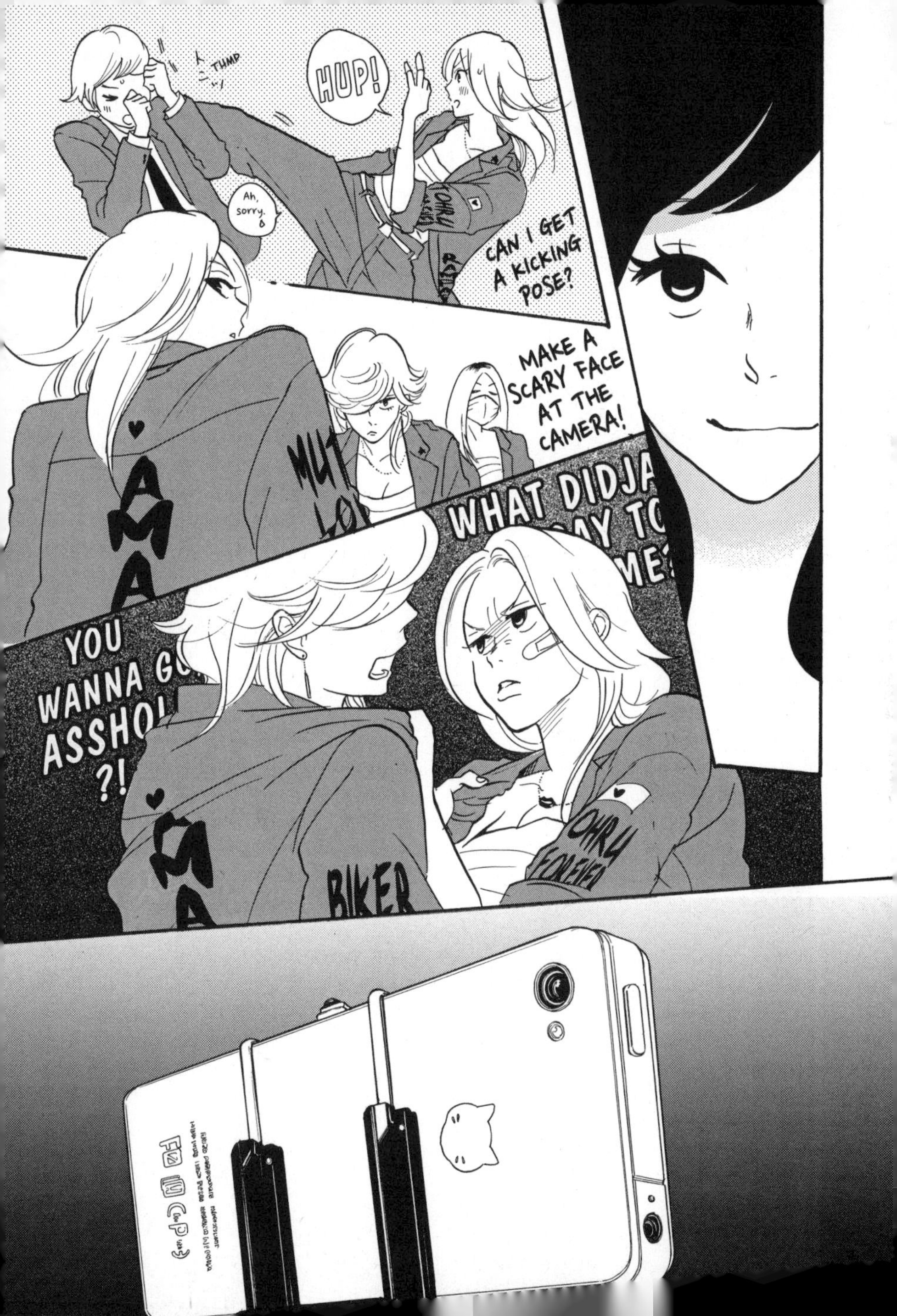
CAN I GET A KICKING POSE?
HUP!
THUMP
Ah, sorry.
MAKE A SCARY FACE AT THE CAMERA!
WHAT DIDJA
AY TO
ME?
YOU WANNA GO
ASSHOL
?!
TOHRU FOREVER
BIKER

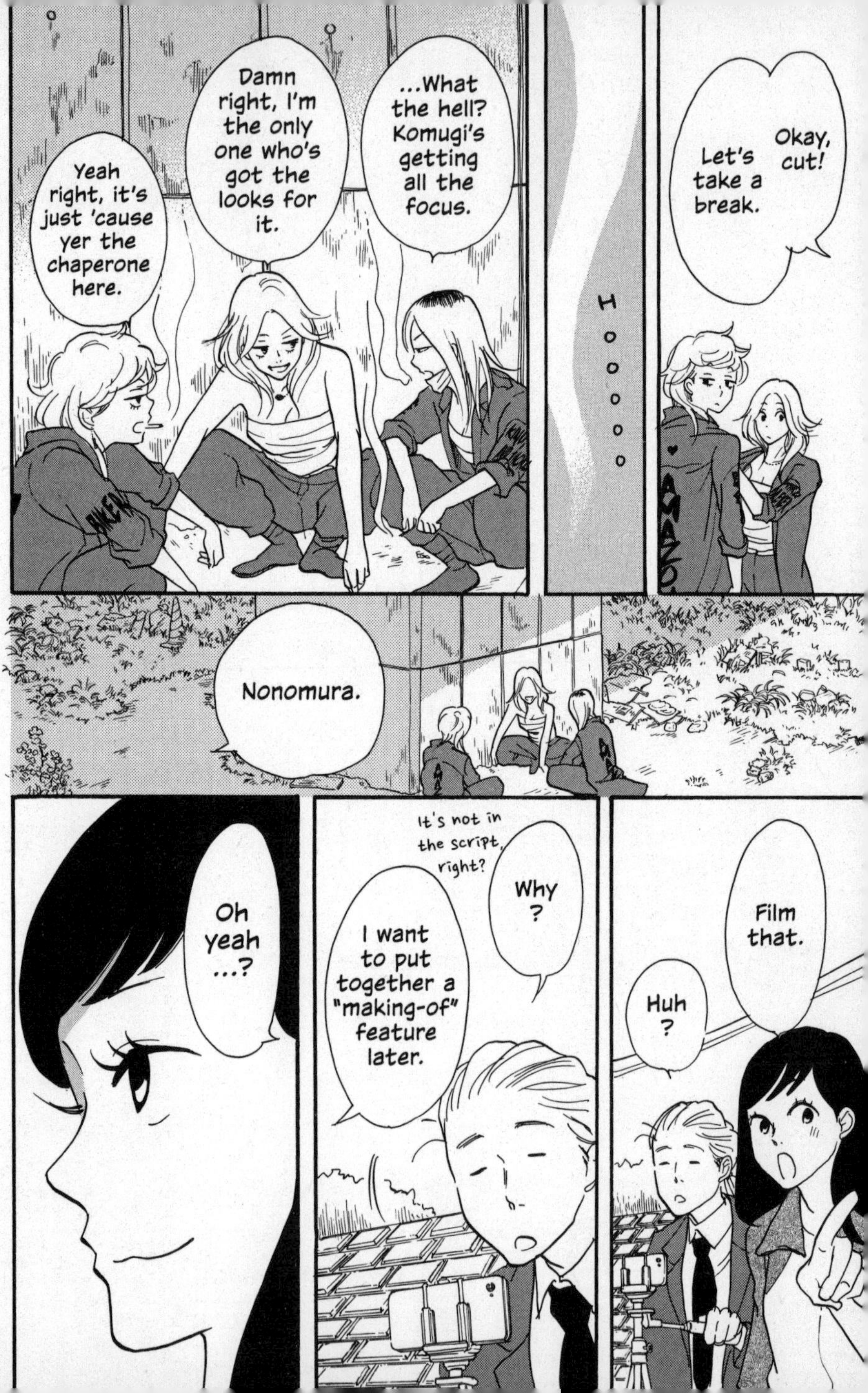
Okay, cut!
Let's take a break.
HOOOOO
...What the hell? Komugi's getting all the focus.
Damn right, I'm the only one who's got the looks for it.
Yeah right, it's just 'cause yer the chaperone here.
Nonomura.
Film that.
Huh?
Why?
It's not in the script, right?
I want to put together a "making-of" feature later.
Oh yeah ...?

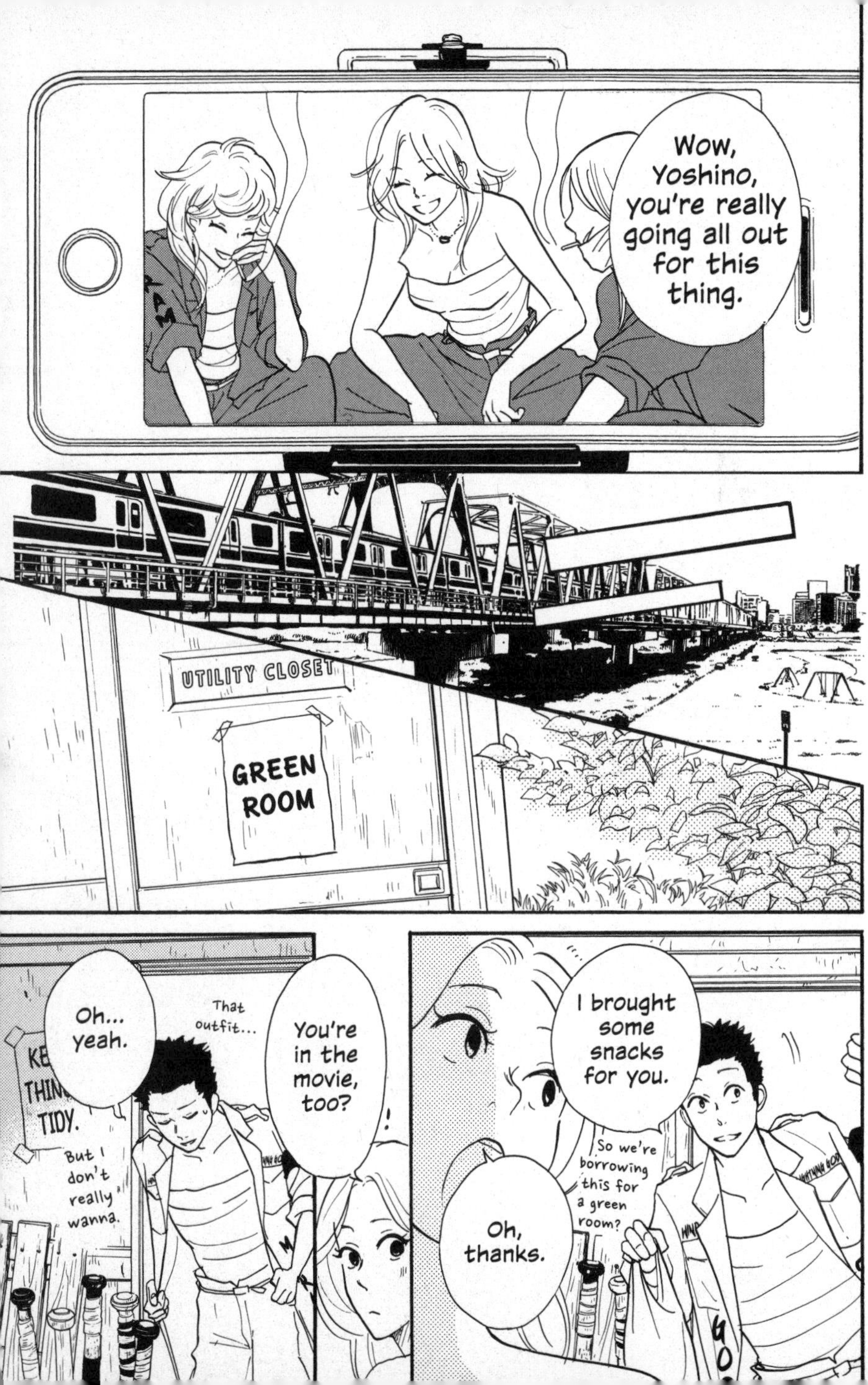
Wow, Yoshino, you're really going all out for this thing.
UTILITY CLOSET
GREEN ROOM
I brought some snacks for you.
So we're borrowing this for a green room?
Oh, thanks.
You're in the movie, too?
That outfit...
Oh... yeah.
But I don't really wanna.

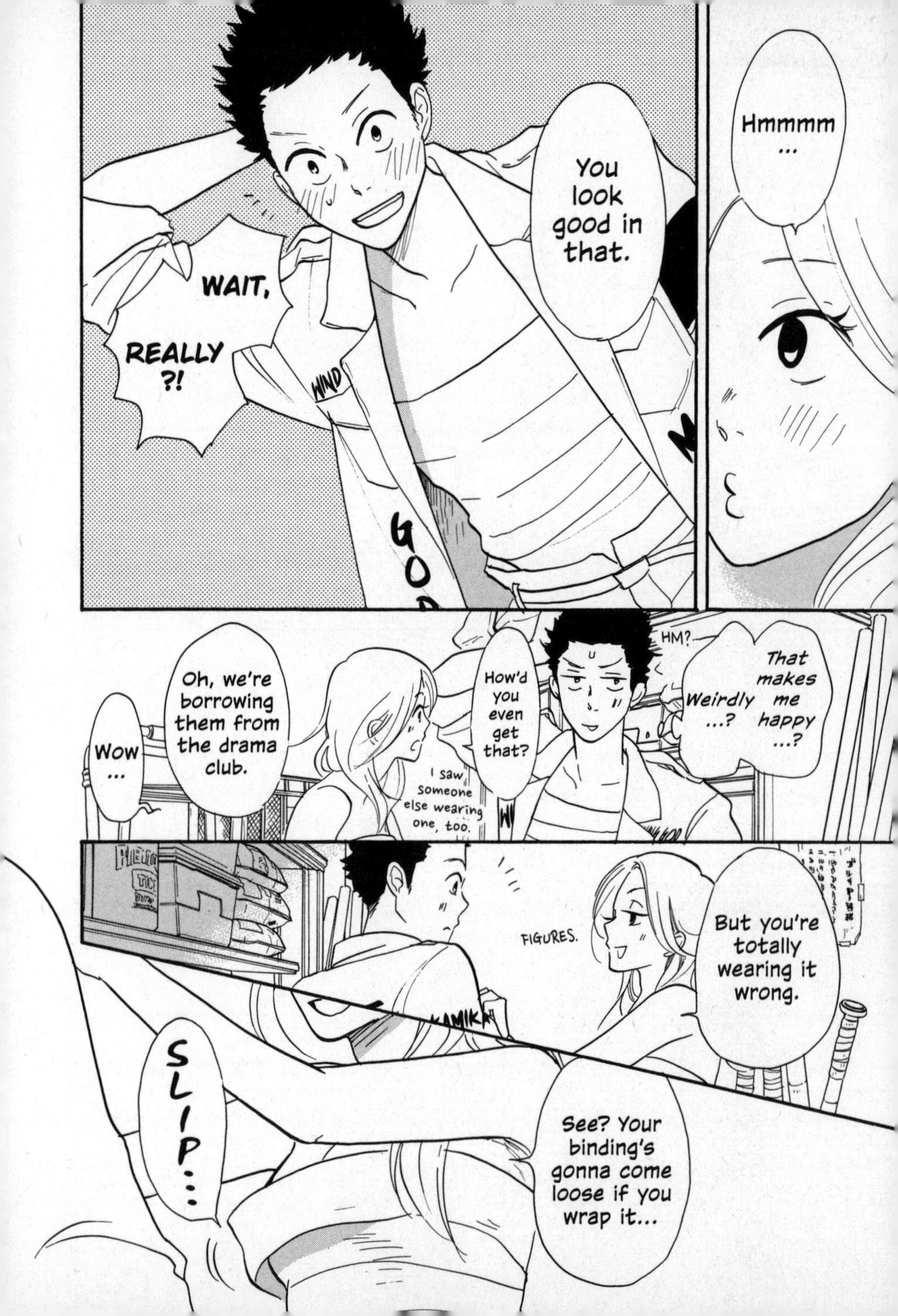
Hmmmm ...
You look good in that.
WAIT, REALLY ?!
HM?
That makes me happy ...?
Weirdly ...?
How'd you even get that?
I saw someone else wearing one, too.
Oh, we're borrowing them from the drama club.
Wow ...
But you're totally wearing it wrong.
FIGURES.
See? Your binding's gonna come loose if you wrap it...
SLIP...

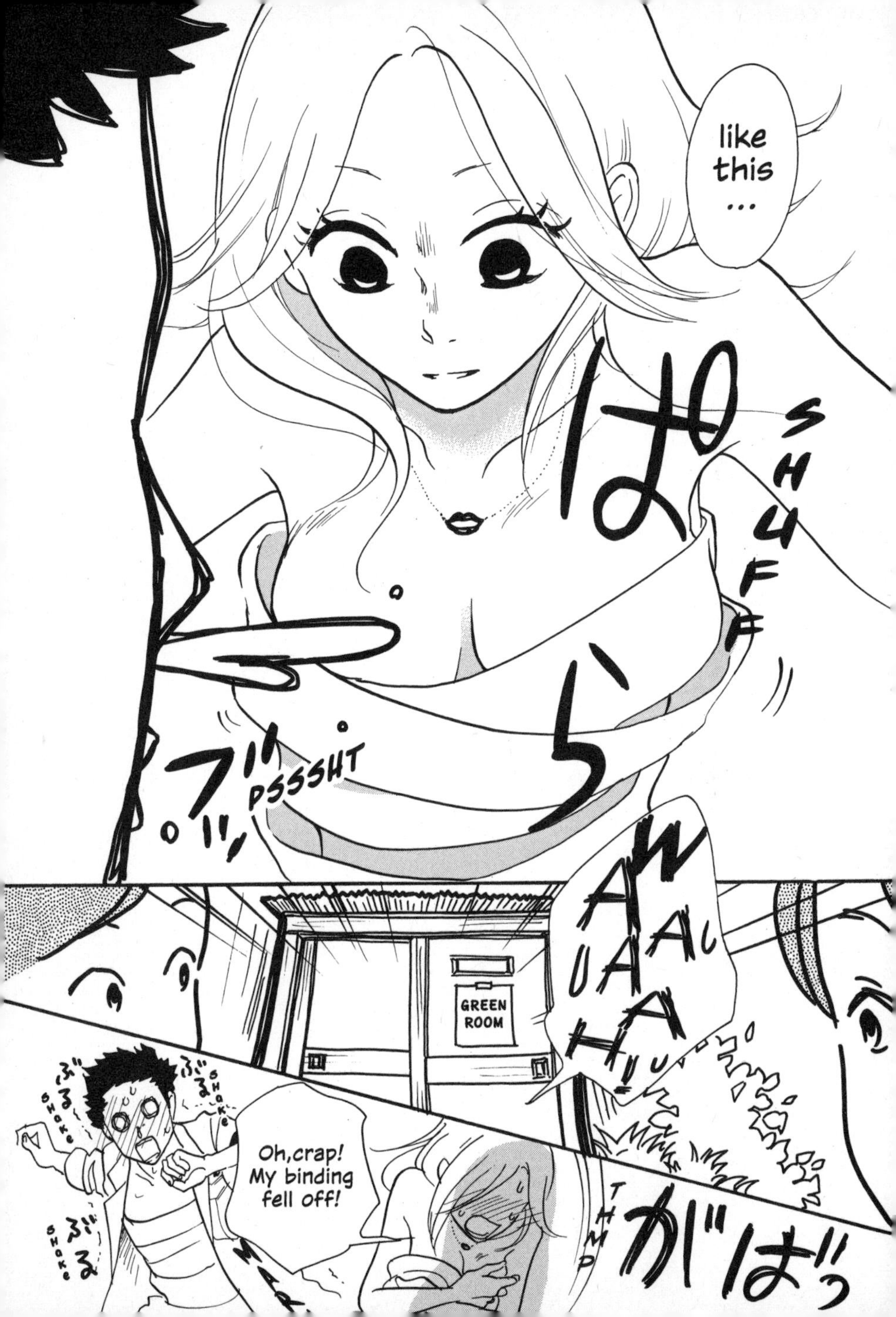
like this...
ぱらっ
SHUFF
ブッ
PSSSHT
AWAAUAAHAHU!
GREEN ROOM
がばっ
THMP
Oh, crap! My binding fell off!
ぶるぶる
SHAKE
ぶる
SHAKE
ぶるぶる
SHAKE

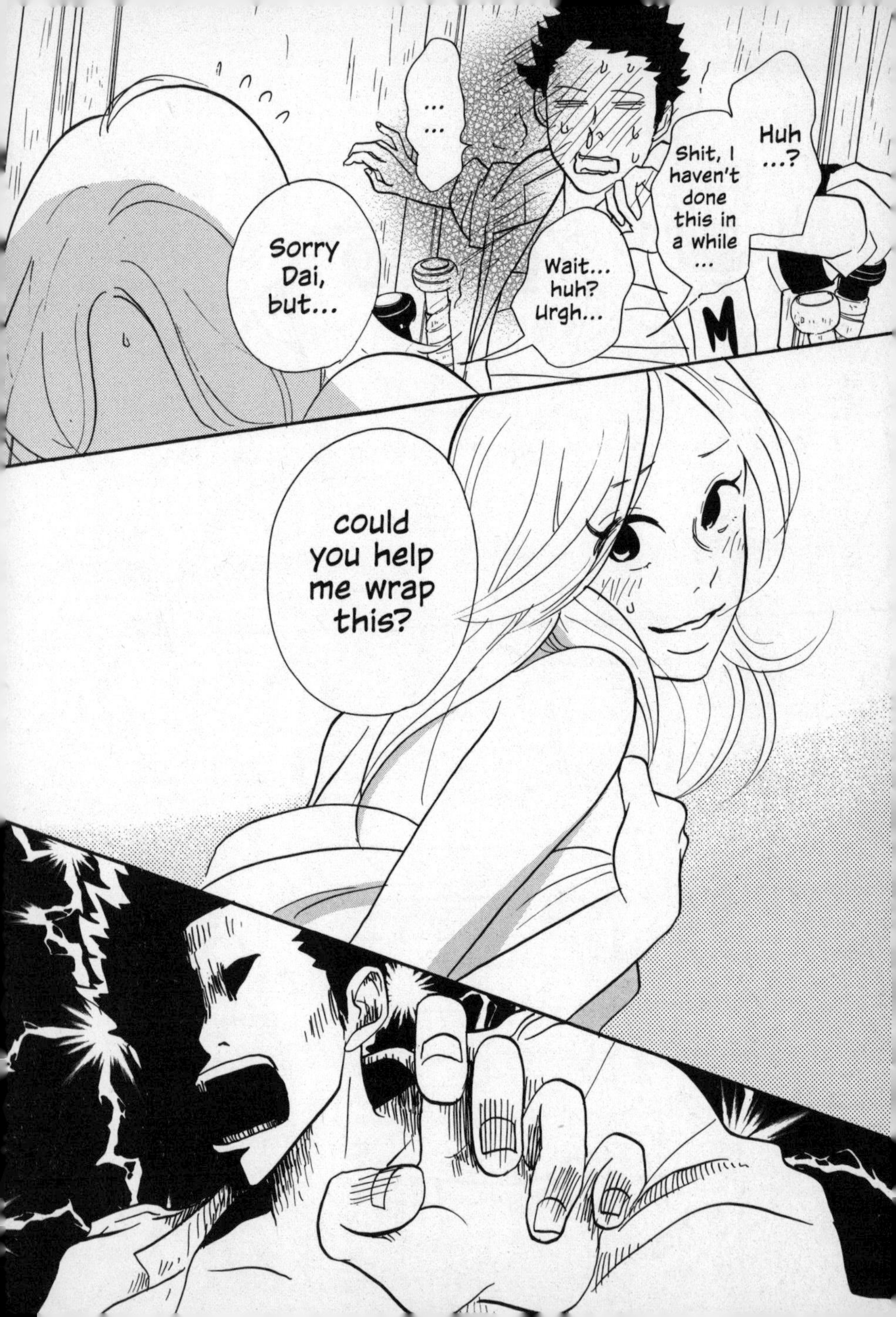

Huh ...?
Shit, I haven't done this in a while ...
... ...
Wait... huh? Urgh...
M
Sorry Dai, but...
could you help me wrap this?

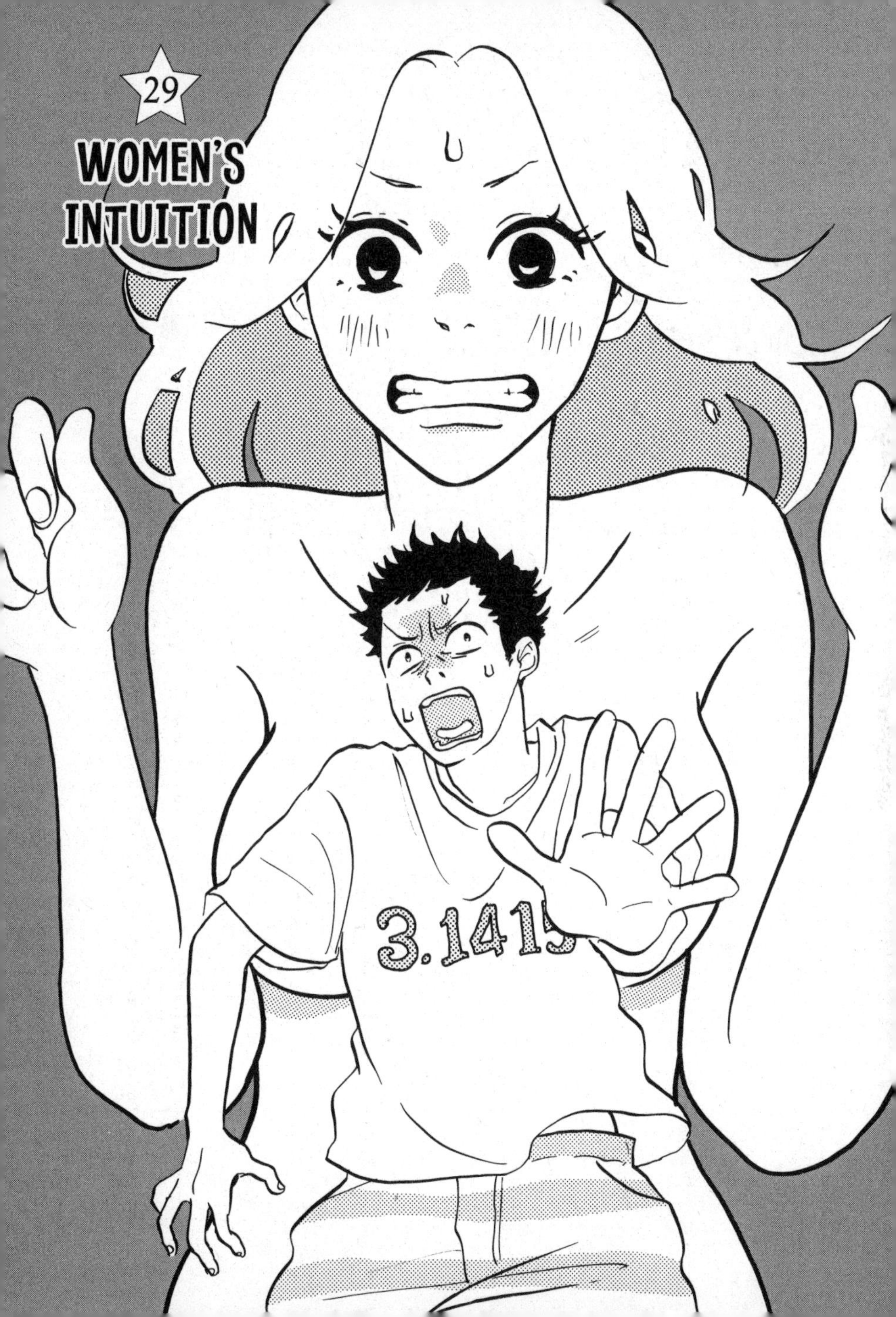
29
WOMEN'S
INTUITION
3.1415

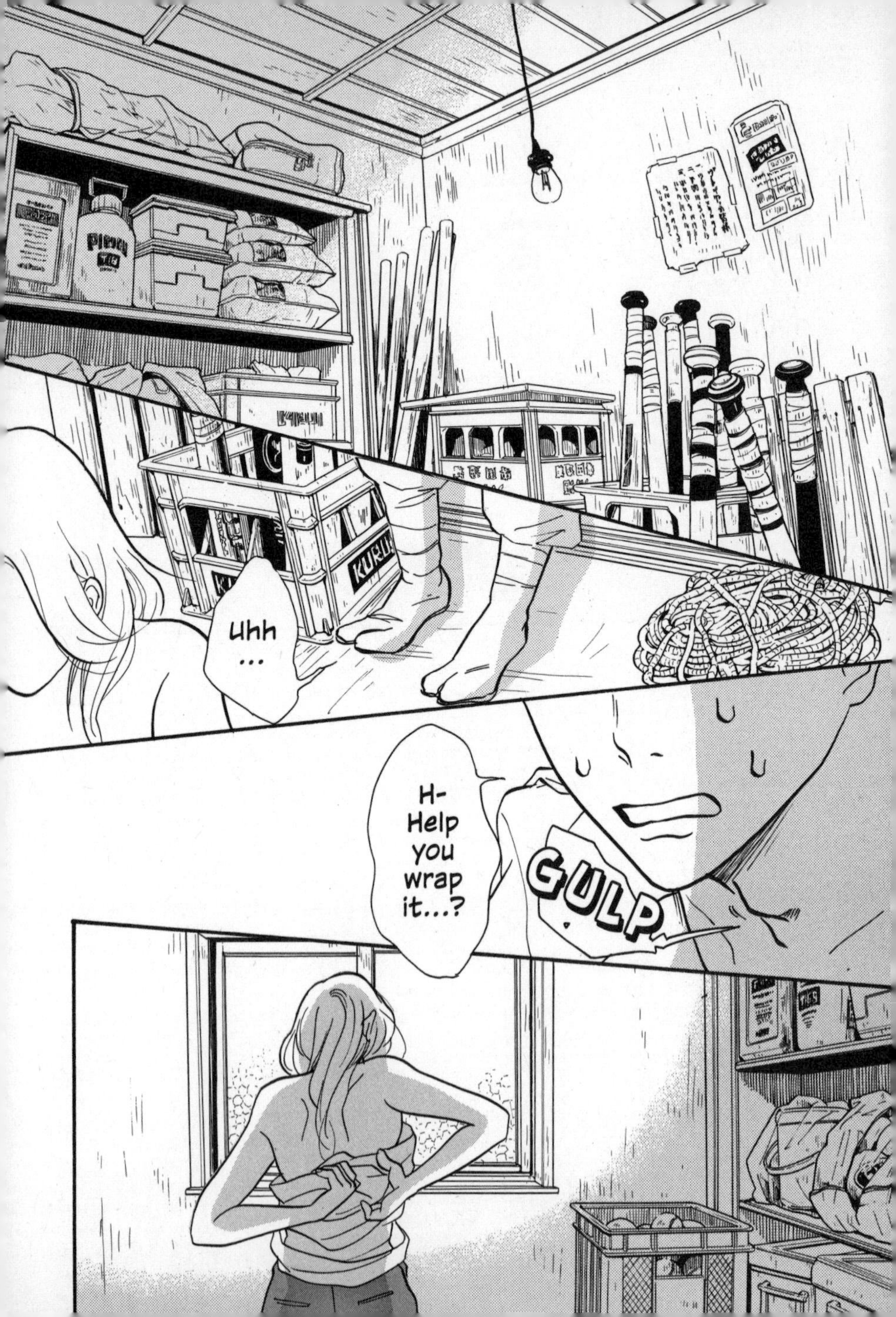
Uhh ...
H- Help you wrap it...?
GULP

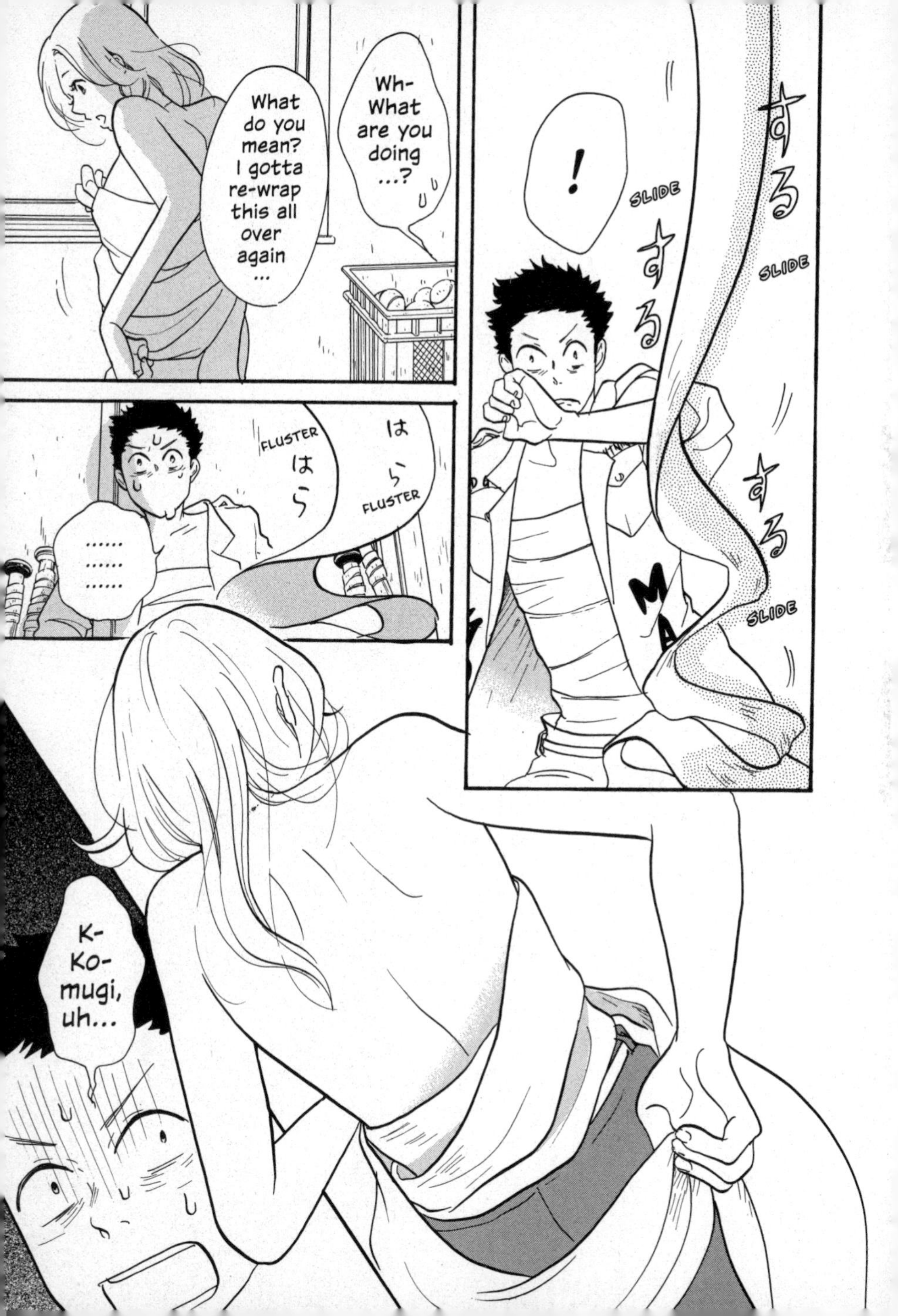

するする
SLIDE
SLIDE
!
する
SLIDE
Wh- What are you doing ...?
What do you mean? I gotta re-wrap this all over again ...
はら はら
FLUSTER
FLUSTER
......
......
......
K-Ko-mugi, uh...

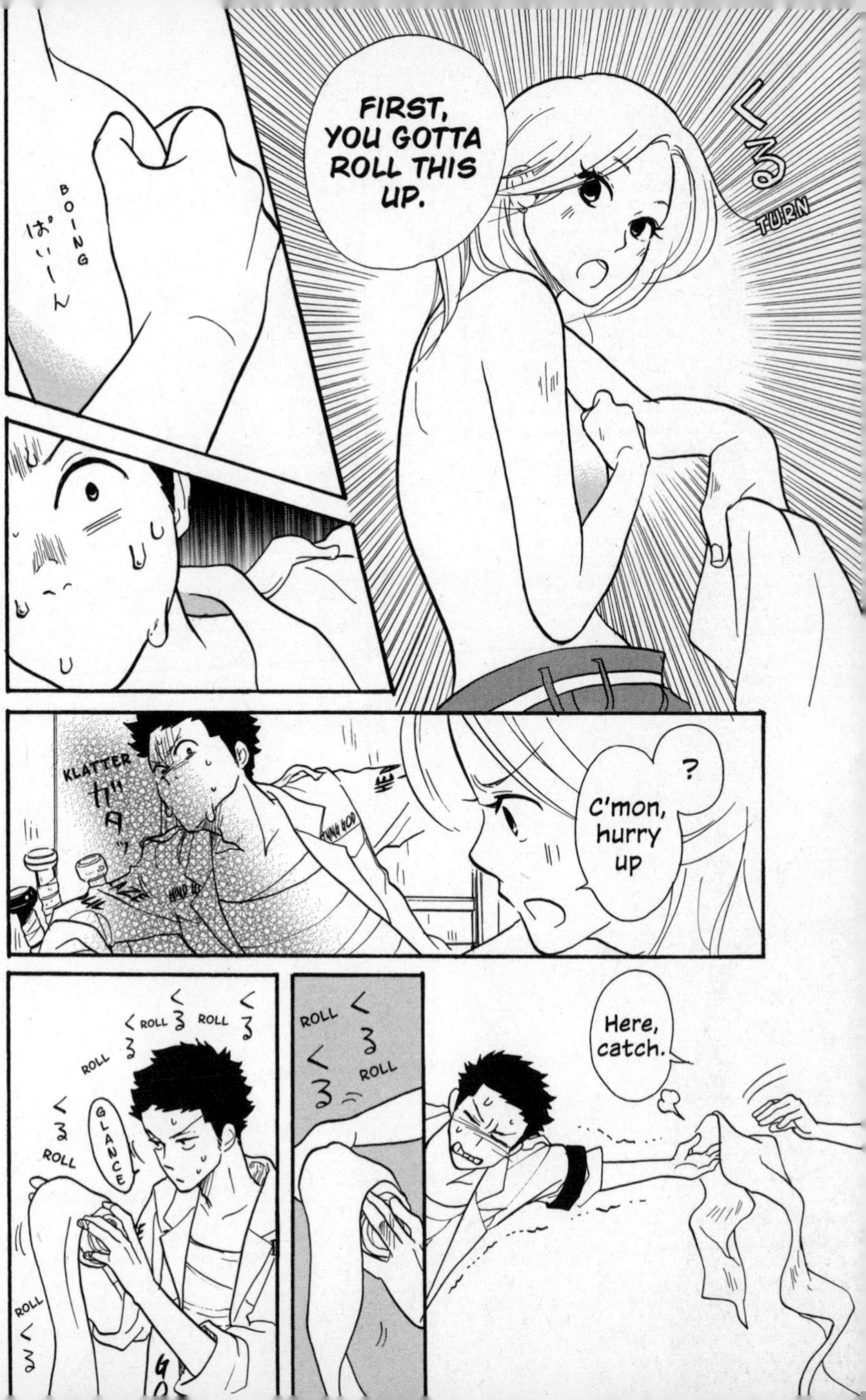
くる
TURN
FIRST, YOU GOTTA ROLL THIS UP.
BOING
ぱいーん
?
C'mon, hurry up
KLATTER
ガタッ
Here, catch.
ROLL
くる
くる
ROLL
くる
ROLL
くる
ROLL
くる
ROLL
くる
GLANCE
ROLL
くる
ROLL
くる

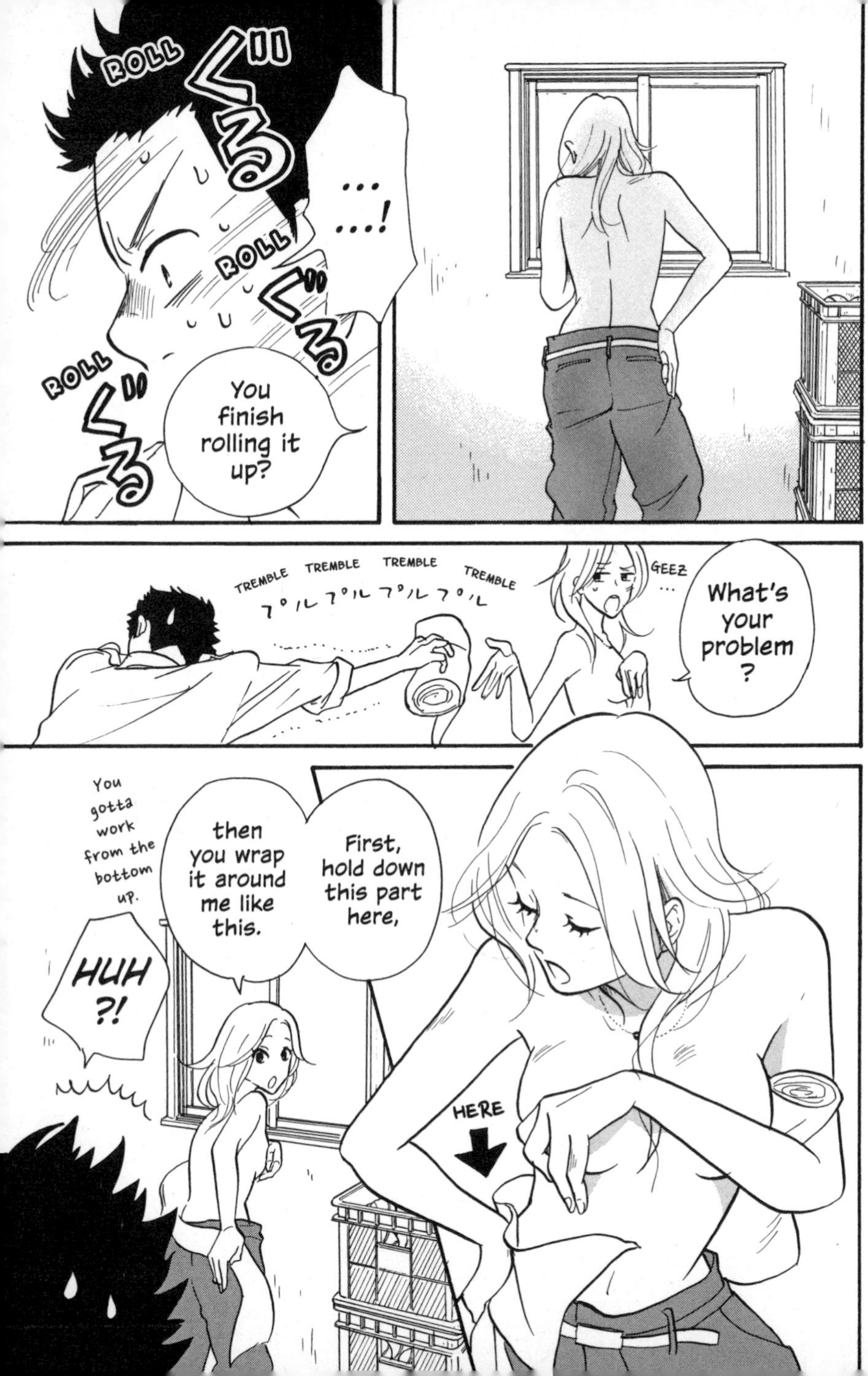
…
…!
ROLL
くる
ROLL
くる
ROLL
くる
You finish rolling it up?
What's your problem?
GEEZ
…
TREMBLE TREMBLE TREMBLE TREMBLE
プルプルプルプル
First, hold down this part here,
then you wrap it around me like this.
You gotta work from the bottom up.
HERE
HUH?!

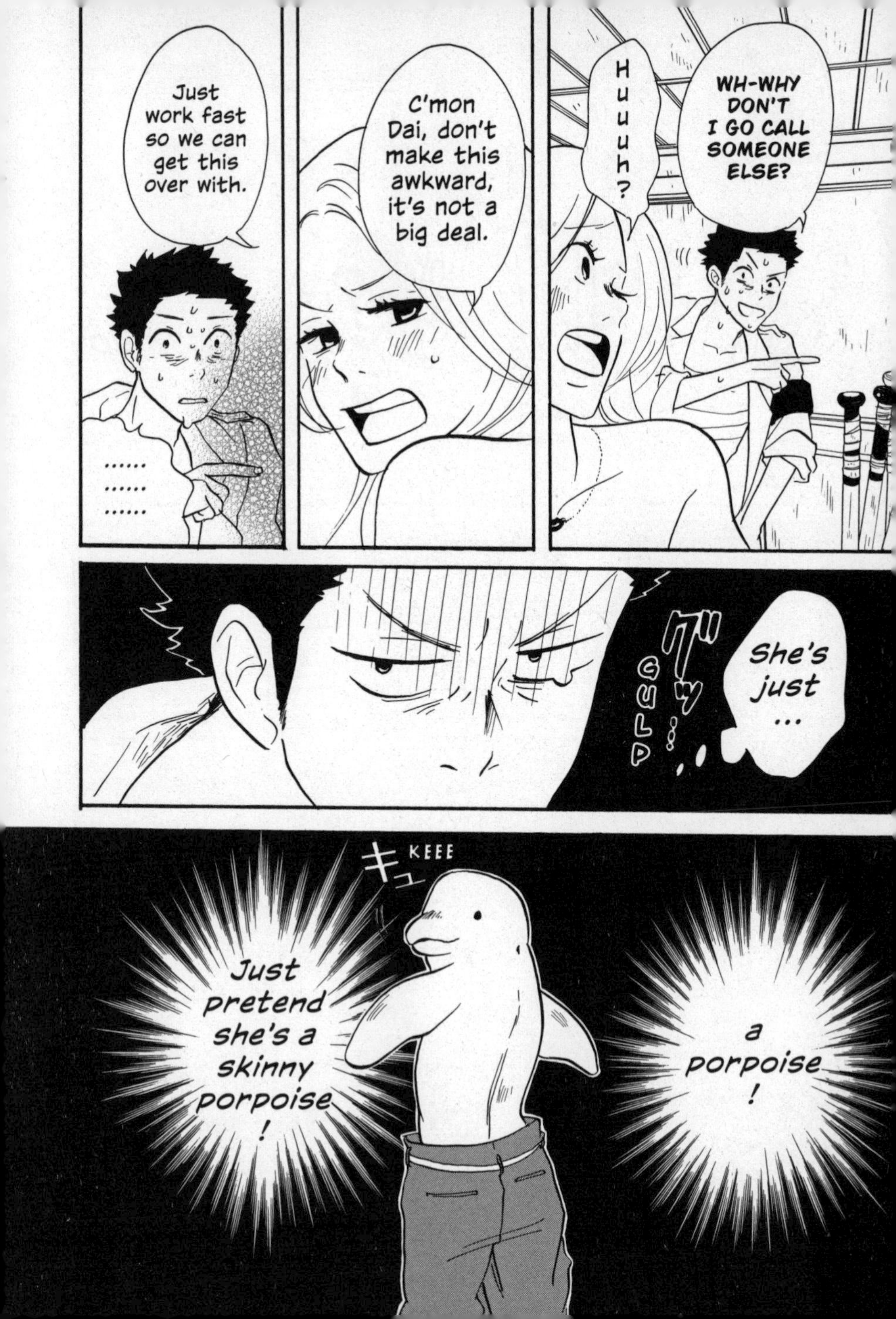
WH-WHY DON'T I GO CALL SOMEONE ELSE?
Huuuh?
C'mon Dai, don't make this awkward, it's not a big deal.
Just work fast so we can get this over with.
....
グッ
GULP
She's just ...
キュ
KEEE
a porpoise!
Just pretend she's a skinny porpoise!

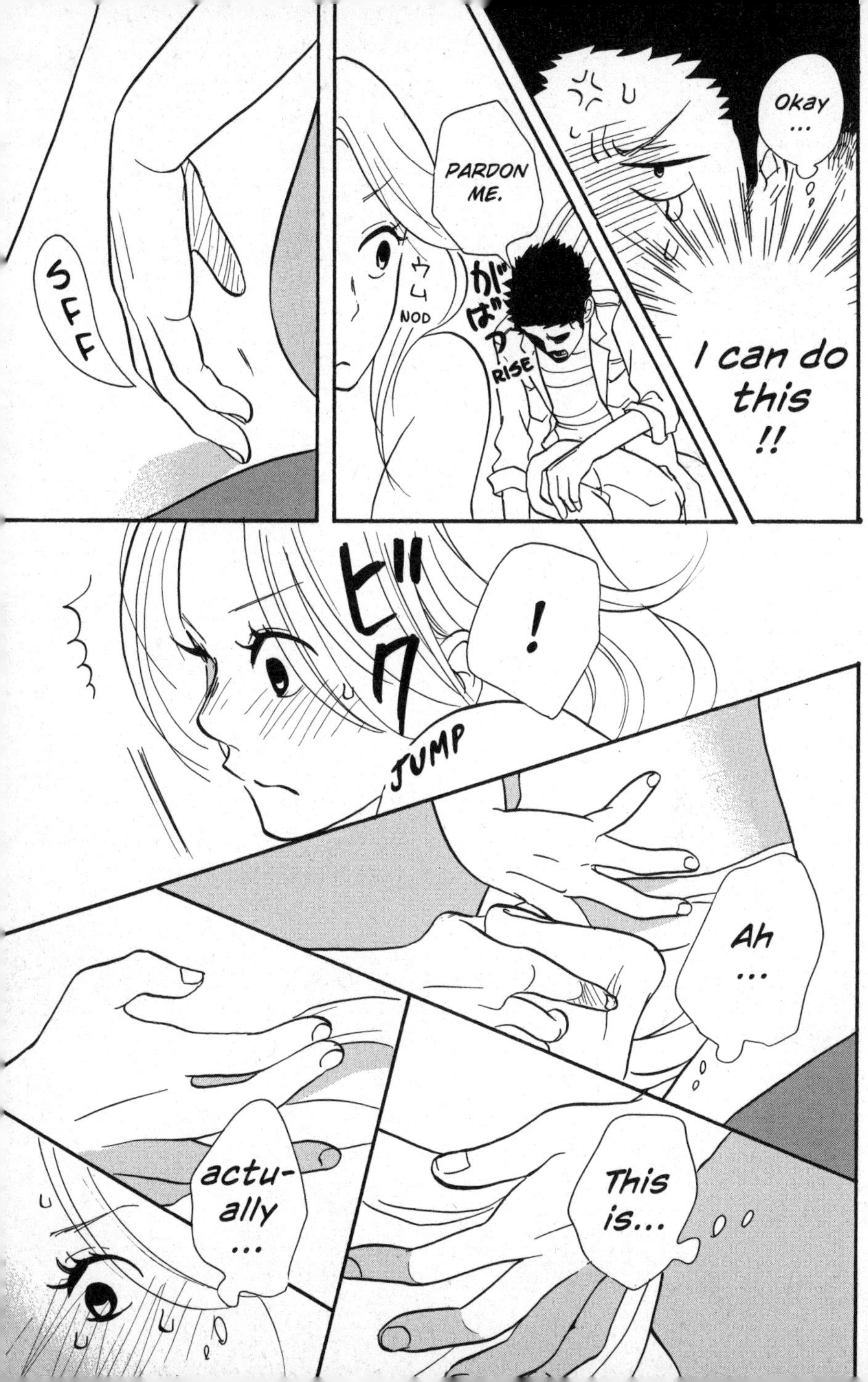
Okay ...
I can do this !!
PARDON ME.
ウム
NOD
がばっ
RISE
SFF
ビク
JUMP
!
Ah ...
This is...
actu-ally ...

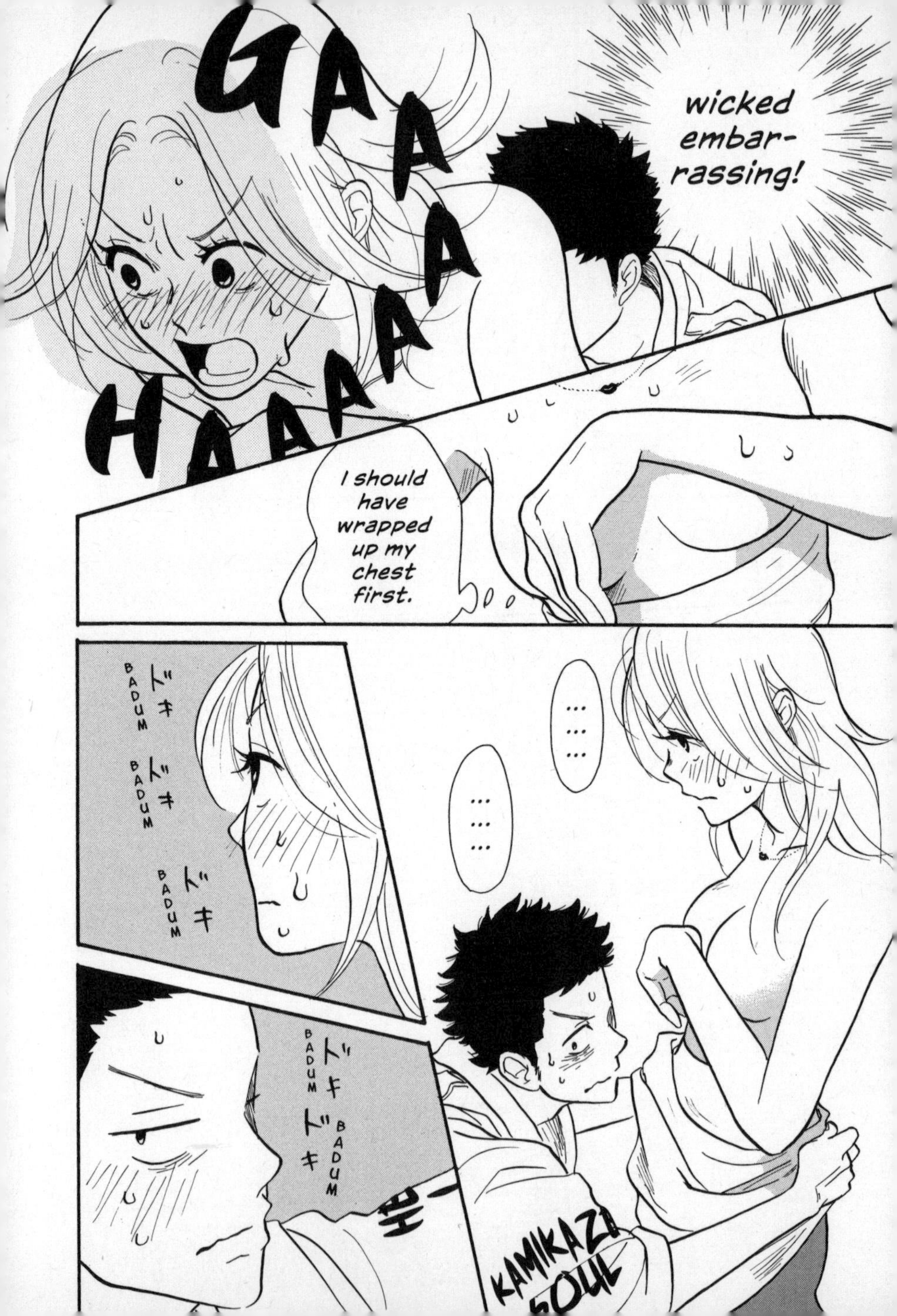
wicked embar-rassing!
GAAAAAA
HAAAA
I should have wrapped up my chest first.
......
......
BADUM ドキ
BADUM ドキ
BADUM ドキ
BADUM ドキ
BADUM ドキ
KAMIKAZE SOUL

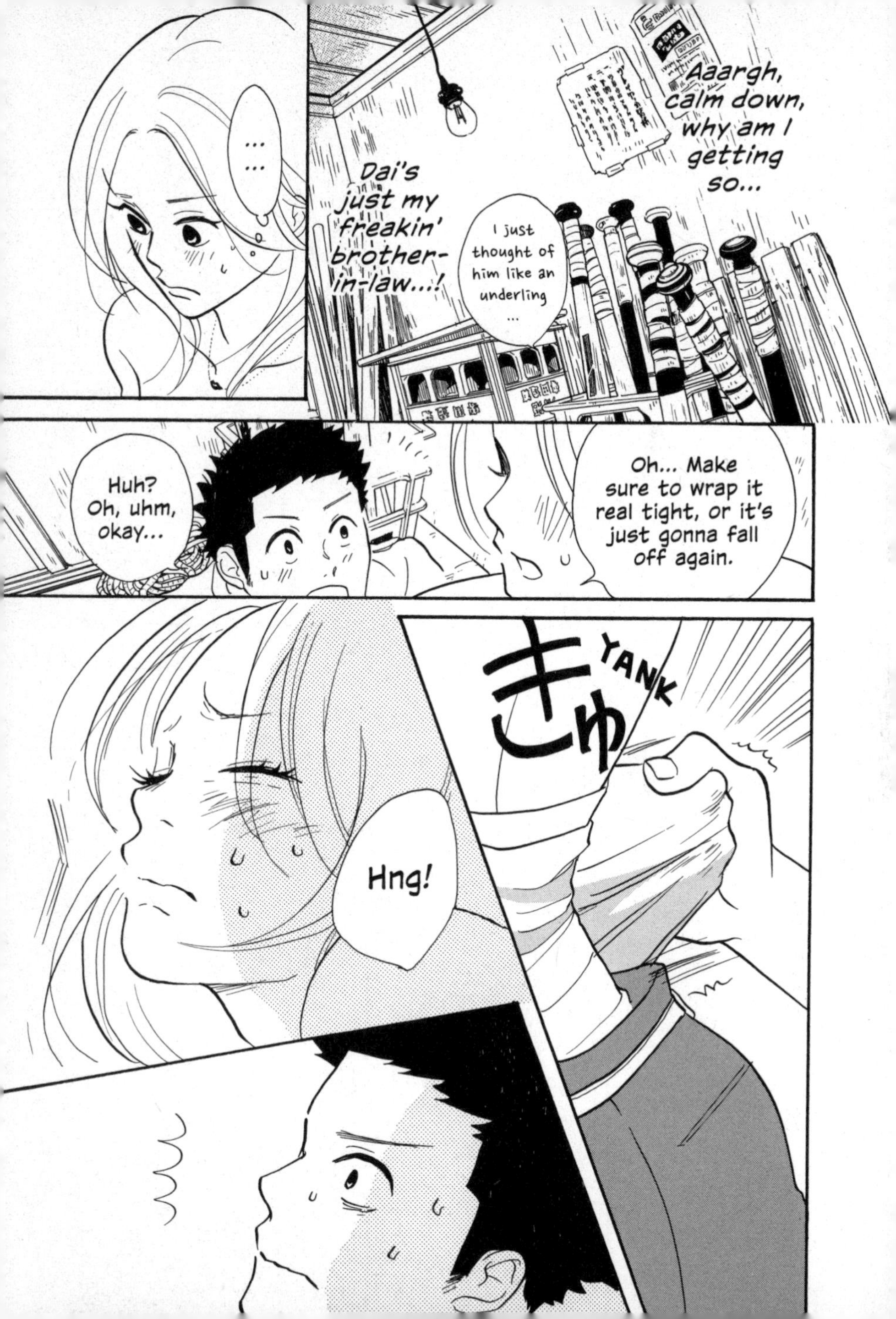
Aaargh, calm down, why am I getting so...
Dai's just my freakin' brother-in-law...!
I just thought of him like an underling ...
...
...
Oh... Make sure to wrap it real tight, or it's just gonna fall off again.
Huh? Oh, uhm, okay...
きゅ
YANK
Hng!

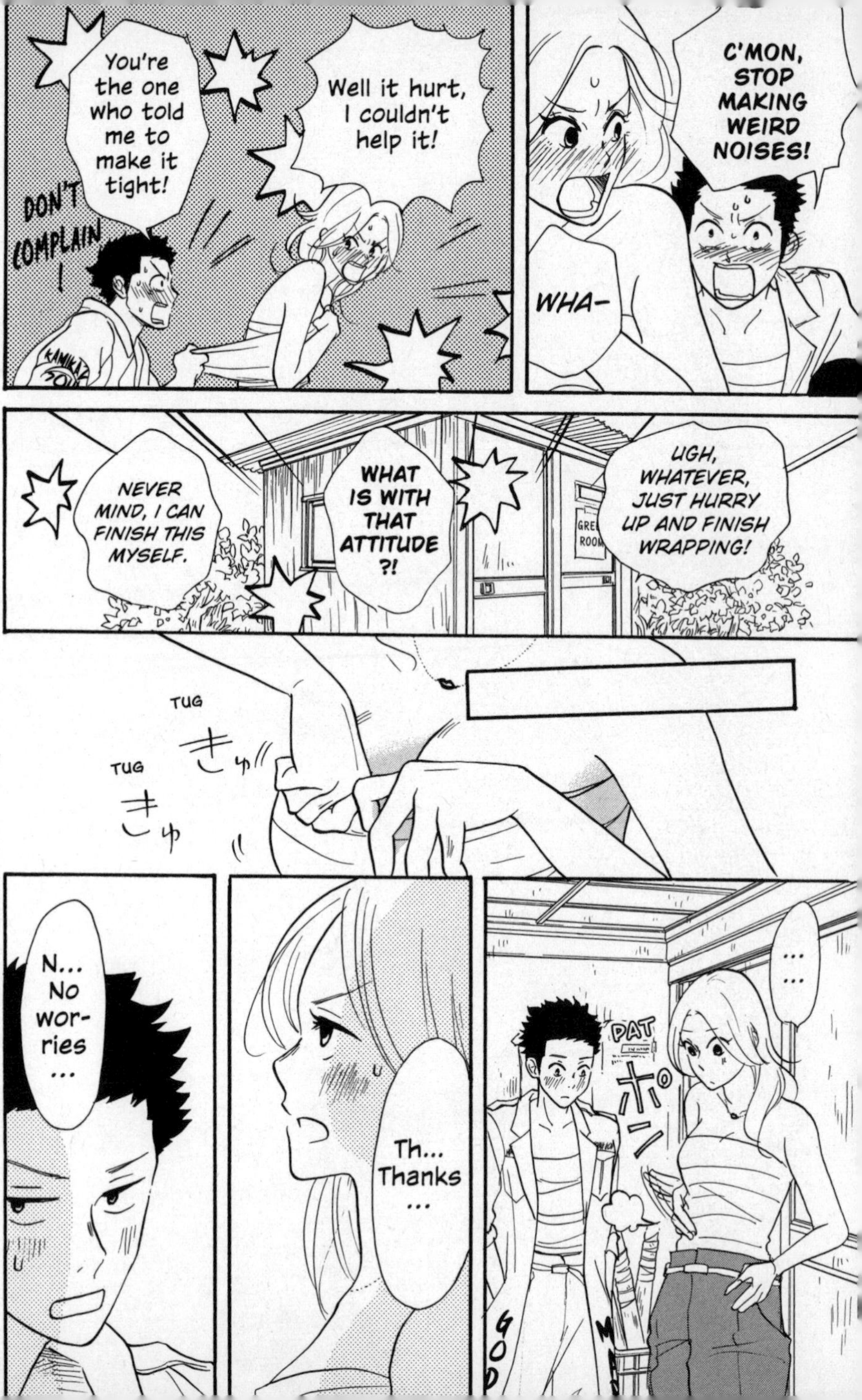
C'MON, STOP MAKING WEIRD NOISES!
WHA-
Well it hurt, I couldn't help it!
You're the one who told me to make it tight!
DON'T COMPLAIN!
UGH, WHATEVER, JUST HURRY UP AND FINISH WRAPPING!
WHAT IS WITH THAT ATTITUDE ?!
NEVER MIND, I CAN FINISH THIS MYSELF.
TUG
きゅ
TUG
きゅ
……
PAT
ポン
GOD
Th... Thanks ...
N... No wor-ries ...

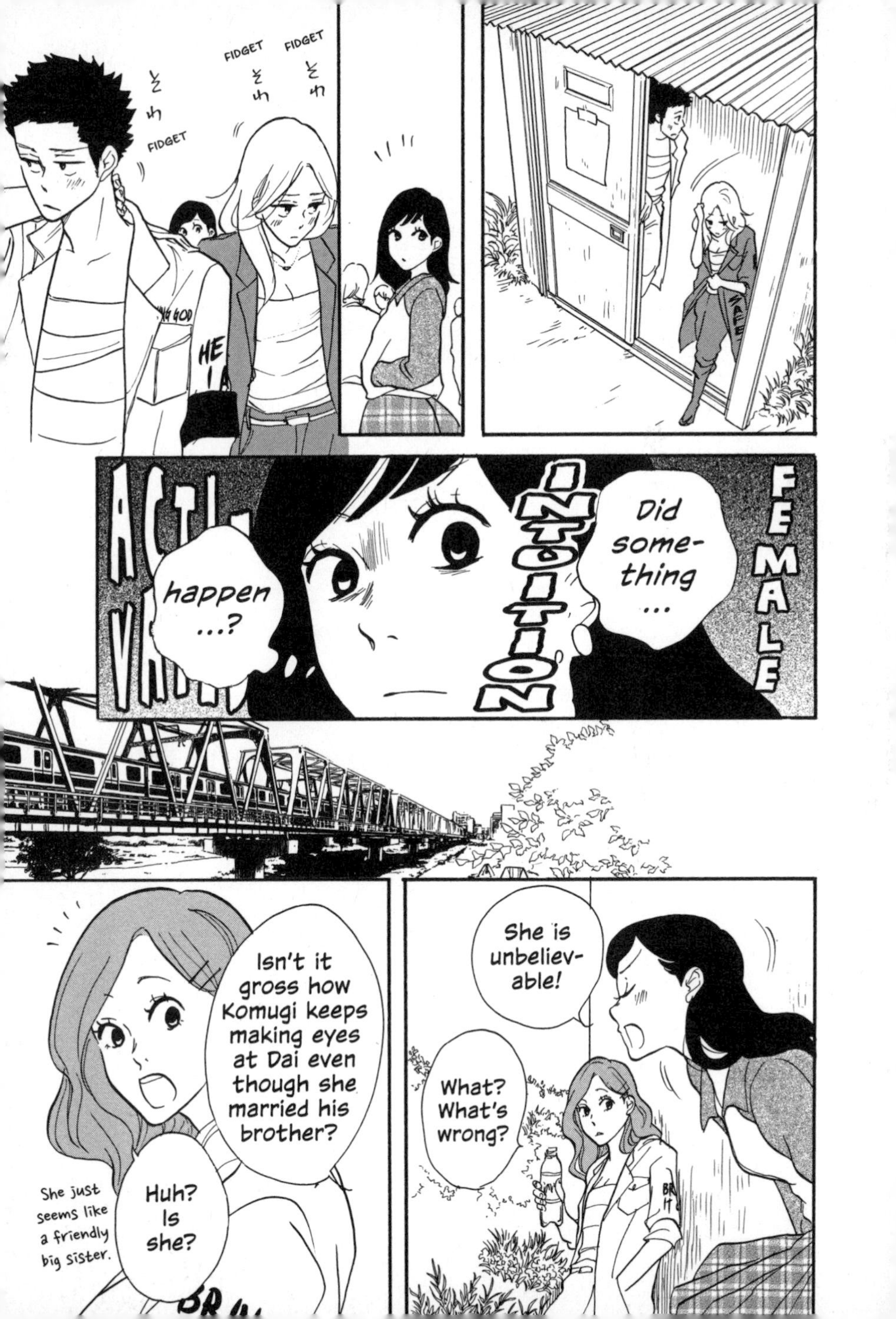
FIDGET
FIDGET
FIDGET
FEMALE
Did something...
INTUITION
happen...?
She is unbelievable!
What? What's wrong?
Isn't it gross how Komugi keeps making eyes at Dai even though she married his brother?
Huh? Is she?
She just seems like a friendly big sister.

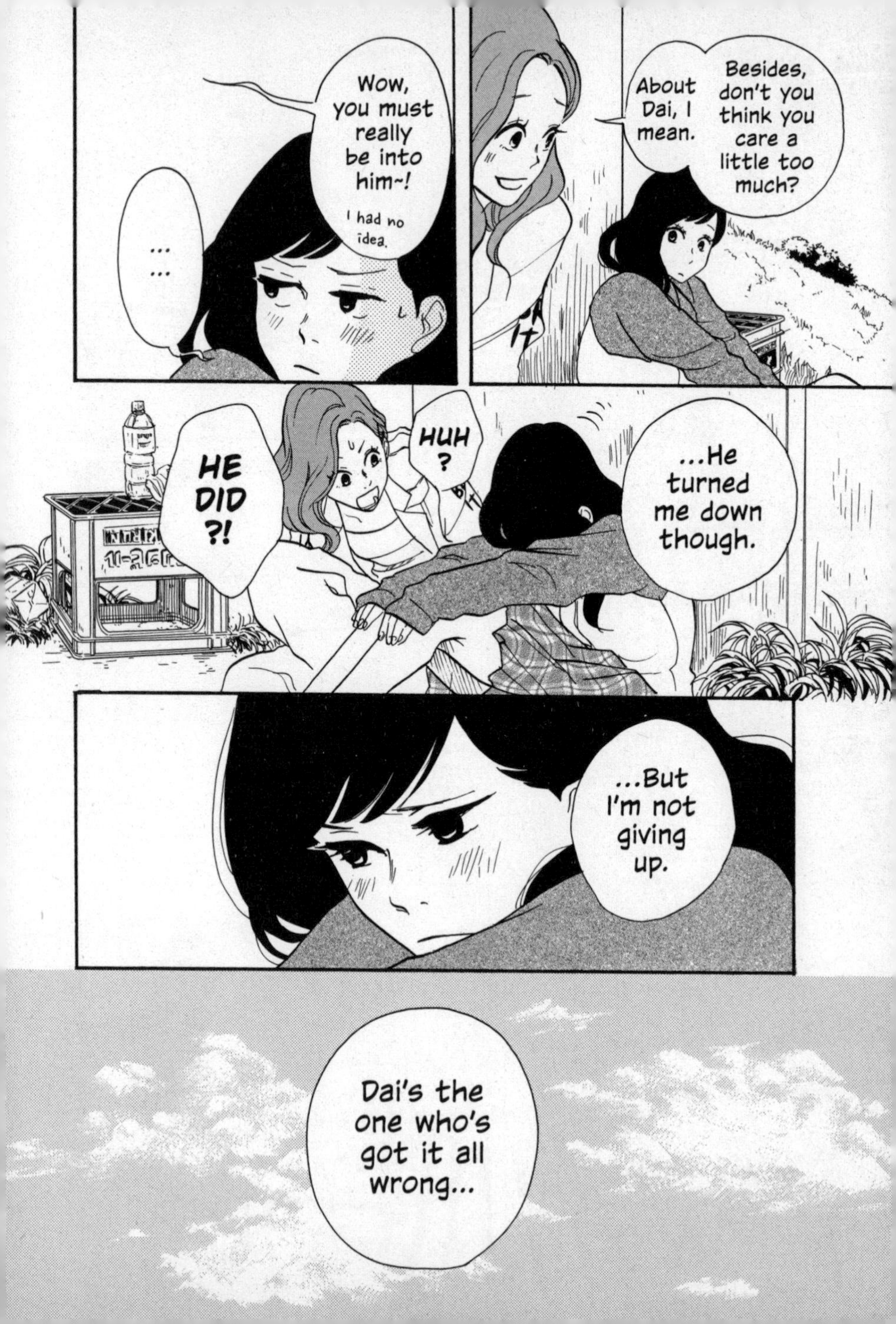
Besides, don't you think you care a little too much?
About Dai, I mean.
Wow, you must really be into him~!
I had no idea.
......
...He turned me down though.
HUH?
HE DID?!
...But I'm not giving up.
Dai's the one who's got it all wrong...

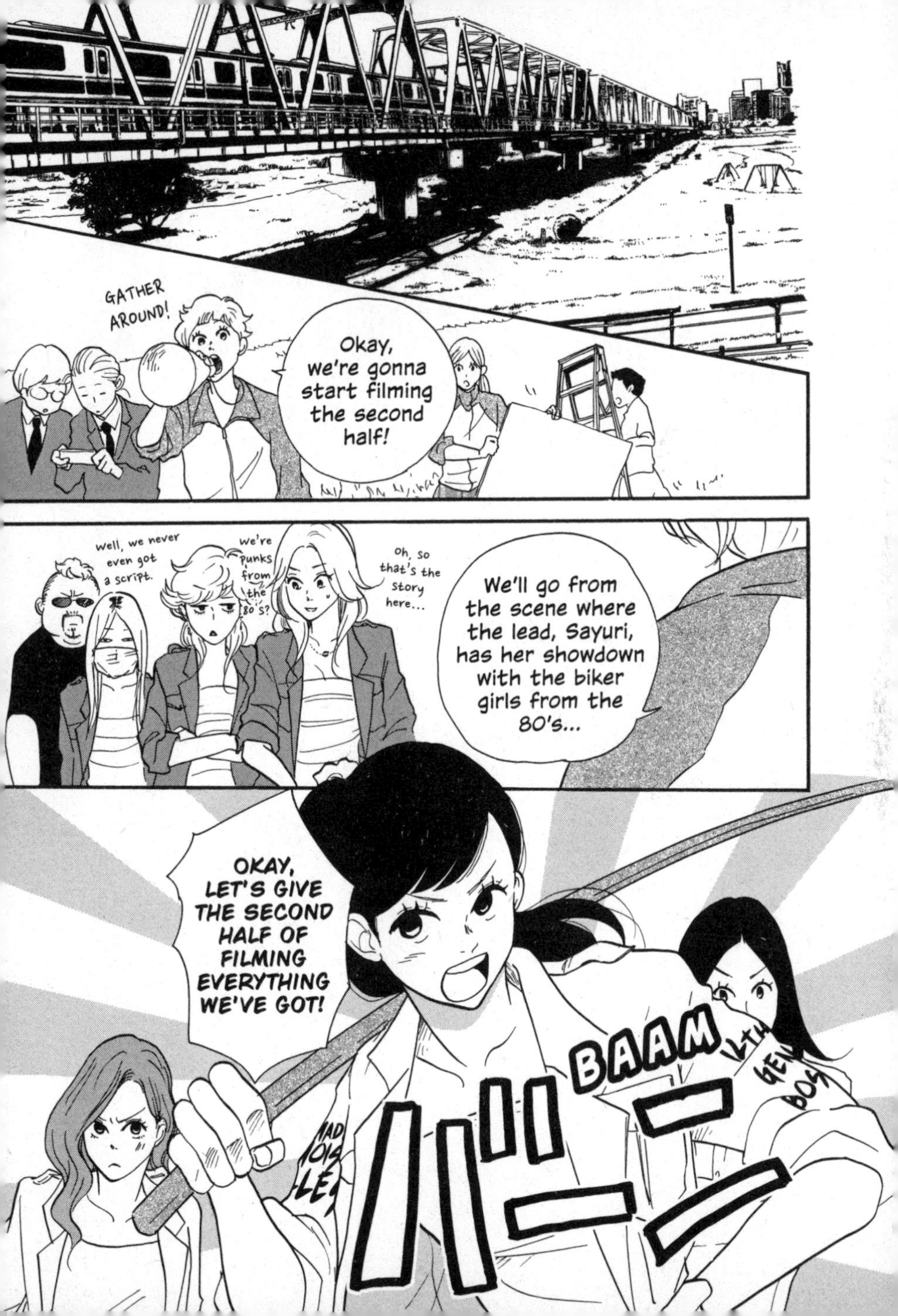
Okay, we're gonna start filming the second half!
GATHER AROUND!
We'll go from the scene where the lead, Sayuri, has her showdown with the biker girls from the 80's...
Oh, so that's the story here...
We're punks from the 80's?
Well, we never even got a script.
OKAY, LET'S GIVE THE SECOND HALF OF FILMING EVERYTHING WE'VE GOT!
BAAM
バーン

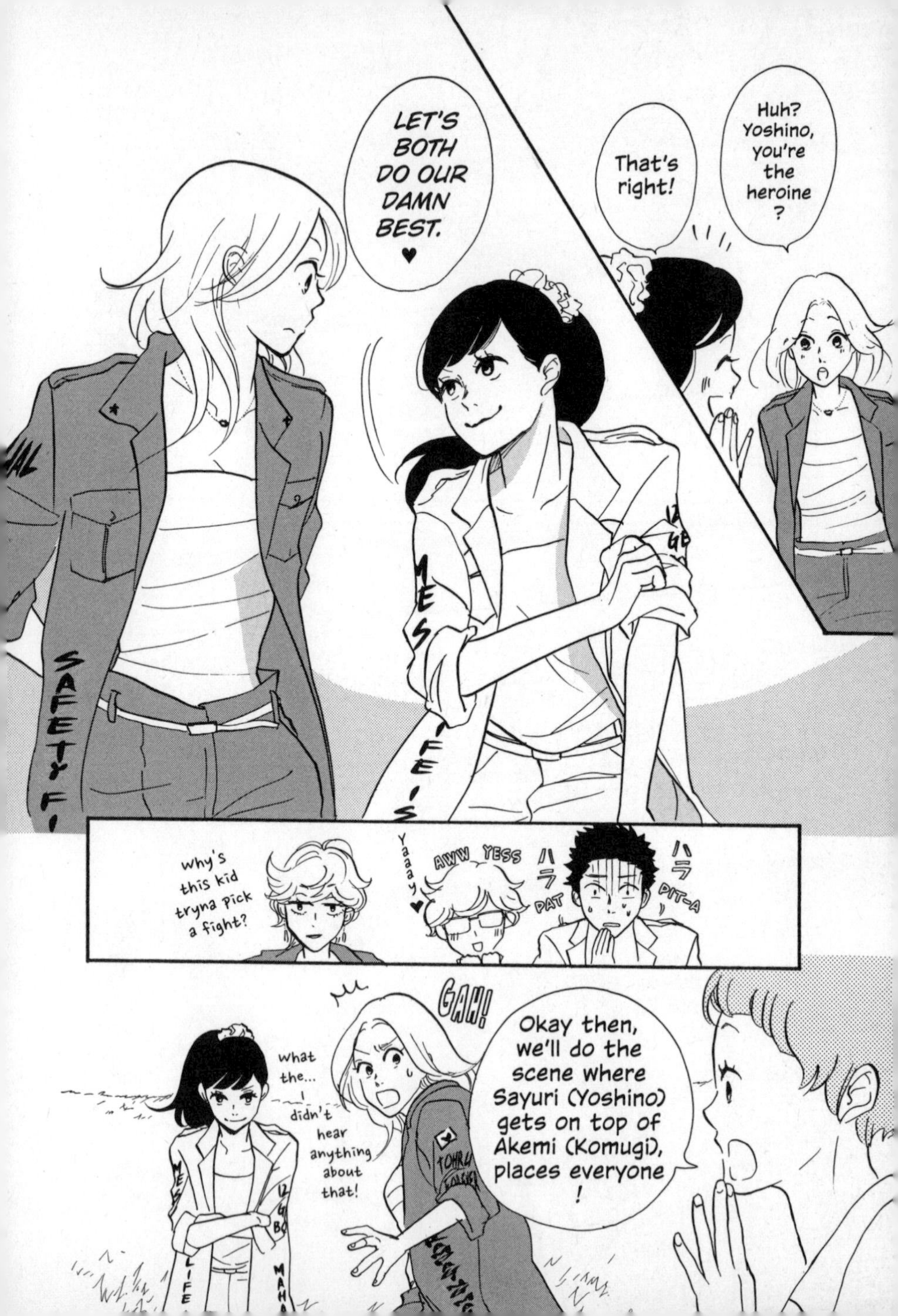
Huh? Yoshino, you're the heroine?
That's right!
LET'S BOTH DO OUR DAMN BEST. ♥
ハラ PIT-A
ハラ PAT
AWW YESS
Yaaaay ♥
why's this kid tryna pick a fight?
Okay then, we'll do the scene where Sayuri (Yoshino) gets on top of Akemi (Komugi), places everyone!
GAH!
what the... I didn't hear anything about that!

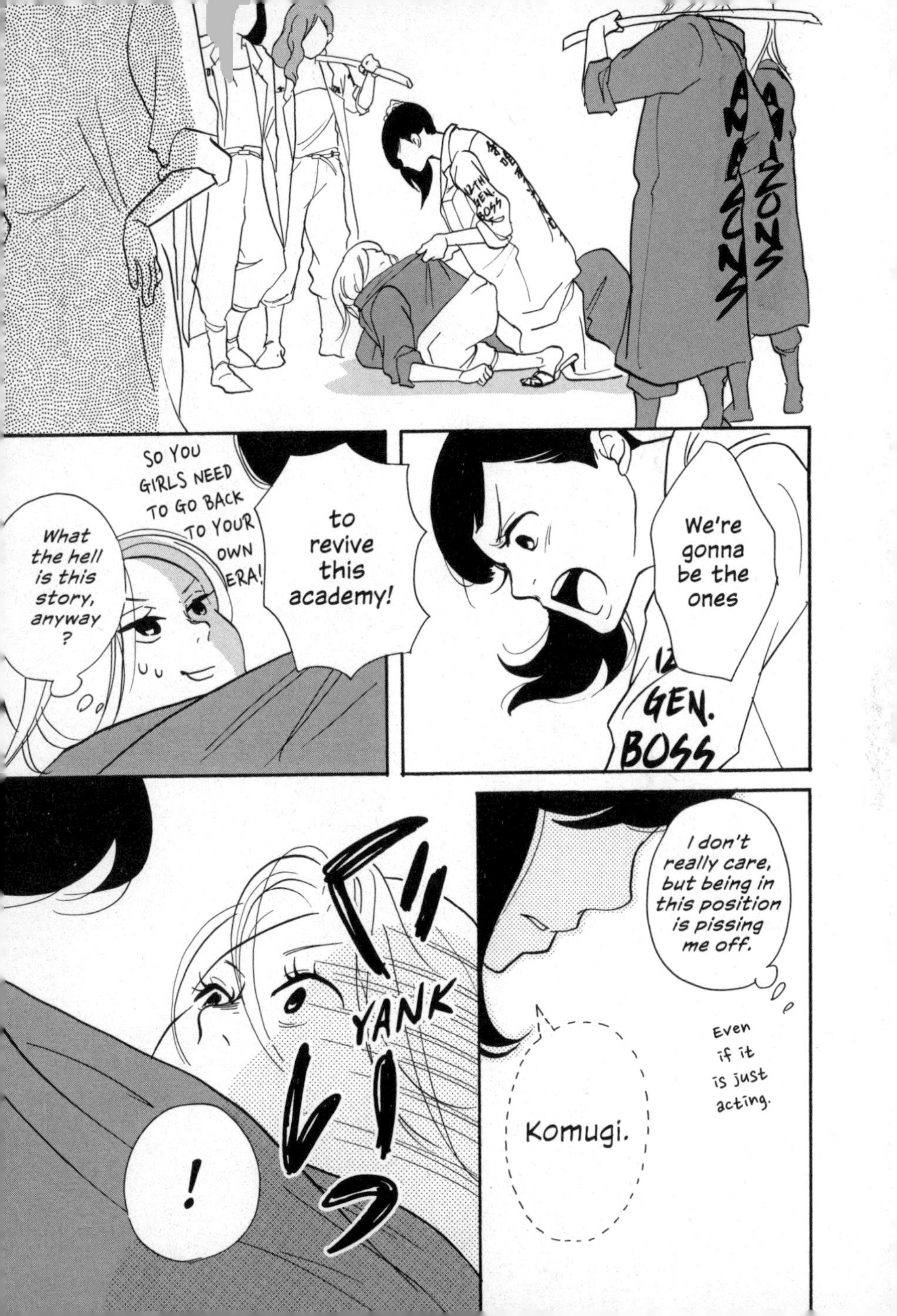
AMAZONS
AMAZONS
We're gonna be the ones
12 GEN. BOSS
to revive this academy!
SO YOU GIRLS NEED TO GO BACK TO YOUR OWN ERA!
What the hell is this story, anyway?
I don't really care, but being in this position is pissing me off.
Even if it is just acting.
Komugi.
YANK
!

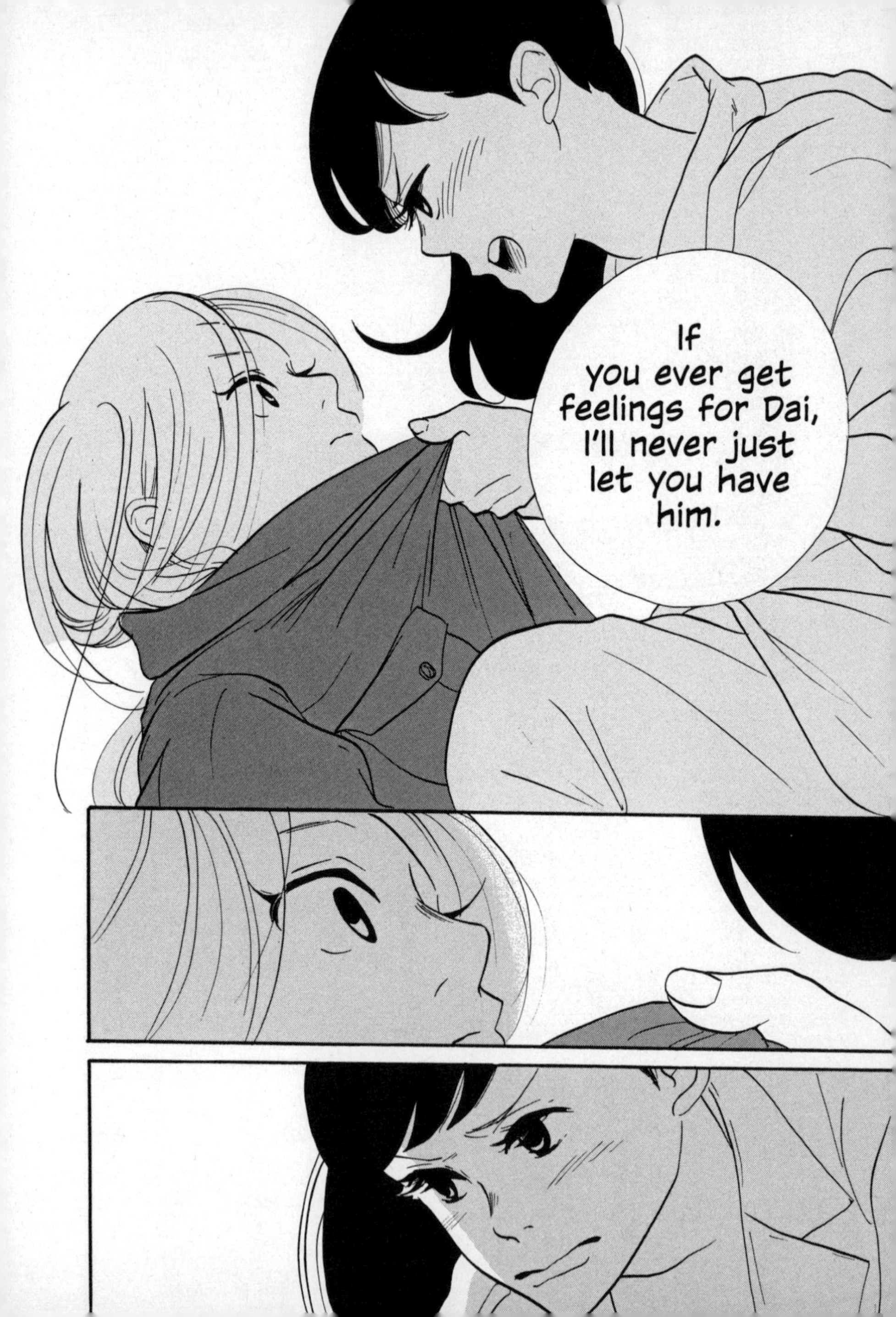
If you ever get feelings for Dai, I'll never just let you have him.

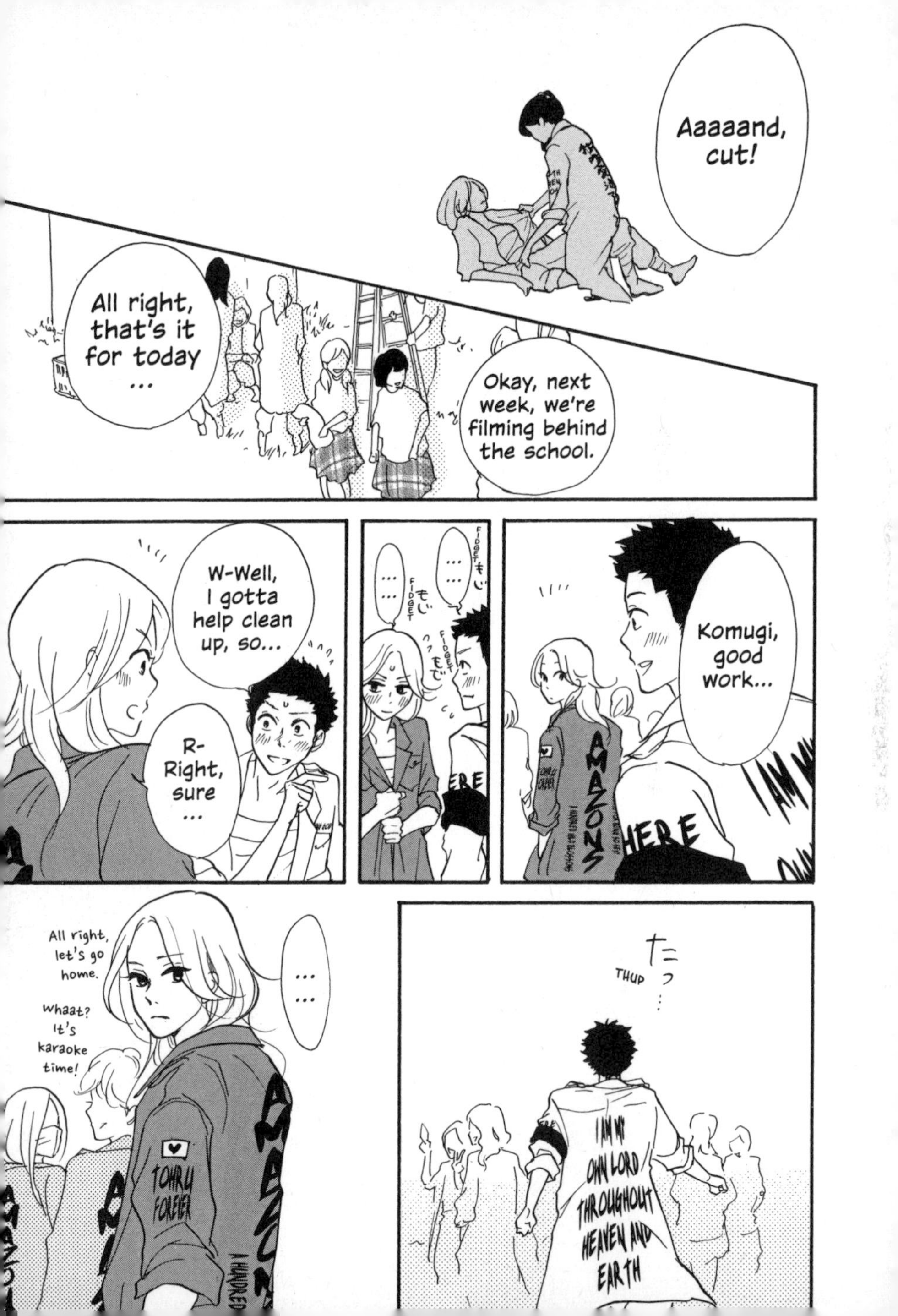
Aaaaand, cut!
Okay, next week, we're filming behind the school.
All right, that's it for today...
Komugi, good work...
HERE
AMAZONS
TOHRU FOREVER
FIDGET
... ...
FIDGET
... ...
FIDGET
HERE
W-Well, I gotta help clean up, so...
R-Right, sure...
THUP
I AM MY OWN LORD THROUGHOUT HEAVEN AND EARTH
... ...
All right, let's go home.
Whaat? It's karaoke time!
TOHRU FOREVER

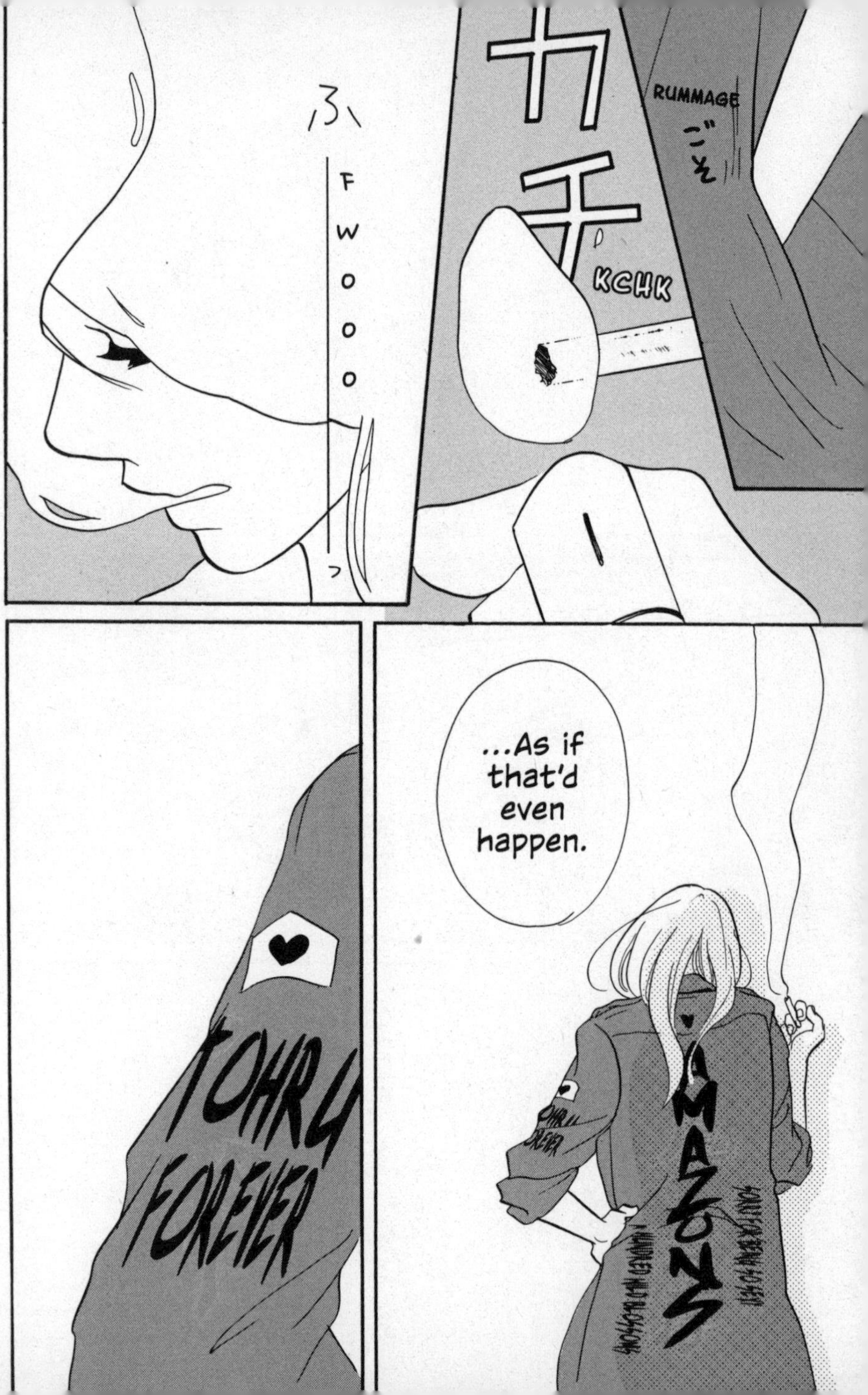
カチ
KCHK
ごそ
RUMMAGE
ふ
FWOOO
...As if that'd even happen.
AMAZONS
TOHRU FOREVER
TOHRU FOREVER

30 DECISIVE MOMENT

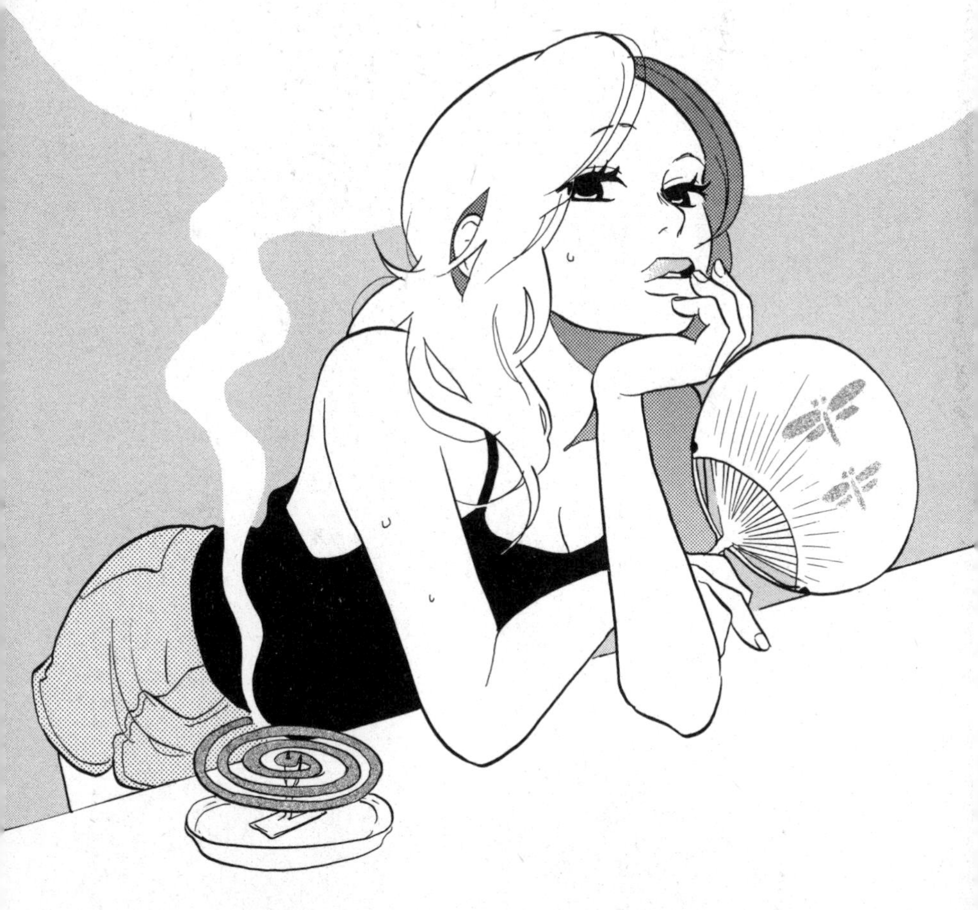

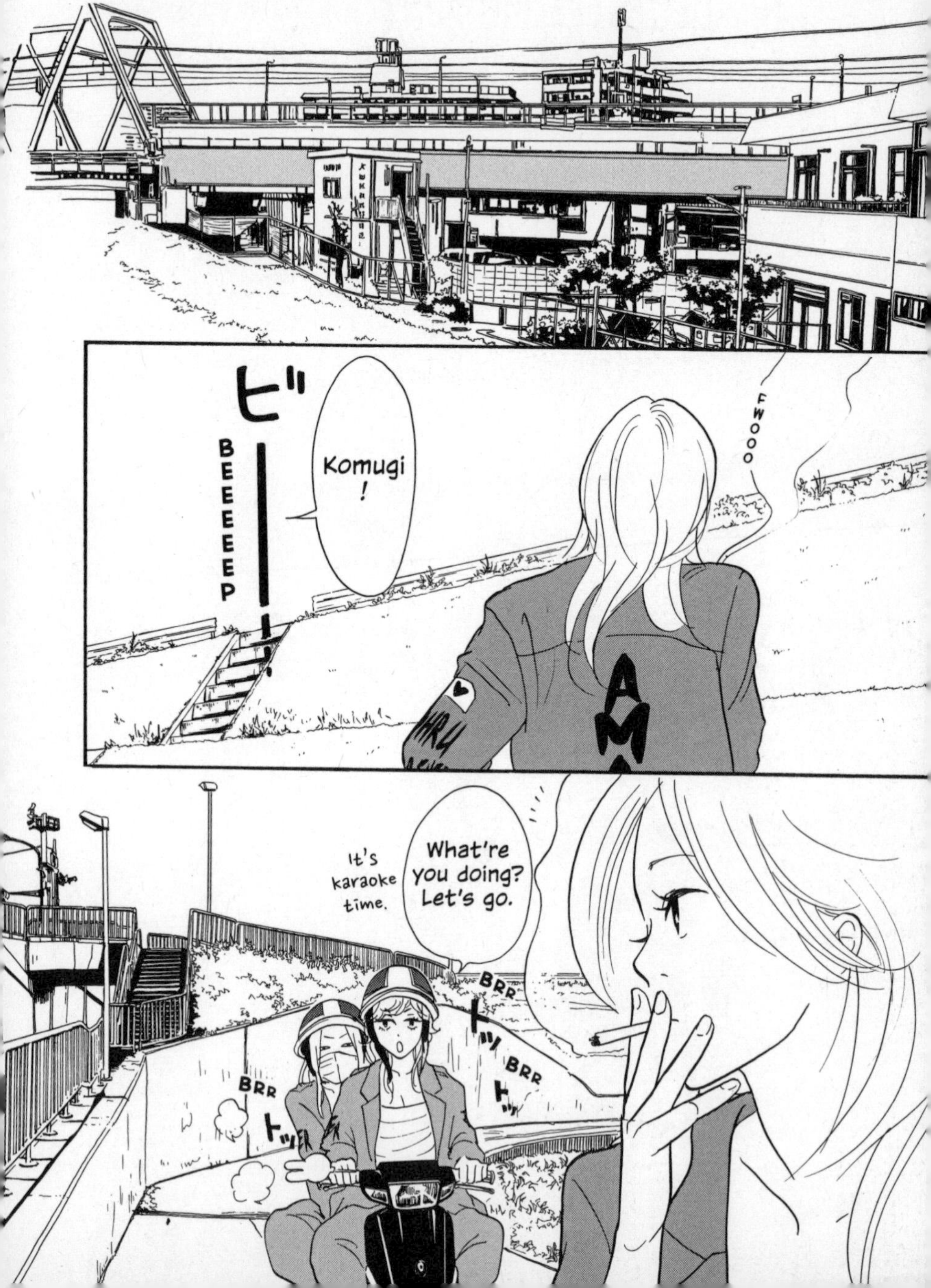
FWOOO
Komugi!
ビー
BEEEEEEP
What're you doing? Let's go.
It's karaoke time.
BRR
トッ
BRR
トッ
BRR
トッ

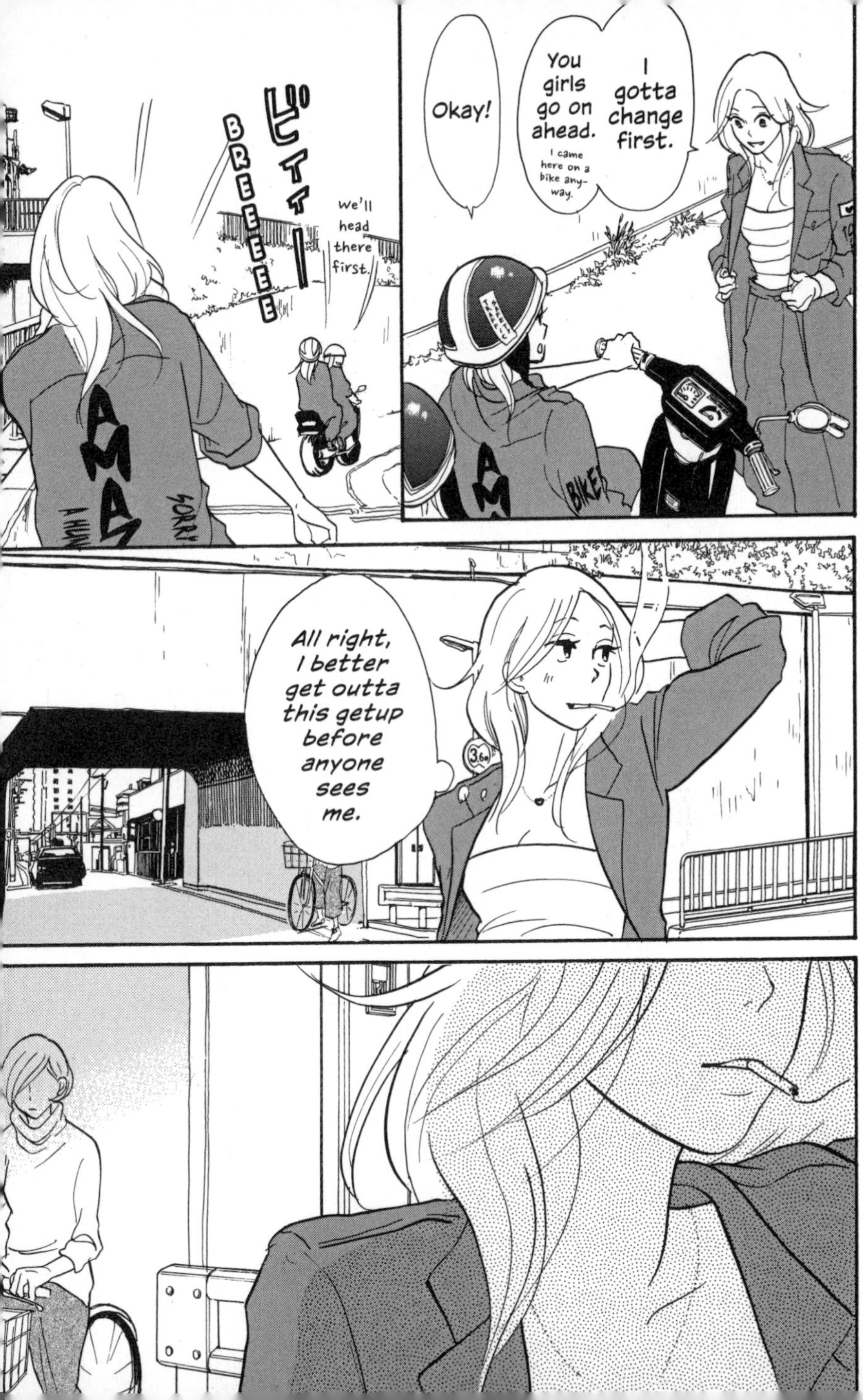
I gotta change first.
You girls go on ahead.
I came here on a bike anyway.
Okay!
BREEEEEE
we'll head there first.
All right, I better get outta this getup before anyone sees me.

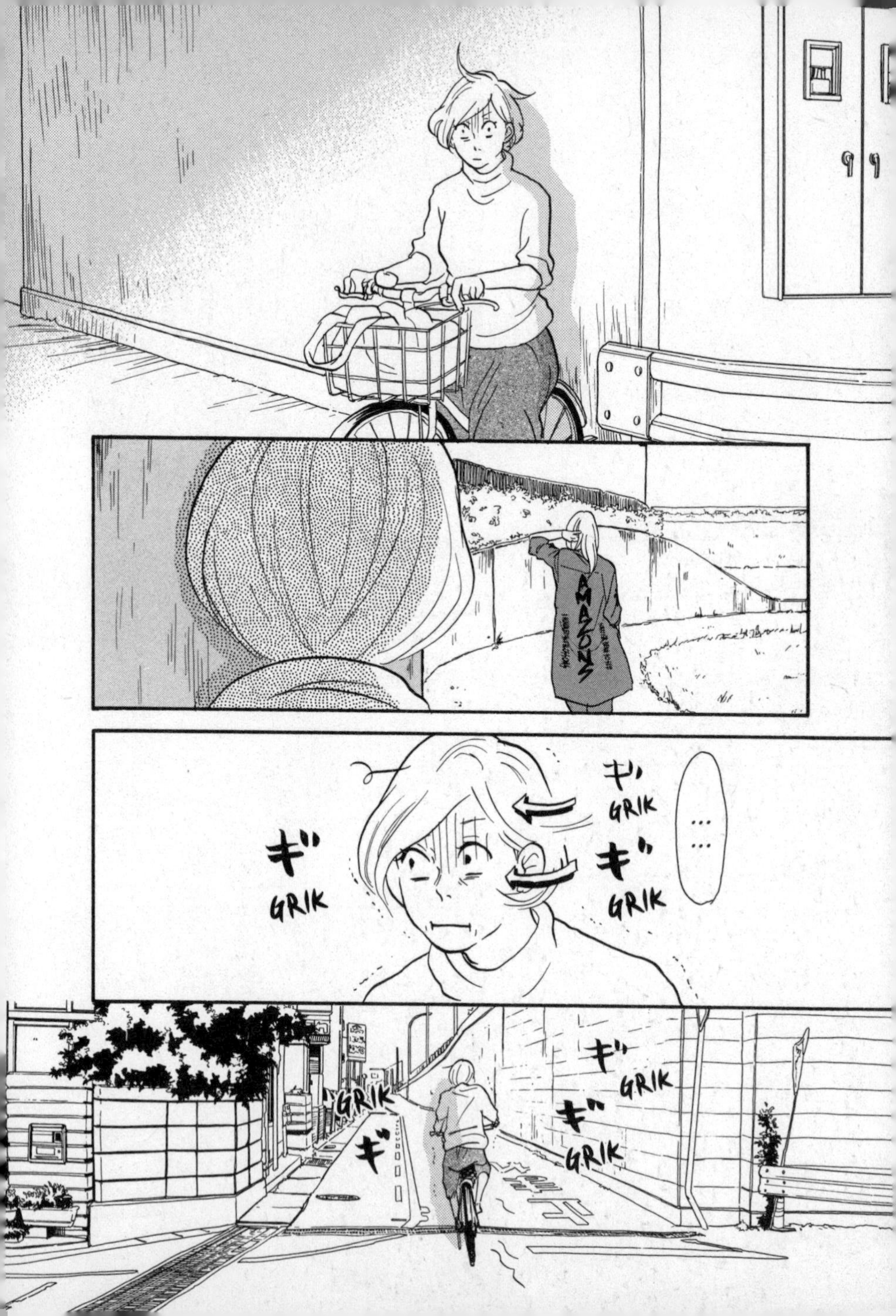
AMAZONS
......
ギ GRIK
ギ GRIK
ギ GRIK
ギ GRIK
ギ GRIK
GRIK
ギ

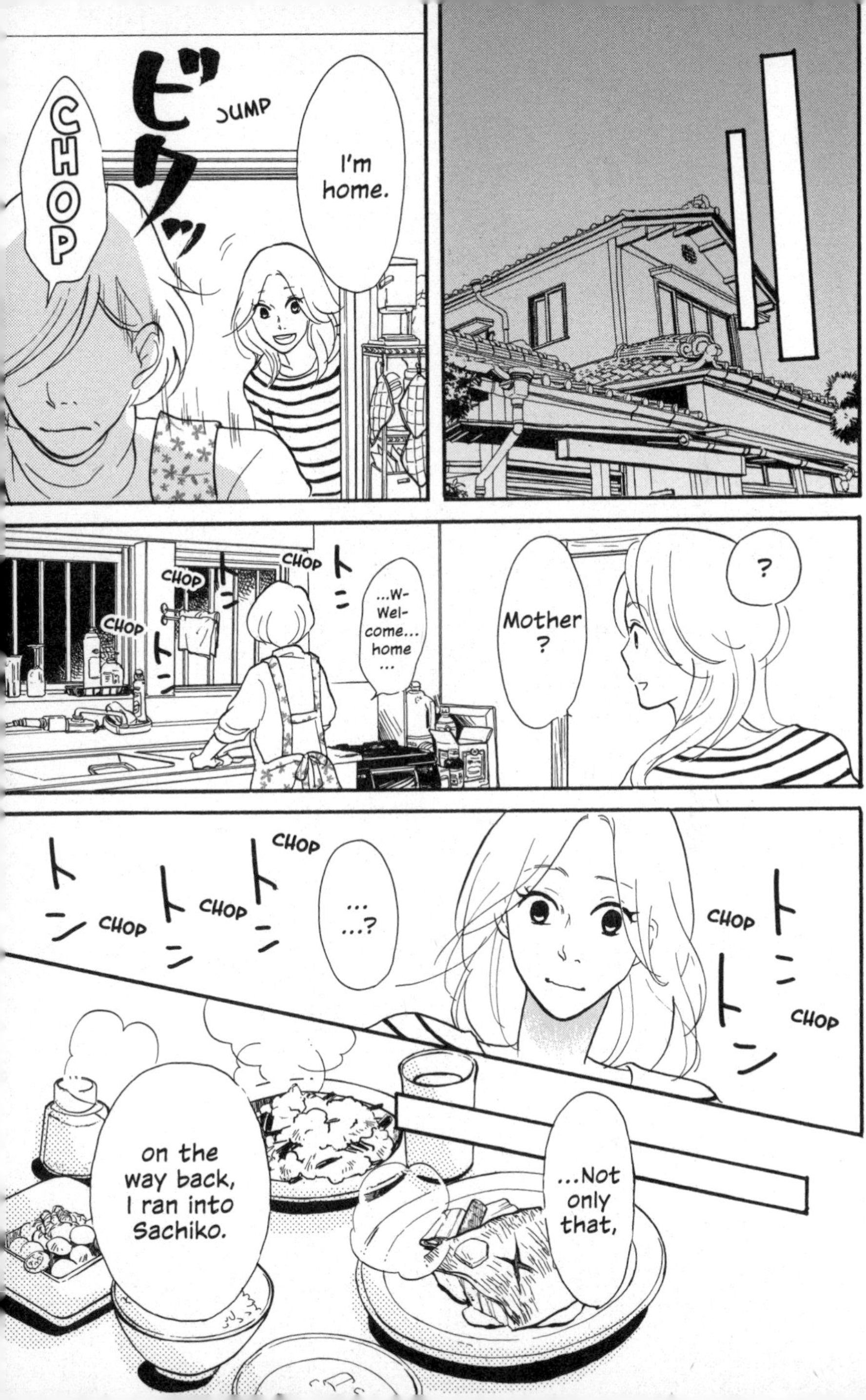
I'm home.
ビクッ
JUMP
CHOP
?
Mother?
...W-Wel-come... home...
CHOP
トン
CHOP
トン
CHOP
トン
CHOP
トン
CHOP
トン
......?
CHOP
トン
CHOP
トン
...Not only that,
on the way back, I ran into Sachiko.

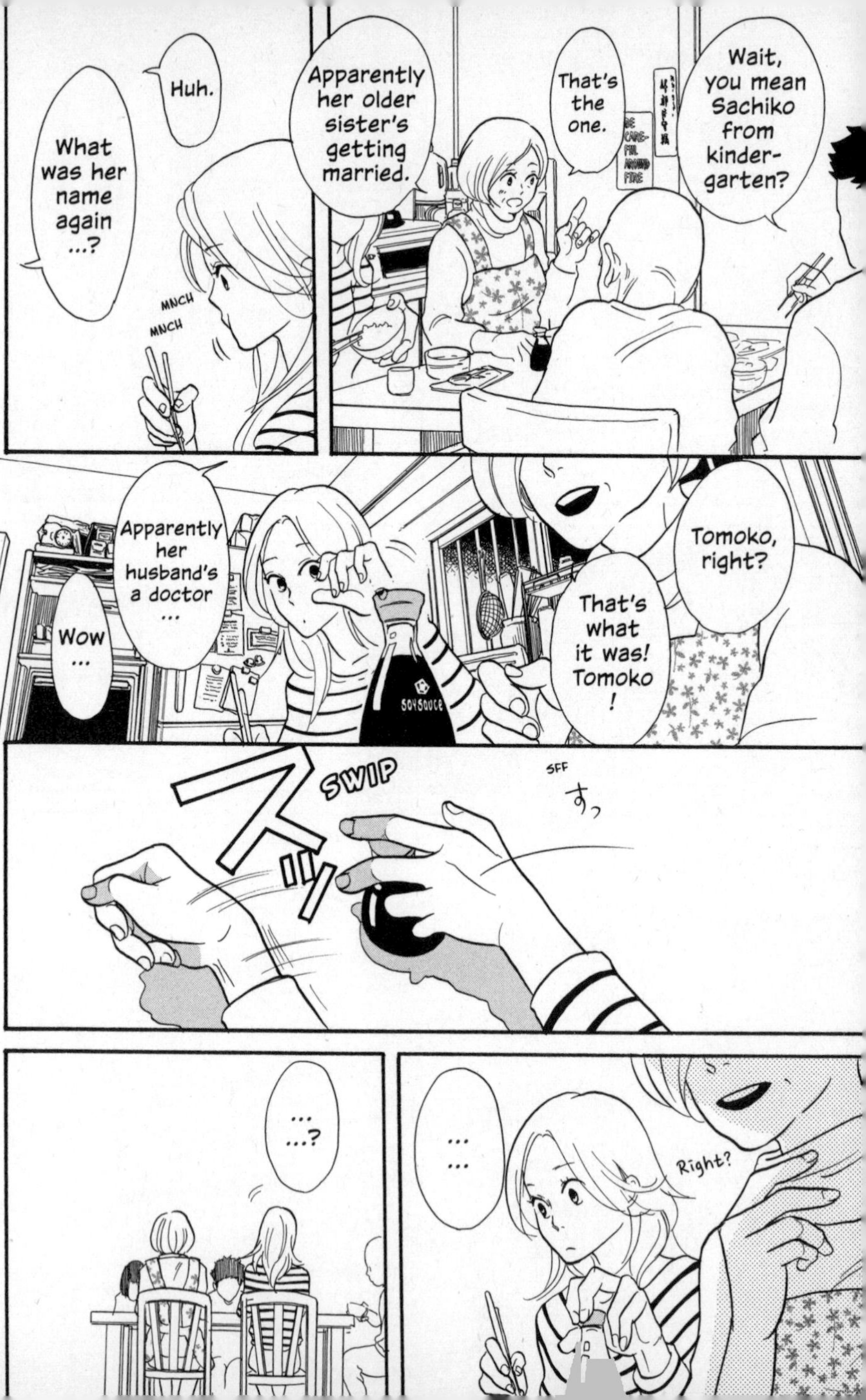
Wait, you mean Sachiko from kinder-garten?
That's the one.
BE CARE-FUL AROUND FIRE
Apparently her older sister's getting married.
Huh.
What was her name again ...?
MNCH
MNCH
Tomoko, right?
That's what it was! Tomoko!
Apparently her husband's a doctor ...
Wow ...
SOYSAUCE
SFF
すっ
SWIP
Right?
... ...
... ...?

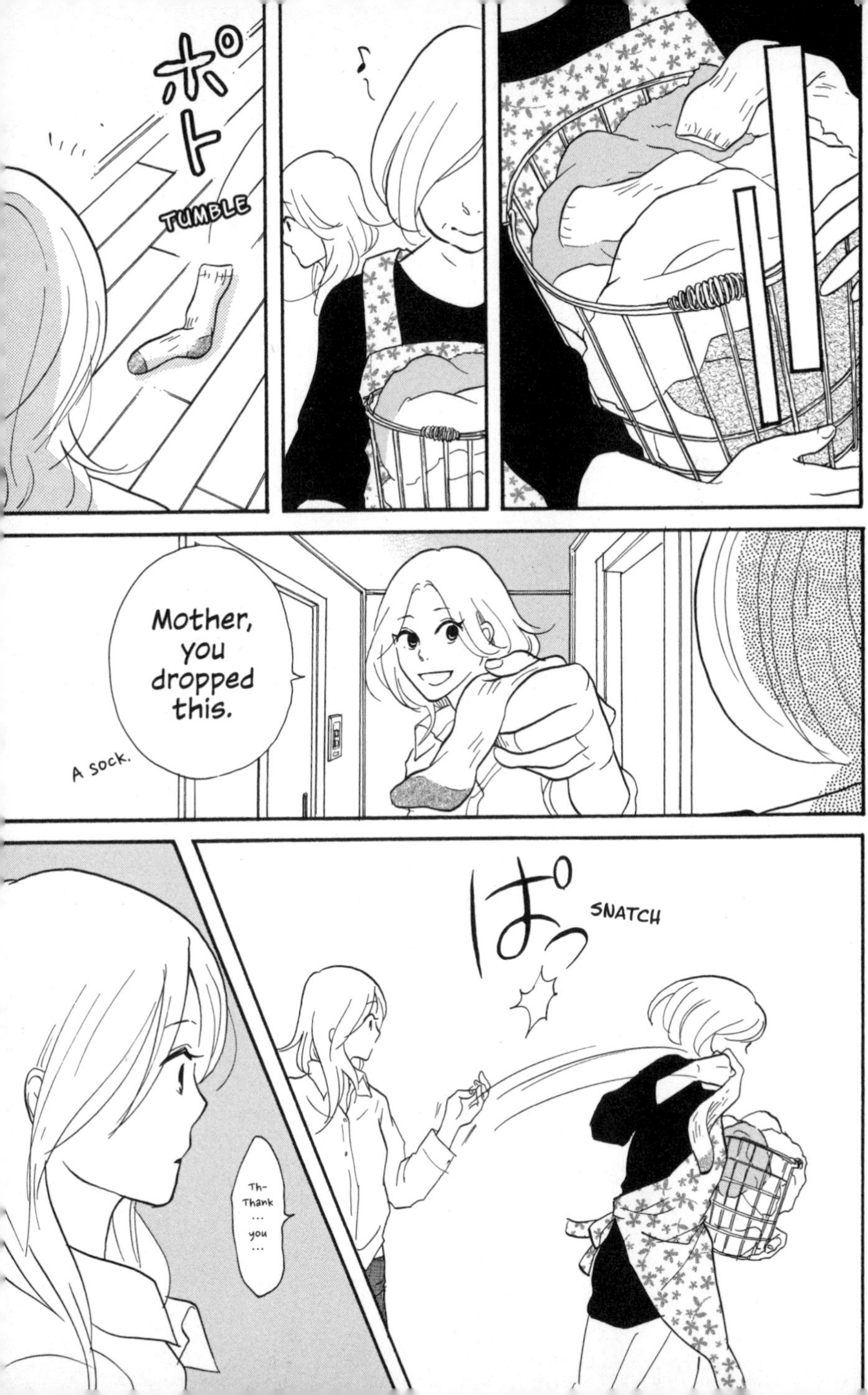
ポト
TUMBLE
Mother, you dropped this.
A sock.
ぱっ
SNATCH
Th- Thank ... you ...

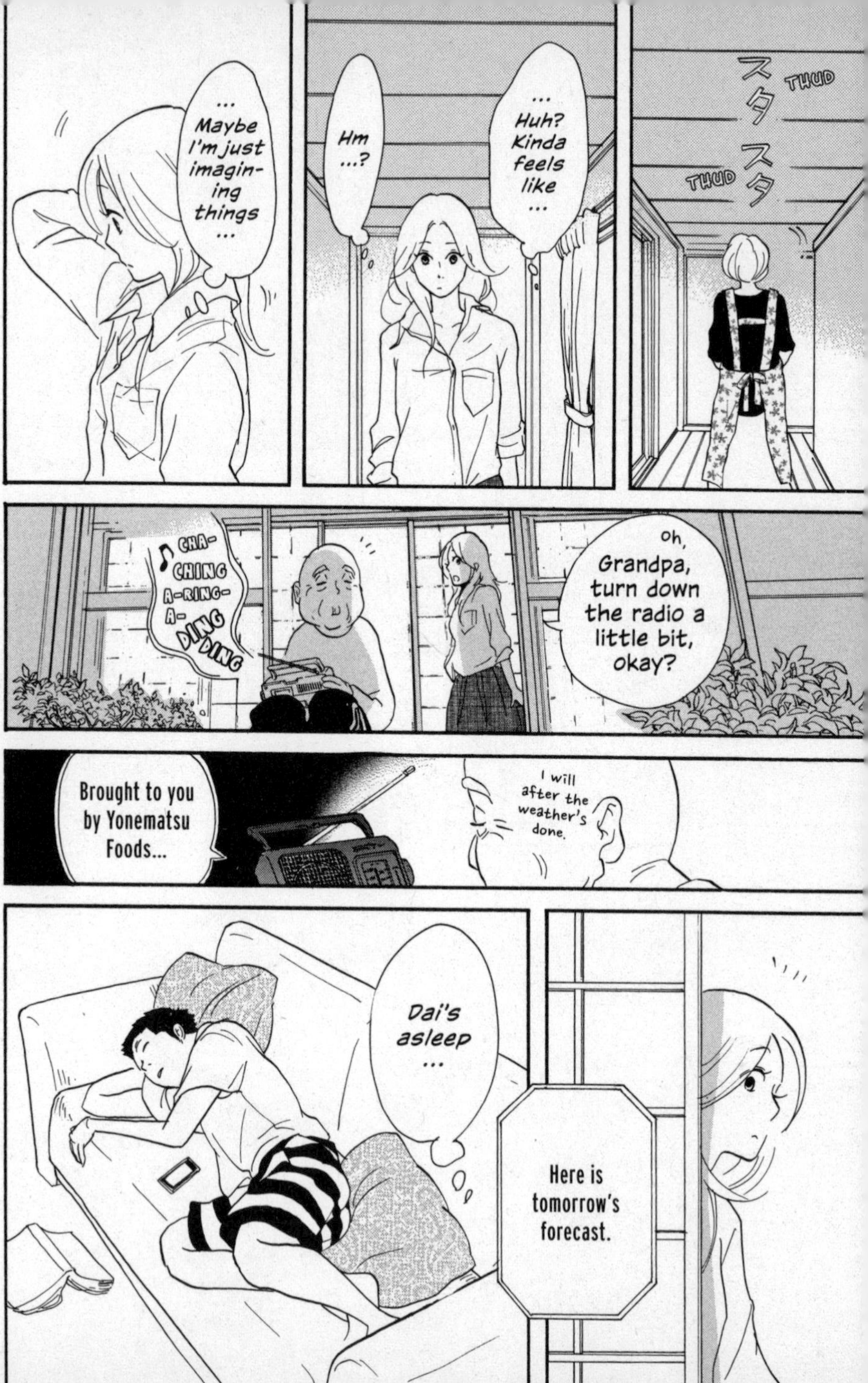
スタ THUD
スタ THUD
... Huh? Kinda feels like ...
Hm ...?
... Maybe I'm just imagining things ...
Oh, Grandpa, turn down the radio a little bit, okay?
CHA-CHING A-RING-A-DING DING
I will after the weather's done.
Brought to you by Yonematsu Foods...
Dai's asleep ...
Here is tomorrow's forecast.

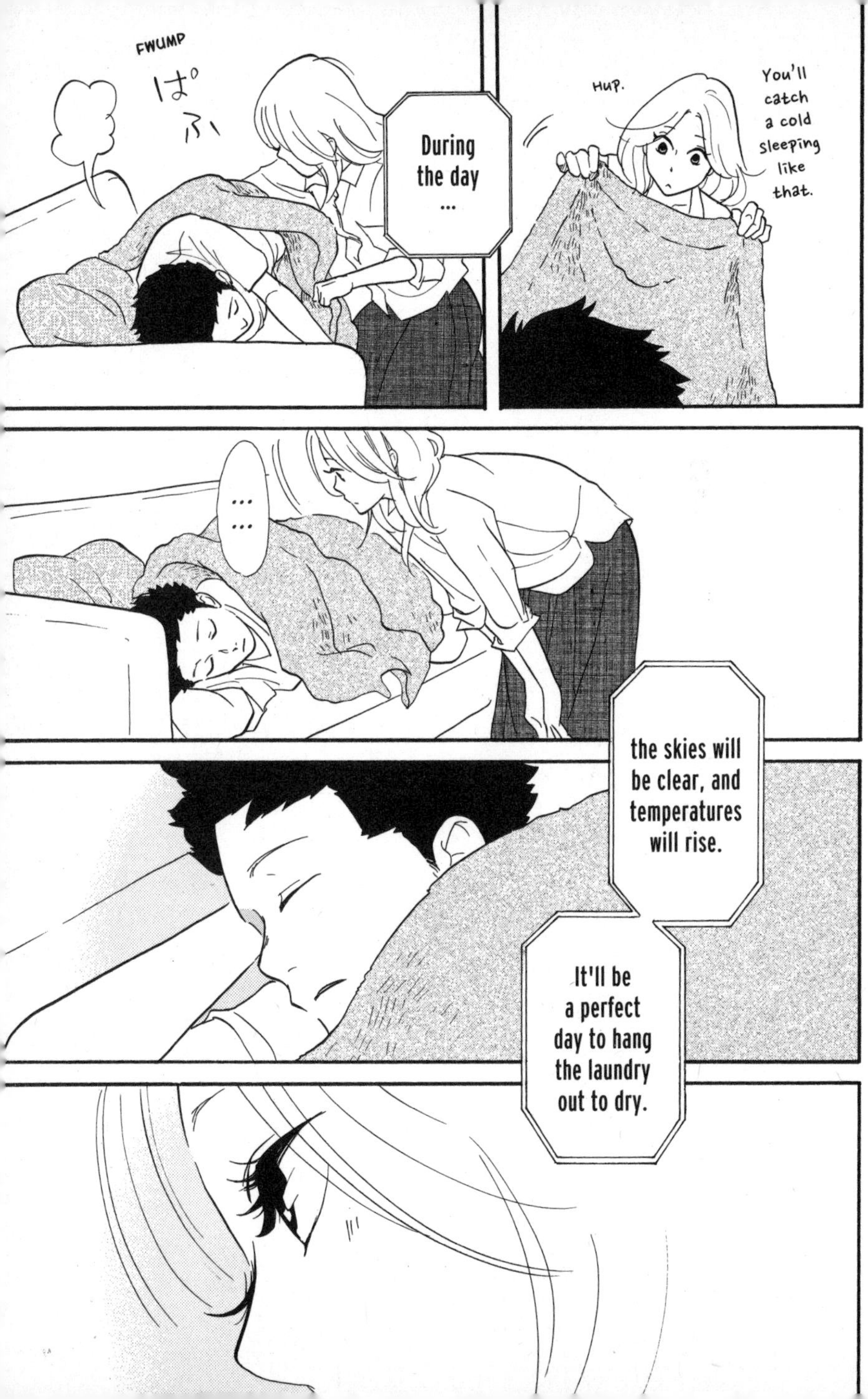
You'll catch a cold sleeping like that.
HUP.
During the day ...
FWUMP
ぱふ
...
...
the skies will be clear, and temperatures will rise.
It'll be a perfect day to hang the laundry out to dry.

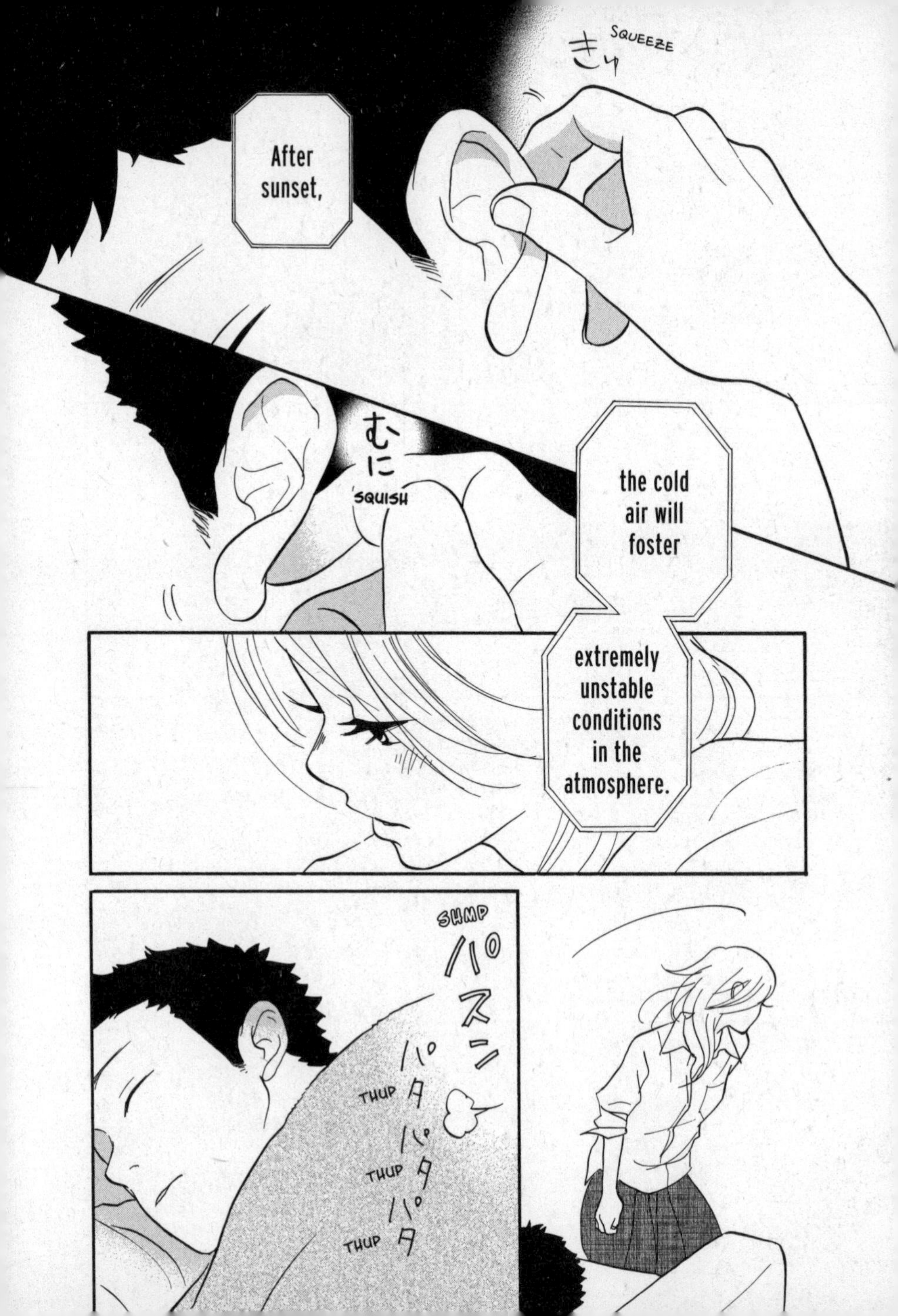
SQUEEZE
きゅ
After sunset,
the cold air will foster
extremely unstable conditions in the atmosphere.
むに
SQUISH
SHMP
パスン
パタ
THUP
パタ
THUP
パタ
THUP

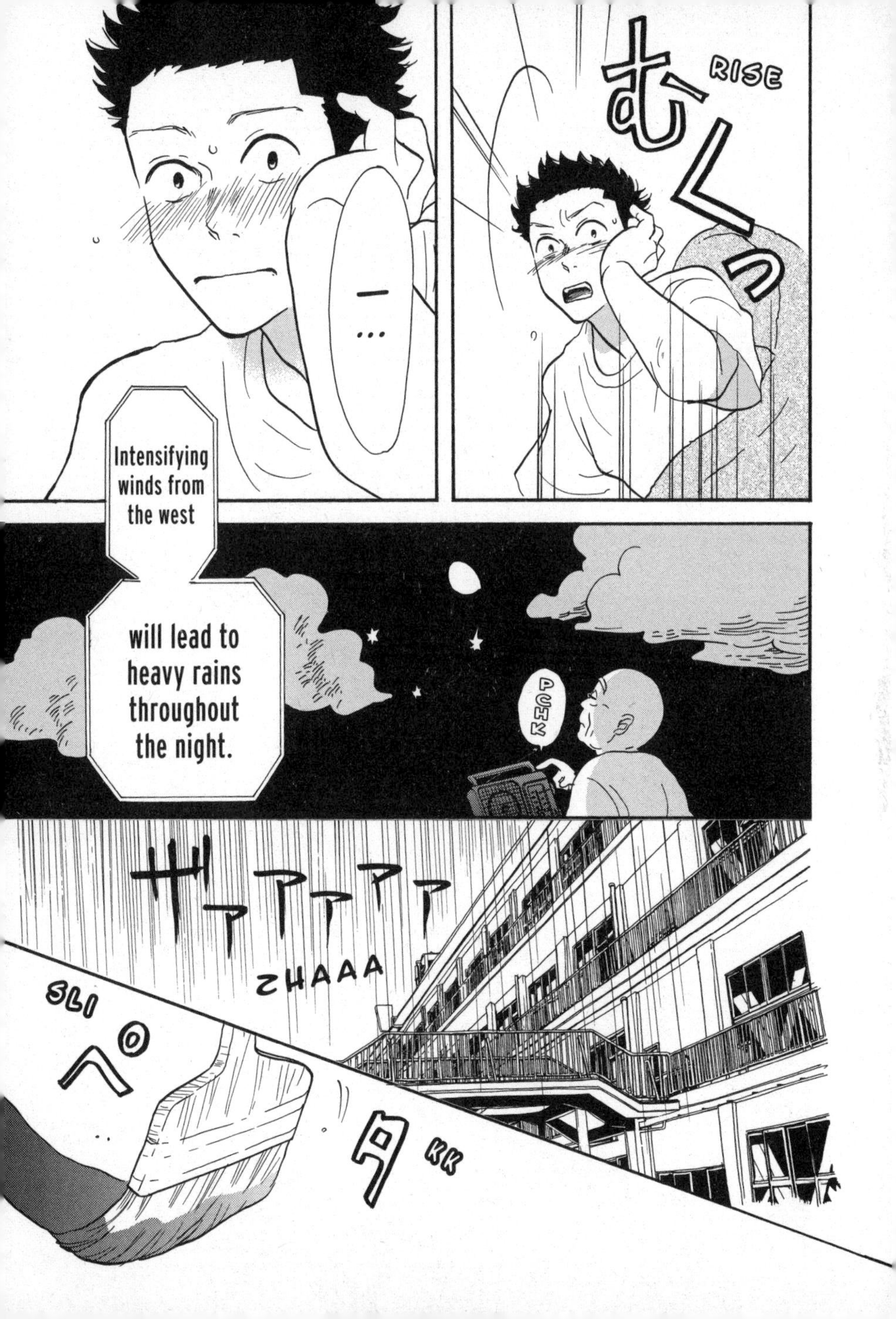
むくっ
RISE
—...
Intensifying winds from the west
will lead to heavy rains throughout the night.
PCHK
ザァァァァ
ZHAAA
ペタ
SLI
KK

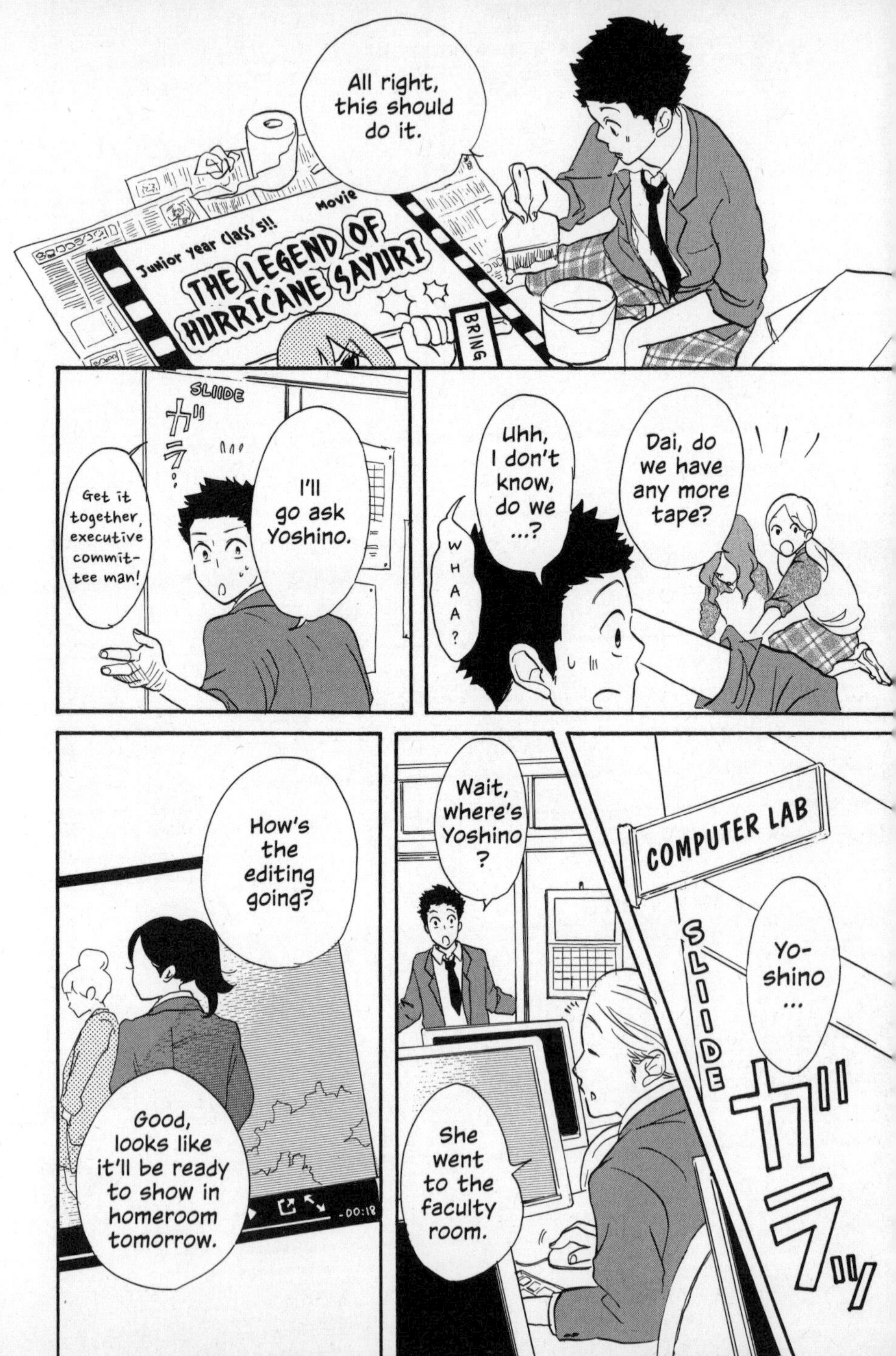
All right, this should do it.
Movie
Junior year Class 5!!
THE LEGEND OF HURRICANE SAYURI
BRING
Dai, do we have any more tape?
Uhh, I don't know, do we ...?
WHAA?
SLIIDE
I'll go ask Yoshino.
Get it together, executive commit-tee man!
COMPUTER LAB
SLIIDE
Yo-shino ...
Wait, where's Yoshino?
She went to the faculty room.
How's the editing going?
-00:18
Good, looks like it'll be ready to show in homeroom tomorrow.

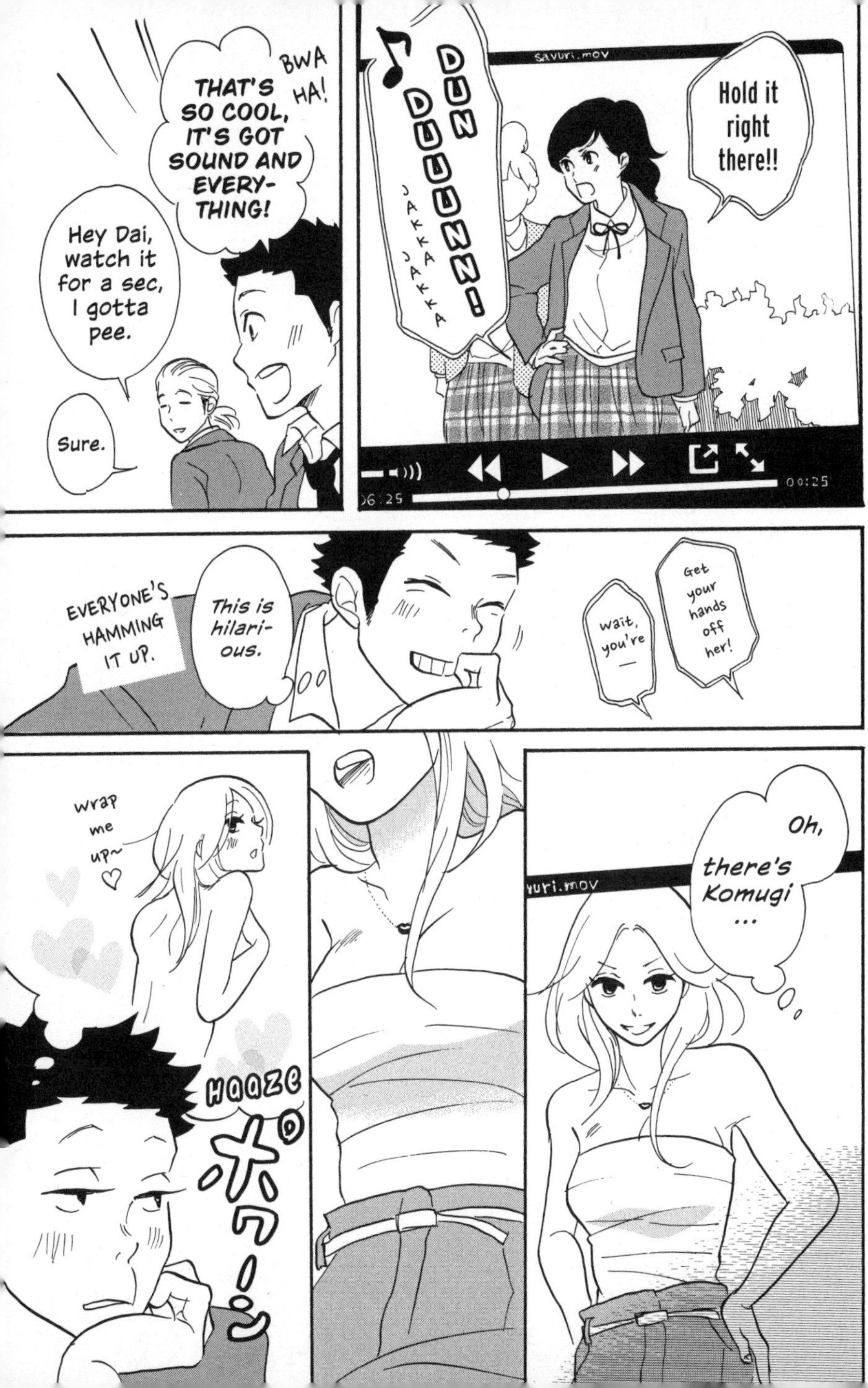
sayuri.mov
Hold it right there!!
DUN DUUUUNN!
JAKKA JAKKA
06:25
00:25
BWA HA!
THAT'S SO COOL, IT'S GOT SOUND AND EVERYTHING!
Hey Dai, watch it for a sec, I gotta pee.
Sure.
Get your hands off her!
Wait, you're —
This is hilari-ous.
EVERYONE'S HAMMING IT UP.
yuri.mov
Oh, there's Komugi ...
wrap me up~ ♡
Haaze
ポワ〜ン

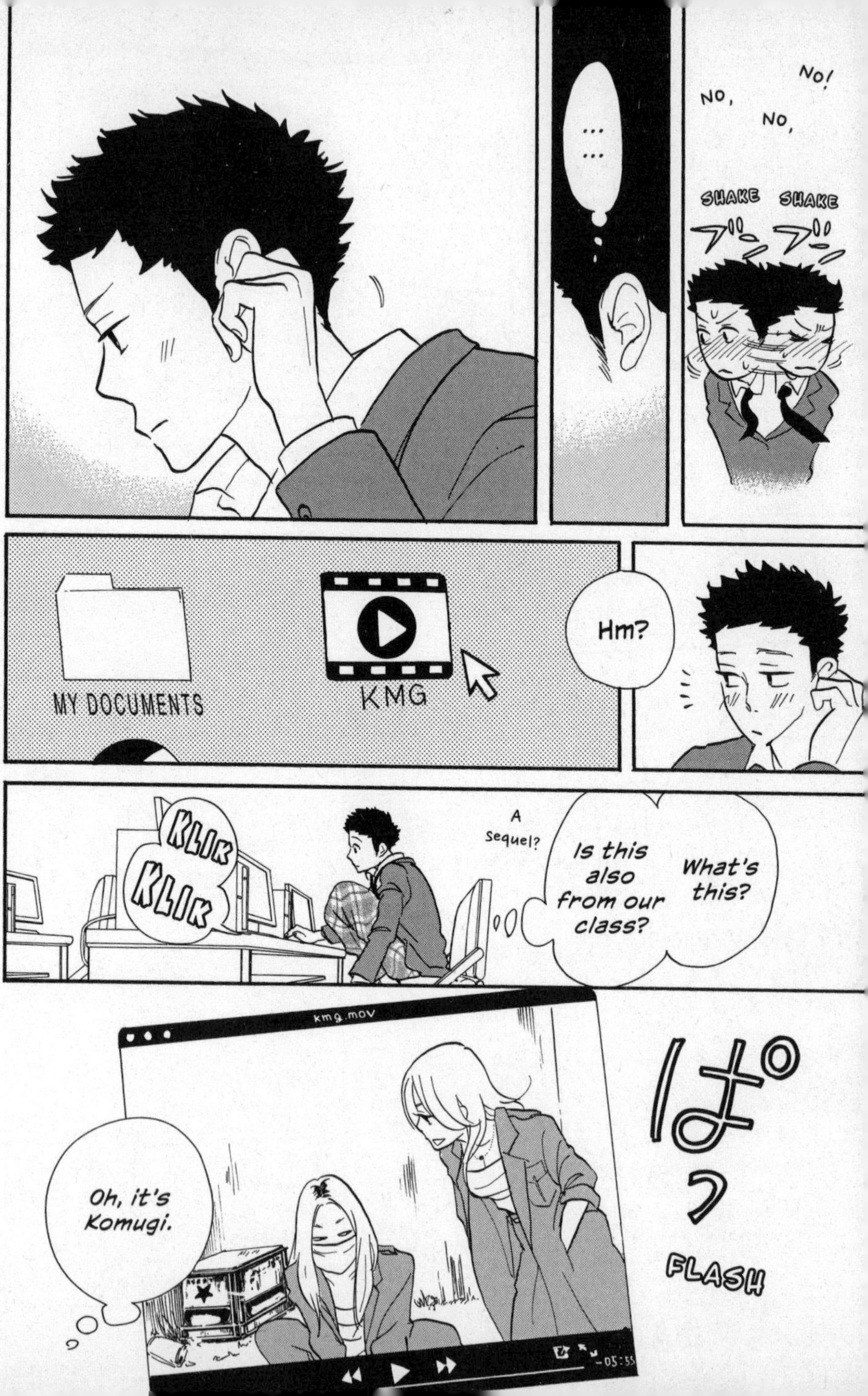
No,
No,
No!
SHAKE
SHAKE
... ...
Hm?
KMG
MY DOCUMENTS
What's this?
Is this also from our class?
A sequel?
KLIK
KLIK
ぱっ
FLASH
kmg.mov
Oh, it's Komugi.

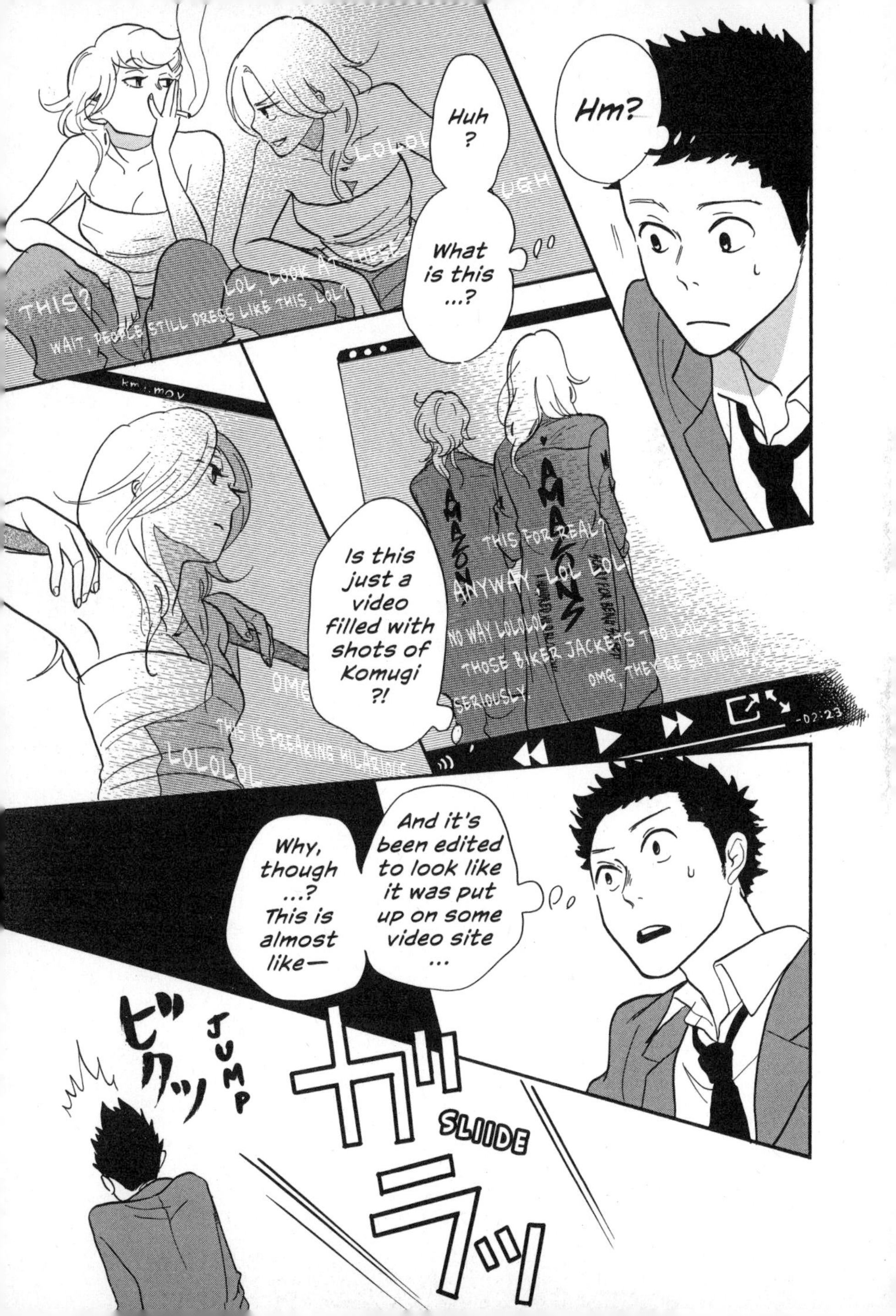

Hm?
Huh?
What is this ...?
LOLOL
THIS?
WAIT, PEOPLE STILL DRESS LIKE THIS, LOL
Is this just a video filled with shots of Komugi?!
AMAZONS
THIS FOR REAL?
ANYWAY, LOL LOL
NO WAY LOLOLOL
SERIOUSLY
LOLOLOL
-02:23
And it's been edited to look like it was put up on some video site ...
Why, though ...? This is almost like—
SLIIDE
JUMP

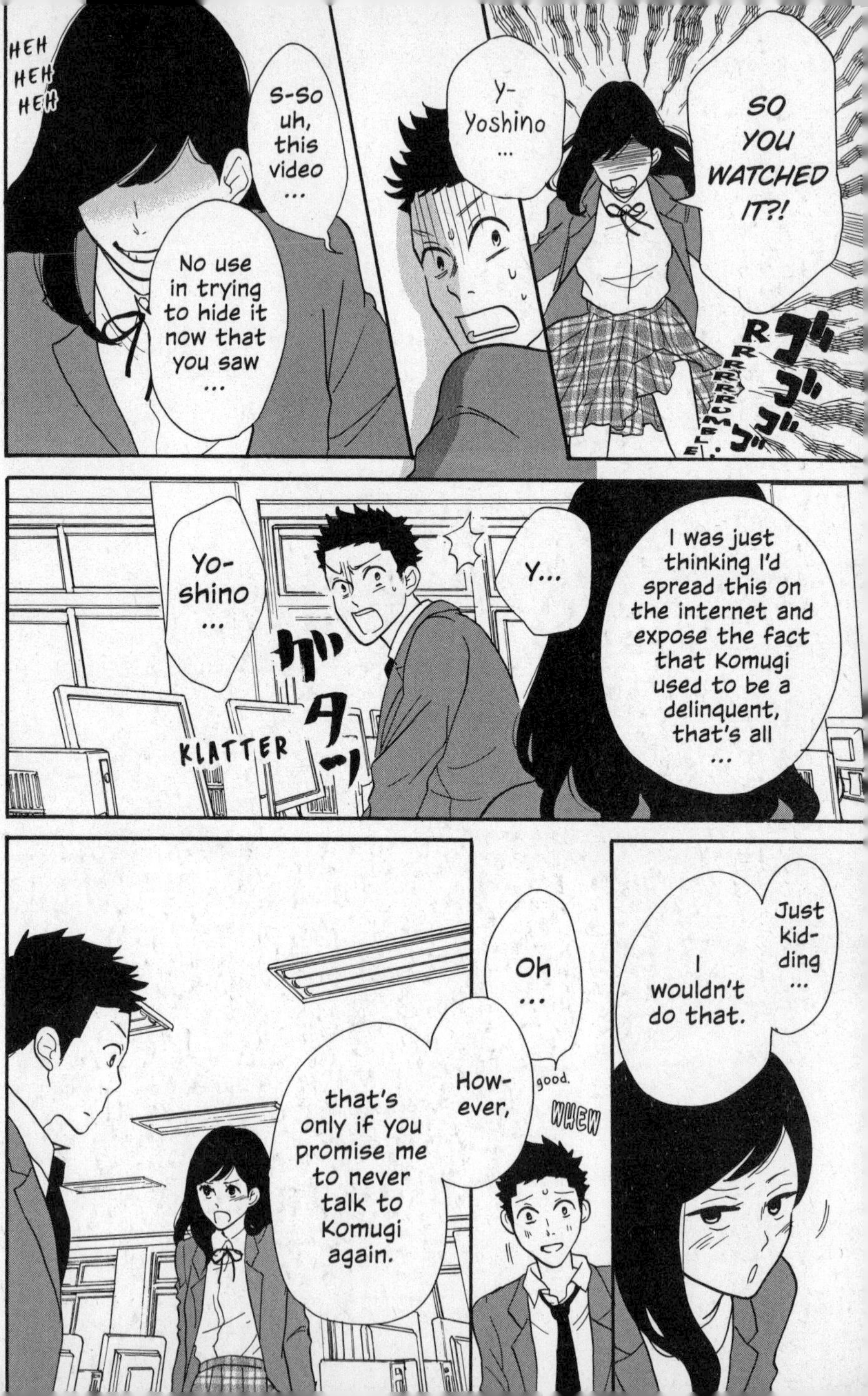
SO YOU WATCHED IT?!
RRRRRRUMBLE..
ゴゴゴゴ
Y-Yoshino ...
S-So uh, this video ...
No use in trying to hide it now that you saw ...
HEH HEH HEH
I was just thinking I'd spread this on the internet and expose the fact that Komugi used to be a delinquent, that's all ...
Y...
Yo-shino ...
ガタッ
KLATTER
Just kid-ding ...
I wouldn't do that.
Oh ... good.
WHEW
How-ever,
that's only if you promise me to never talk to Komugi again.

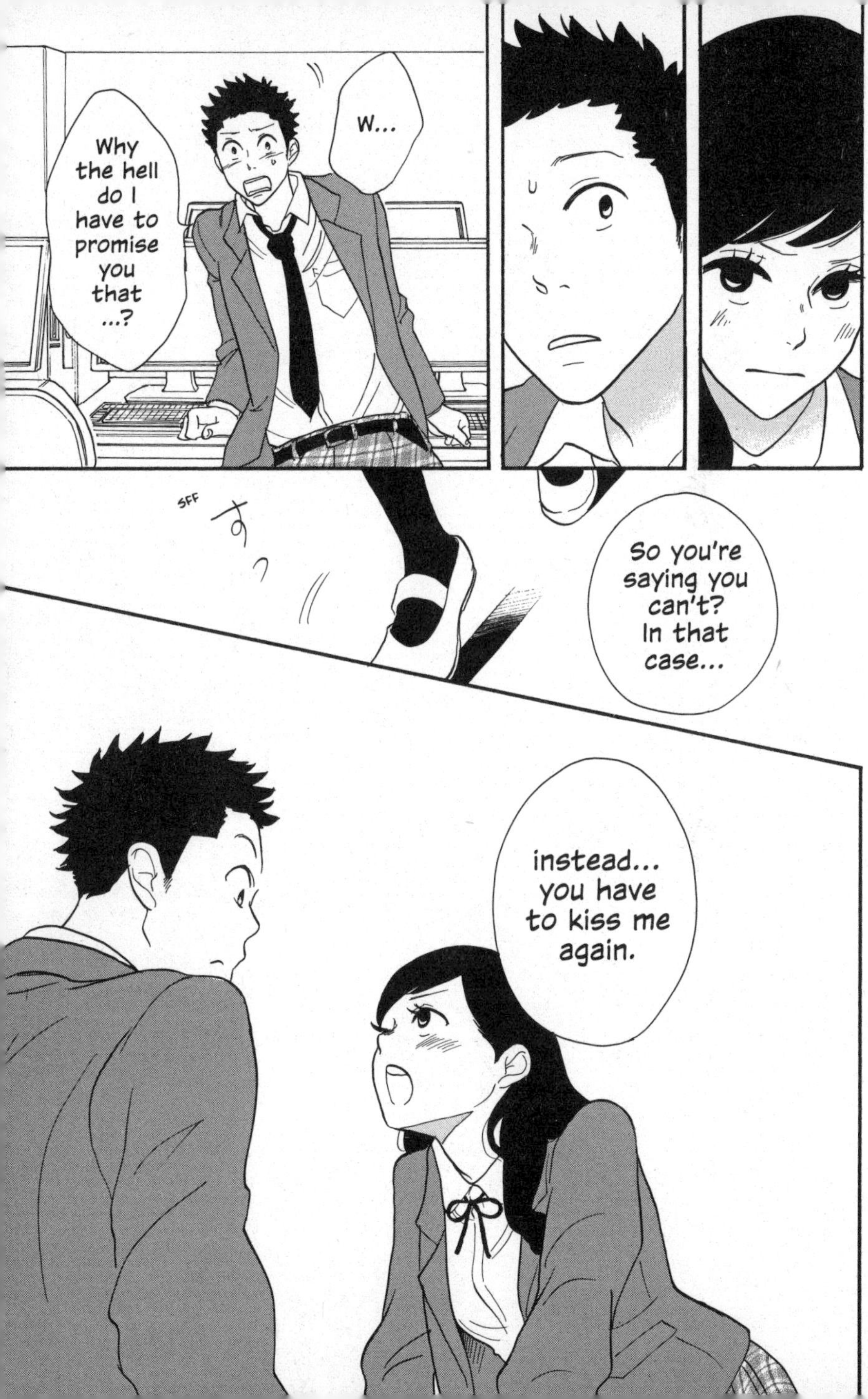
W...
Why the hell do I have to promise you that ...?
So you're saying you can't? In that case...
SFF
すっ
instead... you have to kiss me again.

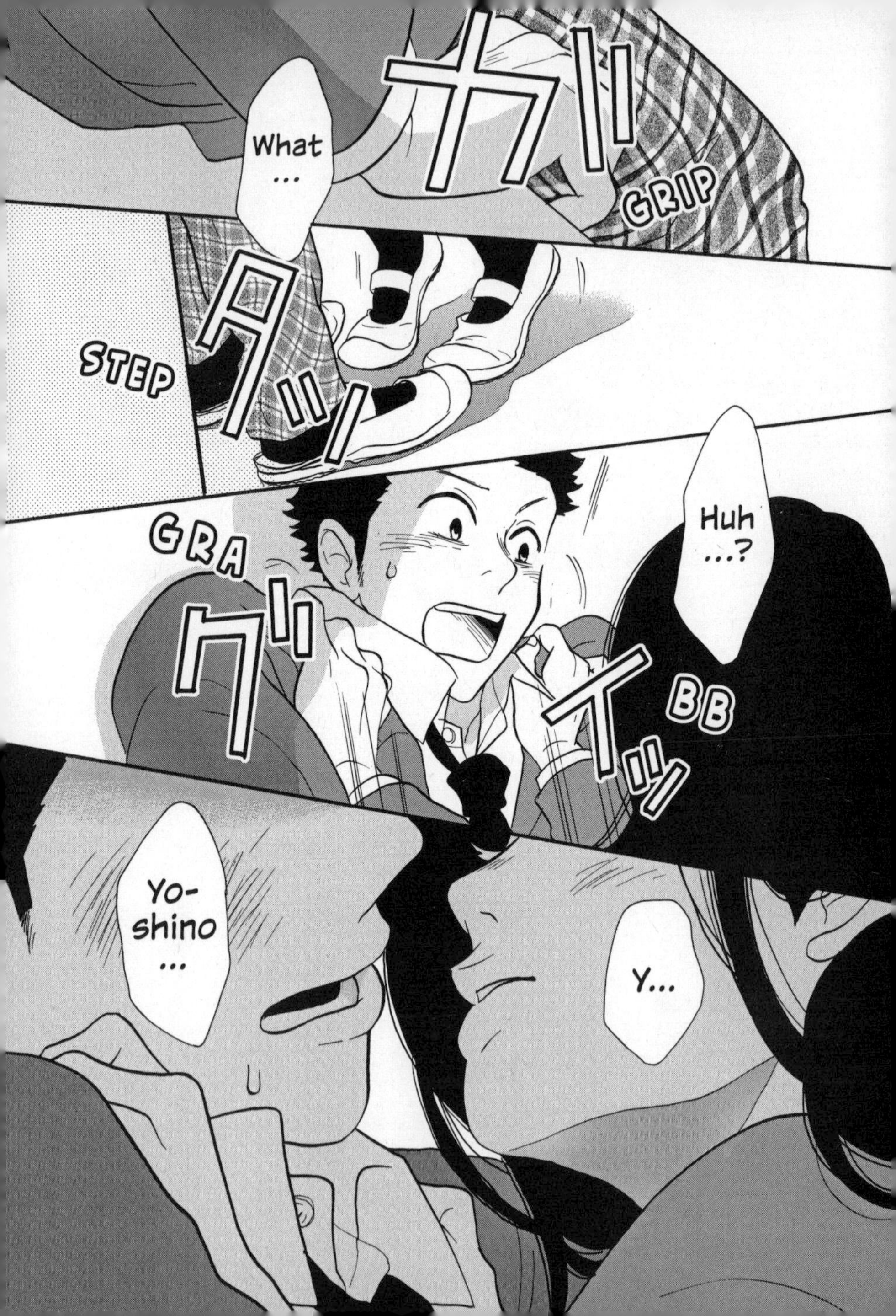
カッ
GRIP
What ...
ダッ
STEP
Huh ...?
グイッ
GRA
BB
Y...
Yo-shino ...

to be continued!

Thank you very much for picking up a copy of The Delinquent Housewife vol. 3! I hope I'll see you all again in vol. 4.

Until then...

-Nemu

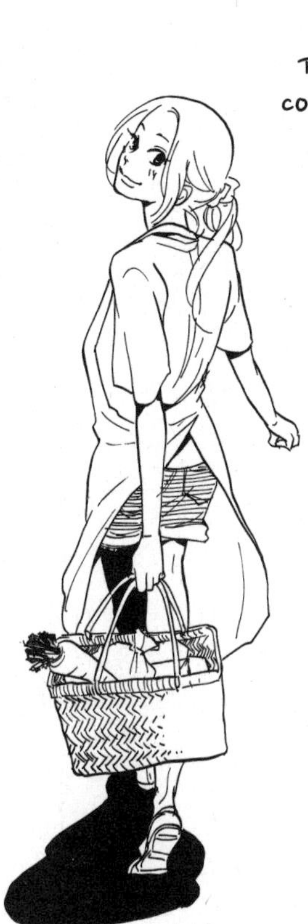

9/2016 Nemu Yoko

SPECIAL THANKS

Tagu-chan Tsune-chan
Noma-chin Yuchika-chan
Dome-chin, my editor
Niikami-sama, the book designer

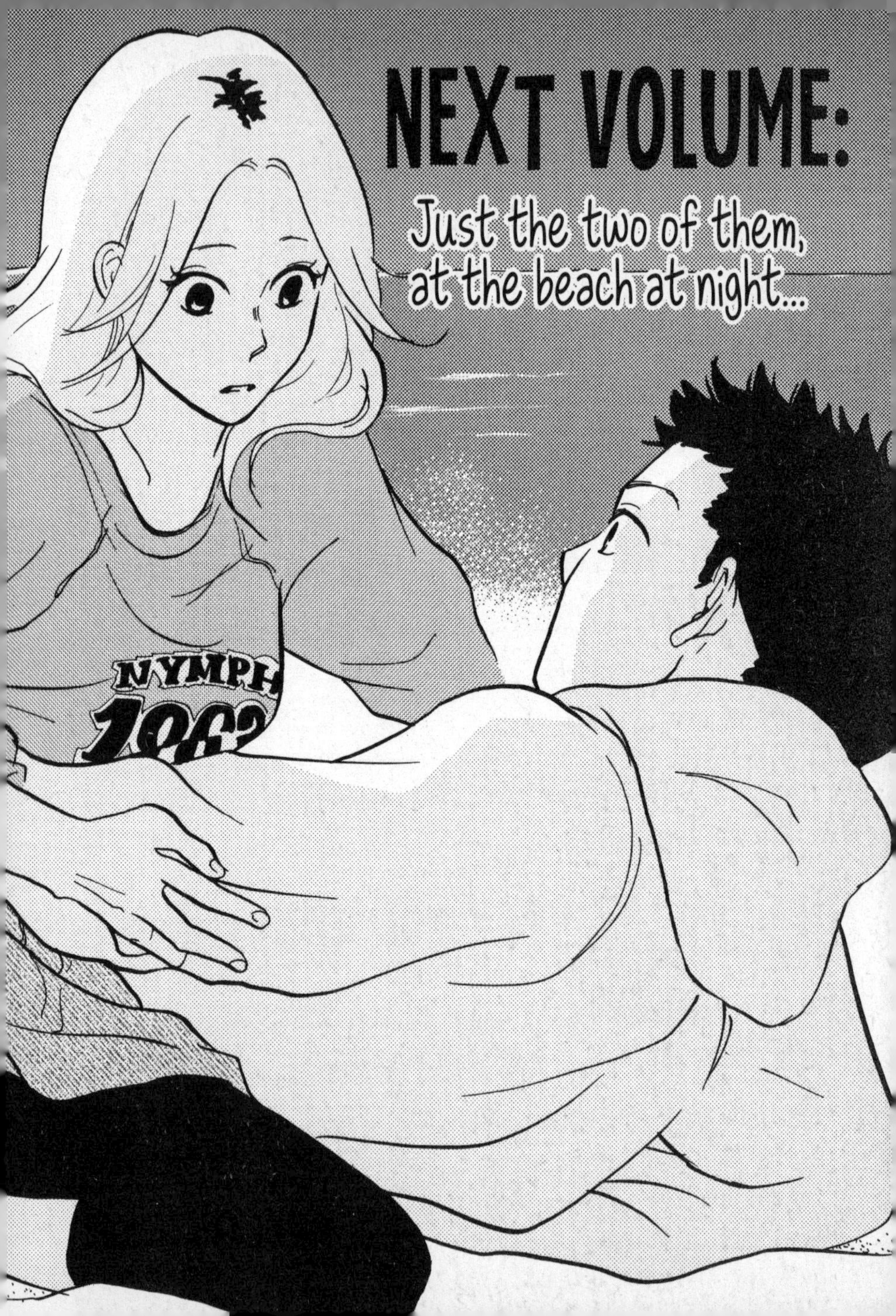
NEXT VOLUME:
Just the two of them, at the beach at night...
NYMPH

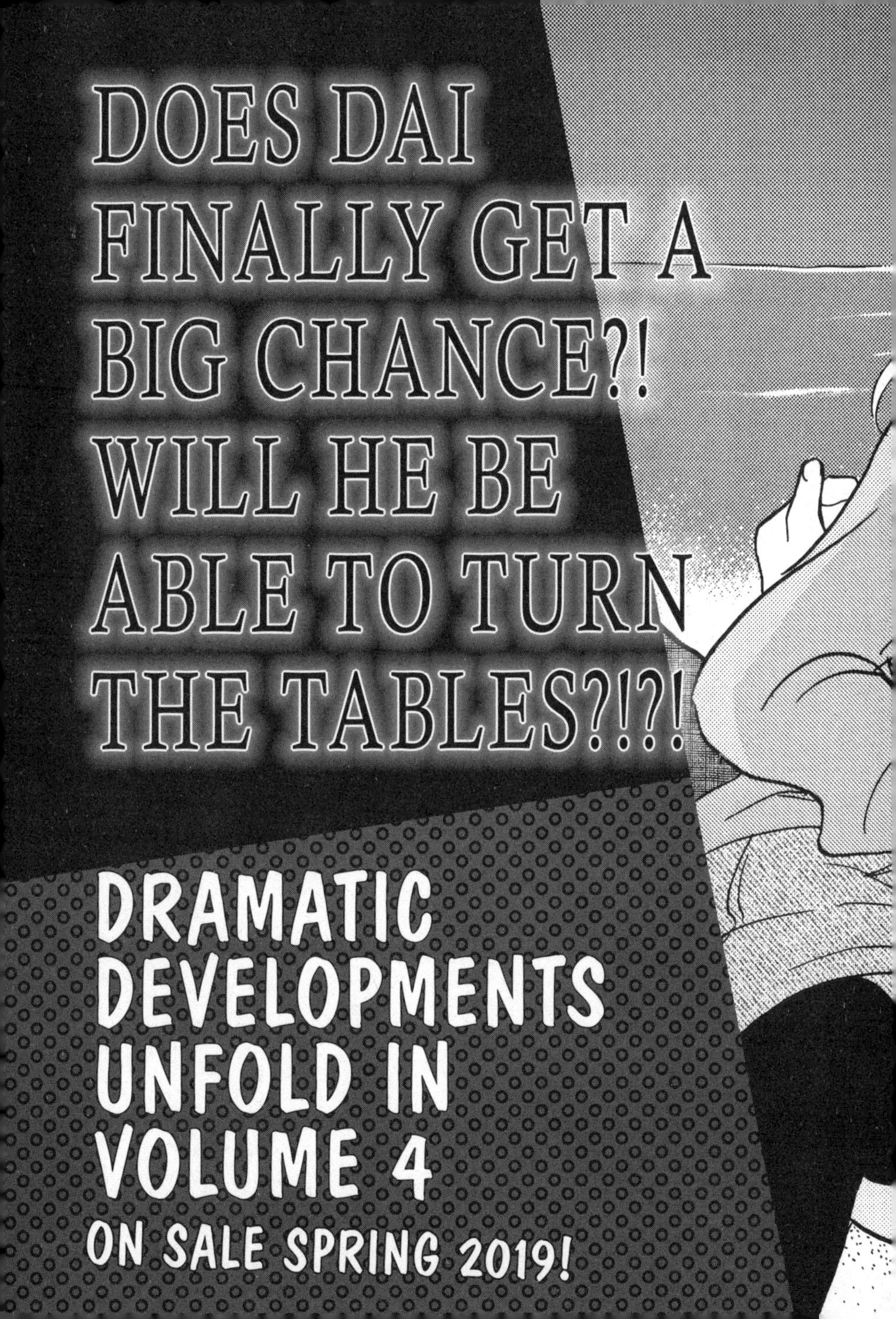
DOES DAI FINALLY GET A BIG CHANCE?!
WILL HE BE ABLE TO TURN THE TABLES?!?!
DRAMATIC DEVELOPMENTS UNFOLD IN VOLUME 4
ON SALE SPRING 2019!

The Basis for the Hit Anime Series!

"*After the Rain* takes a prickly premise and gives us a story about two people with broken dreams that just might be mendable."
— *Japan Times*

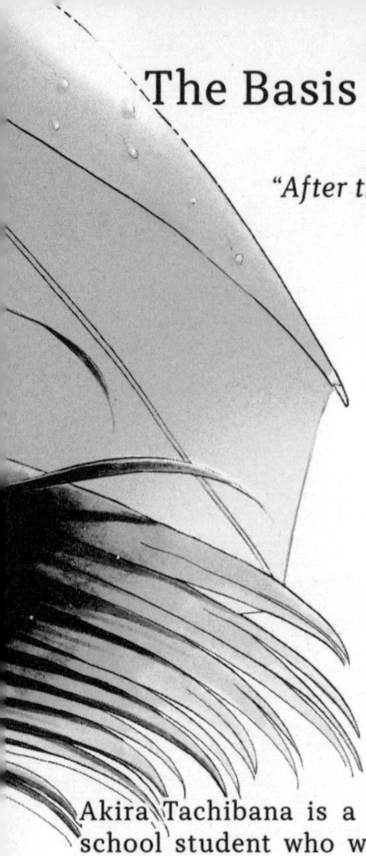

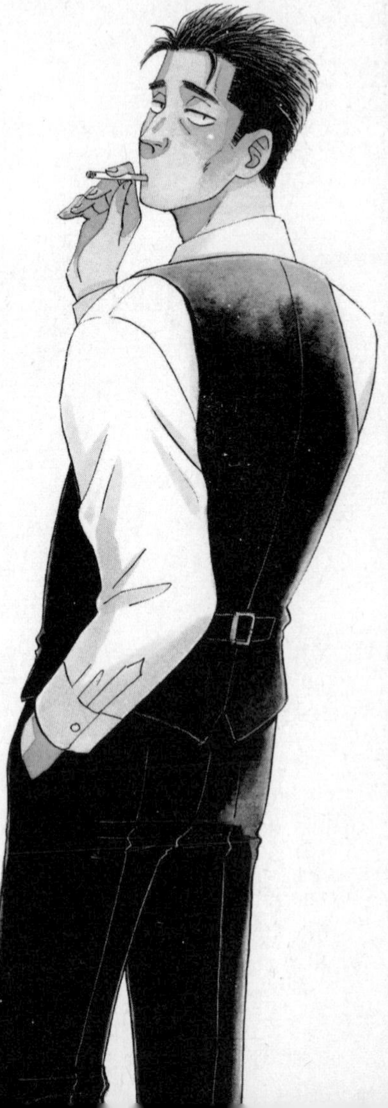

Akira Tachibana is a reserved high school student who was the star of the track and field team but had to quit when she got injured. Sidelined and depressed, Akira stops in at a family restaurant one rainy day, and after the manager—a 45-year-old man with a young son—serves her free coffee, she is smitten, and soon takes a part-time job at the restaurant.

Despite the age gap, Akira is drawn to his kind nature, and little by little, the two begin to understand each other. One day, she decides to finally tell her manager how she feels... but how will he react?

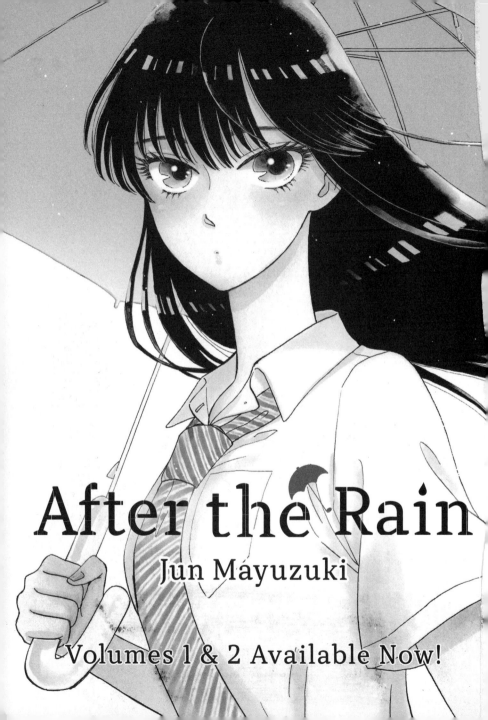

After the Rain

Jun Mayuzuki

Volumes 1 & 2 Available Now!

The Delinquent Housewife! 3

Translation: David Musto
Production: Risa Cho
        Eve Grandt

FUTSUTSUKA NA YOME DESUGA! Vol. 3
by Nemu Yoko

© 2016 Nemu Yoko
All rights reserved.
Original Japanese edition published by SHOGAKUKAN.
English translation rights in the United States of America and Canada
arranged with SHOGAKUKAN through Tuttle-Mori Agency, Inc.

Translation provided by Vertical Comics, 2019
Published by Vertical Comics, an imprint of Vertical, Inc., New York

Originally published in Japanese as *Futsutsuka Na Yome Desuga!* 3 by Shogakukan, 2016
Futsutsuka Na Yome Desuga! serialized in *Shuukan Biggu Komikku Supirittsu*,
Shogakukan, 2016

This is a work of fiction.

ISBN: 978-1-947194-29-8

Manufactured in the United States of America

First Edition

Vertical, Inc.
451 Park Avenue South
7th Floor
New York, NY 10016
www.vert

Vertical books are distributed through Penguin Random House Publisher Services.